Acting and
Character Animation

Acting and Character Animation
The Art of Animated Films, Acting, and Visualizing

Rolf Giesen and Anna Khan

CRC Press
Taylor & Francis Group
Boca Raton London New York

CRC Press is an imprint of the
Taylor & Francis Group, an **informa** business
A FOCAL PRESS BOOK

CRC Press
Taylor & Francis Group
6000 Broken Sound Parkway NW, Suite 300
Boca Raton, FL 33487-2742

International Standard Book Number-13: 978-1-4987-7863-3 (Paperback)
                                       978-1-138-06981-7 (Hardback)

Visit the Taylor & Francis Web site at
http://www.taylorandfrancis.com

and the CRC Press Web site at
http://www.crcpress.com

Printed and bound in the United States of America by Sheridan

Contents

Acknowledgments   ix

Authors   xi

Introduction: Neverland or No End to Childhood   xiii

Part I   The Story of Actors & Acting in Animation

1 Time for Creation: Homunculi   3

2 Chalk-Talking on a Vaudeville Stage   5

3 Magicians and Masquerades   9

4 An Actor's Vision of Optical Poetry   11

5 Shadow Plays and Silhouette Films: The Adventures of Prince Achmed   13

6 Rotoscoping: Dave Fleischer as Ko-Ko the Clown   17

7 The Peak of Character Animation: Walt Disney   21

8 Shamanism and Totemism   25

9 Famous Cartoon Animals   29

10 Animators to Become Actors and Actresses (Sort of)?   35

11 *The Flintstones* and the Age of Television   41

12 Reason & Emotion   45

13 Theories of Acting   49

14 Voice Actors   53

15 Pixilation: Animating Actors or Becoming Animation   59

16 Dancing with Animation   65

17 Acting *with* Animated Characters   69

18 The Puppet Masters   75

19 Animated Characters around the World   91

20 Of Heroes, Antiheroes, Villains, and Men   99

21 Comedy and Comedians   103

22 Acting Against the Odds of Visual Effects and Animation   109

23 *Avatar* and Beyond: The Idiosyncrasies of 3D Animation and the Art of Performance Capture   113

24 A Nod to Computer Games   123

Part II Creativity Training for Writers, Producers, and Animators—A Practical Guide

25 Surprise Me!   131

26 Writing Animation: Role Profiles   135

27 Contradictions: The Key to Great Characters and Stories   143

28 Intercultural Differences between East and West   147

29 Preconceived Characters   157

30 Animals and Anthropomorphism   163

31 Animation, Toys, and Merchandising 167

32 Design, Posing, and Facial Expression 171

33 Understanding Body Language 177

34 The Eyes Have It! 185

35 It's Personality That Wins 189

36 The Score 193

37 Psychological Projection 197

38 The Role of Producer and Director 205

39 Feel at Ease While Animating 207

40 Computer Graphic Characters, Performance Capture Techniques, and the Future of Acting in Animation 211

41 Perceptions Exercises 217

42 Game of Imagination 219

43 Visualization Techniques: Creatures of the Mind 221

Part III Q & A

44 The Animation Film Historian: Giannalberto Bendazzi 235

45 The VFX Artist: Robert Blalack 237

46 The Creator from Italy: Bruno Bozzetto 241

47 The Replacement Animators from Argentina: Alberto Couceiro and Alejandra Tomei 245

48 The Spanish Animation Producer: Manuel Cristóbal 253

49 The Stop-Motion Animator and VFX Director: Jim Danforth 259

50 The Belgian Animation Director: Piet De Rycker 263

51 The Game Expert: Thomas Dlugaiczyk 269

52 The Artist from the Zagreb School of Animation: Borivoj Dovniković-Bordo   273

53 The Animation Scholar from Hong Kong: Daisy Yan Du   279

54 The Disney Expert: Didier Ghez   285

55 The 3D Animator from Germany: Felix Goennert   289

56 The European Producer: Gerhard Hahn   295

57 The Stop-Motion Historian: Mike Hankin   301

58 The Late Stop-Motion Legend Himself: Ray Harryhausen   305

59 The World's Leading Performance Capture Expert: Joe Letteri   317

60 The German Animation Producer: Tony Loeser   321

61 The American Expert in 3D Scans: Karl Meyer   325

62 The Managing Director from Hungary: Ferenc Mikulás   327

63 The German Puppet Animator: Heinrich Sabl   331

64 The Animation Student from Romania: Veronica Solomon   339

65 The Czech 3D Producer: Jan Tománek   343

66 The Experimental Stop-Frame Animator: Grigori Zurkan   347

Selected Filmography   353

Bibliography   363

Index   369

Acknowledgments

In researching the topic of this book, the authors had the chance to talk to and interview at various times Forrest J. Ackerman, Ray Bradbury, Linwood G. Dunn, John Halas, Ray Harryhausen, Dr. Ronald Holloway, Antonín Horák, Paul Christian Hubschmid, Nathan Juran, Sir Christopher Lee, Stanisław Lem, Per Lygum, Dr. William Moritz, Lester Novros, Hal Roach, Curt Siodmak, Dušan Vukotić, Albert Whitlock, Ferdinand Diehl, Gerhard Fieber, Wolf Gerlach, Gerhard Huttula, Heinz Kaskeline, Dieter Parnitzke, Thilo Rothkirch, Karl Ludwig Ruppel, Ernst Joachim Schienke, Herbert K. Schulz, H[ugo] O[tto] Schulze, Professor Bernd Willim, Jürgen Wohlrabe who sadly are no longer with us, directors Luigi Cozzi, Roland Emmerich, Terry Gilliam, Peter Jackson, John Landis, Steven Lisberger, actors Martine Beswick, Caroline Munro, Andy Serkis, VFX supervisors and assistants Volker Engel, Dave Gougé, Joe Letteri (Weta Digital), Richard Taylor (Weta Workshop), Karl Meyer (Gentle Giant Studios), Dennis Muren, John Nelson, Douglas Trumbull, FX make-up artist Rick Baker, 3D FX animators Frank Petzold, Phil Tippett, animation executives, producers, directors and artists Hans Bacher, Peter Bluemel, Bruno Bozzetto, Heinz Busert, Alberto Couceiro and Alejandra Tomei (Animas Film Animations), Manuel Cristóbal (Dragoia Media), Jim Danforth, Piet De Rycker, Pete Docter, Borivoj Dovniković (Bordo), Robi Engler, Dr. Hans Michael Fischerkoesen, Ari Folman, Frank Geiger (brave new work film productions/Little Dream Entertainment), Professor Gerhard Hahn, Herbert Gehr and Neschet Al-Zubaidi (Hahn Film), Rolf Herken, Werner Hierl, Jeffrey Katzenberg (CEO, DreamWorks SKG), Professor Barbara Kirchner, Raimund Krumme, Ralf Kukula (Balance Film GmbH), Tony Loeser (MotionWorks), Richard Lutterbeck (Trickstudio Lutterbeck), Ferenc Mikulás (Kecskemétfilm), Mark Osborne, Maya Rothkirch (Rothkirch Cartoon Film), Dr. Michael Schoemann (Benchmark Entertainment), Georges Schwitzgebel, Nelson Shin

(Akom Production Co., Ltd.), Rainer Soehnlein, Stefan Thies (nfp animation), Jan Tománek (Art And Animation Studio), Wolfgang Urchs, Aygün & Peter Voelker, Tony White, Richard Williams, Juan Pablo Zaramella, our Chinese colleagues Cai Zhijun (CCTV Animation, Inc.), Chang Guangxi, Dong Hang, Wang Borong, Wang Liuyi, Zheng Liguo (President, Jilin Animation Institute), Daisy Yan Du, Gavin Liu, Juan Zaft, Professor R.P.C. Janaka Rajapakse (motion capture specialist, Associate Professor, Tainan National University of the Arts), voice artists Peter Krause (Germany's Donald Duck voice), Oliver Rohrbeck, fellow writers and scholars Klaus Baumgart, Giannalberto Bendazzi, Bob Burns, Dr. Michael Flintrop (Cineways Festival Braunschweig), Dr. Ralf Forster, Joseph Garncarz, Didier Ghez, Jeanpaul Goergen, Mike Hankin, Ed Hooks, Daniel Kothenschulte, Dr. Arnold Kunert, Carsten Laqua, Peter Maenz (Deutsche Kinemathek/German Cinematheque Berlin), Annick Maes and Gerardo Michelin (Cartoon Brussels), Raymond Pettigrew, Dr. Volker Petzold, Nadja Rademacher (Deutsches Institut für Animationsfilm Dresden), Florian Schmidlechner, J. P. Storm, Caroline Hagen-Hall and Christel Strobel (who granted access to the estate of late silhouette film artist Lotte Reiniger), Professor Ulrich Wegenast (International Trickfilm Festival Stuttgart), Thomas Dlugaiczyk (Games Academy), Professor Ulrich Weinberg (Hasso Plattner Institute), Jutta Diebel, Professor Frank Gessner, Professor Felix Gönnert, Dr. Veit Quack, Veronica Solomon, Professor Christina Schindler, Benedikt Toniolo (Film University Konrad Wolf Potsdam-Babelsberg), and Ulrike Bliefert.

Images courtesy of Animas Film (Alberto Couceiro and Alejandra Tomei); Little Dream Entertainment (Frank Geiger); Manuel Cristóbal; Jim Danforth; Deutsches Institut für Animationsfilm (Nadja Rademacher); Film University Babelsberg; Felix Goennert; Hahn Film (Gerhard Hahn and Herbert Gehr); The Ray & Diana Harryhausen Foundation (Vanessa Harryhausen and Connor Heaney—www.rayharryhausen.com); Jilin Animation Institute (Gavin Liu); MotionWorks (Tony Loeser and Jana Wernicke); Primrose Productions Ltd. (Caroline Hagen-Hall and Christel Strobel); Sabl-Film (Heinrich Sabl): J. P. Storm Collection; Benedikt Toniolo; Weta Digital (Dave Gougé); and Grigori Zurkan.

Special thanks are due to Rainer M. Engel, Schrift-Bilder GmbH Berlin, who assisted with formatting images and stills.

Authors

Rolf Giesen Berlin-based screenwriter who specialized in animated feature films and film historian. For more than 20 years curated the stop-motion collection of the late Ray Harryhausen, worked with directors and artists such as Roland Emmerich and Albert Whitlock.

Anna Khan Took acting classes and enrolled in dramatics at Free University Berlin. Experienced actress and director who later got specialized in acting for animation.

Both authors were invited to lecture in universities and academies in China and Taiwan and prepare exhibitions devoted to animation.

Introduction
Neverland or No End to Childhood

Animators should focus on the acting… make the characters think and act… start with the body first, next focus on the eyes, and last focus on the mouth. When reviewing reels we look at the acting first.

John Lasseter[*]

A mosquito flies into the picture. It looks like an insect and at the same time like a human although it wears only a human hat and carries a bag, with big eyes that are neither human nor beastly but are part of the world of caricature. Interestingly enough, the character on screen, like many great cartoon stars, was based on a comic strip where it looked less human, had no hat, no bag: completely insect-like. "Its" or "his" cinematically changed personality is created by the way of acting, lifting the hat with one leg to introduce itself to the spectators, looking around gleefully for a victim that appears in the person of a well-clad, fat, tired, not really likeable gentleman. In anticipation of our spitefulness, we know that what's going to happen serves this man right. The insect follows him to his apartment and gets inside an open door window to the man's bedroom. While the unknowing man sleeps, the mosquito goes to work, sharpens its needle. The man snores. The mosquito sucks blood. Half-sleeping the man tries to catch it but the mosquito is persistent and escapes the man's hand. Finally, the mosquito

---

[*] John Lasseter, Pixar Lecture at the Academy of Motion Picture Arts and Sciences in Los Angeles on November 4, 1996.

is sucked full of blood, its body a balloon. But it hasn't had its fill of body fluid. It's still greedy, sucking more right under the man's nose, scratching its head. The balloon circles above the man's head, landing again, doing a handstand on the man's nose, boisterously performing its antics for the audience expecting applause, sucking again and—exploding: *boom!*, having overdone its job. The whole animation industry as we know it today is based on that little picture because it's the first time that not the novelty of movement and metamorphosis counts but the unique character itself.

Not done by a computer but by ink and paint: consisting of more than 8000 drawings. Five minutes of first-class animation, more than a 100 years old and surpassing most of nowadays' standardized animation. While the few animators in other countries, like Émile Cohl in France, were satisfied to have their simple *Fantoche* characters just moving around, pleased just by movement, Winsor McCay, the creator of *Little Nemo* (New York Herald, October 15, 1905) who did the mosquito in 1912, aimed for good caricatures, drawn in perspective, and above all *personality. How a Mosquito Operates,* a little silent film, nothing else than pencil and ink, never misses its effect on the audience up till today.

The art of acting through animated characters lies in detail, in gesture, in little unexpected things that make a character memorable even after 100 years, maybe not so much the acting itself but rather personality. And these tiny gestures and unexpected movements reflect the personality of the animator as well. Let us quote the late Darlyne O'Brien, widow of the animator who brought King Kong to eternal screen life: Willis O'Brien. She told that she would recognize her husband in every gesture of the famous giant gorilla. Having been close to O'Brien's protégé, stop-motion artist Ray Harryhausen, we only can confirm this sentiment. Having known Harryhausen for 35 years, we watched him mimic in a church in Bologna, Italy, and pounding against the huge gate like mighty Kong against the entrance of the native village of Skull Island. It was imitative behavior inspired by an unforgettable childhood experience. Sometimes, in very private moments, this great animator showed an infecting sense of humor and copied people. He was a fan of comedian Stan Laurel and revealed that at one time he and his lifelong friend and buddy Ray Bradbury planned a pilgrimage to Laurel's home in Santa Monica.

Germany lost a fantastic Hungarian actor in 1933 when the Nazis came to power. His name was Peter Lorre (1904–1964). He was the child murderer in Fritz Lang's *M* and toward the end of his life acted in Edgar Allan Poe films directed by Roger Corman. Colleagues described him as a brilliant scene stealer. When he would walk over a bridge in the comedy version of *The Raven* (1963), accompanied by two other old timers, Boris Karloff and Vincent Price, all eyes would be on him, not on the fellows.

Lorre was born with a *face.* It was director Howard Hawks who once said those actors make the best stars who are easily to be caricatured. Just see the caricatured star portraits (even in animation) of Clark Gable, complete with oversized ears, Katharine Hepburn or Peter Lorre who, alongside Bugs and Daffy, became a mad scientist character in Warner Bros. cartoons *Hair-Raising Hare* and *Birth of a Notion.*

Character animation is about personality, no matter if it's human, animal or, well, unearthly demon. Monsters, the bigger they are, remain uniquely memorable just for their proportion: *Kong, The Beast from 20,000 Fathoms,* the Ymir from *20 Million Miles to Earth,* the intimidating, eye-rolling, nightmarish bugbear of a Cyclops in *The 7ᵗʰ Voyage of Sinbad,* Suffer the Little Children as Stephen King would put it: an extraordinary hybrid creature, goat-legged, lips of a camel, jagged teeth of a boar, nails of a lion, the horn of a unicorn.

Doing research on a Walt Disney favorite, *Fantasia,* John Culhane interviewed master animator Vladimir "Bill" Tytla, called by his associate Lester Novros *the* animator, and asked him how he approached the animation of Chernabog, the powerful monstrous Devil on Bald Mountain. According to Culhane, Tytla would build himself up, like an actor getting back into an old role: *"I imagined that I was as big as a mountain and made of rock and yet I was feeling and moving."**

Although he doesn't do any evil in his scenes, the horned, giant Chernabog acts like *evil supreme.* He unfolds his enormous wings, stretches, summons fire, demons, and harpies. His eyes reflect satanic pleasure, but like Lugosi's vampire the light of the rising sun forces him to retreat.

In Culhane's view, Bill Tytla shared with Disney an overwhelming empathy with all creation that was almost Franciscan. He once said that they approached things with a great deal of emotion. You have to feel yourself to make others feel the same. As an animator, you have to be an emotional character. Tytla was emotional and made us feel with the seven dwarfs, with Stromboli, Pinocchio's puppet master, Dumbo the flying elephant, or Chernabog's predecessor, the giant who rolled a cigarette from a haystack, used the roof of a house as a seat and was conquered by Mickey Mouse, the *Brave Little Tailor.*

The greatest of animators, like Tytla, commanded two skills still highly important, particularly in the digital age: the skill of imagination and the skill to visualize this imagination. Actors act, according to their imagination, visual artists of course visualize it.

Although being no professional actor, Tytla became the character, he felt and grasped the character and enthusiastically filled in, like diminutive Haruo Nakajima became a giant creature inside a *Godzilla* rubber suit at Toho Studios in Tokyo.

Tytla maybe belonged to the first who truly understood the importance of acting in animation, sort of an heir to Winsor McCay's legacy because it was one of McCay's films, *Gertie the Dinosaur,* that inspired and started him on the road. Like McCay, Tytla did his job instinctively by balancing motion and emotion.

---

* John Culhane, *Walt Disney's Fantasia.* New York: Abradale Press/Harry N. Abrams, Inc., Publishers, 1999, p. 194.

Another of Disney's master animators was even more aware of that art. His name: Milt (Milton Erwin) Kahl—and to many he was the best right after Tytla. To Kahl, who animated Pinocchio and Bambi, animation was a very difficult medium that requires pretty good craftsmen who are able to draw well enough to turn things at every angle. One has to understand movement and, Kahl adds, one has to be an actor, put on a performance, and be a showman.

Animation has to do with acting, at least to some degree. But there is no true acting involved, of course not, as animators do not enter the stage themselves, but rather animate the *character that acts*, and if they are lucky they are able to avoid the standardized, mechanical mass production that Richard Williams once called just *animating matches* (but even cheap animation needs a certain amount of characterization). In the best case, actors as well as animators explore and develop characters thoroughly and become one with them. So both, acting as well as animation, is a highly creative process. This is what they have in common. And they have, as we will see, the same origins.

But contrary to film stars who shine on the silver screen (and art that is exhibited in galleries and museums worldwide and sometimes sells to astronomical prices), animators in most cases remain in the dark. Their names are only known to insiders, and in the early years many spectators would naively speculate if Walt Disney was the artist who drew all his animated films himself.

The same is true for actors used in motion or performance capture. Andy Serkis, an exceptional actor, may be the only one whose name is known to bigger audiences thanks to his performances as Gollum in the *Lord of the Rings* trilogy or as Supreme Leader Snoke in *Star Wars: The Force Awakens*.

Vice versa, live actors who share the screen with animated characters have problems, too, to win the "competition." In many cases, they won't. A live actor simply cannot win against animals, kids, or cartoons. They just might catch up as the late Bob Hoskins did in *Who Framed Roger Rabbit*.

This book is divided into two parts: From film history we learn about the importance of actors and the range of personalities and related arts that goes into animation. Then we will turn to the animator's, the writer's, and actor's point of view to describe the various techniques involved.

There might be doubts about mixing history and technical guidance. Some might call the project too academic (don't worry, it's not), more appealing to film historians than animators themselves. Who is this book being written for? Is it for historians, film buffs, and fans? Is it for character animators? Is it for screenwriters? Is it for actresses and actors who might look to animation as an additional source of income? It seems to fall between all these stools. It is no history book in the proper meaning of the word. It is no manual. It is more like a brainstorm of facts and ideas that demonstrate the variety of animation.

The reason for this kind of confusion has mainly to do with our relation to the science of history. Our fast-paced society considers it superfluous to look back to understand what we are doing today. To many viewers, everything that precedes *Avatar* doesn't simply exist. It is predigital, isn't it? Black-and-white film and silent, in the worst case. They forget that animation techniques themselves do depend on neither film nor digital media. So past, present, and future have the same purpose in recording movement. We wouldn't be able to judge and classify what we are doing without the knowledge of the history of moving images. If we don't know where they come from, we don't know where they go to. This prejudice against history transferred to the stage would mean that Shakespeare has no significance in theatre today.

Animated images surround us since a Stone Age artist drew a wild boar with eight legs on a wall in the Cave of Altamira in nowadays Cantabria, Spain. Why did he do so? Because the very idea of animation is in our head, therefore, not necessarily tied to the silver or the computer screen: mentally saving, reconstructing, and re-enacting movement is the objective target. And by re-enacting telling a *story*. While we talked about the effect the shine of fire would have on these, thanks to stone protrusion, almost 3D cave paintings, Tommy Lee Jones, on a visit to Berlin's Museum of Film and Television to promote *Men in Black*, all of a sudden gave a private performance and demonstrated to us how a Stone Age storyteller's shadow would act while speaking and spinning yarns in the shine of fire. One can say that this was the first motion-picture theater.

Since then the field is not exclusively reserved to professional cartoonists and animators (of course not), but in the digital age, in the realm of synthetic media where even acting is artificial, they come closest to the domain of actor-storytellers: from Stone Age right into the future of virtuality.

Animators must bring drawn, sculpted, or digitally created figures to life. Actors must develop characters as well, but they draw on their physical body shape and their gender (although not in every culture: when male actors impersonate females). Animators can portray anything from plant life (Walt Disney's Technicolor *Silly Symphony Flowers and Trees*) to animals, from humans to robots and non-humanoid aliens. For humans it's rather difficult to portray goat-legged satyrs or multi-armed, sword-wielding horrors. When Hollywood planned to film Edgar Rice Burroughs' *John Carter of Mars* stories in the 1960s, stop-motion artist Jim Danforth naturally pleaded for animation to portray the four-armed green giant barbarians who are part of Burroughs' universe, but the VFX supervisor-to-be, Larry Butler, wouldn't sympathize with that idea and would have handled the effect by tying two large basketball players for each giant and having a special headpiece made. The multi-armed silver maid from the 1940-*Thief of Bagdad* was choreographed in a similar way by the same Butler. (Ray Harryhausen would eventually animate the six-armed Kali in a sword-fight sequence from *The Golden Voyage of Sinbad*.) Decades later, when *John Carter of Mars* was eventually produced by Disney, the computer would take over. Animation had become a major ingredient of most American blockbusters with a strong report to VFX. Genuine live-action scenes that hadn't been pixel touched became scarce. Before the digital age, however, VFX and design people antagonized animation, particularly stop motion, for being jerky. MGM's chief production designer Cedric Gibbons despised the studio's decision to have Willis O'Brien come down to Culver City to try a stop-motion adventure titled *War Eagles,* an epic that consequently never was. Of course, there was misunderstanding on both parts. Gibbons' associate A. Arnold Gillespie, for many years in charge of models, ships, planes, and special effects at Metro studios, described the movement of the hanging miniature dolls that filled the stadium to watch the 1925 *Ben Hur* chariot race and were arranged like the tiny players of table soccer as—*animation.* There was not much love lost between live action and animated films. The heads of international film festivals would prefer to walk alongside live stars over the red carpet rather than present themselves with cartoon characters in silly costumes. The Academy of Motion Picture Arts and Sciences rarely would acknowledge animated effects in live-action films up to the 1960s and only would award *Mighty Joe Young* in 1950. Ray Harryhausen, assistant to Willis O'Brien who received the Oscar, was present during the ceremony and felt the tension of the nominated O'Brien. But Ray himself had to wait a long time for his well-deserved Oscar. That signals that animation is different from all other cinematic experiences. Jim Danforth recalls that, in those days, even members of the VFX Academy Award committee didn't understand the intricate Harryhausen process.

The process of animation begins in preproduction with developing the character, a joint effort of specialized writers and skilled artists supervised not exactly by the director but by the producer who in most cases is the project's driving force, in Europe (as we sadly had to learn) with a lot of unwelcome interference from TV editors and distributors, and with devising the model sheets that show posing and facial expression of the respective character. The livelier a single pose is the better. On stage there are art directors, set designers, costume makers, and make-up men who support actors in their performances. The actor himself will contribute what we call emotional expression, using his mimic art, voice, and body movement. But in animation everything depends on the animator provided he is going to work with a solid design of the character that means something to him, that inspires him. In TV mass production, the design is even more important as there is no ambitious detailed animation possible for budgetary reasons and time constraints.

Actors have learned to express emotion by facial expression, gestures, breathing, and voice. The tools actors and animators use are basically the same: body talk, mood, and movement—with the exception that to them this kind of performing is an *out-of-body experience.*

Animators and actors have at least one thing in common. Animators, like actors, are avid watchers. They carefully observe and study animals as well as humans. For *Bambi,* the popular cartoon version of Felix Salten's 1923-book, Disney got real deer, two fawns, christened Bambi and Faline, to his old Hyperion Studios as reference for the animators where they could be studied. The same approach these writers noticed at the animation department of Beijing Film

Academy where they animated a feature about a dog and had a tiny puppy caged in the studio.

Certainly both, animators as well as actors, have to watch. In fact, Augusto Fernandes, Argentine stage director, sent his actors to the zoo to study animal behavior. Animals and nature play an important part in the life of many animators in every country of the world, in every culture. Before animating *Mighty Joe Young*, Harryhausen did just that: going to the zoo and studying live gorillas. *"I even became a vegetarian for some time,"* Harryhausen would say.

But contrary to the actor on stage, an animator is not only copying nature. He can change it. He is almost free from it and the limits of physics. In the world of animated characters, Béla Balázs wrote, nothing is impossible as miracles are part of the daily routine. The drawn lines function in accordance with the shape they assume. Saying that he referred to the antics of Felix the Cat, the screen's first cartoon star that, by the way, was modeled after Charles Chaplin's little tramp with certain characteristics that later were borrowed from and paid for by Buster Keaton. To a creature made of lines, Balázs observed, everything should be achievable. Felix the Cat, for instance, can roll his tail into a wheel and ride off on it as if it were a bicycle. In another case, Felix loses his tail. He wonders what to do and while he ponders, a question mark grows out of his head. Felix seizes it and sticks it on his rump. There you go. These images are absolute. There is no difference between appearance and reality.[*]

With an uncertain nod to the future, Balázs wonders himself, what would be gained if this was to become reality?

Above all technique, however, we must *play*. Play like children. That is being curious and imaginative and having fun doing so.

As children we have looked up to the sky and imagined the clouds to be animals, giants, pirates, adventurers, cowboys, and Indians riding horses. The source of all inspiration is childlike imagination, and Pixar even devoted one of its shorts to simply that, *Partly Cloudy*, creating an anthropomorphic cloud character from pixel animation. It was Max Reinhardt, Germany's great pioneer of the stage, who once said, *"I believe in the immortality of the theatre, it is a most joyous place to hide, for all those who have secretly put their childhood in their pockets and run off and away with it, to play on to the end of their days."*

The same should be true for animators. Children and animators are not necessarily acting. To them it's all like *truly* playing. Playing is also dreaming: great dreams, wishful dreams, and occasionally, as part of the game, nightmares. Playing staggers the imagination.

Hayao Miyazaki, the great *Japanimator*, echoes Reinhardt's sentiments when he says that children aren't interested in logic; to them, all is pure imagination.[†]

It's a dream that is best expressed in *Peter Pan*, James Matthew Barrie's story of a mischievous boy who never grows up, who never will become an adult. He is

---

[*] Béla Balázs, *Early Film Theory*. New York/Oxford: Berghahn Books, 2010, p. 174.
[†] *Anime Interviews*. San Francisco, California: Cadence Books, 1997, p. 31.

the leader of a gang of lost boys and flies to a place behind the clouds: the island of Neverland with lots of imaginary characters like pirates, fairies, and mermaids. In Greek mythology, the god Pan, who idles in the countryside of Arkadia playing panpipes and chasing Nymphs, represents natural life that Barrie contrasts with the effects of civilization.

Therefore, this book is more about *Playing* than about *Acting in Animation*. At least it should be. It's about imagination and about the Pan-like figures that come out of those dreams and begin to live.

It was Ray Bradbury, author and fantasist, who once remarked that Charles Laughton, the Hunchback of Notre Dame, Nero, Dr. Moreau, Captain Bligh and the Canterville Ghost in one and the same person, was the biggest child of them all.

PART I
The Story of Actors & Acting in Animation

1

Time for Creation
Homunculi

Acting and animating are arts of simulation and reproduction: the dream of creating animal and human life by means other than natural reproduction.

The so-called *Homunculus* was the realm of *Doctor Faustus*, the legendary necromancer and astrologer who became a durable character in the literature where he sold his soul to the devil, a predecessor of *Frankenstein*, and it was the realm of the Swiss alchemist Theophrastus Bombast von Hohenheim, otherwise known as Paracelsus, a sixteenth century master of holistic medicine and natural healing, who is said to have been interested in *artificially made human beings*, a concern that in those days came close to *black magic*.

In Universal's *The Bride of Frankenstein* (1935), VFX experts John P. Fulton and David Stanley Horsley created such homunculi optically by miniaturizing live actors while an artist like Ray Harryhausen even animated a (winged) homunculus stop-frame, as an evil magician's aid in his "super-spectacle" *The Golden Voyage of Sinbad*.

Today's alchemists who call themselves scientists create artificial life through genetic engineering and human cloning. Animators, however, accomplish the process in a much simpler way. They create their *little men* (this is what homunculi means translated from Latin) by using digital imagery or simply a pen.

Facing auspicious occasions, animators will have a chance of not only acting but also *creating*. In some early animation, as in the *Out of the Inkwell* series by Max Fleischer, the hand of the animator appears and it looks as if the drawn character was touched by the hand of God. Animators invent characters that virtually do not exist. In such cases, some of them actually might feel like being God and say so. *"Now I know what it feels like to be God!"* Colin Clive screamed when portraying *Frankenstein* in front of James Whale's camera. This attitude was parodied in Chuck Jones' short cartoon *Duck Amuck* (1953) in which Daffy Duck fights the malicious hand of a mischievous animator who turns out to be Bugs Bunny. But sometimes the creations might be more powerful than the creator itself. They seem to develop a life of their own like Pinocchio did.

In 1965, famed Czech stop-motion producer Jiří Trnka (1912–1969) wrote and directed an 18-minute short film, a parable titled *Ruka* (*The Hand*) that dealt with personality cult: A harlequin potter is happy to create his daily output of flower vases, but then a huge Stalinist hand appears that threatens and manipulates him to sculpt nothing else than memorials of a giant hand.

2

Chalk-Talking on a Vaudeville Stage

At the turn of the century, in vaudeville, caricaturists and show-and-swift cartoonists had to have acting ability as they presented their creations live on stage. They were in direct touch with the audience. They were true *animateurs*.

The master certainly was Winsor McCay (c. 1867–1934), "America's greatest cartoonist," the famed creator of the strip *Little Nemo in Slumberland* and an accomplished entertainer. When he entered the art of animation, it was intended to become part of his live act on stage presenting his animation and interacting with it by giving a Brontosaurus lady named Gertie on screen commands that she would follow or not.

This was one of the rare cases that a cartoonist and animator became a true stage actor.

McCay had drawn his *Gertie the Dinosaur* in 1913, accordingly over a period of six months, starting with the key frames and filling in the "in-betweens." He had brought the series of drawings to the Vitagraph Company of America in January 1914 to have them photographed frame by frame. The next month the film was premiered at the Palace Theatre in Chicago where McCay entered the stage, armed with chalk, and began sketching on a blackboard. Personal appearances of cartoonists on stage were part of many vaudeville acts. This was followed by a screening of *How a Mosquito Operates*, *Gertie's* predecessor. Then McCay returned to the stage, cracking a bullwhip like an animal trainer to introduce Gertie, "the only dinosaur in captivity."

Gertie on screen would do, at least sometimes, what McCay ordered her on "tricks" to do on stage. "*Gertie—yes, her name is Gertie*," McCay addressed his audience, "*will come out of that cave and do everything I tell her to do.*" Then, armed with his whip, he would turn to Gertie: "*Come out, Gertie, and make a pretty bow. Be a good girl and bow to the audience. Thanks! Now raise your right foot. That's good! Now raise your left foot.*" A sea serpent rears its ugly head out of the water. "*Never mind that sea serpent! Gertie, raise your left foot.*" But Gertie is distracted. "*You're a bad girl, shame on you!*" When scolded Gertie begins to weep bitterly. "*Oh, don't cry. Here, catch this pumpkin.*" For the first time in imagery live action becomes an interactive part of an animated cartoon. Gertie opens her mouth to catch the pumpkin. "*Now will you raise your left foot?*" Gertie devours a tree and shrieks when a mammoth passes by. "*Gertie, don't hurt Jumbo.*" Gertie tosses the mammoth in the lake. "*Gertie loves music. Play for her and she'll dance.*" While Gertie dances to the music, standing upright on her hind legs, she gets sprayed with water by Jumbo and hurls a boulder at the vengeful mammoth that escapes. After such action, Gertie is tired and takes some rest until a flying reptile turns up. "*Did you see that four-winged lizard?*" Gertie nods. "*Sure? Are you in the habit of seeing things?*" Gertie shakes her head. "*Are you fibbing to me? Will you have a little drink? There's a lake. Take a little drink if you want it.*" McCay doesn't have to tell her twice. Gertie cleans up the whole lake. At the end of the show, McCay goes one step further. He walks offstage and returns in drawn form: "*Gertie will now show that she isn't afraid of me and take me for a ride.*" Gertie would open her mouth and the McCay cartoon character would step in to be lifted on her back swinging his whip while she exits.

McCay's *Mosquito* and McCay's *Gertie*—they are both animals and they act that way. Gertie, however, is more animal than the Mosquito that is unnamed but, although it follows its instincts, has a human personality. It loves to be at the center of attention, and while Gertie bows to the audience at McCay's command, the Mosquito pulls off a feat for the audience at his own request. Gertie is a showcase: the first animated *stage personality*, the Mosquito's stage is man's daily life. His natural goal: to make this life miserable by his blood-sucking antics. Humans have empathy for Gertie as you would have for an overgrown pet. The Mosquito is no pet, never will be, but we like that critter too. He—and it's certainly *him*, not It!—behaves mischievously like a brat and has *fun*. We feel sorry for him when he explodes having sucked too much blood. We don't feel sorry for the sleeper who lost a few drops of blood. The Mosquito is the first screen animal in animation history that evokes human feelings and true empathy.

With the end of vaudeville personal appearances like those of McCay would become rare, and personalities like Walt Disney had to be prerecorded to appear as a host on screen or television together with their cartoon characters. In these recordings you see, however, that Disney had enormous acting abilities. And that his animals, like McCay's, make themselves understood by communicating on a wavelength with the audience. Not only their performances, it's their personality that captures the audience.

3

Magicians and Masquerades

Besides the vaudevillian actor, early *trickfilm* refers to magic as an extension of similar stage presentations. The illusion to let persons and things appear and disappear could be easily accomplished cinematographically.

Trickfilm pioneer Georges Méliès (1861–1938) was a proprietor of the *Théâtre Robert-Houdin* in Paris, where he developed and presented many stage illusions before he turned to filmmaking. In 1896, he used the stop trick (or substitution splice) to create the illusion of the *Vanishing Lady (Escamotage d'une dame chez Robert-Houdin)* on film. The Edison Manufacturing Company used the same trick one year earlier to substitute an actress' head with a dummy to reconstruct *The Execution of Mary Queen of Scots*. It was more than just stopping the camera. The illusion was based on a seamless match cut that linked two separately staged shots.

James Stuart Blackton (1875–1941), co-founder of the Vitagraph Company of America, started as a cartoonist and a chalk-talker like his client Winsor McCay. He seemed to have been one of the firsts to use the stop trick in combination with drawings: in *The Enchanted Drawing* (1900) and particularly *Humorous Phases of Funny Faces* (1906), where he did a lot of stop-framed transformation.

The crude Gaumont-produced metamorphoses created by Émile Cohl (1857–1938), a French pioneer of animation and contemporary, even forerunner of Winsor McCay, showing faces that transformed from young to old, from beautiful to old hag, from human to animal, from 2D to 3D puppet, and from human to object to surreal hybrids, are certainly the prototype of the morphing techniques of the digital age, up to *The Mask*. To Scott Squires of Dream Quest, this show was another big step in CGI development. *The Abyss, Terminator 2, Jurassic Park,* and then *The Mask* took CGI another step the evolutionary ladder. Finally, he said, they were able to take surreal cartoon concepts and apply them to the real world. He was right but only partly. The concept of applying metamorphoses onto human faces is as old as cartooning itself. It's not that revolutionary. It's a magician's illusion: just playing around with the novelty. And so even *The Mask*, although CG was used to transform Jim Carrey into that cartoon face, was only a step ahead in digital infancy.

Masks are a key element in the art of performing. Two masks, dating back to the Greek theatre, symbolize the art of the stage: a comedy mask that was associated with Thalia, the muse of comedy and bucolic poetry, and the tragedy mask associated with Melpomene, the muse of tragedy.

Stage and film director Peter Brook talks about a mask that is life giving. It affects a wearer and an observer in a positive way. On the other hand, he claims that there is a mask that can be put on the face of a distorted person and make him appear even more deformed. Watching this it creates the impression of a reality more distorted than the one seen ordinarily. Both go under the same name: "masks." Even the everyday expression is a mask for it is either concealment or lie. In this regard, the ordinary human face might work as a mask.*

The earliest type of mask, disguise and costume, a covering to hide or guard the face, dates back several millennia. It might have been taken from animals, but the human skull as found in skeletons must have been an inspiration too. The maybe oldest stone mask found so far dates to 7000 BC and resembles just that, a human skull.

There are many ritual masks from all over the world that confirm that acting has a lot to do with religion, that it was kind of a ceremony. Theatre came in later.

Right from the beginning, cinema loved the masquerade. Just think of the Alexandre Dumas' novel *Le Vicomte de Bragelonne*, repeatedly filmed as *The Man in the Iron Mask*. Think of Fantomas and the ancestor of *The Shadow:* Judex, silent serials that were directed by Louis Feuillade for Gaumont in Paris, and of all those ugly horror masks: Frankenstein, Mummy, Wolf Man, and Creature from the Black Lagoon. Think of Zorro, Batman, and of Stan Lee's menagerie of Marvel superheroes.

The *Golem* of Jewish folklore, with a mask created by sculptor Rudolf Belling, became Paul Wegener's most famous screen part in movies made in 1914 and 1920, respectively.

---

* Peter Brook, *The Shifting Point: Theatre, Film, Opera 1946–1987.* New York: Theatre Communications Group, 1987.

Acting and Character Animation

4

An Actor's Vision of Optical Poetry

In a 1915 lecture, Paul Wegener (1874–1948) was the first Berlin stage actor to dream of new developments in animation and an entirely new universe of synthetically created images. The fact that actors reflected synthetic images is unique. Georges Méliès found it easier to star himself in his films instead of hiring a comedian or an actor. These pictures seemed to be too tricky for actors. Wegener, on the other hand, became interested in trickfilm. He played a key role in German silent cinematography and he wasn't even interested in the acting, just in technique and aesthetics:

> You have all seen films in which suddenly a line appears, curves, and changes its form. Out of it grow faces and the line disappears. To me the impression seems highly remarkable. But such things are always shown as an intermezzo and nobody has ever thought of the colossal possibilities of this technique. I think the film as art should be based—as in the case of music—on tones, on rhythm. In these changeable planes, events unreel which are partly identified with natural pattern, yet partly beyond real lines and forms. Imagine one of [Arnold] Böcklin's sea paintings with all the fabulous tritons and nereids. And imagine an artist duplicating this work in hundreds of copies but with each copy having small displacements so that all copies revealed in succession would result in continuous movement. Suddenly we would see before our

very eyes a world of pure fantasy come to life. Such effects can also be achieved with specially constructed little models animated like marionettes—in this field there are great achievements nowadays. One also can change the pace of different movements by shooting too slow or too fast, developing a fantastic vision which will produce entirely new associations of ideas. We are entering a new pictorial fantasy world as we would enter a magic forest. We are setting foot in the field of pure kinetics—or optical lyric as I call it. This field will perhaps be of major importance and will open new beautiful sights. This eventually is the final objective of each art, and so cinema would gain an autonomous aesthetic domain for itself. A movie could be created which would become an experience of art—an optical vision, a great symphonic fantasy! That it will happen one day, I am sure—and beyond that, I am certain, later generations will look upon our early efforts as upon childish stuttering.

This is a vision of a true parallel world created by the manipulation of a sequence of moving images, an illusion put together by the dream machine and mechanics of the cinema projecting a light beam, perceived by the human eye and transferred to the brain. Wegener foresaw a magic forest of optical lyric as he called it. All this was imagined, however, not by an engineering wizard or a technical visionary but by an *actor* coming from the legitimate stage. Paul Wegener had joined Max Reinhardt's acting troupe in 1906 and got interested in the movies right before World War I. He understood that the movies were more than a novelty, more than an amusement attraction. It was a new art form and the manipulation of images was to be a part of it. With the end of the Great War, cinema hit puberty and was acknowledged as a new art. It was cinematographer Guido Seeber's trick photography that enabled Wegener to act with his own *doppelganger* on screen in *The Student of Prague* in 1913 and transforming into the *Golem* in 1915, but it still was Wegener's vision.

The *doppelganger* topic seems to be quite important for understanding acting in animation. The character you are going to animate is not exactly *you*. It is like your *doppelganger*. Ray Harryhausen once said when asked how he would master stop motion art technically: *It becomes your second nature.*

Once, on the quiet, an old-time animation producer told us: *The ones who work behind the camera hate those who star in front of the camera.* This type of envy shouldn't be daily fare. Both can learn from each other. Both are filmmakers. Actors are no cattle. Neither are the drawn or digitized actors on screen. Paul Wegener and Walt Disney (with *Fantasia*) had similar dreams. Today, thanks to digital technology, these dreams come true, at least in terms of technology.

---

* Rolf Giesen, *Der Trickfilm: A Survey of German Special Effects.* Cinefex number 25, February 1986.

5

Shadow Plays and Silhouette Films

The Adventures of Prince Achmed

Another actress, who was encouraged and supported by the same Wegener, was Lotte Reiniger (1899–1981). She created the most wonderful silhouette films like the feature-length *Adventures of Prince Achmed (Die Abenteuer des Prinzen Achmed)*, which premiered in Berlin and Paris in 1926. Lotte adored actors and dancers, particularly dancers with whom she spent many hours watching them in their performances. She even had access to the private box of Wassily de Basil for the performances of his *Ballets Russe de Monte Carlo*. At a young age, Lotte had entered the Theatre School of Max Reinhardt, but only wanted to join the classes for the boys, because they did gymnastics. It was in Reinhardt's school that she developed her paper cutting skills, producing tiny portrait figures with great accuracy, most notably the stars in order to attract their attention. Lotte Reiniger was the first-ever actress to turn her back on acting and become an animator.

During Germany's financial crisis, Louis Hagen, a banker acquaintance, had invested in a large quantity of raw film stock as a shelter from inflation, but the gamble hadn't paid off—and so Lotte was allowed to use it to make *Die Abenteuer des Prinzen Achmed*, a Thousand and One Night Fantasy, in the magnificent tradition of the Shadow Theatre that originated from Asia, from China, India, and

Indonesia, which in fact is one of the founding stones of intercultural synergy between the East and West.

The Adventures of Prince Achmed (1926). (Courtesy of Primrose Film Productions Ltd. [Caroline Hagen-Hall and Christel Strobel.])

Shadow puppetry may be as old as the discovery of shadows themselves. Folk tales, fables, and legends are favorite topics on the shadow screen in any culture and time period.

Shadow puppets were first made of paper sculpture, and later on from the hides of donkeys or oxen. That's why their Chinese name is *pi ying*, which means shadows of hides. Shadow puppetry was quite successful during the Tang and Song dynasties. Under the rule of Kangxi, the fourth emperor of the Qing dynasty, this folk art became so popular that there were eight generously paid puppeteers in one prince's mansion. When the Manchu emperors spread their rule to various parts of China, they brought the puppet show with them to make up for the fact that they could not appreciate local entertainment due to language barriers. Only for a few years, the art of puppetry hit hard times in the Middle Kingdom. From 1796 to 1800, the government forbade the public presentation of puppet shows to prevent the spreading of peasant uprising at the time. It was not until 1821 that shadow puppet shows gained vigor again.

Shadow puppets can be animals, heroes, or clowns. They can involve full orchestras and detailed settings or tell a story with only one or two props. Puppets can be moved with strings, rods, bamboo, or animal horns. And they can be smaller than the palm of your hand or larger than life. The stage for the show is a white cloth screen on which the shadows of flat puppets are projected.

Acting and Character Animation

In shadow plays of the past, a candle or an oil lamp cast a soft golden but unpredictable light. Shadow puppets look similar to paper-cut except that their joints are connected by thread so that they can be operated freely. The scene is basic, simple, and almost primitive; it is the consummate performance that wins the spectators' hearts.

Nicknamed the business of the five, a traditional shadow puppet troupe is made up of five people. One operates the puppets, one plays a horn, a *suo-na horn*, and a *yu-kin*, one plays *banhu fiddle*, one is in charge of percussion instruments, and one sings. The singer not only assumes all the roles in the play but also has to play some of the instruments as well.

In Germany, at the further end of the Silk Road, the art of the shadow play got from stage straight to the moving picture screen.

The technique of this type of film is very simple. As with cartoon drawings, the silhouette films are photographed movement by movement. But instead of using drawings, silhouette marionettes are used. These marionettes are cut out of a black cardboard and thin lead, every limb being cut separately and joined with wire hinges. A study of natural movement is very important, so that the little figures appear to move just as men and women and animals do. But this is not a

Lotte Reiniger and assistants working on *The Adventures of Prince Achmed* (1926). (Courtesy of Primrose Film Productions Ltd. [Caroline Hagen-Hall and Christel Strobel.])

technical problem. The backgrounds for the characters are cut out with scissors as well, and designed to give a unified style to the whole picture.

Describing the process of animation, Lotte Reiniger explained that before any acting there is a lot of technique involved to move the flat silhouette puppets around:

> When you are going to play with your figure seriously, make sure that you are seated comfortably. The shooting will take up a long time and you will have to keep yourself as alert as possible. Don't wear any bulgy sleeves; they might touch your figure unexpectedly and disturb its position. If possible arrange to place an iron or wooden bar 5 in. above the set along your field of action and let your arms rest on it, so that you touch your figure only with the finger-tips, or with your scissors. [...]
>
> The most cautiously executed movements must be the slow ones, where you have to alter the position only the fraction of an inch. A steady, slow walk is one of the most tricky movements to execute. Here the most frequent mistake at the beginning is to let the body lag behind the legs, so that they seem to be running away from under the body. If you touch the centre of the body first and move it forward, holding the legs in the initial position, you will notice that they fall into the next position almost by themselves.
>
> Tall, lean figures are more prone to these errors than round, short ones, which roll along easily, whilst the balance of the long ones is more difficult to establish. [...]
>
> If a figure is to turn round it had best to do so in a quick motion. If you want the movement slower you might partly hide it in a convenient piece of the setting.[*]

Lotte's interest in silhouette films matched perfectly with the fascination with shadows that she shared with Expressionist filmmakers like Fritz Lang, Robert Wiene, Friedrich Wilhelm Murnau, and Albin Grau who had designed both *Nosferatu* and *Schatten* (*Shadows*). Yet she pointed out that there is a difference between a shadow and a silhouette:

> From the early days of mankind shadows seemed to men to be something magic. The spirits of the dead were called shadows, and the underworld was named the Kingdom of Shadows and was looked upon with awe and horror. [...]
>
> The essential difference between a shadow and a silhouette is that the latter cannot be distorted. A silhouette can cast a shadow. When you see trees or figures against an evening sky, you would say, not that they are shadowed against the sky, but silhouetted against it. The silhouette exists in its own right.[†]

---

[*] Lotte Reiniger, *Shadow Theatres and Shadow Films*. London and New York: B. T. Batsford Ltd. and Watson-Guptill, 1970, p. 105–108.
[†] Lotte Reiniger, ibid., p. 11–13.

6

Rotoscoping

Dave Fleischer as Ko-Ko the Clown

Most often, however, actors have become important for animation not as visionaries like Paul Wegener but for acting it out for animators to give them a real-life reference. The technique, originally developed by Max Fleischer (1883–1972), is basically known as *rotoscoping*. Fleischer who was Art Editor for the *Popular Science Magazine* felt intrigued by the new process of animation but thought that he could improve on the jerky movements of the early entries in this field. So he filmed his younger brother Dave in a clown's costume, rear-projected the footage onto an easel covered by glass, and with a pen and some ink traced the photographed images frame by frame onto paper to capture the movement and action of the live actor. Out of Dave Fleischer's vivid performance, a cartoon character named Ko-Ko the Clown evolved *Out of the Inkwell*.

Fleischer first experimented with the technique in 1914–1915. On December 6, 1915, a patent was filed. Dave's clown suit was chosen because the high contrast between the black cloth and the white buttons would be easy to trace. Dave owned that costume. For him a dream came true, although by a devious route, as he always had longed to be a clown. Now he was used in animation to answer his desire. For this early experiment, Max photographed Dave silhouetted against a white sheet, on the roof outside of his apartment. For the first time, animated movements were smooth, fluid, and absolutely lifelike. The premier film took over a year to make although it run only a minute but it was a breakthrough in naturalist animation (as was Eadweard Muybridge's chronophotography).

Fleischer's cartoons were marvels of invention and imagination. His son Richard, who became a famous live-action film director and would later do *20,000 Leagues Under the Sea* for his father's old rival Walt Disney, pointed out that Ko-Ko made his entrance in an almost infinite variety of brilliantly conceived ways: in one cartoon, a drop of ink would transform into the figure of the clown; in another, the clown, only half-finished, would grab Max's pen and draw the rest of himself. Morphing was the key to this type of screen comedy.*

For many years, rotoscoping was also used as a VFX tool in film series like the *Star Wars* saga. Today's rotoscope is called motion or performance capture and is completely digitized, but the objective is still the same: to make humans animated actors and make cartoons more human.

But even traditional 2D rotoscoping has been resurrected recently, for instance, in *Alois Nebel,* a 2011-Czech black-and-white film based on a shadowy Graphic Novel by Jaroslav Rudiš and Jaromír Švejdík: At the end of the Communist era, a train dispatcher somewhere at the Czech–Polish border encounters a mute stranger who confronts him with his own past and a murder that happened right after World War II. *Alois Nebel* was awarded a European Film Prize as Best Animated Film in 2012 but wasn't selected for Academy Awards consideration.

Low-budget filmmakers also used the process in the new film genre of animated documentaries and semidocumentaries. One who belongs to this group of animators is Ali Soozandeh who was born in Iran. His *Tehran Taboo* (2017), an evocative animated feature film, touches grave issues like self-determination, sexual fulfillment, loyalty, and the desire for freedom in a fresh view on Iran's restrictive society. The picture centers on the lives of young Iran people—lives, in which breaking taboos is part of personal emancipation. All characters act on an awkward level of imprudence that may come as a surprise to Western audiences but is part of everyday life.

Pari (32 years) is a single mother. She lives together with her mute little son Elias in a high-rise building in the center of Tehran. To pay her rent and to be able to divorce from her husband who is a convicted drug dealer, she offers sex against money. To keep up appearances, she pretends to be a hospital nurse.

Pari's neighbor Sara (28 years) is pregnant. She lives obediently together with her husband Mohsen and his parents. Patronized by her mother-in-law, she

---

* Richard Fleischer, *Out of the Inkwell: Max Fleischer and the Animation Revolution.* Lexington, Kentucky: The University Press of Kentucky, 2005, p. 26.

Live actors photographed in front of a green screen and rotoscoped for *Tehran Taboo* (2017). (Courtesy of Little Dream Entertainment.)

neglects her own desires. Bored by her life and haunted by a secret, she makes friends with Pari.

In the same area lives Babak (22 years). He studies music and scratches a living by giving music lessons while dreaming of a career as a musician. Because of a one-night stand with young Donya (20 years), he is in big trouble. Donya needs her virginity to be restored prior to her upcoming marriage and Babak has to pay for the illegal operation. Together with his best friend Amir, he tries everything to raise the necessary money.

To peek behind the curtain of Iran's split society, Soozandeh uses the stylistic devices of graphic novels and rotoscope: The fascinating imagery started with shooting real actors in a green screen studio. Then, in one year of hard work, backgrounds were generated and both characters and backgrounds were thoroughly sketched and painted. Finally, all layers were assembled and camera movements were applied in the process of compositing.

But, historically speaking, we are ahead of time and have to return to more conventional, nevertheless highly entertaining cartoons.

7

The Peak of Character Animation

Walt Disney

Like Max Fleischer, Disney's animators traced also directly over previously recorded live-action footage of actors and actresses thanks to the camera magic of Leonard Pickley—although they came to the conclusion that direct tracing as done in *Snow White and the Seven Dwarfs* (a young dancer named Marjorie Celeste Belcher, daughter of choreographer Ernest Belcher, who later would marry animator Art Babbitt, served as live-action model for *Snow White*, and Margie Bell volunteered to become the Blue Fairy for *Pinocchio*) looked stiff and unappealing, realizing that the action of the cartoon characters needed to be caricatured. So in the future, they solely referenced from but didn't trace live-action footage one-to-one as Max Fleischer did.

Disney's animators would run live film sequences at half-speed in their action analysis classes to understand weight, thrusts, and counter thrusts, then for *Snow White* brought in burlesque actors like Eddie Collins who would do Dopey for them. They even started to act themselves.

Art Babbitt would use fellow animator Dick Lundy as a role model for Goofy, film his antics with a 16 mm camera, and use the footage as a reference for his animation.

For the sequence that featured Chernobog, the devil on Bald Mountain of *Fantasia* fame, Disney animation director Wilfred Jackson shot live action of Bela Lugosi, the screen's famous *Dracula*, so that Tytla could study the movements of the devil, the same way Fleischer did with his brother Dave. But the way that Lugosi unfolded his "wings," grimaced and gesticulated was not the way that the master animator imagined these movements. So after Lugosi left, Tytla had Jackson, who in comparison with the tall Hungarian actor was a skinny person, bare his chest and gesture the way that Tytla directed him. Tytla's imagination transferred these movements to the monumental evil.

Sure, the nightmarish devil was no game for kids. Walt Disney once said he didn't make films for kids. He very well made kid's films, but he succeeded in charming adults to become children again and go and see these films. And he wouldn't be afraid to scare their pants off.

The same is true for Jeffrey Katzenberg (who in 2016 left his position as CEO of DreamWorks Animation):

...we make our movies for adults and for the adult who exists in every child.[*]

Although he never took acting lessons, Walt Disney was an actor from early childhood on. Interviewed by David Smith, former Disney chief archivist, his cousin Alice Disney Allen recalled that young Walt, without permission, borrowed Brother Roy's blue serge suit and did a Chaplin act in a local theater. Animator Les Clark said that Mickey was Walt: the laugh, the nervous characteristics at times. Walt would act it out for the animators by pantomime.[†]

Disney was the only cartoon producer who was not only in animation but also, as we know, in live action too. It made no difference to him. If he *could* Walt Disney would prefer to do live action which, thanks to popular stars, was more prestigious and less time consuming in production. The proudest moment of his cinematic career might have been *Mary Poppins* (1963) that contained only a short animated segment.

Jules Verne's *20,000 Leagues Under the Sea* (1954) was first considered as animated feature before it became a live-action CinemaScope picture directed, as we have seen, by Max Fleischer's son Richard. Except for James Mason's Captain Nemo, all the other characters, however, Kirk Douglas as Ned Land, Paul Lukas as Professor Aronnax, and Peter Lorre as Conseil remain cartoons. The liveliest actor was a giant squid prop that didn't work from the beginning but when they decided to place it in a storm sequence, it performed terrifically and stuck in audience's memory as the highlight of the picture.

---

[*] Joanna Moorhead, *Jeffrey Katzenberg: How to Make a Perfect Family Film*. The Guardian, Saturday March 12, 2016, London. https://www.theguardian.com/lifeandstyle/2016/mar/12/jeffrey-katzenberg-how-to-make-a-perfect-family-film.
[†] Didier Ghez, ed., *Walt's People—Volume 12: Talking Disney with the Artists Who Knew Him.* Bloomington: Xlibris, 2012.

Disney's forays into live feature and TV films included Guy Williams as *Zorro*, Fred MacMurray as *The Absent-Minded Professor*, and Peter Ustinov, signed right before Walt's death, as *Captain Blackbeard*. (In September 1959, during the Cold War, when he visited Hollywood, Nikita Khrushchev eagerly hoped to go to see *Disneyland* but much to the Soviet Premier's annoyance he was turned down for safety reasons. Ustinov, a thoroughbred comedian, suggested to Disney he would like to play Krushchev in a film and would use different disguises just to get into *Disneyland*. Alas, that movie was never made. It would have been a hilarious comedy.) Fess Parker a.k.a. *Davy Crockett*, who was the first actor signed to a long-term contract by Disney, however, was unhappy on the lot. He said that Disney treasured his great animators who were in effect the actors in his animated films but that it was baffling to him that Disney wouldn't have had some of the same feeling about the most important actors in his live-action films.*

---

* Fess Parker interviewed by Michael Barrier. http://www.michaelbarrier.com. December 23, 2004.

8

Shamanism and Totemism

What made people think that Disney produced shows for kids were not only his fairy tales but was his constant use of cute animals: mice, cats, dogs, horses, chicken, pigs... you name them: the whole barnyard ensemble up and down. Walt Disney was sort of a barnyard kid himself: A genuine country boy. His boyhood hometown was Marceline, Missouri.

Some of his most famous cartoons are a mix of fairy tales with all kinds of rodents and farm animals on board, and a mix of European style with American rusticity. On his European trips, especially in 1935, Disney would buy all kind of reference books and ask one of his artists, Albert Hurter, who was born in Zurich, to do inspirationals that were authentic to the respective background.

In the process of "(type) casting," Donald Duck would be introduced to *The Wise Little Hen* (which was basically a Russian story), Mickey Mouse would star in *The Barn Dance* before he climbed the ladder of success and was cast as *The Brave Little Tailor* and *The Sorcerer's Apprentice,* a cricket would co-star with *Pinocchio,* and *Cinderella's* helpers would consist of a gang of mice.

For regular actors, it is quite difficult to portray an animal. They need costumes but usually their anatomy is not built the way animals are and the result looks like Bert Lahr's Cowardly Lion costume in *The Wizard of Oz* that was made by British taxidermist George Lofgren who came to America when he was 9 years old and would work with Willis O'Brien and Ray Harryhausen and for Alfred Hitchcock on *The Birds*. Some quadruped dinosaurs like Anguirus (Angirasu), the mutated ankylosaurus from Toho's *Gojira no gyakushu* (*Gigantis, the Fire Monster/Godzilla Raids Again*, 1955), forced the bit players inside the rubber suits shamefully down on all fours, but what they did was more crawling than walking. Special makeup artists Charlie Gemora and Rick Baker came nearest to nature building the best gorillas in film business before the digital age for pics like *Murders in the Rue Morgue* and *Phantom of the Rue Morgue, Gorillas in the Mist* or *Greystoke: The Legend of Tarzan, Lord of the Apes*.

We know that shamans often disguised as animals too and looked like the hybrids of mythology.

It was Ed Hooks who pointed out in his lecture tours that actors as well as animators might have the same ancestor: the shaman. A true priest, said Constantin Stanislavsky (also spelled Stanislavski), is aware of the presence of the altar all the time and the same way a true artist should react to the stage.

Insiders say that to Eiji Tsuburaya, a technical creator of the Japanese *Godzilla* films, the movie studio was a sacred place.

A shaman is a person who enters an altered state of consciousness to travel in a kind of parallel universe, similar of nowadays digital, virtual world. Their healing "shows" are regarded as a source of acting and storytelling. They used to sing, pray, drum, and dance. Animal spirits were their constant companions. As part of their animal worship they believed in the Power Animals that are around us all the time, that take pity on us when we are born, and protect us. Power Animals represent the ties of man with nature and document the human/animal dualism. Often the objective of early cultures was to lock horns with, say, a bull to kill the strongest or fastest animal of the country and drink the victim's blood to absorb its strength and abilities: bear, deer, wolf, and snake.

This mimesis and shamanistic transmutation that involved imitation of animals extended animal concepts into the social domain and is part of *totemism* that we find in traditional economies that rely on hunting and gathering. What you had killed you showed respect to because it was a living being and it feeds us. To a shaman everything is living, even a stone—and that is true for the animator too.

The Power Animal becomes a protective spirit. In the Western film genre, although we notice it only subconsciously, the horse becomes the Power Animal of the Cowboy, for instance, Lucky Luke's horse, Jolly Jumper.

Actors are the direct heirs to shamanism while artists and painters are the ones to record what they did and, more important: what they saw. German anthropologist Andreas Lommel mentioned the man–animal picture known as "the Sorcerer" located at the Les Trois Frères cave in the Ariege. To him it is the oldest known portrayal of a shaman, maybe a shaman disguised in an animal suit. Thus, for the first time, the animal was *humanized*.

A shaman acts as a bridge between different worlds, just like an actor and an artist who guide audiences and spectators to another dimension, a dimension between life and death: to see, explore, and experience the things *behind*. Today, we have the media to revive and re-animate the souls of the dead. It is little surprise that the spiritists of the late nineteenth century, the heirs of the shamans, used man-made technology such as telegraphic and telephonic contact and photographic effects to establish a communication with the world beyond. Hayao Miyazaki's *Spirited Away* (*Sen to Chihiro no kamikakushi*, 2001) is a truly Shamanic film. It shows us the things and ghosts that are behind reality. In the rational world of today, we are not allowed to do so. In children's tales, films, and animation, and in video games where we actually take part in role games we are allowed. Humans are irrational. They need to believe in this other dimension.

A shamanic play is like a healing ritual. After seeing a good movie or a good play, we feel cured too.

Isn't the Walt Disney Company, one of the world's self-proclaimed leading producers and providers of entertainment, based on ancient animism and totemism: founded on the myth of a mouse? By definition totemism is a mystical relationship with a spirit being, with a powerful animal. Disney, however, is totemism that has lost its meaning. We experience it in the Magic Kingdom of Disneyland. In the Internet, we have found a fascinating little Japanese import, a totem pole mug set with Mickey, Minnie, and Pluto, and another one with Humphrey the Bear, Donald, Goofy, and Mickey.

Soviet director Sergei Eisenstein wrote an essay about Disney in which he called the very idea of an animated cartoon a direct manifestation of the method of animism. In that regard, he said, what Disney does is connected with one of the deepest features of the early human psyche. So it is no wonder that Power Animals would early on transform into cartoon stars, with one exception, however: The strong animals of Shamanic visions and journeys, the mighty eagle, for instance, that took the visionary in his trance high above mountains and countryside, are merely supporting players in cartoons while the tiny ones, especially the mice, became the ones audiences would sympathize with.

Occasionally, some animals are even used explicitly in the shamanic way as Power Animals in cartoon series and animated feature films:

Sure Rémy the Rat of *Ratatouille* fame acts as such a power animal[*] to an aspiring young cook named Alfredo Linguini. More on *Ratatouille,* one of the best and most emotional cartoon films ever, later. Earlier Disney used the concept when he attributed a cricket conscience to marionette-to-become-a-real-boy *Pinocchio*.

Disney heroines favorably respond to animal "sidekicks:" *Cinderella* befriends a gang of mice, *Pocahontas* has a pet raccoon named Meeko, Jasmine (*Aladdin*)

---

[*] Not a classic power animal but thanks to cunning the rat finished in first in the Chinese zodiac and appeared on the back of a buffalo in front of Buddha.

is seen in the company of Rajah the tiger, Rapunzel (*Tangled*) has Pascal, a chameleon, as her best friend and confidante, and *Mulan* has a weird but tiny dragon called Mushu.

In a recent series that premiered on Disney Channel in the summer of 2016, *Elena of Avalor,* the fox Zuzu—which acts as a link between the world of humans and ghosts and only can be seen by the heroine princess—is described as a power or a spirit animal by the series' creator and executive producer, Craig Gerber.

9
Famous Cartoon Animals

Animism and animation have the same root.

Let's have a look at all those famous anthropomorphic cartoon animals that are indeed a reflection on shamanism and animism. Very often in the cartoons, humans are compared to animals, same as in the Shamanic vision.

American cartoons most often used cute animals and upended nature to have sheep-loving little David win over the carnivorous barbarian, Goliath.

Mickey Mouse has become a trademark although there are cartoon stars that are more popular. The mouse is seen as a wise animal: quiet, shy, understanding, invisible, stealthy, neat, meek and humble, scrutinizing, and paying attention even to the tiniest detail. In storytelling, the mouse reflects favorably the David and Goliath principle: In small we trust. Be faithful to the little things. In the great American tales, it's quite often the underdog who is the hero while in real life we would consider him beneath contempt. And like Chaplin's tramp, the early Mickey Mouse started out as an underdog but his optimism became a symbol of hope in the time of the Great Depression.

One of the reasons is that Mickey came first, well, not exactly, not even in sound. Even Disney had another character before Mickey (and lost it to Universal): *Oswald the Lucky Rabbit*. But it was Mickey that fit the bill. Ub Iwerks was the first to draw him, construct him out of simple black circles and rubber tube arms and legs, but the personality was invented by Disney himself. Although Iwerks, for a while lured away from the Disney Studio by Pat Powers, tried on his own and invented *Flip the Frog* and *Willie Whopper*, he failed because, although these characters were equally simple, they lacked Mickey's personality. But we shouldn't belittle Iwerks' part. Mickey's sometimes raucous behavior—being very abusive to other animals, being an anarchist—seemed to have been a part of Iwerks' character. Mickey started as an actor, as a parodist. In his first films, he parodied Charles Lindbergh (*Plane Crazy*), Douglas Fairbanks (*Gallopin' Gaucho*), Al Jolson, and absorbed a little bit from everyone to fill his character. Acting and parodying was his forte because Mickey himself was a shy character haunted by the psychological problems of everyday America. One Walther Schneider would even go so far as to describe Mickey as mentally disordered:

> *The chronic movie image of Mickey Mouse displays unmistakable streaks of a paranoid mental illness of its originator. A diagnosis of the spindle-shanked, hydrocephalic, astigmatic and neurasthenic Mickey Mouse reveals particularly disorders in the sphere of face and hearing (commonly called mental delusions). On closer examination, concerning these "pathologically changed perceptions of real objects", one has to decide if this is a manic or paranoid case. [...]*
>
> *Basically, this preposterous behavior (in kitchen, ice boxes, fortresses and deserts) is a kind of paranoia that is characterized by right logic under wrong prerequisites. The "distortion of space, time and causal connections" (in the film plot), the "blurred blending of various objects" (the car that transforms into a living being, the dancing piano stool), the "permanently erroneous repetition of perceptions" (multiplications of young Mickey Mouses) is indicative of youth madness.*
>
> *A psychiatric surveillance of Mickey Mouse that lasted over several screenings leaves no doubt of a serious case of paraphrenia as described by [Emil] Kraepelin (related to Dementia paranoids). The world of Mickey Mouse ideas, voluptuously equipped with fantasy and narrative streaks, represents a marginal case of lunacy psychoses that often leads to severe temper tantrums.*[*]

This revealing "analysis" was published in 1931 in a respected Berlin magazine. Although it seems quite certain that it was maybe satirically meant, there are some words of truth. Even Disney, when he became saturated and conservative, had doubts about Mickey's "mental disorder" and had the character change from *sturm und drang*, storm and stress to *petit bourgeois*. More and more, Mickey lost popularity and simply became a trademark. He had become a suburban citizen like so many of us. Like the viewers changed socially, a number of cartoon characters changed psychologically. In his early films, Mickey was a funny chap and sort of an adventurer, even a slob and rebel. But Disney realized that Mickey was primitive in animation and that made him order to re-design the character and make him more charming, not the animated stick he was in his first pictures.

---

* Walther Schneider, *Micky Maus ist geisteskrank*. Der Querschnitt #10, Berlin 1931, p. 679. Printed with permission of J. P. Storm Collection.

Clothes made the mouse. The early Mickey was almost completely naked except for red shorts and big shoes. The later version was meticulously dressed. Some pictures even show Mickey in a tail coat.

The pursuit of charm and personality, however, for anatomical correctness over cartoony action would change Mickey's character completely and put him in the background. So Mickey became this uninteresting character, a shadow of his early popular self, with his dog Pluto destined to do all the funny things, provide the gags and bring Mr. Mouse in trouble.

Disney story artist and director Jack Kinney called Mickey a bastard to work with: a Boy Scout but what the hell to do with a Boy Scout?

Although simply constructed, the late Mickey was not easy to draw and certainly became boring to act. His formerly rebellious mind was projected onto a gang of sidekicks, like Donald Duck, that became more popular than the original creature.

Disney didn't exactly realize that the figurative simplicity was the key to success, but he had to change the caricature the more he was striving for naturalism. (As many actors were: for different reasons as we will see.) Just consider changing the design of the *Simpsons* or *South Park* kids of today's television.

Nevertheless, many cartoon characters, contemporaries of Mickey, remained zany and crazy. They are like bad-boy avatars of those who enjoy the movies and want to break out of their petty bourgeois existence but are unable to do so.

Woody Woodpecker was nuts when he started out in a supporting part in a 1940 Andy Panda cartoon, *Knock Knock*. Producer Walter Lantz claimed that the crazy bird was based on a real woodpecker that was pecking holes in a cottage. The bird was so disruptive that Lantz' wife suggested to turn him into a cartoon character. It was not Lantz who finished the job but one of his employees, story man Ben "Bugs" Hardaway, fresh from Warners, where he had worked on Bugs Bunny that was originally Bugs' Bunny. Woody was terrible. He was rambunctious, highly aggressive, and had a crazy laugh that was adopted from Happy Rabbit, a predecessor of Bugs. In 1944, this hundred-percent insane character was transferred from the forest right into opera where he did *The Barber of Seville*. This was the first Woody Woodpecker cartoon to feature a refined version of the woodpecker that was designed by Emery Hawkins and layout artist Art Heinemann. The red belly had been altered to white.

Then, however, a change occurred initiated by a shorts director who came straight from less anarchic or no-anarchic-at-all Disney, Dick Lundy, who would make the character more sympathetic. Out went the early day madness. Woody became rational, small, cute, and likeable in a complete turn-around of personality change.

Each cartoon character seems to have two souls: an assimilated and an unassimilated. Cartoon aficionados seem to sympathize with the unassimilated, while cartoon producers usually will go for the assimilated.

Bugs Bunny, on the other hand, was smart aleck, a pain in the ass to his adversaries like Elmer Fudd and Yosemite Sam: *This means war.* According to Frank

Tashlin, one of his early directors, all of Bugs came from a 1934 Disney *Silly Symphony*, *The Tortoise and the Hare*. With one major difference, we might say: The Disney hare is incredibly vain and therefore not at all sympathetic. He is no role model at all. His antics are disgusting. Ten years later, Warners made a spoof of *The Tortoise and the Hare* called *Tortoise Wins by a Hare*, and one sees that Bugs doesn't work very well in that context: being outsmarted by a turtle. Bugs works better as an avenger to those who interrupt his peaceful life. And that would mean that his personality was based on the witty dialogue.

But even a character like him can vary from film to film and from director to director. Just compare the Bugs Bunny of Tex Avery to the one supervised by Chuck Jones, Robert Clampett, or Friz Freleng.

Chuck Jones considered his Bugs quite different from that directed by Bob Clampett who resembled Woody Woodpecker or Friz Freleng. Freleng's cartoons, like *Sahara Hare* (1955), were more physical, with things happening quickly. Jones' version tended to think out his problems and solve them intellectually. But Jones saw his Bugs never as a revolutionary. He understood him as a counterrevolutionary.

One of the best creations conceived by Chuck Jones and his main storyboard artist Michael Maltese was Wile E. Coyote. This character is its own worst enemy. He'd never ever catch the Road Runner. The more frustrated, the more wildly inventive he becomes. Santayana said that a fanatic is one who redoubles his efforts when he's forgotten his aim. Wile E. is that kind of fanatic.

The Coyote is a character not so much by acting but by definition as a complete loser who wouldn't surrender and give up losing (as gamblers don't give up gambling while they lose), enriched by the quality of accidents and *Fast & Furryous* gags. This is why we always identify with the pains the Coyote suffers. It is the same as in daily life: No matter how hard we work, no matter how clever our schemes, we invariably seem to get out-run by someone who hardly tries at all like Gladstone Gander, Donald Duck's comic book nemesis.

Upon leaving Warner Bros., Michael Maltese and Chuck Jones got a hold of Tom & Jerry after MGM had closed down their own cartoon department. Both decided to change the original design particularly of Tom Cat and out came a completely different character. Style changed personality and performance, not to the likes of outspoken Tom & Jerry fans. The facial expression, especially the eyes, produced a totally different cat. The same happened to Mickey Mouse, as we have seen, when he was completely clothed like a petit bourgeois and to the domesticated Woody Woodpecker.

Daffy Duck was different than Donald, the proverbial black duck among the animated duck community: literally daffy, speaking in a lisping, spitting form, schizophrenic, considering himself witty to no end, and trying to outsmart smart aleck Bugs Bunny but failing constantly. But the same as with Bunny, his personality would change from director to director. Best he was portraying an anarchist.

The Pink Panther started out as title character for Blake Edwards' comedies to become a cartoon star in his own right. In pantomime, he equals Felix the Cat but, named after a jewel, he is more elegant. Dignified, cool, and most important: pink he is sure a ladies' man. The Panther developed into a successful series character in television, one of the last famous cartoon animals.

There is one single quality that many cartoon animals have. Regardless of whether they try to kill each other with sticks of dynamite or have themselves steamrolled, they always resurrect as if nothing had happened. They are cartoons and so they are immortal like Gods. They are shining stars and so we admire and envy them.

10

Animators to Become Actors and Actresses (Sort of)?

An animator has to have not only acting and dubbing reference, but inwardly he has to have certain acting qualities himself. In the old days, animators had a mirror in front of their drawing board to study their own facial expression and grimaces.

But when they call an animator an actor with a pen, it's a misnomer. *Inwardly*, yes, as he might use techniques to put feelings into a character, but never ever will he equal a professional actor. There are young aspiring animators who say that they are afraid to act. They don't have to. They never will be actors. They never should be. They are like puppeteers, remaining in the dark. Always will. They have to know about acting (as they have to know about film theory and film history) because they have to judge it. But they are certainly no actresses or actors themselves. They don't have to be afraid; they don't have to enter a stage. Vice versa actors won't become animators. We only know about one Tom Holland, an actor who in the early 1960s would do some stop motion work for a Hollywood company named Project Unlimited, animating a boy and a caveman riding a Brontosaurus in *Dinosaurus!* (1960), Cormoran in a dance miniature (for reference he had himself filmed doing Cormoran's dance steps), and some scenes with a two-headed giant and a harpy for *Jack the Giant Killer* (1962). In 2D animation we don't know any, only directors who would move from animation to live action: Gregory La Cava, Frank Tashlin, Brad Bird, Andrew Adamson, Tim Burton, and Marjane Satrapi who went from co-directing *Persepolis* (2007) to *Chicken with Plums* (2011).

However, the animator must become one with the image he creates. The image will absorb him mentally:

According to a Chinese legend, there was an old painter who had painted a landscape that depicted a beautiful valley, with mountains in the distance. The painter liked the valley so much that he walked right inside the painting and disappeared into the mountains, never to be seen again.

The issue here is very simple. The old Chinaman had simply used his brush to create reality. For that was the belief at the time: things are just as they appear to be. A picture is no longer a picture; it is a reality that can be entered into, something definitive and fixed.

By using pencil, paint, clay, or pixels, the animator has to make an audience emphatically believe in a creation that was voiced for him by a professional actress or actor. Believable acting means that the audience will feel that the character's actions are the result of his own inner emotions and not what the animator might pretend. It means that the character has personality and reflects, even in the tiniest gesture, mood.

If the people could watch the faces of the best animators when caught up in the act of drawing an emotional scene, said Brad Bird, they would see artists as fully invested in the moment as the best live actors:

The difference is that an animator stays in that moment, often working for weeks to express an emotion his or her character takes only seconds to convey on screen.*

The menagerie of anthropomorphized animals in animation based on the work of the great storytellers in history from Aesop to Jean de La Fontaine is impressive as we have seen: all these animal characters require from the animators the combined knowledge of human and animal behavior to express them in the great art of character animation.

For actors, and particularly for animators, it is useful to develop a kinesthetic sense and a thorough understanding of music and rhythm. Frank Gladstone, the former Director of Training at DreamWorks SKG and CEO of his own company, Gladstone Film, feels that an animator is responsible for creating characters that not only fit their own voices but can perform without vocal cues as well. The more keenly developed a kinesthetic sense an actor, dancer, or animator has, the more capacity that artist has to portray various characters and exhibit organic nuances and gestures appropriate to that character.

---

* Brad Bird, foreword to Ed Hooks, *Acting for Animators: A Complete Guide to Performance Animation*. Revised Edition. Portsmouth, NH: Heinemann Drama, 2003, pp. vi–vii.

It's mandatory that above good movement and fluid animation you feel *personality*. Therefore, in the old days, animators were often cast according to characters. At least that was Disney's principle. Like actors particular animators can handle certain parts better than others. In most productions it is not possible to follow this principle, which means that one character might be handled by different persons. In such cases, there never will be outstanding character animation.

First comes movement, then personality, and out of personality comes emotion.

Animator Art Babbitt reminds a memorable scene from Disney's *Dumbo* drawn by the great Bill Tytla, where he comes to visit his mother who is locked up in a cage. Babbitt recalls to have seen this picture in several places around the world and each time people in the audience would weep:

> It could have been so crude and maudlin but instead it was done with great sensitivity and taste. It's assumed you can make somebody laugh with funny little drawings, but to be able to use these funny little drawings and to make a person feel so deeply that he weeps—in my estimation, that is true artistry.*

From Tytla we know that he had read Polish actor-director Richard Boleslavsky's book, *Acting: The First Six Lessons* (1933), and used the book's principles in animation: concentration, memory of emotion, dramatic action, characterization, observation, and rhythm.

Walt Disney said that their most important aim was to develop definite personalities, not just shadows, but something that would provoke emotional response from the public. They didn't want them to parallel or assume the aspects of human beings or human actions. Instead they endowed them with human weaknesses, which they exaggerated in a humorous way. Rather than a caricature of individuals, their work was supposed to be a caricature of life.

Disney was one of the first to enter television. Other animators would follow his example when the production of theatrical shorts became limited. William Hanna and Joseph Barbera had made the Tom & Jerry Cartoons for MGM. Now they had to confine to low budgets offered by Screen Gems, the TV arm of Columbia Pictures. They had to change the characters figuratively. Barbera recalled that it cost $40,000 to $65,000 to make one of the classic MGM Tom & Jerry cartoons. Screen Gems offered no more than $2700 for 5 minutes. Their secret weapon was the "limited" or "planned" animation technique that they had already used to create full-length trial runs of each MGM cartoon. A limited animation test required only about 1800 drawings instead of the 20,000 or 30,000 thousand for the finished product. For television, they needed to refine the technique and developed working procedures that used about 3000 drawings for a 5-minute cartoon.

---

* Ed Hooks, *Acting for Animators: A Complete Guide to Performance Animation*. Revised Edition. Portsmouth, NH: Heinemann Drama 2003, p. 86.

Television was just based on the arithmetic.

In the early days, animation was designed on bodily motion and gestures as way to express individual personality. Even in the early sound films, there was only little dialogue. The tempo was defined by sound effects and music score. That happened at a time when even silent comedians had to tune into dialogue or have been reduced to become bit players.

Some say that character and acting came in anyway by dialogue and that happened even before the feature films. It happened in one of Disney's most beloved short films that became a highlight among the *Silly Symphonies*, in front of the background of Depression and New Deal: In the 1933 *Three Little Pigs* they had three characters that looked alike. So they had to differentiate them by the way they moved, by the way they acted, and the way they spoke and sang. Otherwise, the three of them would have been equal.

Disney didn't want his characters to be just something moving around on the screen and doing funny things, cartoon director Wilfred Jackson said. He would go for more and wanted the audience to care what happened to the characters, and to believe them as real, not just as a bunch of funny drawings.

That was the time when several animators at the Disney studio even enrolled in acting classes.

Generally, at that time, cartoon characters were stereotypes:

Like for instance when they did The Tortoise and the Hare. *It was clearly laid out to have the hare act the way he did, bombastic and boastful, yet talented. That was good, clear characterization. The tortoise was definitely staged as a stupid guy who could good-naturedly be taken advantage of. Actually he won by default. This was the kind of strong characterization that Walt always insisted on. If anybody else had done* The Tortoise and the Hare *it would have been a series of assorted gags about running, one after another.*

They often wondered, Dick Huemer would add, if Disney could have been a great actor or a comedian. The acting in them was what made his pictures so great.[*]

Most of his fellow students at Folkwang School in Essen, Germany, looked down on Andreas Deja. The young graphic designer was not interested in abstract animation but fascinated by Disney's character animation, which he had literally inhaled studying Hans Bacher's Super 8- and 16-mm prints of Disney animation frame by frame. Deja was insistent and applied to Disney. Everybody was flabbergasted when Deja was eventually hired on the strength of some pencil test animation that showed a witch having problems starting a broom and riding off. That means he was hired on the strength of his cartoon acting. During his long stay, he was lucky enough to animate some of the great 2D Disney characters: Roger Rabbit, Gaston in *Beauty and the Beast,* Jafar in *Aladdin,* Scar in *The Lion*

---

[*] Joe Adamson, *With Disney on Olympus. An Interview with Dick Huemer.* Funnyworld No. 17, 1977, p. 38.

Acting and Character Animation

King, and Lilo Pelekai in *Lilo & Stitch.* Deja was convinced that a sure feeling for acting is a vital prerequisite for outstanding animation. He knows that there are good animators around who do nice, polished drawings, but there is no emotion to come over. Some might need to attend acting classes, he says, others, him included, work intuitively. They watch people live and on screen.

In television, however, with the zany action gone, there was no need for nuances in acting. Figures were characterized by more and more dialogue until it became illustrated radio. The classic cartoons had no or not much dialogue. They were based on the variations of a chase like that of a cat and a mouse. But with television, it had to be a human story because it would require dialogue to save action.

The Flintstones and the Age of Television

With the advent of television, animals gradually disappeared from cartoons and were substituted by rough human caricatures. The reason is that TV cartoons had to use more dialogue and less action for budgetary reasons. With the classic cartoon animals, like Tom & Jerry and Coyote & Roadrunner, it was vice versa of course.

The Flintstones are genuine offspring of television. William Hanna and Joseph Barbera, their creators (of Tom & Jerry fame), designed them not only for television, they designed them from television, from the series of family sitcoms that were popular in the 1950s such as *I Love Lucy, Father Knows Best*, and in particular *The Honeymooners*. Looking for the right environment, Hanna-Barbera passed family Pilgrims, Romans, Eskimos, and Cowboys until they hit hard stones and rocked them. The show, starring Fred, Barney, and their wives, started on September 30, 1960, and despite some negative reviews became an instant hit, not so much by character animation but by witty dialogue and a modernized Stone Age that resembled typical American suburbs. The Flintstones were the direct ancestors, Stone Age predecessors so to speak of the Simpsons, an animated sitcom favorite that, like the Flintstones, only works in dialogue, not in animation that was inexpensively executed in South Korea. Homer Simpson's design is that simplistic that inspired animation is almost impossible. But when it came to the colors, one of the animators suggested to render him and his family yellow, and to Matt Groening that looked right. Yellow worked like a signal when people were flipping through the channels. Just by a quick look viewers could see that the *Simpsons* were on. Neither the color nor the characters themselves seemed to be very original: In the late 1940s, Oscar Jacobsson (1889–1945), a Swedish cartoonist, created a character named Adamson that was well known in Europe and looked exactly like Homer.

Now, with so simple animation around thanks to television, the Europeans were finally able to compete with American animation.

Signor Rossi is typically Italian. He was created by Bruno Bozzetto as a cipher for the Italian Everyman. By then, as a result of UPA (United Productions of America), National Film Board of Canada and Zagreb product, audiences' taste had shifted toward mechanomorphic humans who, according to Chaplin's *Modern Times*, have qualities that are similar to those of machines and move that way (which of course makes the process of animation really simple and absolutely limited). They are still 2D but they seem to forebode the digital age when characters and technology would become a standardized one.

Most of the more or less famous European cartoon stars are human, except for André Franquin's Marsupilami, a black-spotted yellow monkey, and Aardman's Plasticine *Gromit* and *Shaun the Sheep* with not many animals around.

Europeans seem to be more interested in history than Americans. They simply have the option to refer to a bigger cultural memory while compared to it America is a rather young country. For some time, Asterix was the leading European cartoon character, both in books and animated films. Asterix was a shrewd, cunning little Gaul warrior living in a small village that opposes the Roman occupants. Thanks to a magic potion that was secretly prepared by village druid Miraculix (or. Panoramix), Asterix gets superhuman strength. The diminutive character itself would not mean much if not in tandem with his sidekick, Obelix. A menhir delivery-man by trade, he is addicted to wild boar. As a child, he fell into the cauldron of magic potion and since then wants to drink more but isn't allowed. Obelix is fat and bulky, while Asterix is small and fast. As with so many comedy teams, they complement each other perfectly.

The Romans, although this fact was denied by their creators, René Goscinny and artist Albert Uderzo, are clear caricatures of the Nazi Germans, the *Boche*, who occupied parts of France in World War II. Interestingly enough, the Asterix comic books and films were more popular in Germany than in the country of origin.

Then there is Tintin, a juvenile reporter created in the late 1920s by Belgian artist Hergé (Georges Prosper Remi), who, travelling through Belgian Congo and other exotic places, is clearly a product of European colonialism. Steven Spielberg was so enthusiastic about Hergé's comics that he filmed one of the *Adventures of Tintin* with performance capture technology.

Most famous abroad, however, are the Smurfs. Their prototypes had been created by another Belgian artist, Peyo (Pierre Culliford), in an animation studio in Brussels during German occupation in 1944 and were refined in 1957 as *Schtroumpfs*. At first glance, they all look alike, and all are blue (while the *Simpsons* are yellow) but on closer inspection we recognize how individual they are, quite similar to the Seven Dwarfs. Besides Papa Smurf, the head of the community, there are, named after their character attributes, Brainy, Greedy, Vanity, Lazy, Clumsy, Hefty, Harmony, and many more.

Marsupilami, Asterix, Tintin, Lucky Luke, and the Smurfs—they all owe their lives to the rich tradition of Franco-Belgian comic books.

12

Reason & Emotion

Reason & Emotion was the title of one out of a trio of anti-Fascist short films Walt Disney produced in 1943, telling of two little guys in the head of each person that symbolize the person's emotions, one of which was brutal and tended to Nazi ideology while reason was rejecting this. The message: Americans should control these emotions inside their head so that the Nazis will have no chance to infiltrate it by means of brainwashing. Pixar director Pete Docter had seen the picture and used the basic premise for the feature-length *Inside Out*. Five little guys symbolize the basic emotions sitting in little Riley's brain, sans reason, and get her into trouble.

Actually, there are seven of them.

The word emotion comes from the Latin *emovere,* meaning "disturb." These disturbances are universal and always tell the truth.

Infants only know two emotions:

- *Anger*: upper lids pulled up, eyes bulging, margins of lips rolled in and pressed firmly
  and
- *Joy*: muscle around the eyes tightened, "crows feet" wrinkles around the eyes, cheeks raised, lip corners raised diagonally

Older persons have five more basic emotions:

- *Fear*: eyebrows pulled up and together, upper eyelids pulled up, eyes open, lips stretch horizontally
- *Disgust*: eyebrows pulled down, nose wrinkled, upper lip pulled up, lips loose
- *Sadness*: inner corners of eyebrows raised, eyelids loose, lip corners pulled down
- *Surprise*: entire eyebrow pulled up, eyelids pulled up, eyes open wide, mouth hangs open, jaw drops slightly

The final one splits the human face:

- *Contempt*: lip corner pulled up on one side and back on the other. Half of the upper lip tightens up.

Audiences empathize with character's emotions. Therefore, Antonin Artaud was right when he said that actors are athletes of the heart. The stronger the human element, the better are the chances of audience identification.

What they act has been written.

Reason is the field of writing. But there is more to emotion. The written situation becomes the criterion for the emotional development of a character, but to empathize with its emotions, there are more elements needed: Spectators must like the design of the character, either a hero or a villain, the score evokes emotion too.

If you have a movie like the ill-conceived *Oooops! Noah Is Gone* (2015), however, also known as *Two by Two* or *All Creatures Big and Small,* a German–Irish–Luxembourg co-production and survival tale about two imaginary animal kids that get lost from the ark, it is easy to like the universal appeal of the story but difficult to empathize with characters that are designed like Asian-manufactured cheap fur fabric toys that nobody wants to have, trashy things you might win at the funfair and then throw away. It comes like a miracle to rescue the life of such miserably ugly guys with too large heads and too small bodies.

Reason brings us values to apply to emotions, and these are different from culture to culture.

Once, at the Berlin Museum of Film and Television, we did an experiment and invited about 150 pupils from a trade school to a screening of Veit Harlan's anti-Semitic *Jud Süss* (*Jew Suss*) made in 1940 on commission by the German Minister of the so-called Enlightenment and Propaganda, Dr. Joseph Goebbels. Although 2 of the 150 young people would declare themselves being anti-Semites (which caused some discussion in the school afterwards), nobody seemed to be interested in the stagy Nazi chamber play propaganda. They weren't emotionally touched by the elite of old-fashioned character actors who would recite their lines with an eye-roll. We also screened Disney's Story of one of "Hitler's Children" as adapted from *Education for Death: The Making of the Nazi* by Gregor Ziemer, one of Disney's anti-Fascist short films, showing the socialization of Hans, a young, very shy German boy in the Third Reich:

Listen to the fanatic cry: "Heute gehört uns Deutschland, morgen die ganze Welt."
- "Today we own Germany, tomorrow the whole world." Hans is now ready for the
higher education as decreed by the Fuehrer.

We see the youth marching, all armed with torches, burning books by Voltaire and Einstein, scores written by Mendelssohn, transforming the Holy Bible into Hitler's *Mein Kampf,* substituting the crucifix with a sword and a swastika.

Marching and hailing, hailing and marching Hans grows up. In him is planted no seed of laughter, hope, tolerance or mercy. For him only hailing and marching, marching and hailing as the years grind on. Manhood finds him still hailing and marching for the grim years of regimentation have done their work. Now he is a good Nazi. He sees no more than the Party wants him to. He says nothing than the party wants him to say, and he does nothing but what the Party wants him to do. And so he marches on, with millions of comrades, trampling on the rights of others for now his education is complete. His education for—death.

We see lines of soldiers chained and muzzled like dogs wandering into war graves.

This did it. This touched them all and evoked emotions, decades after the film had been made.

13

Theories of Acting

Theatrical reality is the opposite from regular, mundane reality. It is compressed in time and space and has a dramatic structure missing from everyday life. To Shakespeare, the whole world was a stage. Reality becomes dream. So far, animation has a lot to do with theatre. And there was another thing that Shakespeare added to drama: His figures were characters that were able to change, and this was what made dramas interesting. In a way, with him we also enter the language of the cinema claims Terry Curtis Fox, an Arts Professor and Chair of the Goldberg Department of Dramatic Writing in the Tisch School of Acting.

Centuries ago, actors and actresses were not well respected.

In the European theatre, tragedy as well as comedy had its origin in the Dionysian Rites of Ancient Greece. Dionysos is the god of fertility, wine, and ecstasy and is associated with disguise and transformation. He would break down boundaries and surround himself with *maenads (mad women)* and *satyrs.*

In *The Republic*, Plato banished actors from his ideal city. The reason: they create appearances rather than reality. Actors masquerade as imitators. This duplicity, if executed succinctly, endangers our perceptions and undermines truth. Acting is synonymous to deception, exploits our weakness for appearances over reality. To him, Plato let Socrates say, all the imitative arts seem ruinous to the mental powers of all their hearers.

In Rome, thespians were part of the slave system. Even those actors who became favorites of the Emperor were denied freedman status. In old Japan, the original all-female form of the Kabuki Theatre was tied to prostitution. In China, actors were considered lower class too. In the thirteenth century, Chinese acting troops were semi-nuclear families that travelled together. They lived hand-to-mouth. In the Early Middle Ages, action troupes were viewed with distrust and disgust. In the seventeenth century, theatre in France and England was considered an institution that acted against God. Actors were imposters and jugglers. They were a travelling circus of buffoons. They were fake fire-eaters. It needed time and a change of mind and society to have these people respected.

The attitude changed in the eighteenth and nineteenth centuries, when theatre became more and more leisure pastime for the new bourgeois upper class. That was when they began to speak about the *legitimate stage.*

At the same time, with the rise of naturalism, the postulate of a more natural way of acting was issued. The bourgeoisie had replaced the outgoing feudal aristocracy and favored a new inwardness. Previously, on stage they applauded the declamation, the louder the better. There was no director around to hold actors back. Actors did as they pleased. They ad-libbed and extemporized.

Now the audience that fancied itself asked for naturalness and hoped to be touched by the actor's art. To supervise this art, a new profession, a dramaturge, was needed.

All drama theory dwells on the relationship between actor, role, and character. One group says that actors have to be taken up in and empathize with their parts, the other demands a distance of the actor from his part.

The ones who placed the director's view in the center of attention were Bert Brecht and Vsevolod Meyerhold. What Meyerhold implemented in theatre is known as biomechania. This biomechania transformed the actor merely into material. His acting theory was therefore very physical. He emphasized dancing and athletic skills. His colleague Brecht wasn't interested in empathy but wanted a play staged and received intellectually. Brecht's plays were meant as *teaching* plays.

The opposite is what Constantin Stanislavsky, co-founder of the Moscow Art Theatre, said. He preferred to explore the players and grant them enough space. The actors should behave naturally, not acting toward an audience but as if there would be a wall between actors and spectators. Actors should be motivated by their personal biography and experiences to express authentic emotion. It's an elaborate process and expensive, but for acting in the movies it is quite helpful. Actors question their parts and bring their characters to life: Where do I come from? Where do I go to? What is my background? What is my personal data sheet? In which situation am I? What is my network of relationships? What are my subject matters?

All these questions are important not only for actors but also for animators.

The Actors Studio in New York was based on Stanislavsky's theory of method acting. The school was founded in October 1947 by Elia Kazan, Cheryl Crawford, and Robert Lewis but the main protagonist was Lee Strasberg. He trained a whole new bunch of actors: Anne Bancroft, Marlon Brando, James Dean, Robert De Niro, Jane Fonda, Dustin Hoffman, Martin Landau, Steve McQueen, Marilyn Monroe, Paul Newman, Sidney Poitier, and Rod Steiger. The list of alumni is long and illustrious.

After they separated from Lee Strasberg and his Group Theatre, Sanford Meisner and fellow actor Stella Adler chose to use imagination to stimulate emotion and involvement in a play's imaginary circumstances. Self-consciousness and self-censorship are enemies to the free expression every actor needs. Sanford Meisner postulated truthful behavior under imaginary circumstances.

If we talk about theatre, there is, of course, a big difference between stage and film/TV. There are no close-ups in the theatre unless you sit in the first row. In the old days actresses and actors tended to overact just to make sure that people in the last row will see what they were doing. These actors had problems in front of the camera. Their way of acting was considered old fashioned and hammy.

Actually, in the early days of the cinema, most legitimate actresses and actors were reluctant to appear on screen. World War I (and the money offered) changed their mind.

On the screen, with a lot of close-ups, the camera decides whom it loves and whom not. You can't explain why some good-looking actors are disliked by the camera while others, not so beautiful, are adored by the mystery of photography. Anyway, in the movies it's all about looks and being photogenic.

Production-wise animation has less connection to the legitimate stage than live-action films. But the production process of live action and animated films is based on a similar premise. While a play is staged from beginning to end, films, live action, and animation are organized in scenes. Actors work so to speak out of synch, from scene to scene, not chronologically. They might start with the end and finish with the beginning, depending on the schedule set up by the production. In animation, the situation is even "worse." If you weren't working at Disney's in the Golden Age of (American) Animation but at one of the poverty row companies, you wouldn't begin or finish with a single character but would be commissioned to handle certain scenes of different characters. No place for method acting.

A real film actor has to be authentic. To him acting is like breathing. This is what you hear from professional actors. Al Pacino said that. Others repeated it.

In animation, there is seldom authenticity. In animation, very often memorable characters come out expressively ugly:

Goofy, Popeye, and the ugliest of them all, Spongue Bob (*"I'm ugly and I'm PROUD"*), have certainly no cute features.

Here are some of Art Babbitt's thoughts concerning an equally ugly character he would often animate for Disney trying to find inside the cartoon figure: a Character Analysis of the Goof who started out as one of Mickey's sidekicks (dated June 1934). Babbitt thought of the Goof as a composite of an everlasting optimist, a gullible Good Samaritan, a half-wit, a shiftless, good-natured colored boy, and a hick. He describes him as loose-jointed and gangly, but not rubbery. A bashful dumbbell who thinks he is pretty smart, laughing at his own jokes because he can't understand any others.*

* Gerald Peary and Danny Peary, *The American Animated Cartoon: A Critical Anthology.* New York: E. P. Dutton, 1980, pp. 235–236.

14

Voice Actors

The closest regular actors could come with a cartoon character is voice characterization. There is even one cartoon character that was solely built around a voice. It was Donald Duck's personality that was created by the quack of Clarence Charles Nash (1904–1985):

Nash said in an interview with *The Times* (1984)* that his interest in becoming an entertainer started in his native Oklahoma, where he had learned to imitate a billy goat. When he left, the goat would bleat in dismay. The sound fascinated young Nash and he tried to convert it to a monologue: *"Mary Had A Little Lamb."* When he moved from Chicago to California, he tried unsuccessfully as a vocalist, animal imitator, and mandolin player but nobody would buy *"Mary Had A Little Lamb."* Nobody—except Walt Disney. Disney was a farm body, same as Nash.

Nash introduced himself to cartoon director Wilfred Jackson as bird imitator. Jackson said: *"We can use them. What else can you do?"* So Nash did his whole act, all the farm animal sounds and *"Mary Had A Little Lamb."* Right in the middle of the recitation, Jackson secretly switched on the intercom. The sound went into

---

* Burt A. Folkart, 50-Year Career: Clarence Nash, Donald Duck's Voice, Dies. Los Angeles Times, February 21, 1985.

Walt Disney's office. Disney came down, looked at the director and said, "*That's our talking duck! That's the duck we've been looking for.*"*

So a goat became a duck.

Originally, Donald Duck was only a member in Mickey's gang but by the late 1930s, when audiences lost interest in the saturated Mickey, he would become a star of his own in his own series.

Clarence Nash said that the Duck's personality was the exact opposite of Mickey's. Mickey was basically a happy fellow, even tempered, and a good buddy. We would call him 1D. Donald was more versatile. His tantrums were his trademark. He was always determined to get his own way. If not he would lose self-control. There were a lot of gag possibilities in such a character. He has problems with everybody and everything. After a short while he would get frustrated and even explode. He likes to bother others but when someone bothers him he gets very angry. In short: while they lost interest in Mickey, Donald was welcomed with open arms by the animators.

The only problem with Donald's voice was that nobody understood the squawking so that other characters had to repeat the important parts of his dialogue.

Other famous cartoon voices:

William "Billy" Bletcher (1894–1979), a diminutive comedian with a big, very strong voice, became Peg Leg Pete and the Big Bad Wolf: In the old days there were not that many actors who would care to do cartoon voices. Bletcher was a regular in slapstick comedies, from *Our Gang* to *The Three Stooges* comedies. One day he was told by Pinto Colvig (who was the original voice of Goofy) that Disney was looking for a voice that would fill the bill of a wolf in the upcoming *Three Little Pigs*. "*Why don't you go over and do this thing for Walt,*" Colvig said. "*They want a guy who can huff and puff and blow your house in.*" So Bletcher would start to work for Disney's short department, sometimes alongside Walt himself who would do Mickey's voice. There is a famous behind-the-scenes clip with Walt as Mickey and to his right Billy as Pete. Sometimes he would do two or three voices at the same time which was not an uncommon habit back then. When he dubbed *The Golden Touch,* a 1935 *Silly Symphony* that told the classic story of King Midas, they would put white on his lips and photographed him that way, as reference for the animators to animate the mouth movements.

Charles Dawson "Daws" Butler (1916–1988) was in his own words a shy young man who began imitating voices: While in high school at Oark Park, a Chicago suburb, he forced himself to appear before groups at amateur contests. His repertoire consisted of a Ford starting on a cold day and included the voices of President Franklin Delano Roosevelt and bandleader-entertainer Rudy Vallée. This self-inflicted therapy worked for him quite well and soon he entered show business. He did radio shows and after World War II, in 1948, joined forces with Stan Freberg to do the TV puppet show *Time for Beany* created by Bob Clampett and also worked

---

* Gregory J. M. Catson, *Clarence "Ducky" Nash. Filmfax,* No. 26, April/May 1991, p. 38.

for Tex Avery (he did the wolf character in *Little Rural Riding Hood*). Since the advent of television cartoons, he performed—a record!—the voices of more than 200 animated characters, mostly for Hanna-Barbera for whom he did *Reddy* of *Ruff and Reddy, Huckleberry Hound, Mr. Jinks* and *Dixie* and *Yogi Bear.*

Sterling Holloway (1905–1992), who appeared in 150 films and television shows, became one of Disney's most popular voices: the adult Flower in *Bambi*, the narrator in *Peter and the Wolf,* The Cheshire Cat in *Alice in Wonderland,* and Kaa in *The Jungle Book*, the last animated feature Disney personally was involved with before his death. Holloway said that his favorite Disney part was *Winnie the Pooh.*

June Foray (born in 1917), a radio voice, created Lucifer for Disney's *Cinderella* as well as Rocky the Flying Squirrel, Granny (owner of Tweety & Sylvester, taking over for Bea Benaderet), and Witch Hazel.

Angela Lansbury came to New York to record Mrs. Potts' songs for *Beauty and the Beast*, particularly the title ballad. She thought *Tale as Old as Time* was a lovely ballad but when she heard it she was afraid that she couldn't sing that, that she didn't have that kind of vocal equipment. She wasn't a singer, she said: She was an actress who sings. That's a difference. Luckily, the late lyricist Howard Ashman wasn't going for the sound, he wanted all emotion and the drama behind it, and this demand Angela Lansbury was highly able to deliver.

The most famous of them all, however, was Melvin Jerome "Mel" Blanc (1908–1989) who did the voices for Warner's cartoon stars, all of them: Porky Pig, Daffy Duck, Elmer Fudd, Yosemite Sam, Tweety & Sylvester, Marvin the Martian, Pepe Le Pew, Speedy Gonzales, Wile E. Coyote, Foghorn Leghorn, The Tasmanian Devil—as well as the original Woody Woodpecker for Walter Lantz (that was continued by Lantz's wife Grace Stafford) and Barney Rubble for Hanna-Barbera's *Flintstones* show. When he started doing cartoon voices, in 1937, he wasn't first choice at Warners.

Blanc had debuted on radio in 1927 and later became a regular on the *Jack Benny Show,* but he had to wait a whole year and a half until he got an audition at Leon Schlesinger's cartoon unit at Warners. Constantly he was told that they got all the voices they needed. When the casting director, a guy named Spencer, passed away, Blanc approached Treg Brown, the man who succeeded him: *"Look, I've been trying to get to Spencer and tell him about my voices, but he's gone now and I wanted to audition for him."* So Brown invited him and guffawed when Blanc auditioned. He called the directors in and they liked what they heard too. One of the directors asked him if he could do "a drunken bull, crocked on sour mash." Blanc answered in drunken voice, *"I'd be - hic - very happy to do a - hic - drunken bull."* *

Blanc's most famous voice was Bugs Bunny:

They showed him sketches of Master Hare and told him that this character was supposed to be a tough little stinker who wouldn't take guff from anybody. Blanc thought of a tough voice that would fit this type of character. The toughest

---

* *Mel Blanc.* Interviewed by Mike Barrier. Funnyworld No. 18, 1978, p. 28.

voices he would find were the accents from Brooklyn and Bronx. So he combined the two and out came Bugs Bunny.

During recording sessions, he actually chewed on a carrot. He had tried apples and celery, but that didn't sound right. But when he got a mouthful of carrot, he couldn't chew it and swallow all of it in time. So they had to stop recording while he would spit the carrot out in the waste basket. When it came to the famous *"What's up, doc?"*, a phrase that was brought up by Tex Avery, he suggested that they have Bugs say, *"Eh!"* first. After that *"Eh!"* he would chew on a carrot. Then they would stop recording so that he could spit out the carrot after which he would add, *"What's up, doc?"*

Some source called Blanc an intuitive method actor. That is a little overstated but else wise you couldn't praise this man high enough.

"Incidentally, (so Blanc in a 1981 TV interview), *they do the voice first and the cartoon after the voice is done. They draw to the voice. Most people don't know that."* Such a voice can be highly inspiring to animators, including the crucial issue of timing.

One of Blanc's best characters was the hysterical Yosemite Sam, a caricature of its director, Isadore "Friz" Freleng. Christopher Lee, a friend of Mel Blanc's: *"Sam was a very small guy but he had that real loud voice."* In this case, the voice makes the whole character. The animation has to follow the voice acting faithfully.

Not to forget, Walt Disney who dubbed, as we have mentioned, his own best creation, *Mickey Mouse's* shy, falsetto voice, from *Steamboat Willie* up to 1946 when his chain-smoking habits prevented him from going on. Disney certainly was the one who established acting in animation.

UPA's nearsighted Mr. Magoo would have been a perfect choice for W. C. Fields although Quincy Magoo, a wealthy retiree, was much more Victorian, not as rough as Fields but there was something both characters had in common. At the time, however, Magoo was conceived Fields had passed away. So actor Jerry Hausner who voiced Magoo's nephew Waldo introduced Jim Backus (1913–1989) to animation director John Hubley (1914–1977). Backus was already fairly well known from the *Alan Young Show* on NBC Radio as the voice of Hubert Updyke, a man so rich he had one chauffeur for left-hand turns and another driver for right-hand turns. Hausner arranged a luncheon at the Smoke House Restaurant, next door to the UPA studio in Burbank. Hubley spoke of this new character he was trying to find a voice for. He didn't want to have to ask Backus to audition for him because it might be an affront to an actor as well established as Backus. At the studio Hubley showed him sketches of the character and mentioned that Magoo was nearsighted and lived in his own little world. All of a sudden Backus said, *"My father lives in his own little world, too, never quite seeing things the way they really are. It isn't that he is nearsighted, but his whole attitude toward life is a kind of personal isolation toward the rest of the world."**

---

* Gerald Peary and Danny Peary, *The American Animated Cartoon: A Critical Anthology.* New York: E. P. Dutton, 1980, p. 245.

Acting and Character Animation

The legacy continues with comedian Daniel Louis "Dan" Castellaneta (born in 1957) as Homer Simpson, Grampa Simpson, Krusty the Clown, Mayor Quimby, and Julie Deborah Kavner (born in 1950) as Marge Simpson in Matt Groening's *The Simpsons*, supported by celebrity guest stars like Danny DeVito, Ringo Starr, Paul McCartney (who decades ago were in *Yellow Submarine)*, Sting, Dustin Hoffman, Michael Jackson, Leonard Nimoy, Elizabeth Taylor, Hugh Hefner, Bette Midler, Conan O'Brien, James Earl Jones, Larry King, Meryl Streep, Dick Cavett, Mickey Rooney, Tony Blair, Paul Anka, Glenn Close, Donald Sutherland, Kirk Douglas, Jack Lemmon, John Waters, Willem Dafoe, Helen Hunt, Rod Steiger, Bob Denver, Tom Hanks, Rupert Murdoch (whose empire controls Fox), Stephen Hawking, Buzz Aldrin, Patrick Stewart, and German film director Werner Herzog.

Nowadays they spend a lot of money to hire big actors to use their names in promotion although we don't know of any movie audiences that would go and buy tickets at the box office just to hear a certain star's voice and justify this nonsense type of name-dropping. Very often it is name above competence. It doesn't add to the quality of a film. These big stars are no Mel Blancs and no Billy Bletchers.

Today's cartoon producers not only record but also film voice actors' dubbing sessions to study the mimic art and facial expressions.

Rocky the Rooster of *Chicken Run* (2000) fame was voiced by one of those big name stars, the contested Mel Gibson. Some of Gibson's characteristics would be used. They had some footage of Mel taken at the recording session, recounts Peter Lord, who co-directed with Nick Park, but he wasn't performing for the camera, and so they found themselves referring most often not to that footage but to *Maverick,* a 1994 Western comedy directed by Richard Donner, in which Gibson played a similar character: *"the classic lovable rogue who's never quite straight or honest, but remains likeable nonetheless because in the end he proves himself trustworthy. It's very difficult to translate live-action into what we do, but aspects of Mel's unique facial mannerisms, such as how he flares his eyes wide to great effect, were used for Rocky on occasion. But for the most part we just drew from his vocal performance."* *

With *Kung Fu Panda* the method of filming an actor worked much better because Jack Black who was cast as the title character at least tried some method voice acting and did the utmost to put himself in the fur of the panda and asking himself, *What's the panda going through? What's his emotional state?* He would take a minute. Said that he didn't like to be rushed. Sometimes he went, *Hold on a second. Let me just imagine it for a while.* And he did some little guided imagery of his own sort of self-hypnosis.

Black was joined by Angelina Jolie (Tigress), Jackie Chan (Monkey), and Dustin Hoffman (Shifu):

For the last several years, I've had the privilege of voicing the character of Shifu in the Kung Fu Panda *films. The process has been one of the most interesting and challenging of my career. (...)*

---

* Kevin H. Martin, *Poultry in Motion*. Cinefex 82, July 2000, p. 126.

Each time I stepped into the sound booth, I found inspiration in the dynamic storyboards and detailed character designs achieved by the artists at DreamWorks Animation. These illustrations were microcosms of information. (...)

*This communal and imaginative vision helped me to interpret the character more fully, and to say that I am greatly impressed by their talent, drive, and creativity would be an understatement.**

We wonder if Hoffman has written these lines himself or if a ghostwriter was used. Nevertheless, voice acting is a tough job.

Some cartoon producers are pretty selective even with recording foreign versions. Disney was. In those days dubbing was almost a science.

In one case, not a voice but sound fx made a character: *Gerald McBoing-Boing,* the boy who expresses himself by imitating sounds, was invented by Dr. Seuss (Theodor Seuss Geisel) and put into cartoons by John Hubley and UPA.

In special cases dialogue can change a whole character. There was that movie about a girl who befriended a tiny star that had fallen from the nightly sky. Originally the filmmakers wanted to introduce the girl as a cranky and not as an upbeat character. She was upset because her family had moved to a new place although she had felt so comfortable at their former home. This version turned out highly unpleasant and annoying. A solution was found to try and change her dialogue in the exposition counting and substituting syllables. But when you carefully watch the animation, you will see that dialogue and acting do not match.

Bruno Ganz' Hitler in *The Downfall (Der Untergang,* 2004), which describes the Fuehrer's end in the bunker under the Reich Chancellery in 1945, introduces Adolf Hitler in an earlier situation as a benevolent old man who even helps a nervous newcomer secretary and puts her at ease. From then on, to the audience Hitler would remain a "human" monster.

Apropos of Hitler and cartoon voices: The Nazi dictator who was an outspoken Disney admirer had three different 35mm prints of Disney's *Snow White and the Seven Dwarfs,* the original version, a Swedish print and a German-dubbed one (that was screened in German film theatres after the war). He didn't know that the German dubbing was done in Amsterdam by Jewish émigrés. Dora Gerson loaned her voice to the Queen who was after Snow White's blood, Kurt Gerron was one of the dwarfs and directed the dubbing. Both were murdered in Auschwitz: Dora (Dorothea) Gerson on February 14, 1943 and Gerron on October 28, 1944. Only Frieda van Hessen who was Snow White's German singing voice survived the concentration camp.

---

* Foreword in: *The Art of Kung Fu Panda 2,* San Rafael, California; Ensight Editions, 2011, p. 7.

15

Pixilation

Animating Actors or Becoming Animation

Pixilation means that actors are transforming into animation, even more so than in rotoscoping, by actually acting frame by frame. Here actors and animators are sharing the performance. Because most actors have no experience in animation, it's a perfect training ground for animators to become animation themselves and do things physically.

Pixilation is a stop-frame technique by which live actors are animated exactly like stop-motion puppets, a variation of object animation that was known since the early days of trick cinematography when Georges Méliès, Segundo de Chomón, Émile Cohl, and others, as if by an invisible hand, moved tables, chairs, and furniture around.

One of the undisputed masters of the process was Norman McLaren (1914–1987) who used it to a great advantage in the Academy Award winning satire *Neighbours* produced in 1952, while the Korean War was going on, by the National Film Board of Canada (and *A Chairy Tale* made in 1957 that shows a young man battling for control over a chair).

McLaren discovered that one not only can animate objects frame by frame at low camera speeds but real people too. He and his colleague Grant Munro started to experiment with the idea. For 3 days they shot a series of technical

Peter Pauli in a pixilation/stop-motion scene from *Café d'Amour* (2015). (Courtesy of Benedikt Toniolo and Film University Babelsberg.)

tests that involved 20 seconds of animation of two men fighting. When they viewed the rushes, they saw that the process worked for humans. Even more, McLaren felt that the fighting scene contained a whole story. Two animators, Munro and Jean-Paul Ladouceur, would star as peaceful *Neighbours* who come into conflict with each other over a flower that would bloom between their adjacent cardboard houses. Wolf Koenig handled the photography, McLaren directed but it would be Munro who termed the process *Pixilation* (from *pixilated*).

Persons shot in this way move in a strange, jerky, stilted, almost surreal way as if they were puppets manipulated by an unseen force. The physical laws and forces of weight and gravity seem to be neutralized.

One of the gems of the genre is a tour-de-force pixilation starring animator Mike Jittlov that became part of the feature film *The Wizard of Speed and Time*. Pixilation, although done frame by frame, seems to be absolutely spontaneous and grows in action like a slapstick comedy while doing it in front as well as behind the camera. The film was intended as a calling card for Jittlov and his friends and just grew from there.

Even in the days of digital animation, this technique is not forgotten. In 2011, Juan Pablo Zaramella, a filmmaker from Buenos Aires, used the technique for his short film *Luminaris* that won 327 international awards and imagines a world controlled by light: A young man (Gustavo Cornillón who co-wrote the script) who works in a factory that produces light bulbs tries to break out from this slave system.

Another short was released in 2016, *Café d'Amour*, which is a magic place that tries hard to bring two people together: Lewis, a street artist, and Coco, a chubby lady. The film was the graduate work of Benedikt Toniolo, a student of Film University Babelsberg.

Coco was played by Ulrike Bliefert. We asked her:

Q: Have you seen a pixilation film before or have you worked already in VFX and trickfilm? What is your background? Why did they cast you?

A: I have been working as an actress for film, television and theatre since the early seventies, but I had never before seen a pixilation movie and I didn't even know the technical term. Nevertheless I knew about the so-called "stop trick" technique, and—in my second job as a writer of youth literature—I have produced a 5-minute short with Playmobile figurines for the online Advent calendar of my editor (https://www.youtube.com/watch?v=W_ly_4RdWVA) in 2014. So I knew that precision and patience would be the overall needs on set.

I don't know why I have been casted, but I think it was mandatory that "Coco" was overweight—in contrast to the spindly male character. As there are very few overweight actresses in movies and TV I guess there were very few competitors for this role. Anyway: You should ask Benedikt Toniolo why he chose me. Maybe there is a more flattering reason for casting me as "Coco…"

Q: While making the movie you as actress had to work under totally different conditions of time and had to subordinate to the requirements of the animation film. Did you have difficulty thinking "single frame?" Did it handicap your performance? Did you feel "mechanical?"

A: I really enjoyed to split my actions and facial expressions into bits and pieces! In doing so, you become aware of every detail of your performance, and you learn to omit unnecessary arabesques. It was a great experience to focus on even the smallest moves and then learn to blow them up in order to achieve the silent movie effect.

Q: What prerequisites should an actor have for this type of film? How did the director support you?

A: Well, after we had finished shooting, I needed a cane (for several weeks!), as my knees hurt like hell. So I think the main requirement is physical health! Imagine standing up from a chair in five or more stages and being forced to freeze in every single position for minutes! In addition to that,

Peter Pauli as street artist and tramp and Ulrike Bliefert as Coco the chubby lady meet in the *Café d'Amour* (2015) that tries to set them up. (Courtesy of Benedikt Toniolo and Film University Babelsberg.)

you need patience: The shooting of one little sip from a teacup may take an hour, and walking through the room and back may take a whole afternoon. So above all you need to keep up a good mood, and you will never succeed to stay good-humored and motivated without the support of the director and his team!

Director Benedikt Toniolo instructs actress Ulrike Bliefert on the set of *Café d'Amour* (2015). (Courtesy of Benedikt Toniolo and Film University Babelsberg.)

Acting and Character Animation

Q: Do you regard this technique as a gimmick or do you think that it opened a new aesthetic dimension to this little love story?

A: I think nowadays people are overrun and jaded by the everyday flood of images. So anything special, anything that breaks the rules of the average TV show, movie or adverts will be welcome and appreciated. Pixilation may not revolutionize film and television, but it offers ways to be playful (!) and inventive and simply have—and offer—fun.

Casting actors carefully for Pixilation projects is mandatory. Body control is the premier prerequisite. Sometimes they have to hold a position up to 5 minutes. So do the utmost to comfort your actors. Dancers and persons who have martial arts experience belong to those who are specially qualified for the job. Actors also should have gestural capacities. They should be patient and concentrated. Before shooting, better test ideas with yourself and prepare a clear shooting plan.

In Pixilation you can create and fill a physical universe of the impossible with its own logic, rich in visual metaphors. And above all, you can master and change space and time.

16

Dancing with Animation

Gene Kelly danced twice with animated characters, in a brief sequence of *Anchors Aweigh* (1945) and in a main sequence of the episodic film *Invitation to the Dance* (1956).

Kelly wanted to create something on film that hadn't been done before. He and Stanley Donen, the director of *Anchors Aweigh,* sat around for days to think of something that would be new. It was Donen who suggested, *"How about doing a dance with a cartoon?"*

The MGM brass was not convinced but Joe Pasternak, the producer, went to bat for them and got an additional budget of $100,000.

Naturally Donen and Kelly went first to Walt Disney, by then the patriarch of animation, to ask for advice and hopefully get some of his artists released to work for them. Disney at that time was experimenting too with animation and live action. In 1944, he had done *The Three Caballeros,* starring the cartoon characters Donald Duck, José Carioca, and Panchito alongside live actors, and would have cartoon sequences in *Song of the South* that was released in 1946. (Afro-American actor James Baskett who played Uncle Remus [*Zip-a-Dee-Doo-Dah*] would sadly be denied to attend the picture's Atlanta premiere but, he was the first male African-American actor to receive an Honorary Academy Award.)

So technically, Disney had no objections and considered the idea feasible but he had no artists available for them as he was busy with his own projects. But his blessings helped to convince MGM's cartoon department to use Jerry Mouse (of Tom & Jerry fame) as Kelly's cartoon partner and the optical department (under Irving G. Ries) to handle the task of compositing the shots. Donen worked it all out jointly with the Director of Photography who would be asked to light and shoot something that wasn't there and would be added later in post-production.

Ray Patterson was one of the MGM animators working on *Anchors Aweigh* under cartoon directors William Hanna (who had a special feeling for music) and Joseph Barbera making Kelly dance with Jerry Mouse. He recalled that they took a rotoscope and that Gene Kelly would take too big steps while the mouse had little feet and problems to follow him. Patterson was afraid and asking himself how the hell this was going to work. Jerry would kind of slide but in the end it all went well. Kelly was going this far, the mouse was only going this far.

Gene Kelly returned to the MGM cartoon unit headed by Hanna and Barbera some years later for the even more ambitious *Invitation to the Dance*, where they would do the elaborate 20-minute long *Sinbad the Sailor* sequence to the music of Nikolai Rimsky-Korsakov's *Scheherazade* in which U.S. Navy sailor Kelly on shore leave purchases an oil lamp in the casbah of an unnamed Middle Eastern country that turns out to be a magic lamp and, rubbing it, summons a genie who materializes in the shape of 10-year-old David Kasday (this might have been a springboard of ideas for producer Charles H. Schneer and Ray Harryhausen for their own juvenile genie Barani in *7th Voyage of Sinbad* played by Richard Eyer who was 12 at the time when the picture was released although Harryhausen himself never mentioned Kelly's picture):

Kelly and Kasday enter the over-dimensional story-book pages of the Arabian Nights and encounter people and animals that are complete 2D animation. In a fabulous valley of diamonds (that indeed is part of the Sinbad folklore), Kelly is threatened by a giant snake but the genie's flute comes to his rescue and makes the jive-loving monster dance. When Kelly takes a gem, two mean looking palace guards wielding swords grab him by the stacking swivel and deport him to the sultan's palace where he out-dances the two and falls in love with a beautiful harem girl that at the end is put into a Women's Naval Uniform (which of course was not part of the Arabian Nights tales).

As guidance for director and camera crew, there was a sketch book at hand that was prepared by artists in the MGM cartoon department illustrating the movements that the animated characters would make in their dance routines.

Carol Haney, credited as one of Kelly's assistant choreographers, would not only appear as Scheherazade but would pose and model as a harem girl day after day on the roof of the cartoon studio. After finishing the show, Haney would go to Broadway and choreograph *The Pajama Game*. She died 6 weeks after the opening of *Funny Girl* at age 39 in 1964.

Unfortunately, *Invitation to the Dance* was too ambitious and flopped at the box office but would win the Golden Bear for Best Film at the 6th Berlin International Film Festival.

Nobody would touch animation and dancing again until Walt Disney himself took a chance. In a famous fantasy sequence of *Mary Poppins* (1963), Dick Van Dyke plays a screever who would invite the titular nanny (Julie Andrews) and two kids to enter the fantasy world of his painting and dance with a comedy quartet of 2D penguin waiters, which was animated by Ollie Johnston and became one of the highlights of the picture.

Dancing itself also became a topic in animation: In *Ballerina* (2016), a French-Canadian 3D fantasy directed by Eric Summer and Éric Warin, an orphan girl named Félicie has the dream of becoming a dance student at the Paris Opera. She flees her orphanage in rural Brittany to follow this passion and succeeds against all odds. The filmmakers worked 4 years on the project and had a budget of 28 million euros. The simple story needs much time to develop emotionally and one might ask why they did it in animation and not used live action. Luckily in the last third of the movie, the audience begins to *feel* the urge of the protagonist and understands why this story was told in animation.

17

Acting *with* Animated Characters

The technique to have a live actor appear with animation was already part of the *Out of the Inkwell* series, with Max Fleischer himself appearing with Ko-Ko the Clown. Walt Disney copied that and extended the concept. Virginia Davis was just 4 years old when she became Disney's *Alice in Cartoonland*, supposed to act on-screen with animated characters that would be matted in throughout the length of a short film.

As an old lady, Virginia still had fresh memories about the shooting of Disney's series. Sometimes they would film in a vacant lot. Walt Disney would have her act out a scene in front of a white tarp that was draped over a billboard to make a pure white background to fill in with animation later on:

> Walt was an excellent storyteller and actor. He would act out the character, so I could see the kind of performance he wanted. He'd say, "Let's pretend there's a lion chasing you. Here it comes! You're frightened! Now, scream!" Or he'd pretend to be a wolf, and roar, 'Aaarrrggghhh!' Because they were silent films, he could direct me out loud while the camera was rolling.*

---

* Pat Williams with Jim Denney, *How To Be Like Walt: Capturing the Disney Magic Every Day of Your Life*. Deerfield Beach, FL: Health Communications, Inc., 2004, p. 26.

There is a lot of talent needed to make a little girl see and believe in ferocious jungle animals. Walt and his company would continue to mix live action and 2D animation occasionally but with 3D model animation, it became a regular feature.

Producer-Director Merian C. Cooper had approached Fay Wray with the news that he had chosen her to be the leading lady in a film about "a discovery of gigantic proportions" and that she would play opposite "the tallest, darkest leading man in Hollywood" who turned out to be not the Gary Cooper or Clark Gable type of star but the O'Brien-animated *King Kong*.

Confronted with the difficult task of opposing a giant monster that was not being seen during live-action shooting, Robert Armstrong, who played Carl Denham, was puzzled and asked Merian Cooper if he really understood him correctly when he said that he would react to a fifty-foot ape. Cooper affirmed, *"Yes, that's right, Bob. Why?" "Well, I've been in this business a great many years,"* *Armstrong answered, "but you tell me how to take a fifty-foot ape big!"*[*]

Part of the challenge of appearing in those stop motion monster movies would have been to act opposite nothing—to cower in front of a giant that's not there, said actor Kerwin Mathews (1926–2007).

Although he wasn't particularly fond of the genre, Mathews was among the most experienced actors in that type of film having worked with Ray Harryhausen twice (and in a Harryhausen rip-off, *Jack the Giant Killer*, 1962). Originally, he was groomed to stardom by Columbia tycoon Harry Cohn himself and inherit the title role in a big-budget biblical epic, *Joseph and His Brethren*, but female co-star Rita Hayworth wasn't pleased with the prospect as she would have preferred another partner and withdrew from the project. When Harry Cohn died in February 1958, the project was shelved entirely. In 1957, with nothing else to do, a disappointed Mathews accompanied Charles Schneer, one of Columbia's B-movie producers, to Spain where they would use the elaborate costumes that had been made for *Joseph* to enhance the realms of low budget and where he had to fence with an imaginary skeleton in *The 7th Voyage of Sinbad* that was added by stop-frame animation months later in a small shop in Los Angeles. To do so, Harryhausen had taken fencing lessons himself.

That sword fight was shot in a cave in Majorca. They started filming one night at sundown and worked straight through for 24 hours, because they could only afford the cave for one night.

Olympic fencing master Enzo Musumeci Greco (1911–1994), an Italian *Maestro d'Armi*, who was in films since 1939 and who did all the big movies (*The Crimson Pirate, Ben-Hur, El Cid*), was put on the payroll on the insistence of *Sinbad* director Nathan "Jerry" Juran, who had worked with him before (on *Le imprese di una spada leggendaria*), and joined the crew in Spain. It wasn't that easy to get him. Juran had asked Charles Schneer explicitly for Greco but

* Orville Goldner and George E. Turner: *The Making of King Kong.* New York: Ballantine Books, 1975, p. 6.

the always penny-conscious producer turned him down first because he didn't want to pay the extra transportation. Juran said he couldn't do without him and when Musumeci finally showed up, he was asking for more money than Charles Schneer was willing to pay. Juran offered to pay the balance out of his own pocket. Schneer was so embarrassed by that offer that he okayed Musumeci's claim. Enzo Musumeci Greco proved a real asset. He laid out the complete swordfight and instructed Kerwin Mathews (and Ray Harryhausen). They worked all night in those in caves Arta. During rehearsals, the Italian sword master took the place of the skeleton, and they printed that for Ray Harryhausen. Projecting the scene, Harryhausen would use Musumeci as a guide and copy his movements onto the puppet of the skeleton. Then, for the actual plate, they just left Musumeci Greco out and had Kerwin Mathews fight thin air.

Nathan Juran admired Mathews who never complained, like Todd Armstrong, the star in another Harryhausen epic, *Jason and the Argonauts* (1963), did: When they finally finished the sequence, Juran noticed that Mathews' sword hand was bloody. The actor had worked so hard that he had scraped off the skin. He always called Kerwin Mathews the epitome of a professional. He gave a hell of a performance.

In a way, the skeleton sequence was achieved by sort of rotoscoping. Only that Ray was not tracing an image but using it as a reference for his model animation (same as Disney).

Harryhausen topped his work in *Jason and the Argonauts* by animating not one but seven skeletons fighting three Greek warriors. One of them was played by Andrew Faulds:

We were told that we were going to have to rehearse this skeleton fight, but I didn't realize what that meant. Over three Sundays, we did rehearsals. The first Sunday we were given the movements, as in a ballet, but more realistic strokes than delicately dancing around. We rehearsed this until we had got the run of the routine of the skeleton fight with some Italian fencers, who had come down from Rome to teach us about how the fight was going to be. On the second Sunday, we did the fight again with the same men, but this time they all were numbered jerseys. They filmed it this time [in black and white] with these men playing the skeletons. Then, on the third and final Sunday, we fought it for real, fighting thin air, following the movements exactly that we had practiced with the men in the numbered shirts. Then it was up to the skill of Mr. Harryhausen to fill in the skeletons where the men in the numbered shirts had been. I had never experienced this in filming before and I thought this was never going to work. I was staggered when I saw the film for the first time.[*]

In an interview conducted by Mark Hamill and Anne Wyndham, Kerwin Mathews recalled his work on *The 7th Voyage of Sinbad* as acting with little reference. To represent the cyclops and other creatures, they only had "monster

---

* Mike Hankin, *Ray Harryhausen: Master of the Majicks. Volume 3: The British Films*. Los Angeles: Archive Editions: 2010, p. 119. Reprinted by permission of the author.

Italian stuntmen substitute for the animated models and rehearse skeleton fight for Ray Harryhausen's *Jason and the Argonauts* while shooting the live-action plates. (Courtesy of The Ray & Diana Harryhausen Foundation.)

sticks," about 30-feet long, tiring to manipulate because they were very heavy. Ray moved those by himself.[*]

Others used this technique too. Among them was Jim Danforth who animated and directed the visual effects for Hammer Films' "sequel" to Harryhausen's *One Million Years B.C.* titled *When Dinosaurs Ruled the Earth* (1970):

> *To establish the size of a dinosaur in a shot, I used dinosaur sticks. These were 2" × 2" wood poles cut to a length equal to the height the particular dinosaur would be if it existed as a live, full-size creature - two poles for each dinosaur. A piece of lightweight rope, equal to the length of the dinosaur, connected the two poles.*
>
> *At the beginning of each take of a dinosaur background 'plate', I had grips stand in the set, and hold the poles, with the ropes stretched tight between them. The positions of the two poles were adjusted to indicate the angle at which the dinosaur would be standing relative to the camera - profile, head-on, forty-five degrees, etc. The slate for the scene would be filmed. Then the slate would be removed, and the dinosaur sticks would be filmed. After one or two seconds, Carlos [Gil, assistant director] would shout, in Spanish, "Remove the poles," and the grips would run out of the shot, while the camera continued to run. When the set was clear, we would start the action.[†]*

This type of direction and actor's work was rather technical and had to be so.

[*] Mark Hamill and Anne Wyndham, Exclusive Interview with Kerwin Mathews, *FXRH* 1, no. 4 (Spring 1974).

[†] Jim Danforth, *Dinosaurs, Dragons, and Drama: The Odyssey of a Trickfilmmaker. Vol. 1.* Archive Editions: Los Angeles, CA, 2012, p. 665. Reprinted by permission of the author.

Necessarily Danforth was allowed to direct the second unit too that would shoot the process plates for the animation but found the director of the first unit, in this case Val Guest, not always attentive to his needs. While the first unit helmed by Guest took its time, Danforth occasionally was rushed and had to content himself with sometimes not acceptable time and working conditions shooting a scene that shows Stone Age Tribesmen capturing a long-necked plesiosaur:

I had two hours and twelve minutes to make my set-ups, rehearse the actors, then film the complicated scenes of the Sand Tribesman pulling on a rope to the plesiosaur's neck, plus the scene of the Sand Tribesmen throwing spears at the plesiosaur, plus the background action for the scenes of the plesiosaur being staked down. If I didn't get the rope-pulling mechanism correctly positioned we would get unusable footage, so I worked slowly and deliberately on this part of the procedure. Aida [Young, the producer] paced nervously up and down the edge of the sand set, pointing to her watch and saying "Time, Jim. Time!" I had to ignore Aida - for the good of the production.

Once the mechanism was correctly in place, we could position the large boulder that would form the stationary-matte area for a Sand Tribesman who would appear to be in front of the plesiosaur's immobilized body. Farther away, I positioned the other Sand Tribe people who would appear to be beyond the plesiosaur, watching or pounding on stakes. Once that was accomplished, I could begin rehearsing the stunt actor who would be seen pulling on the rope attached to the plesiosaur's head. Grips operated the teeter-totter device that raised and lowered like the plesiosaur's head, and to which was attached the vine rope held by the stunt actor. A band of white tape on the vine rope made an easily-seen mark to which I could align the animated miniature rope later. This was important because the forward and backward motion of the plesiosaur's head had to match the corresponding pulls of the teeter totter and the stunt actor. When all was working correctly, I filmed several takes of this action.

Quickly we removed the teeter-totter device and the boulder, then set up a target for the spear-throwing scene. All the actors had to do was get their spears close to the target, and I would later make it appear that the spears had buried themselves in the flesh of the plesiosaur.

When those shots were completed I moved on to the final set-up - the background action that would appear behind the previously-filmed blue-backing foregrounds of Sand Tribe men pulling on ropes wrapped around snubbing posts, to cinch the head of the plesiosaur against the ground. [...]

When we started this set-up it was just after eight o'clock - I had about ten minutes remaining in which to finish all the live action for the plesiosaur sequence. We got the set-up made with about three minutes to spare, and I shot the scene as though I were making a silent movie - talking the actors through the action as the camera ran. "Continue pounding on the stakes - now, on the count of three, I want you all to look to your right... one... two... three. Everyone looking right... Keep rolling... All right... Cut." The camera crew checked the camera gate to be sure there were no hairs in the aperture. The gate was clean. It was a "Print and a Wrap"; we were finished.

* Jim Danforth, *Dinosaurs, Dragons, and Drama: The Odyssey of a Trickfilmmaker*. Vol. 1. Archive Editions: Los Angeles, CA, 2012, pp. 689–690.

Note that neither Harryhausen nor Danforth, who were both pretty knowledgeable about dinosaurs—Danforth's father was a paleontologist—had any problems showing people and dinosaurs live besides each other at the same time.

Usually, films like these are not an actor's favorite dish. It's no big challenge to stand in front of a process, a blue or green screen and react to invisible giant forces. This certainly was true for Robert Armstrong who played Carl Denham in *King Kong* and *Son of Kong*. Armstrong hated to become identified just with that single part. When Kong was shot down and fell from top of the Empire State Building he had that classic line, *"It was Beauty killed the Beast."* He begged Ernest "Monty" Schoedsack, the co-director, to change that line, *"I'll do anything, Monty, but don't make me say that line."*

One of the beauties who confronted beasts was British actress Caroline Munro. Well, she wasn't exactly an actress. She was a model and cover girl and did occasional bit parts in movies. Writer Brian Clemens, who knew Munro from *The Avengers*, recommended her to Schneer and Harryhausen for the part of Margiana, the slave girl in *The Golden Voyage of Sinbad* (1973), who is sacrificed to a one-eyed underground centaur on the lost continent of Lemuria, like Fay Wray was offered sacrifice to Kong on Skull Island. It shows that Munro is no actress but the camera likes her because she is such a beauty. She doesn't have to do anything. Just being beautiful and looking at you with these fascinating eyes seems to be enough "acting" for this type of movie.

18

The Puppet Masters

Ray Harryhausen (1920–2013), the late king of stop-motion animators, took acting lessons in the 1940s, which taught him about movement and building character, and even went out to the zoos to study for hours animals, among them a huge gorilla, for his work on *Mighty Joe Young*. Ray always said: *Being an animator you have to be totally dedicated.* When he animated Joe Young, he even lived on vegetables and couldn't eat meat.

On *Mighty Joe*, Harryhausen was chosen to assist his mentor, Willis O'Brien, who had pioneered the art of dimensional animation in *King Kong*.

We mentioned earlier that Darlyne O'Brien, the widow of the animator, later claimed that she could recognize her husband's personality and characteristics in every tiny gesture of the creature. (Actually, OBie had voted for a slightly more human version of *Kong*.) Harryhausen:

Possibly, Mrs. O'Brien says that a lot of OBie came out in Kong's mannerisms. Undoubtedly, a lot of my idiosyncrasies—the way I look at things—do come out. I have a rather macabre way of bringing statues to life, and I suppose that dates back to a silent film that frightened me as a child when it showed a gigantic sculpture falling on the sculptor. You could say that I am acting out some things, I suppose, but I don't come home and tear my wife apart after having done a violent swordfight between

Kali and Sinbad. Actually, with animation you are acting through another medium. I wanted to be an actor in my early days. I studied drama and was in junior and senior high school plays. But I always had the terrors on opening night, and I couldn't see the rest of my life with lumps constantly forming in my throat. So I found a way to act through animated figures. You have to act and react to the live action: so I have, in essence, found a way to be in acting without actually being an actor.[*]

Harryhausen did everything he could to study human and animal movement. He watched his pet dog named *Kong*. He would go out to see ballet and study famous movie actors. He was particularly interested in Stan Laurel, one-half of the team of Laurel & Hardy. Laurel's facial expression and slight body movement would speak volumes.

The Black Scorpion (1957) is another proof of O'Brien's insight into animal behavior. There is a scene where one of the giant scorpions (there were three stop-motion models, one king-size and two smaller ones) that are unearthed by

Armature (one leg missing and used for another model) from *The 7th Voyage of Sinbad* crafted by Fred Harryhausen. (Author's Collection.)

---

[*] Vic Cox, *Ray Harryhausen—Acting Without the Lumps*. Cinefex 5, July 1981, p. 18. In another interview, Harryhausen (*Man Behind Monsters Makes Mighty Scenes*. In: *The Animal World*. Movie Pressbook. New York: Warner Bros., 1956) said that he often had to act (!) the role of a dinosaur, or an ape, or a flying saucer to feel how to move the models in portraying a certain kind of scene.

volcanic eruption tries to sting a huge metal bucket to death that had been lowered on a long cable into an eerie underground cavern.

Harryhausen could animate anything. He had a set of small flying saucers made by his father, Fred Harryhausen, from aluminum. He animated them on a special rig in front of the process screen, and the animation made those saucers as vibrant and lively like insects.

Interestingly, Ray Harryhausen only covered a niche in animation although basically he was an animator. He always was acknowledged as a master of visual effects, a term that since his screen credit in *The 7th Voyage of Sinbad* was connected with his name. As an animator he was only credited once: for the dinosaurs in *The Animal World* (1956). In 1999, we were going to prepare a series with him, *Ray Harryhausen's World of Myth and Legend* that was going to have introductions filmed with him and feature a legendary tale such as *Ilya Muromets* or *Theseus and the Minotaur* (written by Jim Danforth) entirely in stop motion. Harryhausen wouldn't go for stop motion by and large but with that so-called *reality sandwich* he was known for: live action with an animated character inserted. In his days, he did the blend by a clever way, with miniature background projection and a split screen matte that would put the animated character, say six-armed Kali in *The Golden Voyage of Sinbad*, right into the live action.

Ray avoided to use the term puppet or puppet animation and preferred to call it model animation as he was once asked by a man if he wasn't too old to play with dolls. Our intention, however, was to work with puppets. Finally, the project was vetoed by Harryhausen himself.

Actually, Hero of Alexandria in the second century wrote manuals on how to fabricate images of god that would move. He would rotate statues and design a miniature puppet theatre—not for entertainment's sake but for religious purposes. To create a god was to perform theurgy to attract divine engines: giving life to inanimate objects. The tradition of gods animated carried on in the fascination with puppets.

"*Never have a model standing still,*" Ray said. "*Have something move all time even if the character stands still.*"* If you watch the reptilian Ymir from *20 Million Miles to Earth* (1957), you will notice that even if it stands still at least its tail is moving.

The most interesting Ymir scenes are those showing him little, before growing to giant size, on a table blinded by light. He's reptilian but cute and innocent: a poor, tormented soul as Harryhausen called him. Bill Warren, a film historian devoted to sci-fi and fantasy epics, acknowledged that this maybe was Ray's best animation but then he began to criticize the design as too slender, with hands too large and clumsy. Harryhausen repeatedly has animated creatures, says Warren, that lean slightly forward from the waist, thrusting out the head, and pulling back the arms at the elbows.

To the best of our knowledge, there are only two Harryhausen creatures that act that way: the Ymir, the strange Venusian creature from 20 million miles away

---

* Harryhausen, personal communication.

that stranded on Earth and grew to gargantuan proportions in the atmosphere of Earth, and the Cyclopes from *The 7th Voyage of Sinbad*. Actually, one of the two, the smaller one that had two horns, was made re-using the Ymir armature as a puppet skeleton.

But in one point Warren is right. The Ymir might be the best animation concerning stop-motion techniques but Kong, not that good animation, is the better character, memorable and touching. So it is not always the technical quality of the animation itself which decides about the emotional acceptance of an artificial character.

There is a classic German fantasy tale titled *The Sandman* written by E. T. A. Hoffmann in 1816 that describes a girl a man falls in love with until he realizes that she is not human: The man's name is Nathanael. He has abandoned Klara, his down-to-earth fiancée, for a beautiful girl he has seen from his room in a neighboring building where the girl, Olimpia, does nothing else than sitting motionless in her bedroom. She plays however, as Nathanel learns, piano and dances with perfunctory precision. When Nathanael talks to her she only responds with a gentle "Ah, ah!" To our horror, we realize that Olimpia is a life-size mechanical doll fabricated by Spallanzani, Nathanael's physics professor. Olimpia's eyes are made of glass. Inside her body is a clockwork mechanism that controls her movements and dancing.

The episode is an interesting forerunner to the age of psychoanalysis. It tells of a case of narcissistic love. Nathanael rejects the love of Klara who is spirited and highly cultivated and has only eyes for an artificial creature, which is a reflection of him. Because she has no soul herself, Olimpia mirrors the movements of Nathanael's soul.

Many performers are narcissists and self-obsessed. They want people to look at them, love and adore them. It's part of their personality. In a certain way, this literary analysis describes pretty much the sentiment of an animator toward his creation too. The relationship with the puppet is narcissistic. I (RG) once met a famous female marionette maker who carved hundreds of puppets for stage and TV shows. Suddenly I realized the similarity between this old lady and her puppets, particularly the wooden noses, and told her that sculptors in a way always portray themselves. She was not amused, and our conversation came to a sudden end.

Same is true with Harryhausen, a man with a great sense of humor. Everybody who has ever met him will describe the man as modest and humble which he certainly was unless it came to his art and recognition and his screen credits. Starting with *The Beast from 20,000 Fathoms* (1953), he was always credited on screen and on posters. He told me how furious he became when Sam Katzman, the notorious executive producer of *It Came from Beneath the Sea* (1954), was going to deny him his well-deserved screen credit. In such a case, he was not a person to be trifled with. It was *Technical Effects Created by Ray Harryhausen* or it was not. Ray Harryhausen was a man who had to have *his* way. Sure, he was able to compromise—to a certain degree.

Bust from *Clash of the Titans,* the largest of Harryhausen's animation models. (Author's Collection.)

From *Jason and the Argonauts.* (Author's Collection.)

Holger Delfs (left) and Giesen (right) arrange a Harryhausen display at Filmmuseum Berlin. (Author's Collection.)

Harryhausen was not that much interested in his models although they were highly insured when they went on display somewhere. Otherwise he seemed to be proud only of his bronzes that would survive him and his decaying models. In his vast Kensington home in London that once belonged to director Michael Powell and after his death was sold for a high sum, he had this tiny workroom under the roof with two wall closets and a cabinet in which he stored the rest of his lifetime achievement of original models. Like a magician, for some years, he had become pretty secretive about his work, at least until his retirement. In his own *Film Fantasy Scrapbook* that saw several editions, he didn't reveal that much. What was important to him was only the process of life-giving, of animation itself. Then he could be self-critical too.

He shuddered when he saw the Cyclops making his first entrance in *The 7ᵗʰ Voyage of Sinbad* and lamented: "*If only I would have had more time….*"* The one-eyed creature, with a single horn on his head (the original sculpt was more like a devil with two horns), had satyr's goat-legs, an old favorite of Ray's, and so the acting was based on his strange walk. He would stride out, stop, roar, and proceed. "*It's all in his walk,*" Harryhausen would say. Later, Ray would reject his own grotesque design and say that Cyclopes are no more than overgrown people. He drew one for me: "*Don't make him a Devil Demon.*"* I (RG) don't have the little pencil drawing anymore, that the giant face with a half-bald head resembled Ray himself.

In a way, in his darkroom, where he walked for miles back and forth between camera and stop-motion setup in his active days, he felt creating like god and always spoke of his "Zeus complex." It was more than a joke. (Remember the early 2D animation that we mentioned where you see the animator's hand holding a pen like the hand of a giant god.)

---

* Harryhausen, personal communication.

Many of the younger generation of VFX artists were heavily influenced as kids by Harryhausen and so tried to copy him. One of those youngsters, Dennis Muren, who went to see *The 7th Voyage of Sinbad* eight times during its first week in 1958, wasn't very fond of his own experiments with stop motion. He became a cameraman and had to photograph the stop-motion animation of other youngsters like David Allen and Phil Tippett which must have been depressing. Eventually, Dennis found a way to substitute the frame-by-frame stop-motion animation by more lifelike, kinetic GC animation.

Originally they intended to use stop motion in *Jurassic Park* (1993). But then they decided that stop motion, even the Go Motion process they had used in *Dragonslayer* (1981), was not lifelike enough to put into use in Spielberg's film.

When Ray Harryhausen first saw scenes from Disney's *Dinosaurs* (2000), it was not the lifelike animation or the creatures' textures he noticed but the sheer number of dinosaurs involved in certain scenes while he himself had only four of them in the *Valley of Gwangi* (1969). Concerning the movements, however, he didn't notice that many differences to his own approach from previous days. Nevertheless, these *Dinosaurs*, as typical for Disney, were humanized—what Harryhausen wouldn't have dared. *King Kong* yes, but dinosaurs? (Humanized dinosaur kids appeared already in Spielberg's *The Land Before Time* series that was started in 1988 by Don Bluth.)

Contrary to Harryhausen, his mentor Willis O'Brien did funny dinosaurs in his early slapstick silents, and Jim Danforth would design some for *Caveman* (1981) starring Ringo Starr and Dennis Quaid, particularly a sluggish tyrannosaurus that was totally different from any previous version:

> I sculpted it, painted it, put the eyes in it—everything. When you're designing something in this vein, you don't necessarily want to take your subject too seriously. You don't want to be rigid and say: 'Well, gee. A tyrannosaurus is scary, it's always been scary and I'm not about to do one that isn't.' So I decided to make him kind of sleepy-eyed and snaggle-toothed. And fat so maybe he can't run quite as fast. But he's still big and he can always fall on you. Dangerous, but... What I wanted was an old, fat, degenerate tyrannosaurus. And I got it, I think. So I was real happy with it. Strangely enough, when I showed a photograph of it to Ray Harryhausen he didn't like it at all—not at all. He kept saying, 'Looks like it's pregnant!' *

Nevertheless, the puppet spoke to the animators. Once you had seen it, you knew how to move it. There would be no different way. This tyrannosaurus was a caricature.

But Danforth wouldn't go for lifelike images. This is the difference between him and Harryhausen. In fact, he compared stop motion with ballet. And he was the one to truly acknowledge the art of Czech puppetry and Jiří Trnka.

---

* Scott Vanderbilt, *Caveman—The Real Stars.* Cinefex 5, 1981, p. 56.

Jim Danforth sculpts Siegfried model for a proposed stop-motion project. (Courtesy of Jim Danforth.)

While puppets are not likely to become Stanislavsky method-actors, the motivations for what they do and how they conduct themselves are derived from the situations in which they are depicted. Trnka's cowboy in Song of the Prairie (1949) behaves in an exaggeratedly heroic manner because it has been established that he is a caricature of a Hollywood western hero in a parody of that genre. Occasionally he may be stupid and require rescue by his horse, but he is always in character.

In the films made by O'Brien or Harryhausen, puppets were merely used as special effects devices. It was the clear objective of their makers to let them appear like creatures of nature. Trnka and his predecessor Ladislas Starevich, however, would aim for sheer puppetry, instead of using the strings that manipulate their marionettes frame-wise.

Puppets and puppet films, as Trnka saw them, would stand on their own feet only when they don't mingle with live-action films. He pleaded for stylization of the scenery, the artificially heroic look of the human actors, and the lyrical content of the theme.

Trnka's ambition was moving 3D figures of puppets in space, in contradistinction to the heroes of 2D cartoons. From the beginning, he said, he had his own conception of how puppets could be handled. Each of them should have an individual but static facial expression, as compared with the puppets that by means of various technical devices can change their mien in an attempt to achieve a more

---

* L. Bruce Holman, *Puppet Animation in the Cinema: History and Technique.* South Brunswick and New York: A. S. Barnes and Company. London: The Tantivy Press, 1975, p. 73.

Acting and Character Animation

life-like aspect. In practice, this hasn't enhanced realism, but rather conduced to naturalism.

The puppet faces in Trnka films would remain mostly static. The puppet would act just by movement and body stance. George Pal's replacement animation was totally different. It was like squash and stretch with these puppets. While Trnka wanted to get away from cartoons, Pal, who started out as a 2D animator in his native Hungary and in Germany, aimed for wacky cartooniness. Everything, every step was preplanned and carved in wood before it got to the animators:

> *Every animator was given a detailed cue sheet, prepared by Pal, with each movement laboriously illustrated and synchronized to previously recorded music and dialogue. This setup meant that when the foot of a model touched the floor or a facial reaction occurred, the action was perfectly timed to the music. The model builders constructed sectioned boxes holding the various parts of every character, all coded to match the cue sheet. According to the cue sheet, the animator would replace parts of the model in sequence to produce movement.*
>
> *Pal's meticulous planning was to allow several animators to work on the same sequence without any noticeable variation in style. Hence, the animators were given little room for individual expression, with each move worked out to the smallest detail on the precise cue sheets. The system only occasionally allowed "freehand" animation [...]* *

Pal switched to model animation when he was commissioned a commercial for Oberst Cigarettes in 1932. A heavily damaged print was recently found in the vaults of the Berlin Cinematheque:

A cigarette tobacco leaf standing on two legs, complete with Plasticine mouth movements, is going to introduce the process of cigarette production that is shown in live-action documentary scenes.

Not by drinking (from a small milk bottle), they are kept moist the humanized lead tells us. They generate moisture from the air to keep themselves smooth.

We see female workers sort out leaves.

From the process of shredding, the leaf returns, from the netherworld so to speak, in ghostly 2D animation, to continue its narration. Then it is rolled into the paper.

Finally, we have a humanoid cigarette, with wire legs and arms and clods for feet and hands.

This stop-motion cigarette takes over as Oberst, i.e., Colonel, and, with paper mouth movements and a small paper hat as helmet, proceeds to command a small army:

> *Stand at attention!*
> *Eyes front!*
> *Count off!*

---

* Mike Hankin, *Ray Harryhausen: Master of the Majicks, Volume 1: Beginnings and Endings.* Los Angeles: Archive Editions, 2013, p. 199. Reprinted by permission of the author.

Gold filter soldiers count off and form a marching column:

Six cigarettes in front, six in the middle, and two behind, with the colonel marching ahead to Prussian and Bavarian march music.

In 1933, Pal who was Jewish was forced to leave Germany and founded a new production facility in the Netherlands. In one of his early Gasparcolor Puppetoons, made for Philips Radio in Eindhoven, he had two airplanes front up and used cock's cries to underline that they were enemies. Ray Harryhausen

Replacement puppets by Alberto Couceiro and Alejandra Tomei: *Automatic Fitness* (2015). (Courtesy of Animas Film, Berlin.)

worked for Pal in Hollywood in the early 1940s, but to him it lacked individuality. It was more like a small manufacture. Everything was predetermined and choreographed to even the tiniest step and move.

Harryhausen tried his hand on fairy tales after the war: *Mother Goose Stories, Little Red Riding Hood, Hansel and Gretel, Rapunzel* for which he would have less replacement faces than Pal but just change facial expression by dissolves and would animate the body completely instead of substituting it frame by frame. In one of these shorts, *The Story of King Midas*, he copied his favorite actor, Conrad Veidt, whom he had admired as Jaffar, the sinister grand vizier in *The Thief of Bagdad* (1940).

George Pal, as we have seen, came from drawing and cartoons. His goal was to transform puppetry into cartooning. This was the reason why he chose replacement animation. He wouldn't go for anatomically correct armatures. He would have prepared a different puppet or puppet part for each frame.

Ladislas Starevich (1882–1965), on the other hand, came from natural science. In the early days of cinematography, he started to animate insects to film the fight of stag beetles.

A film creator like Starevich can afford what no man of the industry can afford: He can wait for inspiration. He can play with his figures and thoughts. Although completely playful on the other hand he builds up his films strictly logical. He is natural scientist but one who observes nature with the eyes of a poet and with the perception of the fairy tale: at the same time real and symbolic, concrete and transcendental. The development of a film happens with him as kind of a process of crystallization. He makes an observation while he goes for a walk or observes a community of insects which hits him, infiltrates his mind and moves his imagination. This observation or the thoughts deduced from it he will enrich by new ideas. [...]

He is the actor of all his characters. If he is in the right mood he carefully can start and freely follow his imagination: the elastic, malleable material that provides the "sculptures animées" as he likes to call them and allows any nuance of mimic and gesture. It allows him to remain in the mood and to immediately realize each idea. [...]

Of these enchanting effects of images one can assume what Starevich says: that he can make entirely visual pictures. Occasionally he animates advertising films to make some money. But this is not his ideal "because there is no heart in it." He wants to touch emotionally—children and adults alike—, to make them sad or happy. Although he esteems Disney and doesn't minimalize him he dislikes hand-drawn films. They are not to his taste. Drawings in a film, he says, will remain caricatures: with all amusing characteristics, yet caricatures. They are not living entities who touch the soul. The flatness doesn't allow expression of soul. The drawing cannot have a soul, therefore you need a body. The body alone is bearer of the soul, it necessitates three dimensions. In a hand-drawn animated film a man's head can be ripped off and moved back again, and the audience will laugh. To living sculptures you cannot do that: "On sent de la peine," one will feel pain. Contrary to Disney, the animals are no little machines but living entities, almost human.

Who has seen [Starevich's feature-length] Renard the Fox and who knows Disney will find this differentiation very affecting. Starevich's film, compared to Walt Disney's *animal grotesqueness, has the advantage of an unlikely higher level of liveliness and naturalism. In his finer, tender, saturated tone of fairy tale, he is nearer to our feeling. Against the saucy, clean step of civilisation of the American, the Pole* [Starevich was born in Poland, worked in Russia and after the revolution emigrated to France] *represents convincingly the old Europe with its culture grown in emotion and so rich in tradition. About Disney one can laugh and marvel but Starevich one has to love.*[*]

Maybe this was one of the reasons why Disney strived for 3D realism in his 2D cartoons. Disney himself tried to introduce a stop-motion unit once but, according to Jim Danforth, he ignored how to set up puppet animation correctly and make the puppets stand (!).

Jürgen Clausen, who remained managing director at the Gasparcolor plant in Berlin after the Brothers Gaspar, like George Pal, had fled anti-Semitism, agreed with Starevich's sentiments and unsuccessfully tried to establish a color puppet film production in Nazi Germany with technicians and artists who had previously worked with Pal in the Netherlands:

There are two ways to see pictures: the "flat" and the "dimensional" kind. Instead of "flat" in this case we might better term it: "plakatig" [graphic, poster-like], and instead of "dimensional": "in depth." As far as I enjoy poster-like (hand-drawn) trickfilm I am regarded more an intellectual-witty kind of man without the right sense of humor, also superficial (this is no rating). As far as I am going to enjoy puppet or dimensional trickfilm I am a spiritually sensual man and have humor. Everybody who has the ability to watch himself will agree to this. Hand-drawn animation addresses more the intellect. The ideas or improvisations (the American calls them "gags") have only little to do with humor but more with its brilliant superficiality, the joke. Hand-drawn animation most often deals with malicious caricatures and likes to parody (the cheap kind to get a feeling of superiority). It is not childlike but more childish. For this reason, notabene, as long as hand-drawn animation will remain poster-like it will provide an awkward situation to retell German fairy tale content in this particular style (see Snow White by Disney!). It doesn't seem advisable at all to film fairy tales, legends and also novels in this way for each content is tied to a certain expression, on its form.

Hand-drawn animation has more to do with distortion than with grotesque, it invites more to bemusement than guiding us to bonhomie which is reflected in the smile (actually about oneself, i.e. about the own humanness which steps out of the mirror of artwork). [...]

Americans have transferred the idea of moving posters hand-drawn animation to its highest degree. This style comes from feuilletonistic comic drawings. [...]

Now what is the puppet trickfilm?

Here the matter is totally different. Like feature film, as "photographed theatre", has a tradition that dates back to old-age cultural spaces (tragedy, mystery or miracle play, cult dances and so on) the dimensional trick is tied to everything that has to do with moving puppets. A cultural value so far which is as old as culture itself. If we

---

* Frank Maraun, *"Poet am Tricktisch" Besuch bei Starewitsch*. In: Der deutsche Film, September 1938. Collection of J. P. Storm.

Acting and Character Animation

think of the wooden Egyptian crocodile with its movable mouth—from the second mil-
lennium, or the Turkish and East-Asian shadow plays or the mechanical playworks of
the 16th century (Peter Döpfer, Daniel Bertel for instance), the Kasperle hand puppets
and marionettes (about these Kleist has made a final statement) and last but not least
about the masks of South German Perchten Runs, yes—the nativity plays, gargoyles,
chimes figures up to the truly world-dominating German toys—all this lives in us,
excites us and binds us when we start to think about making color puppet trickfilms.[*]

Then Clausen, who was a member of the National Socialist Party, proceeded
to spread kind of racial ideology:

The puppet or dimensional trick is located in European cultural space and no other
country can be its more natural home than Germany. The German is deeply dimen-
sional-romantic, profoundly imaginative, he is dreamy and contemplative. None other
succeeds that well in humorous grotesque (see Wilhelm Busch) so definitely that one
can count it almost into classic art—classic in a sense of perfection of expression. All of
this means a splendid, not to say decisive predestination for the dimensional trickfilm
and—an obligation. Dimension and depth oblige the German-Nordic identity.[*]

Besides Starevich and Pal, there were the Brothers Ferdinand and Hermann
Diehl in Munich. The Diehls focused their attention on puppet films using realistic human figures. Their style was backward: homage to the *Biedermeier* period.
Hermann designed the puppets and carved the heads, while Ferdinand animated
and directed. For Ferdinand Diehl, the work required a combination of artistry,
technique, and concentration in the extreme:

The stop-motion animator must train himself to be entirely consumed by his work,
as every artist must do, he said. He must have a sympathetic understanding of the
puppet's character to animate it correctly. His concentration must be absolute. The
puppet animator has to memorize each preceding frame in his mind. (Back then
they had no monitors for checking the effect of the animation immediately.) *I*
have placed myself in front of each puppet and got mentally inside of each puppet
to memorize exactly what I had done and what I had to do now. You see, with real-
istic puppets it isn't sufficient for example to just move the foot to have the puppet
make a step. For if the left foot and the leg move forward then at the same time the
right shoulder has to move backwards and the head has to look straightforward.
But if the right shoulder of a puppet is moved backwards the head doesn't stand still
straightforward but moves to the right side too and has to be moved carefully into its
original straightforward position so that the step would be natural. Walking natu-
rally the whole puppet experiences a movement in itself. The animator must know
this angular, pivotal motion, this angular momentum exactly and must memorize
exactly what he has done on the puppet in the previous frame. This is the difficult
part of each stop motion.[†]

---

[*] Jürgen Clausen/Herbert Pohris, Memorandum: *Color Puppet Trickfilm*, 1941. Collection of J. P.
Storm.
[†] Files: Diehl Film, Munich-Gräfelfing.

Once, Diehl recalled, he had to work with sixty puppets simultaneously on a puppet documentary *Assault on a Medieval Town (Die Erstürmung einer mittelalterlichen Stadt)*, produced in 1943: To him, this work was very fine and very healthy. Here one learns best to concentrate truly. *"Usually, though, they had to hold me fast between exposures, because several times I walked right into the shot. My concentration on the animation was so intense that I had forgotten all about the shooting technique."*

The Diehl Bros. Films were presented regularly for soldiers in World War II front cinemas and seemed to have left an impact on the troops fighting for Hitler's perfidious cause:

> *In our front cinema which regularly screens cine-films from local film rentals at first we have seen two films from the German fairy tale world: Tischlein deck dich [Table-Be-Set] and Stadtmaus und Feldmaus [The Town Mouse and the Country Mouse]. At the beginning my comrades smiled a little bit. But then there was evidence that the fairy-tale pictures had to offer a lot more for the soldier. Not only was it an hour of entertainment, forgetting all sorrows and trouble of our battle. Many thought deeper. Since the days of our childhood for the first time something plastically rose before our very eyes. We recalled the long forgotten days of our childhood and youth. Our comrades who are family fathers thought about the content of the pictures and at the same time were reminded of their wives and children at home. Because of that the fairy-tale films moved anybody notwithstanding the deeper meaning behind the plot. We said to ourselves that these too are cultural treasures of our people which we must preserve for a future generation by defending our native country, even by risking our life. War last not least is fought not only for material but for cultural goods. And therefore these films have conveyed to the soldiers the meaning of their present life task and have awakened their enthusiasm...*[*]

Not alone the soldiers at the front, also the Hitler Youth found something in these fairy tales that got a timely meaning. A pupil of eighth grade who saw the Diehls' version of *Tischlein deck dich* wrote a school essay:

> *Yesterday to much laughter of the undergraduate class we saw the picture Tischlein deck dich [Table-Be-Set]. For us grown-ups the fairy tale, however, provided more than entertainment and joy. For in every fairy tale there is a deeper meaning. Today we discussed with our teacher the deeper meaning of this fairy tale.*
>
> *Two tailor's sons acquired, according to the fairy tale, by hard work prosperity and wealth, one in the form of a "Tischlein deck dich" [Table-Be-Set], the other in the form of an "Eselein streck dich" [Gold-Donkey]. Happily they returned home. But the evil and envious landlord robbed them of prosperity and wealth. Luck seemed to have deserted them.*
>
> *The third brother, however, put an abrupt end to the fraud of the host through the "Knüppel aus dem Sack" [Cudgel-out-of-the-sack]. This demonstrates that for the maintenance and security of prosperity and wealth a strong Wehrmacht [German*

---

[*] *Märchenfilme bei den Soldaten.* In Film und Bild, Reichsanstalt für Film und Bild in Wissenschaft und Unterricht, Issue 4/5, 1 May 1942. Collection of J. P. Storm.

Acting and Character Animation

Wedding ceremony from *Memory Hotel*, a feature-length stop-motion project that takes place right after World War II. (Courtesy of Heinrich Sabl.)

military] is necessary, just a Cudgel-out-of-the-sack. It alone is able to regain for the others the lost treasures.

The three sons of the tailor come, as the fairy tale tells us, from Dingsda [Dingbat]. Dingda, however, is somewhere in Germany, it can be anywhere. So the three brothers represent our whole German nation which has to master life as the three apprentices do. The little goblin, however, that lives in fairy-tale land and gives the brothers work and pay, represents the luck that everybody needs. For a time it seemed as if luck had abandoned the good three brothers; but then it returns to them forever.

The treacherous host, who hoped to get rich by employing swindle and meanness, faced the fate of punishment. He resembles the eternal Jew who wants to profit from the work of the diligent and capable without moving a single finger. He is a Schmarotzer [parasite] who only wants to suck the others and exploit them. In spite of his smartness he can't escape punishment; for there is the Cudgel-out-of-the-sack.

So at the end of our review we have come to the conclusion:

1. *By work German people acquire prosperity and wealth.*
2. *The evil Jew wants to rob the German people of prosperity and wealth.*
3. *German people, however, secures its prosperity and wealth by a strong army.*
4. *Only a hard-working nation is lucky in the long run.*

So this fairy tale strengthens and invigorates us in our unruly belief in the Endsieg [final victory] of Germany in this war. Its "Cudgel-out-of-the-sack" drums heavily on the back of our enemies until all who have called upon the cudgel will buckle like the malicious host did.

There are valuable lessons children can learn from fairy tales, but there is always the danger that different interpretations of these popular tales are abused to indoctrinate the young generation.

---

* "*Knüppel aus dem Sack*" School essay—recorded by Ferdinand Josef Holzer. Deutscher Kulturdienst, July 4, 1941. Collection of J. P. Storm.

19

Animated Characters around the World

Most of the classic cartoons star anthropomorphic animals that are in some way influenced by *Aesop's Fables*, a collection of stories credited to Aesop, a slave who lived in ancient Greece between 620 and 564 BCE. These stories, later known under titles like *The Town Mouse and the Country Mouse* or *The Ant and the Grasshopper*, connected modest incidents that happened in flora and fauna with great truth in human life. Quite often Aesop's animals have human characteristics. There was even an early cartoon series under that title (*sugar-coated pills of wisdom*) suggested by actor-turned-writer Howard Estabrook and produced by Paul Terry that was launched in 1921 with *The Goose That Laid the Golden Eggs*.

Besides the habit of quoting Aesop, however, there are big differences concerning various cultures and time periods. Animated characters can vary from studio to studio: The product of Disney differed from the Looney Tunes or Woody Woodpecker. Not only is European animation different from U.S. output but different from country to country too: the tradition of Franco-Belgian comics, Italy and Spain, the Czech Republic, Hungary and Croatia, Germany, Denmark, and Sweden. Although early Chinese animation copied heavily from Russian and Japanese productions, it has its own cultural background, following the requirements of the so-called Cultural Industries, while artists like Hayao Miyazaki are

Japanese in style but story-wise sometimes rely on European culture (TV series *Heidi, Girl of the Alps;* animated features *Kiki's Delivery Service, Porco Rosso, Ponyo,* and *The Secret World of Arrietty* based on a series of novels titled *The Borrowers* and written by English author Mary Norton).

Osamu Tezuka (1928–1989) was a great Japanese master without whose efforts there certainly would be no anime, at least not the way we know and appreciate them. In spite of the passion he had for Disney and other American works, Tezuka was not completely satisfied with their "slapstick" approach, with musical comedies, or fairy tales. He was convinced that animation needed a type of story construction and staging that are inevitably necessary for live action dramas as well.

He wanted to get rid of the clichés that had been accepted until then in animation. Consequently, he began to adapt his series *Tetsuwan Atom (Astro Boy)* that was published from 1952 on as manga and premiered in anime format on Fuji TV on New Year's Eve 1966. Astro Boy is created by the head of the Ministry of Science, Doctor Tenma, with the intent to replace his son Tobio who died in a car accident. *Astro* is the predecessor of *Ghost in the Shell* (1995) that linked the tradition of Asian ghost stories (Japan has a complex history of *yurei*= ghosts that took shape in woodblock prints, the *ukiyo-e* genre of art) with the sci-fi idea of cyborgs and cyberbrains. The diversity of the camera angle became a trademark of Tezuka's Mushi Productions and nowadys is to be found in all Japanese anime productions. So the evolution of Japanese anime was different from American productions. Ralph Bakshi told Tezuka that he had been stimulated by seeing this type of staging when he was just starting out.

Japanese didn't handle their cartoons like cartoons but like live action dramas. Some artists said that they didn't have budgets that would have been sufficient to produce live action. They eagerly would have welcomed live action but had to content with *drawing* live action in manga publications as well as in anime. It wasn't meant to be animation.

One can see, however, that Japanese and other Asian artists are more interested in style and design than in characters. This helped to overcome the limitations and transform long takes, slow motion, only partial animation of body parts, and freeze frame into aesthetic expression. Some of their characters are as static as robots. They really like robots as they resemble so much the armored samurai of their own history. Human characters they copied very often from foreign feature films starring Errol Flynn or Steve McQueen. He had always liked Steve McQueen from the time he was in the *Wanted: Dead or Alive* series, says Ryosuke Takahashi who started with Tezuka's Mushi Productions.[*] These characters for sure didn't come from a real life. They came from screen and TV.

This is true for Chiyoko Fujiwara too, the female protagonist of Satoshi Kon's *Millennium Actress,* a Studio Madhouse production released in 2001 that

---

[*] Ryosuke Takahashi interviewed by Takayuki Karahashi (1996) in *Anime Interviews: The First Five Years of Animerica Anime & Manga Monthly (1992–97).* San Francisco, CA: Cadence Books, 1997, p. 166.

followed the sex thriller *Perfect Blue*. Chiyoko, who is said to have been a once famous star of a prestigious but bankrupt film studio, was modeled after two screen goddesses, Setsuko Hara, well-known from her roles in films directed by Yasujiro Ozu, and Hideko Takamine, favored by director Mikio Naruse, in her youth billed as Japan's Shirley Temple. The picture opens with a TV interviewer and his cameraman who let Chiyoko travel through her memories. It is a sad picture projecting Kon's sentiments. The director made no more than four feature films. He died of cancer in 2010. He was only 46 years old.

When it came to technical detail and design, the art of the anime was flawless. When Hayao Miyazaki recalled his early steps, he said that it wasn't *mecha* so much. It was military that appealed to the offspring of this once very militaristic nation back then. Miyazaki who described himself as a shy boy found a way to express his boyish yearning for power and strength in drawing tanks and warships. Today, he says, it would take the form of air guns, video games, remote-controlled craft, and the like. Not to forget motorbikes. But growing up it's the capabilities and shape of the machines that are fascinating. Luckily Miyazaki's interest shifted to the dramas of the people who build them and made use of them, particularly in *The Wind Rises* (2013) that tells the life story of a dreamer who becomes chief engineer of many Japanese fighter designs of World War II, including the Mitsubishi A6M Zero fighter: Dr. Jiro Horikoshi who passed away in 1982.

Considering drama, Miyazaki interviewed by Roger Ebert mentioned the poetic "stillness" in some movies: not to advance the story but only to give the sense of time and place, in contrast to nonstop action with no breathing space at all. Miyazaki said that they had a word for it in Japanese. It is called *ma: emptiness, gap, the space between two structural parts*—an idea that might have been inspired by the practice of *Zen* meditation that was developed to give insight into the emptiness of inherent existence and open the path to a liberated way of living. What really matters are the underlying emotions.[*]

If you watch closely, there is more posing than character movement in many anime, including Miyazaki's, which seems to be part of a different "stillness" that might have to do with low budgets that didn't allow full animation. So everything, facial expression, emotion, and so on, is defined in a still or key frame, not part of fluid movements. Yes, it sure helps save money but on the other hand adds a softness and thoughtfulness to animated characters.

There even is some "stillness" in Disney's action-filled *Snow White and the Seven Dwarfs:* The sequence that showed the dwarfs crying besides Snow White's bier was critical. It was solved by the decision to have the characters, with watery eyes, move as little as possible. Frank Churchill's music carried the scene.

"Stillness" was also an issue in the films of Japan's greatest stop-motion animator, Kihachiro Kawamoto. In a great example of intercultural inspiration, he travelled to Prague in 1963 to study puppet animation under the master Jiří

* Roger Ebert, Hayao Miyazaki Interview. http://www.rogerebert.com. September 12, 2002.

Trnka. Trnka wisely advised Kawamoto to focus on Japan's own cultural heritage (what an American producer never would have done).

In the Soviet Union, Soyuzmultfilm started the series *Nu Pogodi! (Just You Wait)* starring a wolf (*Volk*) who constantly fails trying to capture a hare (*Zayats*): The series was originated in 1969 by three artists, one of whom, Felix Kandel, later immigrated to Israel. According to Kandel one higher official in the state-run film studio tried to give the series an ideological slant, by making the rabbit into a brave young Pioneer with the red neckerchief and the wolf into some symbol of evil capitalism. Luckily, the series was successful enough to beat off any unwelcome fun-killing change.

Children might have seen in the rabbit the young pioneer but that made him clearly the boring part of the duo. All the young viewers identified with the villain Kandel said.* Well, this *Volk*, this wolf stole cars, chain-smoked, bullied little furry characters, and tried his hand in vandalism. Nevertheless, kids adored him.

The interesting future market for animation is China. In 2006, while promoting *Flushed Away*, Jeffrey Katzenberg was asked by this writer (RG) if he ever would consider working in China. Although at that time he had *Kung Fu Panda* in preparation, he denied any ambition of cooperating: Never ever would he work in China. Chinese, he said, are repetitive, they like to imitate, don't speak English, and what else. Since then, he has changed his mind and did a 180. In 2012, designated general secretary and president of the People's Republic Xi Jinping met with Katzenberg in Glendale, California. Business in mind, Katzenberg changed from Saul to Paul and became a partner of Oriental DreamWorks based in Shanghai. Externally trying to find a balance between Eastern and Western cartoon characters it seemed to be more about outsourcing and cheap labor and—after Katzenberg left the "parent company"—will definitely need a restructure.

DreamWorks, Disney, and Universal—they all line up in China producing toys and merchandize, co-producing, and opening theme parks without paying respect to Chinese culture, however. It's all over the same kind of global standardization, even in China.

The situation was different when former premier Wen Jiabao found his grandson watching Japanese animation and sensed, to cite the late political scientist Samuel P. Huntington, a clash of civilization. During a visit to the South Chinese Jiantong Animation Studio, he complained and demanded a change: "*There are times when I watch TV anime with my grandchild but all he ever watches are foreign works like Ultraman and the like. He should watch more Chinese cartoons. We should be cultivating a domestic anime industry.*" Then he advised the assembled animators: "*Your work is meaningful. You should play a leading role in bringing Chinese culture to the world. Let Chinese children watch more of their own history and their own country's animation.*"†

---

* David Shipler, *Russia: Broken Idols, Solemn Drama*. New York: Crown, 1983.
† Rolf Giesen, *Chinese Animation: A History and Filmography, 1922–2012*. Jefferson, NC: McFarland & Company, Inc., Publishers, 2015.

Following the Premier's advice, the whole industry went ahead and expanded to gigantic proportions. Chinese animation focuses on preschool and young audiences in general. There are so far 370 million kids—a clear target group for the biggest toy manufacturer in the world. Above all, Chinese government wanted to create a situation for the manufacturers to save the high license fees from being paid to Disney and other American or Japanese cartoon suppliers and create their own brands. But up till now, in spite of all protectionism, no true cartoon star has emerged that could compete with Mickey Mouse, the Simpsons, or Garfield. In television, they were going for mass-produced, long-running series like *Blue Cat*, sort of a blue version of Felix the Cat but the Chinese feline was lacking character and suffered from ill-conceived stories.

There was, of course, once a great tradition in Chinese animation. Some of it wasn't based so much on animation and characters but mainly on style. A political caricaturist who wasn't interested in frame-by-frame animation at all and left that part to his assistants, Te Wei (1915–2010), was chosen to head the Shanghai Animation Film Studios. Again it was a politician, Vice-President Chen Yi, who, while visiting an exhibition dedicated to film animation in 1960, encouraged animators and suggested to animate the work of painter Qi Baishi (1864–1957), famous for the illustration of fish and shrimps. Te Wei went on to do a little film in the traditional form of brush-painting and started a trend of ink animation: *Where Is Momma?* The picture begins with simple and elegant Chinese paintings on screen, just like opening a book. The audience is led into a beautifully lyrical inking world. There are small watercolored tadpoles that have been just born and are curious to find their mother. They meet and ask a goldfish, the white belly of a crab, a tortoise, and even a large catfish until they find their mother—a frog. It's a well-known Chinese Aesop-style story. The tadpoles are lively and lovely moving in the water, just like a bunch of innocent kids. So each culture has its own way to approach to the beauty of movement.

The most dangerous fiend to cultural differences is globalization because globalization is the big equalizer: globalization plus available technology. (At the moment, we register a strong countermovement that manifests itself in different kinds of fundamentalism, from America and Europe to the Near, Middle, and Far East.)

When we went to visit Disney's Shanghai branch, they told us that they had just purchased the international distribution rights to a Chinese hit series *Pleasant Goat and Big Big Wolf*, the only real animated success on Chinese TV, but they didn't know how to release it because it was not only cheap and too Chinese but the humor was astonishingly naive. The perennial but vain attempt of a gray loser wolf (Wolfy) who lives with his narcissistic tyrant wife queen, known as Red Wolf or Wolnie, in the ruins of an old castle tower to catch a flock of sheep that happily lives in their village on pastoral Greengrass Land: Pleasant Goat or Happy who wears a small bell on his neck is the witty main character of the series. His friends include Slow Goat (Slowly), the Mayor of the village, who also is their teacher; Lazy Goat (Fatty); Pretty Goat (Beauty); Fit Goat (Fitty); Warm Goat (Gently); and Soft Goat, the ancestor of the goat family. The Wolf Queen who constantly commands her husband to go after these lovely goats resembles certain Chinese wives and, being over-demanding and abusive, gets some laughs at least in Asia.

In China, the brand is titled *Xi Yang Yang Yu Huitai* and was created by Huang Weiming, Lin Yuting, and Luo Yinggeng.

Technically, the series is simple Flash Animation. It was never mentioned but besides being a bizarre, cheaply animated series imitating elements from the *Coyote and Roadrunner* series as well as the *Three Little Pigs*, the whole thing being a poor copy of the aforementioned Belgian *Smurfs,* with the tiny blue dwarves who live in mushroom-shaped houses in the forest replaced by sheep and their nemesis, Gargamel the magician, by the wolf couple. That would have been a solution for marketing the series outside China but Disney gave up right from the beginning. They weren't interested in the series at all. For them it was just a try to strengthen ties with the economically more and more powerful China.

Examples of Chinese animation: *Fei Tian* (top image) and *Chicken Wants to Fly* (bottom image). (Courtesy of Jilin Animation Institute, Changchun.)

Examples of Chinese animation—*Chicken Wants to Fly* (top image) and *Frog Kingdom* (2013, bottom image). (Courtesy of Jilin Animation Institute, Changchun.)

Disney's first try to fraternize with Chinese culture was *Mulan*, a 1998 animated feature film, based on the Chinese legend of Hua Mulan, a female warrior who lived in Han Dynasty. Chinese audiences, however, disliked what they saw. Mulan's design was considered by them not Chinese but Korean! In the meantime, Disney has learned his lesson and by offering a Disney Princess series transforms little Chinese girls into *Western* princesses. We will talk about this idea later.

A great example of successfully depicting a different culture is *The Book of Life* (2014). Directed and co-written by Jorge R. Gutierrez, who had studied at CalArts, and exec-produced by Guillermo del Toro, this fantasy that makes us feel what *La Muerte*, the Day of the Dead, means to Mexicans: not only grief and mourning but an exercise in high spirits.

20

Of Heroes, Antiheroes, Villains, and Men

Heroes might be in conflict with themselves. This is the case in new superhero movies, as a matter of course in all superhero comics of the Marvel generation, the generation after World War II. Spider-Man is an ordinary teenager bitten by an atomic spider. Before World War II, the attitude was different. To the new antiheroes their special qualities come like God given fate: by accident. In Greek tragedy, fates are decided by the pleasure of the Olympian gods. The first antihero of Greek tragedy was Prometheus, a Titan who antagonized Zeus and sided with the humans by stealing the power of fire from the immortals and bringing it to the mortals.

There is a song by The Stranglers, an English rock band, titled "No More Heroes."

If we watch the news media reports, it's mostly bad news. To the media, we are a deeply pessimistic society. Instinctively, we don't believe in the good of people and, after World War II, we don't believe in heroes anymore as mythologist Joseph Campbell described them: A hero is someone who has given his or her life to a bigger cause. Heroes' last stand is the fantasy world of *Star Wars*. Even movie stars that we worship turn out to be drug-addicted and alcoholics and are thrown in jail. If something really good happens we doubt it immediately and tell ourselves, "It seems too good to be true they must be hiding something." There must be a lot of skeletons buried in people's closets, especially in Tinseltown.

Kenneth Anger has devoted a whole albeit in terms of research rather superficial book to the history of virtual film heroes and called it aptly *Hollywood Babylon*.[*]

In a world of global economics, multinational corporations, and shifting moral, there seems to be more space for the antihero. And Francis Ford Coppola's Don Vito Corleone of *The Godfather*, portrayed by Marlon Brando, became an admired character bigger than life.

Nevertheless, there are new-type heroes. They need a well-defined social surrounding to have audiences identify with them. In Japan, they have succeeded in doing so. Manga and anime seem to be an exception. Here we find heroes who are human and quite ordinary and even flawed. Their heroism is defined by the dedication to their cause although even that one might be suspect. To fight for the wrong cause does not damage their noble mindset.

Sure a good hero needs an adequate villain. But the villain should be constructed along the same lines. A villain considers himself not the bad one. To him the reasons he has for acting this way are absolutely justified and good.

There is a habit, at least in Europe, to tell animation stories destined for preschool kids without antagonism, which is being considered harmful to the children's mind. This would be the same as if to tell classic fairy tales and eliminate all opposition, magicians, witches, or dragons. When he created the evil witch for *Snow White and the Seven Dwarfs*, Disney deliberately scared kids and created a long-term nightmare.

Not only did Disney have virgin-like heroines, he also had some of the most memorable, almost misogynic villainesses that were all flamboyant and eccentric: Lady Tremaine, *Cinderella's* wicked stepmother, and Maleficent, *Sleeping Beauty's* evil fairy, both voiced by Eleanor Audley, as well as Cruella De Vil who plans to have *One Hundred and One Dalmatians* skinned. She was voiced by Betty Lou Gerson and rivaled, as Thomas and Johnston would put it in their book, Donald Duck for emotional outbursts and temperamental tantrums.[†]

Mohammed Atta and the other suicide assassins believed in Allah and thought themselves heroes out of religious motives when they committed what everybody else called one of the biggest crimes of the century: 9/11. There even was a Telegate commercial produced and broadcast in Germany shortly before 9/11 that showed an airplane crashing into a skyscraper but nothing happened to people as everything was "meant for fun." The commercial was stopped immediately and nobody could explain the reason for its production. They just wanted to create a big bang to get a lot of attention and thought they had a hit in their hands. Obviously, there was something in the air. Certainly, the producers of the spot

---

[*] Kenneth Anger, *Hollywood Babylon*. San Francisco: Straight Arrow Press (distributed by Simon & Schuster), 1975.

[†] Frank Thomas & Ollie Johnston, *Disney Animation: The Illusion of Life*. New York, 1981: Abbeville Press Publishers, p. 506.

Acting and Character Animation

didn't consider themselves evildoers and don't think to this day. Their violence was simply "meant for fun" but exploded into a terrorist firestorm.

Again, an actor as well as a person who works in animation has to defend his or her character. Actors long to play *Richard III*. There are always motives for what turns out evil. Only in 1D, highly naïve tales there are super villains who rise in the morning and think about what evil they can do today. Of course, this is a dilemma that cannot be solved by the actors. It is the duty of the playwrights to create empathy for the victims and expose the evildoers.

Ed Hooks and Edwin Rutsch discussed this matter on YouTube. Hooks claimed that an actor even would have to defend Adolf Hitler if he would be cast in the part. Yet nobody would like to empathize with that devil of a man. Hooks mentioned Swiss actor Bruno Ganz who played the dictator in a 2004 German movie titled *The Downfall (Der Untergang)*. To render the monster human, the scenarist used a trick. In the exposition, he introduced a friendly Hitler who comforts overly nervous Traudl Junge who is applying for a job as Hitler's secretary.

Hooks' perspective on this matter is: Unless we feel empathy, we won't know anything. We won't recognize the next Hitler who might already wait around the corner. No, although he is gone we have to worry about the potential Hitler imitators in the world. Hooks would rather portray Hitler as a man who had a dream: a dream that turned out a nightmare for millions.* The writers of *The Downfall*, however, cut out the suffering of millions to focus on what became the Passion of Hitler on screen. There was nothing the actor could do about that. He followed the rules of his craft. Tennesse Williams, the great playwright, claimed that there should be no painful people, at least not on stage. All cruel people, he said, describe themselves as paragons of frankness.

But there is not only the archetype of the supervillain, there are ratbags in everyday life as well. Just take Pixar's *Ratatouille*. France's top restaurant critic, Anton Ego, modeled after French actor Louis Jouvet and voiced by Peter O'Toole, isn't a sympathetic character, but when he asks they should surprise him and tastes what has been prepared by an unknown rat cook, he has a flashback and transforms into the boy he once was when his beloved mother served him just that, *Ratatouille*. All of a sudden, we understand him. The negative character transforms into a positive human being. If a villain at all, Ego is a comedy villain.

* *Empathy for Actors and Animators: Ed Hooks and Edwin Rutsch.* www.youtube.com, 2015.

21

Comedy and Comedians

Remember Leonardo di Caprio standing on the bow of the *Titanic* yelling, "*I am king of the world*"?

That's drama.

Now imagine he would lose his pants.

Then the same scene would transform into comedy.

Comedy is drama heightened, oxygenated, says Ed Hooks, and it can even include death as we know from the work of Woody Allen.

Well, in Mexico they ridicule death (children included who are shielded from the impression of death in the big industrial countries).

Jim Danforth remembers that while animating the dragon from MGM-Cinerama's *The Wonderful of the Brothers Grimm* (1962), he was told by Gene Warren, his boss at the animation studio Project Unlimited, to animate the pathetic death scene in a funny way because it should be a comic dragon. Then in came producer George Pal and Danforth told him how funny the dragon's death scene would turn out. Pal remained calm and disappeared in Warren's office but when he left, Warren was pissed off. The death scene was executed differently then, in a most dramatic way.

There were two masters of movie comedy.

Charles Chaplin came from British music hall tradition.

The other, Buster Keaton, was trained in American vaudeville.

Keaton was illiterate. He was a child born and conditioned backstage. At young age, his father used him on the vaudeville stage, threw him around, hurt him, and told him to show no emotion to the ill-treatment. That might have been child abuse. No, it might not have been, it sure was. Keaton became deadpan and a poker face. His screen image was created by early childhood trauma. It was laughter created at a child's mistreatment and the art of self-control. Keaton "excused" it by calling his old man an "eccentric." It all was, as he said, the result of a series of "interesting experiments" conducted by his "Pop." Joe Keaton began his vaudeville act by carrying him out on the stage and dropping him on the floor. Next he started wiping up the floor with the little "Human Mop." When Buster gave no sign of minding, "Pop" began throwing him through the scenery, out into the wings, and dropping him down on the bass drum in the orchestra pit. The audience was amazed that the little boy didn't cry. In his autobiography, Keaton claimed that he didn't cry because he wasn't hurt. He even enjoyed himself. All little boys, he says, like to be roughhoused by their fathers. To support the act, little Buster would look miserable, humiliated, hounded, and haunted, bedeviled, bewildered, and at his wit's end.*

What Keaton is doing here is whitewashing his childhood experiences. He certainly was humiliated and became a heavy drinker, same as Lon Chaney, Jr., who, according to late writer Curt Siodmak, was tormented by his famous father, the *Hunchback of Notre Dame* and *Phantom of the Opera*.

Chaplin, on the other hand, brought emotion to superficial slapstick: Other comedians might have stumbled into a bucket and just shove it away, but Chaplin, ashamed, would try to hide foot and bucket and turn not so much the mishap but the following embarrassment into fun and laughter.

Chaplin was looking for empathy and Keaton for sympathy.

Of course, there are other great comedians to study. Harry Langdon, a slow-paced, baby-faced actor (and caricaturist), who would do things in an innocent way so that only God could help him as Frank Capra, one of his writer-directors, would remark. When sound came in, they tried to make him faster and that completely spoiled his comedy timing. Some characters are fast. Some are slow. Comedy always is a question of timing. Most cartoon characters are fast. Some are too fast. But the biggest laugh in Disney's highly successful *Zootopia* (2016) gets a sloth named Flash (!) that works at the Department of Motor Vehicles where customers usually have to wait in long lines. Flash reacts to a joke in super-slow-motion, his eyes widening, his mouth opening until after what felt like an eternity he finally bursts into laughter. It's not so much the quality of the animation (which is quite good, of course, but it could be cheap as well and the gag would still work) that makes the character a hit but the identification of a slow,

---

* Buster Keaton & Charles Samuels, *My Wonderful World of Slapstick*. Garden City, NY: Doubleday, 1960, pp. 12–13.

single-minded person with a very slow animal. It works on a satirical level. It's a social comment. Being slow can be funny, very funny. You don't have to rush characters.

Harold Lloyd was no natural comedian. Keystone's Mack Sennett didn't consider him funny at all. But Lloyd was a great doer and, above all, passionate actor and therefore immensely popular with audiences in the 1920s. His comedy was based on challenge and acting abilities. To stand out from other comedians, he abandoned the trademark of the moustache. To transform, he just needed a pair of glasses. The rest was proper acting. Lloyd's forte was dangerous comedy situation such as climbing a skyscraper in *Safety Last*.

By the way, Sennett as well as his main competitor Hal Roach, Harold Lloyd's producer, occasionally would use cartoon effects animated by Walter Lantz, Pinto Colvig, or Roy Seawright to enhance slapstick action.

In modern days, there is Rowan Atkinson as *Mr. Bean*, like Lloyd an actor who gets into funny situations, also no natural comedian and in Europe more popular than in the United States.

As a comedian you have to create a character that fits you: Chaplin started to create his screen personality by looking for the right clothes that made him a tramp and adopting a walk.

Cartoon characters have a lot in common with these great clowns and comedians as we know from Ko-Ko the Clown.

Animation pioneer Pat Sullivan (1887–1933) was able to contract with Charles Chaplin for a cartoon series based on his screen character released in 1916. Chaplin himself was delighted with the results and realized the value of the promotion. He had sent them three dozen photographs of himself in different poses.

When they went on with a cartoon star of their own, *Felix the Cat,* they would still use Chaplin and copy his moves: the walk, the subtle gestures. Otto Messmer (1892–1983), who would work with Sullivan on both, the Chaplin films and the *Felix* series, did most of the animation, he even designed the cat, made it all black so he didn't have to worry about outlines. He recalled (most likely a legend) that after seeing one of Chaplin's films he went straight home, sat down, and drew an angular black cat with big wide eyes to fill the white screen. Under the impression of Chaplin, he patterned the cat's facial expressions and funny movements after the little tramp. Audiences adored Felix the same way they loved Chaplin. But there was a big difference between Felix and Charlie besides that one was a human, the other a feline stray: The animated character did things that Chaplin couldn't do. In *Felix in Hollywood* (1923), the cat detaches its tail and uses it like Chaplin his cane. Felix develops a moustache and keeps on walking like Chaplin offering his service to a film producer—until the real Charlie (as animated character, of course) intervenes and stops the cat, *Stealing my stuff, eh?!* (As we have seen, Chaplin himself felt flattered when his mannerisms were projected onto an animated cat.)

Entrepreneur and marketing expert Lawrence Weiss (1925–2008), better known by the stage name Larry Harmon and through *Bozo the Clown* franchise

(Bozo was later caricatured as Krusty in the *Simpsons* show), purchased the rights to the Laurel & Hardy characters from Stan Laurel and Oliver Hardy's widow and used them in an Hanna-Barbera animated TV series run of 156 episodes and in comic books that were started in 1969. In 2015, Gaumont Animation in France decided to produce and distribute an all-new 2D animated series for kids based on the icon characters and purchased the rights from Larry Harmon Pictures Corporation. Another famous comedy team that became animation was Abbott & Costello: first as two dumb cats named Babbit and Catstello that encounter the prototype of Tweety Bird in Bob Clampett's *A Tale of Two Kitties* (1942), later in the half-hour animated TV *Abbott and Costello Cartoon Show* (1967–1968) by Hanna and Barbera.

After a while, early American animation became metonymic with slapstick comedy. Comedy action was on a similar level. Of course the humans were substituted by all kinds of animals, including a Coyote chasing a Roadrunner. Chuck Jones, the director, admitted that he learned a lot from Keaton who was the most inventive among silent comedy's physical gag specialists, for instance, the little eye-flicks toward the camera, which he would use whenever the Coyote realizes that something is inevitably going to fall on him and the action stops for a moment. Or Keaton's footwork: As Keaton wouldn't act with his face that was frozen he would act with his feet, Jones said.

The main difference, however, was that you couldn't get Chaplin in a milk bottle as Tex Avery put it once. That was the reason why cartoons survived and the old slapsticks didn't. Cartoons are fast and furious.

But same as comedians Bug Bunny or Daffy Duck weren't particularly funny to watch as characters. Neither are they that original. Disney had similar characters on the screen. If you see Woody Allen, Chaplin, or Laurel, they are not funny to look at. They are funny by the way they move. That is, Jones would emphasize, the whole point about character animation. It's how they move what makes them special.

That's important when it comes to create comedy out of a character's personality. A *slow burn*, an exasperated facial expression, performed deliberately, can be funnier than the gag that has gone before. Comedian Edgar Kennedy was a *slow burn* master.

Cartoonist Charles R. Bowers (1887–1946) who was involved in the early *Mutt & Jeff* series adapted from Bud Fisher's comic strip even became a silent film comedian himself filling his shorts with cleverly, surreal animated dimensional gags. In *Egged On* (1926), for instance, he played an eccentric inventor who has an unbreakable egg in mind. When his machine is finished and has laid the hoped-for eggs, he transports the eggs in the hood of a Model T Ford—and out of the eggs roll miniature Fords. Bowers used animation for transformation and metamorphosis and also played with strange stop-motion characters such as a metal eating bird (*It's a Bird*). In *Believe It or Don't* (1934), he had a lobster playing xylophone until he is blown up by dynamite, with the body parts spelling out the end title.

Sylvain Chomet, who did the *Triplets of Belleville* (2003), bowed to another grandmaster of comedy, Jacques Tati, and animated a script that Tati had left behind: *The Illusionist* (2010).

Comedy is more than just a handful of gags. Comedy is a narrative structure. There are different types of comedy that follow certain rules and all became part of animated films:

- *Slapstick* (the field of Keaton et al.)
- *Parody* (*West and Soda*)
- *Spoof and Mockery*
- *Satire* (*Animal Farm*)
- *Irony* (they say kids don't understand irony)
- *Sarcasm* (*Terkel in Trouble*)
- *Farce*
- *Black comedy* (*Hell and Back*)
- *Surrealism*

Essential is the comedy timing and what Stan Laurel called the magic of the first moment.

According to actor Henry Brandon (born Heinrich von Kleinbach), who was with Laurel & Hardy in *Babes in Toyland* (1934), the comedy team would rehearse but then the first take was *it*. Chaplin, on the other hand, was a perfectionist who would need sometimes up to 60 takes until he found that the scene and his acting were right. (Most of this footage has been destroyed on Chaplin's demand later by his cameraman Rollie Totheroh although he kept some footage that proves that some of the earlier takes were more emotional and therefore funnier.)

22

Acting against the Odds of Visual Effects and Animation

In the history of VFX movies, there rarely was great, memorable acting. In many of those films, we just saw the "pointers." They would look and point at a marvelous effect and just say, *Hey, look at that!* Then there were the guys running away from a monster on the loose. That wasn't a challenge for the actors either.

There are only a few cases when VFX and acting merge in a symbiotic way. One might recall Disney's classic live-action feature *Darby O'Gill and the Little People* (1959) that had Irish Albert Sharpe's character acting with leprechauns thanks to forced perspective, special lenses, an enormous amount of lighting equipment, and the Shuftan mirror process. In 2016, made possible by elaborate green screen shots, French actor Jean Dujardin became a person of rather restricted height, just 4 ft 5 in, who fell in love with normal-sized Virginia Efira in Laurent Tirard's *Up for Love (Un homme à la hauteur)*. What is fun on screen, however, is a nightmare to actors while shooting. (Some critics, however, suggested it would have been better if the filmmakers would have hired a diminutive actor. They were wrong. It wouldn't have been that funny.)

Occasionally, a live actor becomes an animated effect too.

In *The Invisible Ray* (1936) and *Man Made Monster* (1941), two entries of Universal's classic series of horror films, female animators under the supervision of John P. Fulton would have to create painstakingly a glowing halo frame by frame round the bodies of Boris Karloff (as Dr. Janos Rukh exposed to "Radium X," the radiation of a meteor) and Lon Chaney, Jr. (as Dynamo Dan, the Electric Man), respectively.

Modern-day films like *Spider-Man* (2002) starring Tobey Maguire resemble digital and mechanical bits and pieces, with the star only partly involved in the virtual environment.

Actors in front of green screen shooting *Tehran Taboo* (2017) by Ali Soozandeh. (Courtesy of Little Dream Entertainment.)

The film was shot on soundstages in Los Angeles, where the air-bearing wall rigs mostly became the props for Chris Daniels who doubled Maquire in three pictures. A special harness was what helped him to swing through the air in his special superhero costume. The straps went around his legs, waist, and chest while clips attached the harness to a cable. Daniels moved his arms and legs as if swinging from a spider web. The wires were removed digitally in post-production creating the illusion the performer was supporting his own weight. According to Daniels, the scariest moment came when he had to jump off a building about 200 ft and trusting that the rig was going to work.

More or less, Tobey Maguire contributed only his face for close-up green screen elements. The wire from Tobey's shoulder occasionally crossed his face so that they had to rebuild it using Adobe After Effects and Pinnacle System's Commotion, sampling textures from the other side of his face, replicating his surprised expression and animating wind moving his hair. Sony Pictures Imageworks would then create the final composite of Maguire swinging against a rushing background of digital buildings.

British actor Bob Hoskins was driven to the brink of insanity by his part in Disney's *Who Framed Roger Rabbit*:

I think I went a bit mad while working on that. Lost my mind. The voice of the rabbit was there just behind the camera all the time, you just had to know where the rabbit *would be at all times, and Jessica Rabbit and all these weasels. The trouble was: I had learnt how to hallucinate. If you do that for eight months it becomes hard to get rid of.* *

Despite a thunderstorm of VFX, the blockbuster that the Warner Bros. moneymakers made out of J. K. Rowling's *Fantastic Beasts and Where to Find Them* (2016) was disappointing. There are enough stars, including Eddie Redmayne, Johnny Depp, Colin Farrell, Ron Perlman, and Jon Voight, but only supporting roles, no true main protagonist, and no Harry Potter on board. The result was confusing.

Doctor Strange, a former neurosurgeon and the Sorcerer Supreme who protects the Earth from magical and mystical fantasy threats, is another of the legion of comic book superheroes created by Stan Lee and Steve Ditko in 1963. The film *Doctor Strange*, released the same year as Warner's *Fantastic Beasts*, although naïve and completely trivial, is nevertheless highly entertaining, not only thanks to extraordinary VFX but to the actor who portrays the title hero, a well-defined protagonist: Benedict Cumberbatch, who trained in a *Sherlock Holmes* TV series, is intelligent and witty enough to play an intellectual and also acts with understatement. That makes the movie much more entertaining than the usual stupid superhero rough-and-tumble. And Mads Mikkelsen sure is an equal adversary. This entry proves that actors and actresses indeed can master VFX and are not necessarily squeezed against the (green) wall.

---

* *Hoskins: "Roger Rabbit Drove Me Mad."* WENN, October 27, 2009.

23

Avatar and Beyond

The Idiosyncrasies of 3D Animation and the Art of Performance Capture

Many 2D animators remained skeptical when computers were introduced. Decades ago, Tony White wrote:

> *Without the varied idiosyncrasies of a human personality, the computer is incapable of giving a living spirit to its creations, and this is the secret ingredient of all great animation. As long as audiences continue to want subtle, sophisticated, and entertaining character animation—where we actually believe that the drawings we see are alive and real—then the role of drawn animation in filmmaking is assured.*

We know, of course, that he was proven wrong over the years. To the great disappointment of fundamentalist 2D animators, 3D has become the standard. There still is a lot of 2D, particularly in Japan, but the mass has transformed three dimensionally. We are literally swamped by it. Unlike 2D, 3D animation is never individual. 2D is more individual. It isn't changed that much after the artist has done a scene. 3D, on the other hand, is easily to be changed during production: details, gestures, facial expressions, and so on is based on the committee decisions.

---

* Tony White, *The Animator's Workbook*. Oxford: Phaidon Press Limited, 1986, p. 158.

Above all, there is a main difference between traditional film and computer-generated imagery (CGI): For film the content was decisive, the content of photography, or the play, which is depicted in moving images.

With CGI, it's not the content, it's (to quote Marshall McLuhan) the medium itself. The content is less important than the fascination with the technological medium itself that sometimes absorbs and "devours" the viewer.

Visually 3D or computer animation is related to stop-motion animation because it's dimensional. But in its execution and possibilities to overcome gravity it's next to 2D. There are still animated caricatures but, other than *Felix the Cat* and his heirs, they are not subjected to a world of drawn lines on a piece of paper. Thanks to nonlinear interpolation, 3D animation is fluid, smooth, and flowing. It's not so much stylized animation, it is realistic simulation. Concerning the characters, there is a lot of building and rigging to be done, but imagery, camera angles and movement, and editing certainly have the quality of live action. The characters resemble us. We accept them as equals, as "people" like us.

The digital media transform the simulation of nonexisting realistic worlds to a daily affair. What digital simulation has achieved is not so much realism, it is *photo*-realism. It's an incredible world of make-believe. The objective is not to copy our sensuous and physical experience but the image of it. Eventually, it will become the world dominion of imagery.

This is a dilemma because particularly American 3D animation strives for the utmost in naturalism. So there is no distance anymore to fantasy content. Fantasy isn't any more special. It's down-to-earth and plain, like a daydream.

Everything has to become "lifelike." That was the main goal right from the beginning. It was not about good acting, it was about capturing the image as naturalistic as possible. The first actor to get a digital *doppelganger* in a feature film, *Futureworld* (1976), was Peter Fonda. They projected a raster onto Fonda's white painted face that was photographed from two angles. The result was used as a reference for the computer model to get a rotating robot head that transforms from a simple polygon model into a plastic-like shining actor's head. The image was created by Triple-I in cooperation with computer graphics pioneer John Whitney, Jr. Similarly, not only the head but the complete body of actress Susan Day was remodeled for an appearance in *Looker* (1981).

The process to depict real people at that time for more than a few seconds as in *Futureworld*, however, proved too difficult. There were some late film stars resurrected thanks to the business acumen of their heirs. W. C. Fields and Marlene Dietrich were among the firsts to become "immortal" that way. But even the proprietors of the Berlin Film Museum that covered much of Marlene's career, costumes, and memorabilia rejected the Dietrich clone for their shrine. The digital face was awkward, totally artificial, and bore no resemblance to the movie star. So the virtual Dreamsmiths took appropriate steps and turned to different breeds of characters that were easier to cast digitally. Even God didn't start his creation process with man. If there were to be human shapes at that time, the digital artists had to content with robots (Robert Abel's 1985 *Sexy Robot* TV commercial) or toys.

Just let's look back at the advance of computer technology (which isn't too far ago): After Steven Spielberg's and Dennis Muren's digitally created dinosaurs in the 1993 *Jurassic Park* (the first, as *Gertie the Dinosaur*, came to us in 2D animation), after John Lasseter's *Toy Story* 2 years later, after *Ice Age* (2002) mammals and Scrat, the acom-obsessed saber-toothed squirrel, and after *Finding Nemo* (2003) and other fish, the evolution of animation brought caricatures of human beings and eventually "lifelike" people. In their striving for photo-realism, Americans still seem to have problems to reproduce believable human beings but in the long run synthetic actors are unavoidable as we all need those ghostly avatars representing us in the world wide web of digital images. That is where live actors come in again.

Frank Petzold worked as a visual effects supervisor for the Tippett Studio. One of his early tasks was to render Kevin Bacon transparent in Paul Verhoeven's *Hollow Man* (2000) by using digital means:

To realize every aspect of the idea, Computer Graphics lends itself as perfect tool. We were aware right from the beginning how difficult it would be to show something that is invisible. In the storyboards the Invisible Man would get visible solely through elements like water, fire, rain, blood and dust.

One from a technical point of view particularly difficult scene was the death of a general who drowns in his swimming pool after an underwater fight with the Invisible Man.

But what does an Invisible Man look like underwater?

In the preliminary discussions with Phil Tippett and with my colleague Craig Hayes we decided to do some extensive test shots as a first step to learn more about transparent bodies. After an endless series of underwater experiments with bubbles, chemicals and a transparent plastic human we were able to get an idea of Hollow Man and could define the assignment and discuss the VFX we wished to realize in preproduction with the director.

Shortly afterwards, the final underwater fight with both actors, Kevin Bacon as Invisible Man and William Devane as General, was shot in a specially for these scenes constructed swimming pool inside Sony Studios in Hollywood. An enormous expenditure of water-protected computer technique and VFX cameras was necessary, not to mention the five days I had to spend in a diving suit to photograph motion references of the actors. During the shoot back at Tippet Studio they worked on further layouts and project-related software to offer Paul Verhoeven suggestions how to solve certain scenes.

The idea to develop an invisible human required the production of an artificial human model for Computer Graphics. Kevin Bacon had to be scanned from head to toe with a laser system and had to perform 250 different facial expressions in a photo studio in New York. Meanwhile Tom Gibbons, our animation supervisor, and his crew had instructed the CG character how to walk and released the first animation for virtual lighting in the computer.

Soon we registered that our Hollow Man didn't fit easily into the background. To solve the problem I turned to traditional film technique and shot additional elements in our studio. In front of a green screen we filmed bubbles, blood splatter and smoke elements for compositing. After wrapping the shot we couldn't use this studio for weeks because everywhere stuck film blood. We had to clean our hardware repeatedly.

Now I could focus on the character animation, virtual lighting and the compositing of the effects with the background. The insert of the CG character into the original background required a trained eye for color and contrast so that the final product was still watchable after numerous film and video prints.[*]

In the history of animated films, we had Max Fleischer's rotoscoping process that allowed artists to copy human movements exactly on drawings, a technique that found a new domain in digital imagery. In digital animation, we got from biomechanics to what we now call motion analysis and motion capture.

Biomechanics organizations monitored and tracked the human body's motions for medical research. Multiple cameras were synced to a computer to monitor and register the body's motions for medical research. Reflective or bright markers placed on the body's main points of motion (elbows, wrists, and knees) could help track movements.

The video game industry was among the first to introduce this system to the entertainment industry, and John Dykstra used it for creating a digital double of Val Kilmer in *Batman Forever* (1995), produced by Tim Burton and directed by Joel Schumacher.

Jeff Kleiser was among those who spearheaded the process. In 1986, while working at Omnibus Computer Graphics, he used an optical system from Motion Analysis to encode martial arts movement for a test for Marvel Comics but back then the result was disappointing. When Omnibus closed down, Kleiser joined forces with Diana Walcazk, an expert in sculpting human bodies, and together they founded Kleiser–Walczak Construction Company with the clear objective to build and animate *Synthespians* including the digital stunt doubles for Sylvester Stallone, Rob Schneider, and others in *Judge Dredd* (1995). They also created Jet Li's evil double from a parallel universe in *The One* (2001). This is when motion capture came in.

There were digital extras on board of James Cameron's *Titanic* (1997) and in Ridley Scott's *Gladiator* (2000). Then they applied the technique to fantasy creatures: Ahmed Best, the actor digitized for Jar JarBinks, acted on the set of the *Star Wars* prequels in front of a blue screen opposite the other performers. He wore a special suit with markers and a Jar Jar headpiece.

Sinbad: Beyond the Veil of Mists, a not too successful and meanwhile completely forgotten co-production between India and the United States, used the technology in 2000 for a completely 3D-animated picture. They had two sets: one for the mo-cap performers and one for the voiceovers. It was a little bit like the

---

* Frank Petzold cited in Rolf Giesen/Claudia Meglin, ed., *Künstliche Welten*. Hamburg and Vienna: Europa Verlag, 2001, pp. 199–202.

early days of sound film when they did different language versions with foreign actors behind the set to speak the lines.

Mocap actor. (Courtesy of Weta Digital.)

The breakthrough of CGI came with director Peter Jackson, Andy Serkis, and the *Lord of the Rings* trilogy.

The process of evolution brought this technique then from the background to the foreground.

It reminds of a story written by Jack Finney in 1954: *The Body Snatchers*. It was four times filmed, the first version *Invasion of the Body Snatchers* directed by Don Siegel, and also inspired a bunch of dopier imitations like *Invasion of the Pod People*. Back then, in Cold War McCarthyism, the Pod People were meant to represent the "Communist Menace." But there is a deeper meaning.

Finney's "pod people" you will find everywhere in society: Unspeakable "Demons" who are going to take possession of friends, parents, relatives, and neighbors. According to Finney, even lovers turn inexplicably cold, succumb to depression, or become victims of dementia—and we fear that we are next in line to lose our mind and soul!

Mo-cap is the magic word. Mo-cap absorbs totally.

Motion capture records facial expression and movement of actors such as Andy Serkis playing Gollum in Peter Jackson's superior *Lord of the Rings* and *Hobbit* saga and the chimp hero in *Rise of the Planet of the Apes.*

Mocap actors check performance. (Courtesy of Weta Digital. All rights reserved.)

Serkis was born and brought up in Ruislip, West London. He studied visual arts at Lancaster University and became heavily involved with the theatre studies department, which had a broad-based approach including design, lighting, staging, as well as history and acting theory. In 1985 he appeared at the Dukes Playhouse in Lancaster in plays such as *Volpone, The Good Person of Szechwan* (Brecht), and *A Midsummer Night's Dream,* followed by work in touring companies. Eventually he was associated with the Royal Exchange Theatre in Manchester, the Royal Court Theatre in London, and the prestigious Old Vic. Film and television work followed until, in 1999, he was offered the performance capture part of Gollum: *"Gollum is an incredibly physical role. And it's a combination of physicality and of course vocal. They're so entwined with each other, so meshed with each other. [...] You don't suddenly change the type of acting you do. You're playing a character. You're embodying that role in the way that you would if it was a live action character. It's just that it happens to be a different set of technology that records the performance."**

Ralph Bakshi's version of J. R. R. Tolkien's *Lord of the Rings* (1978) came too early, technologically speaking. Jackson did the same, but he had a better, more

---

* James Rocch; Interview: Andy Serkis of "The Hobbit: An Unexpected Journey." MSN Entertainment, December 17, 2012.

refined technology at his disposal than Bakshi who would rely heavily on over-worked 2D rotoscoping although the promotion for the film tooted its own horn and termed it an "entirely new technique in filmmaking:" *the first movie painting.* To Bakshi it was like making two pictures for a relatively modest budget of $4 million.

Nevertheless, Bakshi had scenes rotoscoped for the same purpose as Jackson. In the past the rotoscope was used to exaggerate live action, to render live action cartoony. Bakshi (and Jackson) strived for bloody realism in the battle scenes. But Jackson's *Lord of the Rings* trilogy (2001–2003) had the advantage of 3D realism that pulled out all stops and used, impossible to do in 2D, a custom-built artificial intelligence animation system called "Massive" with up to 220,000 Humans, Orcs, and Elves in some scenes following a complex set of rules how to move, fight, and die. The crowds alone were justification enough to use the 3D process.

Group of Mocap actors simulating a ride. (Courtesy of Weta Digital. All rights reserved.)

For the crucial scenes involving Gollum, Jackson used a three-stage process. First, Serkis would play the scenes with the regular actors, then those actors would perform without Serkis, and finally, Serkis would act all by himself wearing his motion-capture suit.

A total of 25 CCD video cameras would be placed throughout the stage. Infrared lights would shine onto Serkis' markers that were attached to all key joints, small plastic balls that were covered in a highly reflective material, which would reflect the light back to the cameras, syncing his motions into the computer. These result in black images with a big number of moving white dots. Out of the dots of several camera angles, the computer has to triangulate the data to determine the exact position in a 3D space. Eventually, no markers would be placed on Serkis' face so that the animators would have to study the actor's facial expressions. (Usually, the actor has to wear hundreds of markers.) In Peter Jackson's *King Kong* remake (2005), however, markers were added to Serkis' face to track the muscle movements.

Each marker of the live performer needs to be mapped onto the respective part of the body of a digitally created character that generally absorbs up to 80 percent of the actor's performance.

The evolution of digital actors include steps like *Final Fantasy: The Spirits Within* (2001); *The Polar Express* (2004) starring the virtual doppelganger of Tom Hanks and *A Christmas Carol* (2009) starring former *The Mask* Jim Carrey as Scrooge and the Charles Dickens ghosts that "torment" him, both films directed by Robert Zemeckis. *I, Robot* (2004); *The Adventures of Tintin* (2011); *Jack the Giant Slayer* (2013); and *Man of Steel* (2013) are milestones in this technique as was British actor Bill Nighy's performance as Davy Jones in *Pirates of the Caribbean: Dead Man's Chest:*

> *Davy Jones FAR surpassed Gollum as a CGI character. Now I know what many of you are saying "But John, Davy Jones wasn't a CGI character." While it's true that the CGI in Pirates was BUILT ON TOP of the actor instead of REPLACING the actor as they did with Gollum, the former is actually more difficult to pull off, and the end results were mind blowing!*[*]

Synthetic actors, *Synthespians*, might not only absorb our physical identity and movements but even will command artificial intelligence someday that would make their appearance in an interactive scenario much more interesting and unpredictable. In interactive environments that are by now more successful than the story-wise analog, linear product of the movie industry one better works with digital actors, as they most easily transfer from one medium to another.

A phalanx of actresses and actors so far was scanned and digitized by Karl Meyer's Los Angeles-based company *Gentle Giant*. And even Willem Dafoe did appear in an interactive drama action-adventure titled *Beyond: Two Souls* (2013) although he is coming out not that well in an otherwise sophisticated and well-designed game.

Out of once primitive video and computer games, true parallel worlds will evolve one day, brought to life by digital actors.

When we speculated about that science fact on German radio, people felt insecure and filled Facebook pages: "*There is nothing better than the old Planet of the Apes films*, they wrote. *If this is the type of digital superiority actors don't have anything to fear.—They never will surpass live actors.—There are always actors behind the digitized characters, it's only something like digital make up.—Why should a*

---

* John Campea, Visual Effects Oscar Should Be Pirates Booty. *The Movie Blog*, www.themovieblog. com. November 16, 2006.

digital character portray a human being better than a human being?" Well, that's not the question. The question is not about quality, it's about standardization of products, which includes the standardization of humans too. Some airlines use these incredibly bad digital characters to promote safety rules. Why don't they use real people?

Avatar (2009) was the peak of performance capture. Over the next years, the saga will continue. Sequels are announced. The technology will be refined. Director James Cameron used performance capture extensively for *Avatar.* He used wraparound cameras to better record facial expression and what they call a "virtual camera," which streamed the actors' motions in CGI.

A picture like *Avatar* wouldn't have been possible at the time when it was actually written. They had to push the technology over a year and a half until they reached the point where *Avatar,* partly inspired by the shelved Merian C. Cooper/Willis O'Brien/MGM project *War Eagles* (1939) of which Cameron as former stop-motion buff sure was aware, was finally possible to make.

They had enhanced the size of the performance capture stage, called The Volume, to six times the size previously used and incorporated a real-time virtual camera, which allowed Cameron to direct the CGI scenes as he would doing live-action scenes. He could see his actors performing in real time, and he could move his camera to adjust their performances.

In conjunction with Weta Digital in New Zealand, *Avatar* also pioneered facial expression capture, which would spare the actors the discomfort to spend hours in makeup chairs. In the beginning of the process, actors would have glued hundreds of tiny spherical makers to their faces and so couldn't touch their own faces throughout the shooting day. With the new system, a lightweight head-rig could be donned minutes before shooting.

This rig consisted of a small skull cap, made from a cast of the actor's head, as a base for a strut, which resembled a concert microphone. Instead of a mike in front, however, it had a tiny camera to record the actor's facial expression and mimic art.

Cameron assured that actors needn't to feel threatened by this development and said it wouldn't replace acting. On the contrary, it was designed to empower acting and directing and give it a niche in a new age, support the actor against traditional computer-generated animation, which uses only the actor's voice, and in which a committee of animators performs the character, operates the camera, and does the lighting.

On the other hand, we got the concept of *blending motion* that allows you to use the movements of an actor to create a completely different digital character. It's the same as in photography. Photos are no more the exclusive work of photographers. They are more or less digitally enhanced. Acting is being used in digital disguise.

Absolutely astonishing, nothing short than a quantum jump technically speaking, are the animals in Disney's *The Jungle Book* 3D (2016). They are incredibly naturalistic and lifelike, with eyes that reflect human emotion, although sometimes this illusion is destroyed by mostly unimaginatively used human voices that do not sound like animals. They are even better than Neel Sethi, the boy actor they got as Mowgli successor to Indian boy Sabu in the 1942-live action *Jungle Book*. (Sethi got puppets for interaction supplied by Jim Henson's Creature Shop.) Director Jon Favreau and his team that included VFX supervisor Rob Legato and mo-cap expert Mike Stassi did their homework and studied animals. Yet scenario-wise there is not much to laugh. The creatures are so photo-realistic that they forgot the funny tale and the gags. Most of the action is played straight and humorlessly. All the comedy and songs that made the 2D *Jungle Book* (1967) so memorable are gone.

3D has become standard but it's only technology. It creates texture and lifelike performances but isn't sufficient to create better performances or design better characters. In the world of computer games, however, it is indispensable.

24

A Nod to Computer Games

Computer games create characters that define themselves through action and challenge the gamer. It's a lucrative field handled by an industry on the way up.

Name actors we know from the cinema screen don't hesitate to turn and rush to the games to loan their vocal talents.

Gary Oldman and Kiefer Sutherland were in *Call of Duty: World at War,* Sean Benn and Patrick Stewart in *The Elder Scrolls: Oblivion,* Seth Green and Martin Sheen in *Mass Effect,* Charles Dance was in *The Witcher 3: Wild Hunt,* Ron Perlman in *Halo 2 & 3, Fallout,* Malcolm McDowell and Liam Neeson in *Fallout 3,* Mickey Rourke was the *Rogue Warrior,* James Woods and Samuel L. Jackson voiced *Grand Theft Auto: San Andreas,* the late Dennis Hopper was in *Deadly Creatures,* Christopher Walken in *True Crime: Streets of LA,* and John Rhys-Davies in *Dune 2000.*

Of course, that's only name dropping to sell the games (that became a bigger industry than movies or television) and spend some of the big money on stars.

The main problem with computer games is not so much that they are narrated against all rules of Western scenario tradition: in a nonlinear way, not straight storytelling but round the corner so to speak. Many kids seem to have problems thinking in straightforward, logical manner likewise. They are more attached to all kind of details than an overall view. They are constantly distracted. An incredible amount of images and impressions crosses their mind daily.

In a TV conversation that the late Norman Mailer had with French philosopher and journalist Régis Debray, the author of *The Naked and the Dead*, complained about modern-day kids who have problems to finish even watching a TV show. They are frustrated to no end, Mailer said, because they don't carry through even such trivial things. This, he concluded, would make them aggressive: an eccentric but interesting statement.

We once discussed the topic of a frustrated, disillusioned youth with a police officer, an expert in teen crime. He said that films, TV, or games will not stimulate people who are already socially displeased, bored, and aggressive but will influence and inspire them, give them ideas how to commit aggressive acts at the peak of society's rise. Many of them seem to be aggressive for no special reason. It's just a matter of undetermined cultural anxiety. He mentioned two girls, maybe 15 or 16 year old, who tormented a younger girl and brutally stubbed out cigarettes on her skin. When interrogated why they did such an atrocious act, they claimed the victim talked crap!

Besides television that even runs the most brutish, inhuman crime films on Christmas, cultural pessimists suspiciously eye first-person shooters. These games are only one part of computer games but certainly the most prominent. The watershed moment for the violent video game debate was the 1999 Columbine massacre. Most times suicidal teenage killers that appear the media tell us that they were avid gamers.

Psychologists maintain that violent video games negatively affect kids when played *consistently.* They might desensitize gamers because the mind is conditioned and violent acts become the most natural thing in the world to get attention and recognition in the mass media and in social media. But you won't become a little bit more of a jerk each time you shoot yourself through a video game—unless you already have the antisocial seed in you.

And believe it or else: What might be called antisocial today might become part of the world of tomorrow. There are institutions and groups that need insensitive persons. Interestingly some of the top gamers and hackers are meanwhile beguiled by the armies of the world. They are not touched by emotion but by affects.

Titles like *Halo: Combat Evolved, Modern Warfare* or *Call of Duty* signal that a goodly portion of these games is about war. Remember John Badham's *War Games* (1983) which appeared at a time when most of us didn't foresee personal computers. A year later, in July 1984, one of the first big CG movies was released: *The Last Starfighter.* Written by Jonathan R. Betuel it starred Lance Guest as a teenager who becomes a crack in playing the computer game *Starfighter,* the highest-scoring player, and is recruited to become a fighter in a moronic extraterrestrial war.

In the meantime, Hollywood has rediscovered *The Last Starfighter,* and there is a rumor that everybody, including Spielberg, wants to remake it. If this is true, the subject matter of the movie is up to date: Gamers and hackers are wooed for the war and cyber games to come.

First-shooter games are flickering projections of militant ghost images and defy the rules of scenario tradition. Gamers sure don't need what storytellers regard essential: *empathy*. It would be a burden to them. Why should they show empathy with the enemy?

Soldiers wear uniforms. Members of paramilitary troops in Africa and the Middle East present themselves hooded. They look equal. You can't have warm feelings for these guys. They are all equal, just numbers on your hit list.

Under such circumstances, the players might lose devotion of their own mortality because in the game they remain immortal. They might feel like demigods. Even if they are going to lose the game, there always will be a next chance to stay alive. So they are conquering death a thousand times.

Above all, computer games are fast. There is no time to think about the motives of the enemy, about his childhood, and his family—it's just him or you!

The gamer cannot even empathize with his own image, his own avatar. Nevertheless, there are such things as *empathy games*.

Interactive empathy games focus on everything from being depressed to coming out. But can a 15-minute flash game provoke feelings of understanding and compassion?

What is Empathy All About?

Obviously there is intellectual empathy that makes you feel what response another person needs. And there is emotional empathy that focuses on an affective response to an emotional stimulus. According to Dr. Mark Davis, a behavioral scientist and empathy expert, face-to-face contact can be a powerful empathy stimulus, *"It's not that far a step to go to a virtual reality game where you'd see and hear what the target you're evoking empathy for would see or feel."* So can empathy games make players more compassionate? One of these games is called *Syria,* an immersive virtual reality experience that mediates the fights and screams of injured children in Aleppo. The creator, Nonny de la Pena, the "Godmother of Virtual Reality," claims that this one makes people cry as they directly connect to Syrian refugee kids.

Well, alliances are based on reason, not emotion. There are not many prosocial games commercially available, but there is a lot of aggression to buy. And it doesn't need even good virtual acting, only efficient weapons.

Maybe in the future they will simulate empathy artificially, when brain–computer interfaces will be the rule of brainwash. The same could be said for violence.

But we should see the positive effects of computer games too.

Remember the words of stage impresario Max Reinhardt: that acting should be a process to return to childhood. Computer games can be a wonderful *playground*. In 1938, Johan Huizinga, a Dutch cultural theorist, published a book about the *Homo Ludens* that focused on the importance of the play as one necessary module for the creative development of culture and society. To him, *Homo Ludens: Man the Player* is next to *Homo Faber: Man the Maker*. His "Play Theory" was echoed by Roger Caillois, a French intellectual and sociologist. In his book *Man, Play and Games,* first published in 1958 as *Les Jeux et Les Hommes,* he built (critically) upon Huizinga's writings and described six core characteristics of the play: that it is free (voluntary, as Huizinga puts it); occupies its own time and space; that it is uncertain; unproductive, and different from ordinary activities and not interested in material values; governed by rules that suspend ordinary laws, and, most importantly, creates imagined realities that stagger the imagination (which to many sounds escapist of course). Huizinga adverts to secrecy and disguising which is a main part of acting. Caillois distinguishes a number of games: one of which is *mimicry* where the player tries to escape from himself and become another. This is one of the reasons why superheroes are so popular with younger audiences. But what can we tell about social media? We know that they create a digitized parallel society. On *Facebook* you may have one thousand and more friends, but you still will be lonesome. Social networking occupies a lot of time but the way how it contributes to human society is serpentine.

The main difference is to be found in the terms *play* and *game*. Games maybe stimulate but do not liberate the human mind.

Homo Ludens, however, needs complete freedom of mind to play and be creative.

PART II
Creativity Training for Writers, Producers, and Animators—A Practical Guide

A book called *"The Legend of Centopia"* allows Mia, the young heroine of an Italian/German/Canadian TV series titled *Mia and me* to enter a world of magic and animation. The key to this world is made of imagination plus creativity.

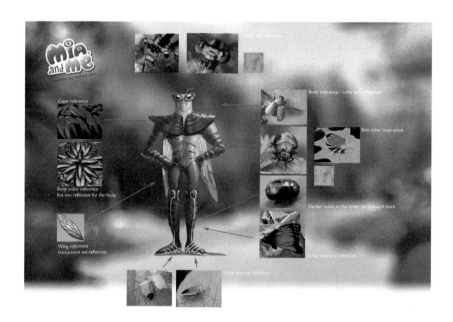

Fantasy character development and design at different stages. *Mia and me* is a German-Italian-Canadian TV series created by Gerhard Hahn that opens a fantasy world of winged elves, pans, unicorns, and dragons for Mia, a teenage girl. (Courtesy of Hahn Film/m4e Productions GmbH.)

25

Surprise Me!

The difference between actors and animators: Actors do, while animators describe. Animators have to project their acting like a puppeteer would do but there is, other than stop motion, no physical puppet they act with but pencil drawings or digits, bits and bytes. So they need to visualize their feelings and emotions *frame by frame*, with their brain constantly focused on motion analysis.

The character on screen is *not* the animator. Nevertheless, the animator has to see the character with the audience's eyes. An animator should cooperate with the character, says Ed Hooks, not dictate to him. The best animators allow their figures to be independent. Then they will be surprised of what cartoon characters are able to do.

This is the key. An animator might take some acting classes but he is a visual artist. He will not have enrolled a drama school. But in the best case, the character will speak to him/her and he/she will be able, just by communicating with the character, to find out about it.

No, animators are no actors. Animation is not acting. However, it is serving an animated character that will be explored with a pen in hand or a mouse click.

Storyboard sketches for proposed *Siegfried* project. (Courtesy of Jim Danforth.)

Acting and Character Animation

Ed Hooks, who wrote one of the most important books about *Acting for Animators*[*], is no animator himself. He started out being an actor and offered acting classes. Once, in San Francisco, he was approached by one of his pupils if he wouldn't be interested to come down and talk to some animation folks who were doing their first movie. This was in 1996. Hooks agreed and when he got there he realized that the company was DreamWorks. The animators sat around and listened to him. But he couldn't help much as he didn't understand the process of animation back then. They tried again and he told them that they have to show him what they were doing and then, maybe, he could comment and give advice. He knew about acting but had to learn the basics of animation. And after a while, this worked. He began to understand their needs. Finally, they were on the same wavelength. The main difference between actors and animators, he realized, is time. Actors are in the present moment while on stage (well, film actors also play in present moment but divided in hundreds of takes) while animators are not. They need a long time for a small moment that lasts on the screen maybe only a few seconds.

If you visit one of Ed's classes (highly recommended because of the entertainment value), you see that he is acting it out for hours and has an immediate audience feeling. Audiences love him.

As animation is teamwork, there are many parties contributing to it. And this happens, with big pictures as well as cheap series, starting with preproduction. This is the time of exploration, in some cases too short and in others sufficient to provide a superior result.

In all cases, animated characters are basically developed in preproduction and refined in the process of animation. There can be real good, inventive characters in cheap animation too. An important part of the preproduction process is the writing although, in a way, there is more drawing than writing.

And with the preproduction, the storyboard and animatics completed the picture itself if timed and finished even before actual production is started.

---

[*] Ed Hooks, *Acting for Animators: A Complete Guide to Performance Animation*. Revised Edition. Portsmouth, NH: Heinemann Drama, 2003.

26

Writing Animation
Role Profiles

Case Studies

Acting is first and foremost storytelling. And mankind is a storytelling species. We are primates with a storytelling mind. We are *homo fictus*, the fiction man. Stories are vital to train our survival skills. Stories make our life from childhood on: stories to warn kids of misuse of fire. Stories might even tell of huge floods: Noah and his predecessor Utnapishtim, a character in the Epic of Gilgamesh. Plato's tale of the doomed Atlantis. Stories of past, present, and future. Science Fiction stories about the conquest of space. *Star Trek* and *Star Wars* transform future into mythology like Homer did with the Trojan War. We empathize not only with each other but share emotions with totally fictional characters.

In ancient times, the shaman was both storyteller and actor. Early on, there was a cave artist around to illustrate the shaman's stories.

In a modern society, except for the fundamentalist faith communities, the shaman's healing powers have passed over to medical practitioners and psychologists, the doctors of the soul, the storytelling part has become the privilege of actors and writers vice versa. And the cave paintings are alive on the cinema screen, in TV, and on the internet.

In animation, the archaic animistic tradition continues and reunites the shamanic purpose of acting, art, and foremost storytelling. Storytelling is the main ingredient of both expensive and cheap animation.

Particularly digitally standardized, limited TV animation is rushed into production and cannot rely on intricate character animation. These series rely on moving caricatures like Bruno Bozzetto's Signor Rossi. Nobody can claim that *South Park* is a miracle of animation. Animation-wise this series is a shame. Cutout-style animation was digitized. Here were (stereo) types animated, no true characters. What did it was the basic idea, was the saucy dialogue. So these characters have to be established mainly by writing and dialogue and by the memorable simplicity of the caricature. Good animation has become a secondary feature on TV.

One of the first to realize this was David H. DePatie, who ran a cartoon studio with Friz Freleng. He said that a lot more creativity is nowadays going into scripting, a lot of thoughts. He and Freleng didn't need it. They were working on the animated TV series *The Pink Panther*, a popular series that was done without dialogue and simply based on gags.

One of the early limited cartoon characters, UPA's Mister Magoo, created in 1949, got his funny background from being nearsighted, which made him to outsiders act like a lunatic. It's all in the writing and the dialogue, not so much in subtle movement and animation, which was impossible to do considering the low budget.

There are different methods how to do story work for animation, different from country to country and different from studio to studio. There are really no writers in animation. In many cases, concepts are developed visually by storyboard artists, not by the writers. There is no single formula that works.

Derek Hayes and Chris Webster tell of a visit while *Shrek* was in preproduction and they had problems, almost thinking of canning the whole project. But then a new storyboard artist came in who did a sequence in which Lord Farquaard tortures the Gingerbread man. The new approach obviously changed the mind of DreamWorks CEO Jeffrey Katzenberg.

Working as a screenplay consultant on an animated feature film in Germany, I (RG) asked the producer to see their role profiles. There were four characters in the film, two main and two secondary characters. What they sent me was one single page, one single page for four characters, estimated for a budget of millions!

Very often the character descriptions are 1D. In Europe, they often make the mistake not to aim their animation at family audiences but preschool kids who, they say, don't understand irony and shouldn't be harmed by antagonism and violence. (The morals enforcers were shocked when Porky Pig and Bugs Bunny entered European TV screens in the early 1970s.)

Over a period of several years we attended the *Cartoon Forum,* a European TV pitching event organized on a yearly basis by Cartoon Media Brussels. Most of it consists of preschool projects, mainly 2D or 3D computer, introducing characters such as *Caiman,* an inquisitive 5-year-old crocodile, *Charly Vet,* who wants to become a veterinarian, same as his father, Baba, Dada, and Boo, three undefinable kids who are shaping and coloring their world and re-inventing their own universe, or the humanized dragons of *Dragon Troubles,* a bizarre entry from Bulgaria: *…the adventures of an odd dragon family in the conservative city of Dragonville. The main idea of the project is to show, with lots of humor and no drama, how hard it is to stay good and polite, despite the fact that you are different, even gifted, but not accepted by the society….*[*]

I (RG) asked the author of favorite children's book fare that became an animation series to name the Dad and Mom characters of his stories. He looked me straight in the eyes, smiled and said, "Mom and Dad." He didn't know. He didn't care. He might be successful but his series never will be truly great. It is difficult to work as a writer under such circumstances.

Role profiles, however, should be biographies. We need to know all about the character. We need to know even things that won't make it into the movie. Actors work the same way to find into their parts.

There is outstanding writing. There is writing so imaginative that you see the images while reading, for instance *King Kong's* tragic end at the top of the Empire State Building as described by Edgar Wallace in his first draft script dated January 25, 1932, submitted 2 weeks before his untimely death:

> *CLOSE SHOT of Kong. He closes his eyes, sinks down on his knees, down and down until he is crouching right against the flagstaff. With an effort he rises again. Blood is now showing on his left breast. He stands up erect, beats his breast in one last defiant gesture and collapses. [...]*
> *CLOSE SHOT of Kong, with his head against the wall. Kong opens his eyes, picks the girl up, holds her to his breast like a doll, closes his eyes, and drops his head.*[†]

Such is even more the case when animators themselves do the writing, as Jim Danforth did when he wrote *Theseus and the Minotaur,* based on one of the most famous mythological tales of ancient times, written on spec for a proposed but, alas, never made series of all-puppet films exploring the world of myth and legend. Danforth animated a lot of fight scenes in his career such as the encounter of a two-headed giant Galligantua and a tentacled sea monster in *Jack the Giant Killer* or Buddy Hackett slaying a dragon in MGM-Cinerama's *The Wonderful World of the Brothers Grimm.* We quote from the description of the nothing but spectacular *Theseus vs. Minotaur* scenes with Jim's kind permission:

---

[*] Cartoon Forum, September 13–16, 2016, Toulouse e-catalogue edited by Cartoon Media Brussels.
[†] *Kong* by Edgar Wallace (alternatively titled *The Beast*). First Draft Script Copied by RKO Stenographic Dept. Corrected as of January 25, 1932. In Mike Hankin: *Ray Harryhausen: Master of the Majicks. Volume 1: Beginnings and Endings.* Los Angeles: Archive Editions, 2013. p. 327.

Jim Danforth animates puppet of ancient sky god Wotan for a test. (Courtesy of Jim Danforth.)

ENTRANCE TO THE CENTRAL ATRIUM—THE LAIR OF THE MINOTAUR
The CAMERA slows from its rapid progress and comes to rest at the entrance of the Minotaur's lair.

A shaft of daylight stabs down through an opening in the ceiling of the atrium. The corners of the large, rectangular room fall away into shadow. An indistinct form can be seen in the center of the room.

The Minotaur raises its head and sniffs the air. It emits a growl and then rises to its feet behind a pile of straw and human bones. The head is the head of a bull—the torso that of a powerful man. The Minotaur steps out from behind the pile of bones, revealing that the legs of the monster are those of a bull. The MINOTAUR roars a challenge to the foe he senses is approaching.

AT THE ENTRANCE OF THE ATRIUM
Theseus stands in the doorway. The CAMERA moves to a close shot.

THE MINOTAUR
Fixing his gaze on Theseus.

THESEUS ENTERS THE ATRIUM

THE MINOTAUR WATCHES THESEUS WARILY

THESEUS AND THE MINOTAUR CIRCLE ONE ANOTHER
Theseus gives the Minotaur a jab to the jaw... and another. The Minotaur grabs for Theseus. Theseus ducks—leaps back.

ANGLE ON THESEUS
He picks up a thigh bone from the pile.

WIDER
Theseus and the Monster circle. Theseus flings himself at the Minotaur and beats at him with the bone.

THESEUS & THE MINOTAUR
They struggle. The bone weapon breaks.

WIDER
The Minotaur flings Theseus against the wall of the atrium. Theseus leaps up and dives at the Minotaur, catching him off balance and knocking him down.

ANOTHER ANGLE
Theseus grabs a shoulder blade from the bone pile and attempts to hamstring the Minotaur. The bone is not sharp enough. The Minotaur kicks Theseus back. Theseus gets to his feet and leaps at the Minotaur, knocking him down.

WIDER—THESEUS & THE MINOTAUR
The antagonists roll over and over as each tries to get on top of the other. They roll into the shadow of the unlit portion of the atrium. After a moment, Theseus is hurled back into the light.

ANGLE ON THESEUS
He lands near a pillar, then quickly leaps to his feet.

FULL SHOT—ATRIUM—THESEUS & THE MINOTAUR
The Minotaur comes charging back into the light and dives toward Theseus.

THESEUS—DOLLY IN
He leaps aside and the Minotaur crashes into the column.

FULL SHOT—ATRIUM
The Minotaur is stunned. Some chunks of stone fall from the ceiling.

THE MINOTAUR
Starting to get up.

THESEUS
He picks up one of the chunks of stone and smashes it down on the Minotaur.

WIDER—THESEUS & THE MINOTAUR
The Minotaur kicks out at Theseus—knocks him back.
As the Minotaur groggily tries to stand, Theseus leaps past the Minotaur and runs to the door of the atrium.

THESEUS
He pauses for an instant, looks at the Minotaur, and then runs into the corridor, disappearing from sight.

ANGLE TOWARD THE MINOTAUR
He staggers to his feet and roars, then starts after Theseus.

TOWARD THE DOOR
The Minotaur heads toward the door, following Theseus.

IN THE CORRIDOR—LOOKING BACK TOWARD THE ATRIUM
The Minotaur bursts into the corridor and stops just outside the atrium. He stands, silhouetted in the doorway, looking for Theseus.

WIDER
Theseus is perched above the entrance to the atrium, standing on the corbels of the arch. The Minotaur starts to move farther into the corridor. Theseus leaps onto the Minotaur's back and grabs his horns.

CLOSE ON THESEUS & THE MINOTAUR
Theseus tries to twist the Minotaur's head to break his neck.
[This clearly is a quote from the Kong/tyrannosaurus fight in the original *King Kong*.]
WIDER
The Minotaur tries to scrape Theseus off his back by smashing him into the walls of the corridor.

SEVERAL REPEATED INTERCUT SHOTS OF:
(a) Theseus trying to break the Minotaur's neck.
(b) The Minotaur trying to dislodge Theseus.

ANGLE ALONG THE CORRIDOR
Ariadne hurries forward, toward the sound of the struggle. She stops as she sees:

POV—THESEUS ON THE MINOTAUR'S BACK
Finally, the Minotaur succeeds in dislodging Theseus.

THESEUS
Lands on the ground.

THE MINOTAUR
Turning toward Theseus.

THESEUS
Rolling aside.

THE MINOTAUR & THESEUS
The bull-man overshoots his target.

THESEUS
Scrambles back, trying to get to his feet.

ARIADNE
As she runs forward, she raises the sword of Daedalus.

THE MINOTAUR & THESEUS
The Minotaur turns to charge again. Theseus runs back into the Atrium.

INSIDE THE ATRIUM
Theseus runs toward the bone pile and picks up a skull. The Minotaur enters the atrium. Theseus flings a skull at him, then another.

THE MINOTAUR
Momentarily distracted as the skulls bounce and shatter against his head.

FULL SHOT—INTERIOR OF ATRIUM
Theseus runs to one side as the Minotaur, temporarily blinded by the skull fragments, lunges forward with a bellow.

CLOSE ON THE DOOR OF THE ATRIUM
Ariadne appears in the doorway.

THESEUS
He sees Ariadne and turns toward her.

ARIADNE
Ariadne flings the sword, hilt first, toward Theseus.

THE SWORD
Flying through the air—soft-focus Minotaur beyond.

THESEUS
He catches the sword and follows its momentum, pivoting around, as the Minotaur charges past.

WIDER—THESEUS & THE MINOTAUR
Theseus continues his arc and brings the sword down on the bull leg of the Minotaur. The Minotaur tries to take another step, but collapses, hamstrung.

INTERCUT: CLOSE ON THE MINOTAUR'S HEAD
A scream of pain.

THESEUS & THE MINOTAUR
Theseus leaps onto the fallen Minotaur and plunges the sword into its chest.

ARIADNE
She turns away from the grisly sight.

THESEUS
He rises into the frame as he stands up, triumphant.[*]

---

[*] *Theseus and the Minotaur.* An animated puppet-film scenario by Jim Danforth. A speculative submission for Dr. Rolf Giesen's proposed series of heroic myths & legends of the world to be hosted by Ray Harryhausen. 1998.

This exciting piece of writing leaves you breathless. It sure is animated writing that defines each move of the animation. Like a protocol of something that has to be made yet. While reading it one might recall David and Goliath. Some scenes are quite gruesome and of the horror caliber.

As this is a producers-driven medium, many producers regard themselves heirs to Walt Disney's throne. One European producer started a project on a subject matter that dealt with fear, which held some little children in its grip. A big topic but the producer succeeded in making it a small one. He reduced a little boy's fright and suggested as reason the fear of some bullies who participate in a soccer game and a janitor who took away the boy's ball and hid it in a cellar. That evokes dream monsters in the boy's mind that lie in wait for him down there. The producer, a soccer fan himself, didn't care for the boy and didn't take any to study and fully explore him. A confiscated ball as reason for nightmares?

A better method is to study the possibilities and develop the story out of a character. This takes some time but it works.

A good exercise is to have a drawing and invent some story around the character drawn on paper.

27

Contradictions

The Key to Great Characters and Stories

Animators love to work around contradictions. So characters, if intended to be memorable and able to carry a whole series, should have two sides: one that corresponds with the expectations of viewers and one that doesn't, that comes as a surprise.

While working for the Terrytoons Studio in New Rochelle, New York City, in 1942, with the sensational *Superman* comics a hot topic but *Spider Man* way ahead, story artist Isadore Klein came up with a concept that was quite interesting at that time.

In the story department, they were putting up ideas for a new cartoon they were going to do. Then and there *Superman* crossed Klein's mind. As most of the animated cartoon characters of that period were humanized animals and insects, Klein decided to use a fly as a substitute for Superman. He had read that a fly, for its size, had super strength and that strength, in the imaginary world of cartoons, could be multiplied many times over. He started to sketch a fly wearing a Superman type of cape holding up with one arm an enormous pole, which, related to its size, seemed like a telegraph pole but actually was an ordinary pencil. In a second sketch the Super-Fly was flying against the front of an automobile, causing the radiator to buckle, and bringing the car to a forced halt.

When studio head Paul Terry entered the room and looked at the drawings, a little bit puzzled but interested, Klein talked about the *Superman* comics and explained his idea. Terry looked impressed, but he wouldn't agree to make a super-creature a fly. He turned the innovative idea of a super-fly into a commercial one that would combine Superman with Mickey Mouse.

So out of Super-fly grew Supermouse and because they couldn't name it Supermouse (for the "Super" in those days belonged exclusively to Superman), they named the character Mighty Mouse.[*]

The strangest choice of an animal whose avid desire was to enter the stage (!) was the whale who wanted to sing at the Met. *Willie the Operatic Whale*, a segment of Disney's *Make Mine Music* (1946), is about a whale that truly sings opera's greatest arias (voiced by Nelson Eddy) but is killed with a spear gun by a misunderstanding impresario who thinks that the giant of the sea has swallowed an opera singer. But Willie's singing spirit lives on in heaven. In 1955, Chuck Jones made a parody that some called the *Citizen Kane of Cartoons: One Froggy Evening*. Inside a cornerstone, a construction worker finds an amazingly dancing and singing frog, but each time he wants to present it in public, with dollar signs in his eyes, the frog stops dead.

Nobody likes rats in the kitchen for reasons of health and hygiene. Exactly that taboo was broken with Disney-Pixar's *Ratatouille* (2007): A living rat not only in the kitchen where it shouldn't be but cooking there the most delicious meals! And audiences didn't hate, they adored that little rat, Rémy, voiced by stand-up comedian Patton Oswalt, with the magnificent, lovely background of Paris, which plays a part in contributing to a really charming story. There is a scene with Rémy on the roof overlooking the nightly city that wins the heart of audiences all over the world: a little creature that sets out to whet the Parisian gourmet scene's appetite.

Ed Hooks considers interspecies communication a fascinating challenge for animation: The first try of communication between Rémy the Rat and Linguini the red-haired boy is rather tentative. At first, they do not know how to proceed and establish their relationship as this is the first human–rat communication both have experienced. They have to find a mutual like and that is: cooking (not killing as in those infamous horror thrillers, *Willard* and *Ben*).

Humans are at the top of the food chain, Ed Hooks argues, so with animals and humans in the same story, the humans must remain at the top of the food chain. Although Rémy is on par with or even better than human cooks, the natural barrier between animal and human world is kept. Communication between them is something of a hat trick. The rats are no humans. They remain rats.

Linguini and Rémy cannot talk to each other. They pantomime, use sign language and speak with the eyes, contrary to DreamWorks' *Bee Movie*. Here bees and humans talk to each other and therefore ruin the whole project with superfluous, stupid rubbish dialogue:

---

[*] Danny Peary & Gerald Peary, *The American Animated Cartoon: A Critical Anthology*. New York: E. P. Dutton, 1980, p. 176.

You have got
to start thinking bee, my friend.
- Thinking bee?!
Me?

Dialogue can build up but also slow down and destroy a lot. Why must humans and bees talk to each other and then such crap?

The purpose of dialogue is to move a story forward and make a character understood not to deliver idle chitchat and boring formalities (provided the character in question is not particularly wooden). On TV, to save and economize visual gags, they often go for funny dialogue. Well, that's okay—if, yes, if the spoken word is *really* funny. (In many cases, it is supposed to be but it isn't.)

Actors as well as animators must understand and fully absorb their characters: their incentive and motivation, their personality and logic. (And the dialogue should match their sentiment and way of thinking. Very often it is important *how* a person talks and not *what*.)

Actors must find a reason for each step, every action, and even if they transform into an animal in a children's play. Their personality must flow into that character. Theatre people say: You have to defend your character. This means one has to understand the personality of the character completely. One has to make that character to his or her own. You have to like the character and identify with him, even if he is awkward or stupid or evil as we have seen when we talked about screen villains. A criminal sure has a reason why he became that way. Maybe his parents didn't have time for him while he was a child, and so he did everything to gain their attention. And by being mischievous, he succeeded and stayed that way. By completely identifying with that character and discovering how one would act as he does, one eliminates the barrier between actor and character. One is supposed to "be," not to "act."

Actors have to wear mask and special makeup to become ugly. An Animator will use the pencil to design an ugly character. He or she has to have the skills of a makeup artist. But the real transformation, as in *The Hunchback of Notre Dame*, is part of the story construction. *Rango* is a chameleon that is constantly faking his character and suddenly finds himself lost in a desert town pretending to be a great gunman when he is not.

There never ever was a character uglier than this chameleon that found himself in an exceptional situation. The story sounds good but the character is even better. They really have worked on that role profile. The character experiences the story, not the other way round. The character is a bundle of contradiction: torn between Wile E. Coyote and Carlos Castaneda. The Western setting is not new, the character is modeled clearly after Clint Eastwood in Sergio Leone's Dollars Trilogy with the difference that Eastwood was, at least back then, quite handsome.

Contradiction makes the character, and it makes the story.

Usually, however, series that feature cartoon characters are not created in an ideal atmosphere. There are many cooks around, too many. Once there was a story about a little monkey that found a violin in the jungle and started to exercise producing sounds and eventually music. No monkey would play music. That was a good premise. (Disney's TV producers call the first draft outline, which is no more than a brief synopsis a *premise*. If it doesn't work, well, forget it. Go to work on another premise.) We thought it would be a great topic for a little series: having a monkey with a musical background right in the jungle. We hoped some of Disney's *Jungle Book* would rub off on us, but then the TV editor turned up and prescribed slapstick, not music. Out went the melodies and songs and with them the whole reason why these series should have been made. A strong-willed producer would have objected, but there are not too many cartoon producers who are strong willed. They go for the money and the easiest way to get it and won't fight for a good idea.

And above all, people don't like apes as movie stars, excepting *King Kong, Planet of the Apes,* and China's *Monkey King.*

Selecting the right characters is a difficult task. The Chinese wanted to do a different version of the American *Kung Fu Panda* celebrating the Year of the Rabbit and decided on *Kung Fu Rabbit,* directed by the head of the Animation School of the prestigious Beijing Film Academy, Sun Li Jun. Yet the rip-off was ill-designed and boring to watch from the first minute, an overgrown, cumbersome, horribly uninteresting rabbit in a dry story. If you miscast the hero, you can't save the story anyway. And if you have a great hero, as Howard Hawks had when casting Humphrey Bogart as Philip Marlowe in *The Big Sleep,* there is no need to chop your way through the undergrowth of Raymond Chandler's somewhat confused story construction.

Today, there is a tendency to cast plastic faces in feature films and rather surreal characters in animation.

Some of the strangest cartoon characters, besides *SpongeBob,* are the 3D-animated sausages and vegetables of a rather odd and sexist, but also existentialist tale titled *Sausage Party* (2016). They all believe that customers will take them out of the store to the wonderful *Great Beyond,* the paradise for food and cuisine, but eventually one sausage named Frank finds out that there is no such thing as eternal life, least of all for hot dogs and potato chips, but that they are being eaten and consumed. The result is a revolution in the supermarket. The movie is by no means any good but it is irritating and annoying, very down on overconsumption and the American Way of Life, and completely different from anything Disney-Pixar would do. It marks the end of the *American Dream.*

There are contradictions too that do not work. A very expensive example was *The Good Dinosaur* (2015) that proved disastrous for Disney-Pixar. A talking apatosaurus (brontosaurus) named Arlo that looks like rubber in front of almost natural backgrounds befriends a boy called Spot. The dinosaur is the cultivated, almost human creature, the boy the wild one with no speech. That sure is contradiction, but it doesn't help to make the characters likeable. Both are completely out of character in a way that you won't go to spend an afternoon with them.

28

Intercultural Differences between East and West

Contradictions work very well in an intercultural context. An animator must not be afraid of contradictions.

Po is the best example. Po, DreamWorks' *Kung Fu Panda,* usually appears lazy, undisciplined, and drugged-up, a naive teenage boy: sure a cool role model for young audiences because eventually he proves the opposite, developing unconventional ideas and longing to become the fastest martial arts hero that ever lived. A lot of his dynamics comes from the acting input of voice actor Jack Black who was chosen to become the vocal godfather of this character.

Kung Fu Panda went a long way through many hands, from Asia to America and back. Originally, in the 1990s, the forerunner was to become a sweet Chinese cartoon character, *Panda Jing Jing,* a poor man's Andy Panda, one Walter Lantz character that only achieved some prominence in the late 1930s because a panda hadn't been used before and seemed to be fresh.

When we asked Wang Borong, a former deputy of Shanghai Animation Film Studios, why Chinese animation hadn't come up with anything like *Kung Fu Panda* itself, he told us that they already had started work on *Jing Jing,* but at that time *Jing Jing* was supposed to be a panda that had escaped from an American (!) zoo and crossed the Pacific Ocean on board of a freighter to return to his beloved bamboo home. While Mr. Wang wanted to show the ancient evolutionary power of a heroic animal character, co-producers in the United States understandably weren't pleased with a slightly anti-American prospect and not willing to invest in what they considered political propaganda that demonstrated the strength and patriotism of a Chinese animal. They were going for a cute Disney-like pet. Production on the revised project was begun but eventually stopped when the Chinese backed out. Some Hong Kong partners tried to improve the pile of fragments. They had the bright idea to combine the little cute panda with their most favorite screen goods, martial arts and kung fu, and so Jing Jing would transform into *Kung Fu Panda*. But he was still a nice boyish smart aleck. It needed more thought and DreamWorks to step in, to create a clumsy version of a panda that under all circumstances wanted to become the fastest and do kung fu fighting. And to add to contradictions, a gander became his father with him thinking he hatched from an egg. This absurd idea kept many people busy trying to correct the situation biologically and made a topic in *Kung Fu Panda 2* and *3*. (We all felt sorry to see this wonderfully absurd idea go by being explained rationally.) Although Po was an Americanized panda, the makers had done so much research on Asian customs and philosophy that Chinese audiences accepted Po immediately as one of their own and, by setting up Oriental DreamWorks in Shanghai, made him one of their own.

Teenage kids are the same all over the world. They oppose to rules and want to break them. So the way of acting them out is universal.

Teaching at the Animation Institute of the Communication University of China in Beijing, I (RG) asked the students: What is it that Chinese and people anywhere in the world interests most—besides food? The answer came immediately: *cars*. Cars are a universal topic and a topic dear to the heart of many Chinese. So I tried to create together with my Chinese students a character that is a driver but has problems with his way of driving all around town: a man of contradictions.

We gave him a name, inspired from Jackie Chan: Charley Zhang. A character should have a name so that one can communicate with him. (The students really came alive when finding names for the figures.)

Charley Zhang (a.k.a. Zhang Fei, his Chinese name), Beijing Cab Driver No. 123456. And, 1 year before the big games, we had a setting that was truly international and intercultural: the Beijing Olympics. Our trademark would have been: Five Car Tires arranged as Olympic Rings. Painted in capital letters on the door of his cab: *English speaking taxi*. Mr. Zhang greatly improves his English during the Olympics and since then fails to master it. Incidentally, Charley Zhang has a secret identity. In his wildest dreams, he and his fictitious "Fellali" (known throughout the world as *Ferrari*) join the daring Formula 1 and mostly win. Sadly, more than once, however, this likeable man confuses daydreams and reality.

His main disadvantage—and here we hit the proverbial nail on the head and found a disaccord that would be a challenge for any driver: Charley, like Mr. Magoo, has an insignificant eye defect, which only causes trouble when he is upset or hits heavy traffic. That is at least once a day. Then he transforms into a cross-eyed madman. His pupils dilate and wander around wildly.

We sure recognize in Charley Zhang a Chinese version of Homer Simpson.

Family is most important in China. So we got him a Chinese Simpson family, for the Chinese students even more important than Zhang himself.

Charley Zhang and wife Singsong: pencil designs for Chinese students' project *The Misadventures of Charley Zhang* (2007). (Author's collection.)

Although he understands himself as a Jack of all trades (and master of none), Mr. Zhang's monthly income is modest. This is where Mrs. Zhang—*Song Mei Li* (Singsong Zhang to her friends)—takes over. She changes her professions like other people their shirts and blouses: Episode per episode we might see her in a new job. One time she owns a small restaurant: *The House of Flying Chopsticks*.

But most time she likes to deal: with cosmetics, then with umbrellas, household appliances, toys and other kind of merchandise, and during the Summer Olympics with all kinds of winter sports articles. Her business method consists of asking her husband to present the respective fares the latest of her low-quality products. What she does not sell ends up in her store and that's a lot. The Zhang family flat is filled up to the ceiling with all kinds of junk and rubbish.

Zhang Xiao Mei (Mei-Mei), the Zhang's daughter is about 8 years old (and clearly ideal for identification purposes of young audiences). Not only does she have an English pen friend who is much older than her (in fact he doesn't know how young she is), she is also familiar with all things that are mechanical. Charley Zhang always claims she got it from him, but in fact he is the one to watch Mei-Mei practice and repair his poor battered, broken car more than once.

The Zhangs have a pet as well. Instead of paying high taxes for an ordinary dog, the Zhangs have a wheeled robotic pet, an unfortunate left-over from Singsong's big business activities: *Dian Dong No. 68* (short: No. 68), which only works part-time, mostly produces strange noises but occasionally (preferably at night) funny songs too: "The Moon Represents My Heart." At time transforms into different shapes. (*Transformers* was the first American TV series being broadcast in China, so the Chinese love it.) Mei-Mei constantly has to repair it.

In a different course at the Communication University of China, we wanted to know from the students if they liked superheroes. All nodded. Sure they said. I became interested and wanted to know if they had any modern-day superheroes of their own in China. Alas, no, they replied.

So why shouldn't we create our own Chinese type of *Spider-Man*, our *Captain China* (instead of *Captain America*)?

We invented a good title, *Shanghai Super Kids*. Ordinary kids from Shanghai should perform in capes and even clean outer space from waste. But it wasn't right.

Then, in Zurich, we told Swiss students about the title and that the students' project wasn't going to performing right.

The Swiss students suggested a topic that was not about super-guys flying around with super-speed in funny outfits but dealing with water and environment. Both topics are popular and seriously discussed by young people who are aware of climate change. Chinese teenagers are environmentally conscious, and everything that has to do with fish, especially in Asia, is considered synonymous to sexual interest. We have realized that Chinese animation students often use the symbol of fish unconscientiously to express their sentiment that they are outgrowing childhood. So the combination of both had a personal and political meaning.

Shanghai, the Pacific Ocean, and the environmental dangers should be the main topic.

The world's oceans, including the Pacific Ocean, were under assault and we were the guilty party.

From this premise, we went on not to story construction but to think about the main characters. These kids should be aware of the dangers and engage themselves against pollution of the Pacific Ocean by using certain powers that would make them superhuman. Immediately the students started to draw Western characters. I told them that what they had drawn were not Chinese kids, particularly not the females. They had designed blondes right out of the world of fashion and advertisement. Next try: Suddenly the Chinese looked like characters from Japanese manga or anime. But we didn't give up. I suggested that they study photo books with the faces of ordinary Chinese kids that would meet our role profiles.

These were the three "S" that made the Shanghai Super Kids:

Sue Ling: She is stubborn but also a true companion, a good sport. Once you know her, once you penetrate her armor, her shell, you will find her a very warm and a romantic character. She likes to play piano and distastes hip-hop or rap. Also claims not to be interested in fashion. But behind her glasses shines beauty, at least for those who have eyes to see. Sue Ling's father is specialized in aquacultural engineering. Her mother is in the environmental protection office and often leaves the country to attend congresses abroad. At school Sue Ling is very good at natural sciences. Her parents' job has made her aware of ecology, pollution, and the dangers to marine life.

Sue Ling from Chinese students' project *Shanghai Super Kids*. (Author's collection.)

Nobody Song: Nobody Song's trademark is a cap ("No Fish"). He is a lazy character that occasionally seeks a feud but otherwise remains mostly nonverbal. He warms up only to hot music. Chinese rapper. He constantly tries to leave a cool impression but inwards is highly sensitive.

Song's father is an official in the fishing industry while his mother runs a small seafood restaurant. But the parents are in a state of getting divorced and indirectly

Nobody Song with bowl of noodles: *Shanghai Super Kids.* (Author's collection.)

blame their son. For Song this is unforgettable. He has this predicament. In a way, that's part of the reason why he prefers to keep his mouth shut when not rapping. Out of protest he wears a T-shirt: "I hate Fish." Prefers beef noodles to fish.

Both characters detest each other at the beginning. They both crept from different molds. But they get together while fulfilling their mission.

There was a third character inserted:

Sheng "S. T." Tao: Addicted to Manga and comic books, he is a dreamer and sense-of-wonder kid who is wonderfully creative. Some nickname him Monkey King because of his looks and movements (a mix of Sun Wukong and the Japanese Astro Boy), but he himself prefers to be called S. T. His favorite book is almost a collector's item, Jules Verne's *20,000 Leagues Under the Sea,* with some tremendous illustrations of the deep sea and its bizarre creatures that fire the boy's imagination. He is not bad at drawing and likes to draw comics himself. The nightmares of the boy who is water-shy are haunted by water-breathing Gill Men who populate the ocean floor and by Aquamen with extreme comic super power. Today, with all digital tools around, we would make him game-addicted but back then comic books were still attractive.

The premise had Nobody Song organize a fishing trawler to have a swimming contest out there. S. T. almost drowns but suddenly becomes part of a huge jellyfish swarm mysteriously approaching the shore. Sue and Nobody rescue him and are infected themselves by some strange chemicals in the water.

While Peter Parker was bitten by an irradiated spider in its death throes, these three kids are transformed by jellyfish and strange chemicals. Gradually they begin to change and mutate until they realize that they are able to get absorbed by different species of marine life mentally and telepathically. For them it is like acting in an interactive game of second life nature. For a moment, they feel like shaman's apprentices who will enter other species spiritually, not by super power

5.1

Sheng Tao: *Shanghai Super Kids* project. (Author's collection.)

but by sheer mental power in a state of trance. And they find out that the marine life is a more powerful weapon than any superpower.

Superheroes always are contradictory characters. They have a secret identity to hide. Now the Shanghai kids have their secret too.

By using 5-foot-long battery-powered robo fish and mini subs, they explore the Pacific Ocean to fight (and here come the stories) specters from the deep sea, oil spill, nuclear waste, the great dying, the great Pacific garbage patch, or the Pacific Ring of Fire.

Man is a land animal, but he is also closely tied to the sea. The hero kids may be among the first in the evolution of future mankind who are willing to return to live on the Ocean Floor with environment on earth's surface polluted and destroyed. In 2009, *Shanghai Super Kids* would have been China's first ecologically motivated animated series but, alas, it was just students' work and, like *The Misadventures of Charley Zhang*, a students' exercise.

While working on it, we found that there is more to cultural differences than costumes and the color of the skin.

French sociologist Marcel Mauss who spoke of "techniques of the body" observed that differences in walking and swimming are cultural. While hospitalized in New York, he noticed nurses and girls walking in distinctive ways. He divined its origin. At last Mauss realized that they adopted this walk from seeing movies. After repatriation, he recognized the same phenomenon in France and realized that this "technique" had spread through cultural contact and "prestigious instruction," learning from a trusted authority.*

---

* "Trusted authorities" also may be family members who dominate others in the family with the sound of their voice that is then being imitated by the others.

Returning to France, I noticed how common this gait was, especially in Paris; the girls were French and they too were walking in this way. In fact, American walking fashions had begun to arrive over here, thanks to the cinema.

A good albeit sometimes rather didactic example of a very interesting inter-cultural project is the animated German-Irish-Canadian TV series *The Travels of Young Marco Polo* (2013): Marco Jr., by way of the Silk Road, on the track of his famous father, accompanied by his faithful friend Luigi and a Chinese princess named Shi La Won.

The Travels of Young Marco Polo (2013). (Courtesy of MotionWorks.)

There are, however, not only differences between the West and East but East and East as well.

In the 1960s, the most ambitious project of Chinese animation was *Havoc in Heaven* by the Wan Brothers, which was based on the prologue of one of the Four Great Classic Novels of Chinese literature, *Journey to the West*, written in sixteenth century Ming Dynasty by Wu Cheng'en.

The reason for this production might have been a Japanese animated feature film produced by Toei Company and released in 1960 as *Saiyu-ki*, a year later by American International Pictures under the impossible title *Alakazam the Great* as one of the first anime movies that hit the United States.

In the Japanese feature made from Osamu Tezuka's manga version Sun Wu Kong, the Monkey, is a young, cute, and brave monkey, more American than Chinese.

* Marcel Mauss, *Techniques of the Body* (1935). *Techniques, Technology and Civilization*, ed. Nathan Schlanger. New York: Berghahn Books, 2006, p. 80.

Acting and Character Animation

This the Chinese could not tolerate. Why should the Japanese touch Chinese national heritage? They needed their own version and show the world. Their Monkey King is an acrobat, a witty revolutionary and fighter, no cute Disney animal. Jin Guoping, later to become the formal head of Shanghai Animation Film Studio, describes him as a vivid and attractive being.

The Chinese version was produced between 1960 and 1964, initially to be distributed in two parts although back then the second part could not be released due to a change in the politics of art and culture that led to the so-called Cultural Revolution. During this period, the Shanghai Animation Film Studio was among the institutions criticized. *Havoc in Heaven* was accused to shake Chairman Mao Zedong's throne. The Monkey King was seen as a rebel not only against Heaven but against Mao's supreme authority leading a Cultural Revolution himself. He was independent, witty, and a free spirit.

Only a few of the tens of thousands of animation drawings survived the raid of the Red Guards. The artists did not escape persecution either. Wan Lei-Ming, the director, was detained. The co-directors, Ms. Tang Cheng and Yan Dingxian, were sent to the countryside for re-education and reform through hard labor. As a complete feature, *Havoc in Heaven* was released not before Mao's death.

Chinese producers still copy foreign product and don't rely too much on their own cultural history (except for kung fu). Japan, on the other hand, has exported samurai culture in a way that the world couldn't ignore but copy. Akira Kurosawa's *Seven Samurai* became *The Magnificent Seven*, Toshiro Mifune transformed into Clint Eastwood, and Godzilla toys belong to the inventory of many children's rooms around the world.

Well, it isn't easy but there are people from the West who take time to understand Asian culture. One of the more recent releases of renowned 3D stop motion producer Laika Entertainment, *Kubo and the Two Strings* (2016), certainly does Asian culture more justice than Disney's *Mulan* did two decades ago because it truly captures the Japanese spirit. Thanks to his witch mother, Kubo, a young magic boy, is able to perform charming miracles with origami figures and tell fantastic stories about the adventures of his late father, a samurai warrior, who fought all kind of evil. But his grandfather, the ghostly Moon King, is vengeful because his daughter fell in love with a mortal. He tries to get the boy's right eye (the left eye he stole when Kubo was still an infant) and make the boy forget his human roots. So he sends his two other daughters to kill their sister and get hold of Kubo. Dying Kubo's mother uses her remaining magic skills to transform her son's talisman into a monkey who would protect him and, together with a samurai beetle, the spirit of his father, indeed two power animals, and a tiny origami warrior, locate his father's magical suit of armor. On the skull of a giant skeleton there is the *Sword Unbreakable*, on the ground of the sea they find the *Armor Impenetrable* and finally the *Helmet Invulnerable*. The samurai warrior was certainly modeled after Mifune but Kubo himself is different. He summons the magic of a shaman to recruit the spirits of the dead to demonstrate that human memories are the strongest magic of them all and change the dreaded Moon Beast into a benevolent human.

The fact alone that all this wasn't done by using a computer but with traditional, hand-made stop-motion puppets and replacement heads is amazing. Sure *Kubo and the Two Strings* is one of the best animated feature films ever: sheer wizardry with stunning performances that are as good as live action albeit stylized. Above all, *Kubo* is the proof that intercultural topoi still have a chance on the big screen: A picture with a deeply humanist message that will be understood universally.

29

Preconceived Characters

Many producers who don't have the time or the money to work from scratch and create entirely new characters go for well-known characters and titles, some of which are in public domain. Yet even then they might slip on a banana skin.

Regarding its 3D product, nWave is known particularly for the stereoscopic quality of its product, like *Fly Me to the Moon* or *Sammy's Adventure*. Even Dennis Muren mentioned it when he had seen *Fly Me to the Moon*. Looking for a safe harbor, an American writer got nWave's attention to Daniel Defoe's *Robinson Crusoe*. So they made it in 3D (2016) and it turned out to be, story-wise, a disaster because they shifted their interest from the main character to secondary animals. Although Robinson's name is on the posters, he has not much screen time and when he appears he proves a 1D character. Instead they had some animals fight around. On the island there is one animal of each species (so they are damned to extinction) and greedy cats from the sunken ship that multiply and mix them up. It became an animated feature starring sidekicks.

Many fairy tales and legends have been filmed all over dozens of times. One of these fairy tales would make a gorgeous background for an intercultural story by the way. It would add a fresh angle to an often-told tale. Studying Bruno

Bettelheim's famous book about the *Meaning and importance of fairy tales,*[*] we have found that one universal tale comes from China. Not many, neither in China nor in the Western world, know that the tale of *Cinderella* originates from China. This fairy-tale character is indeed known all over the world: in Europe as well as in India, Africa, and America… In 1697, Charles Perrault adapted it for French readers as *Cendrillon ou La Petite Pantoufle de Verre* (which contained all the ingredients Walt Disney needed to produce his 1950-animated feature). The Brothers Grimm of Germany retold it as *Aschenputtel*. Ludwig Bechstein, another German, titled it *Aschenbroedel*.

The Chinese version of *Cinderella* predates any Western version by almost 1000 years. The story of Chinese *Cinderella, Yeh-Shen* (or *Ye Xian*), was conceived in the Tang dynasty and more or less offers what all versions have in common. It's about the initiation of a young girl to womanhood. A girl who is living in the ashes and feels neglected by her (step) mother and sister will grow up and marry (as it is a fairy tale, the bridegroom has to be a prince or a king).

From China the tale wandered the Silk Road and so became sort of world cultural heritage. It is known as *Ashpei, Ashpitel, The Brocaded Slipper, The Jewelled Slipper, The Broken Pitcher, La Cenerentola* (Italy, transformed into an opera of the same title by Gioacchino Rossini), *Cenicienta* (Spain), *The Cinder Maid, Conkiajgharma, Essy Puttle, Finette Cendron, Grattula-Beddattula, Katie Woodencloak, The Little Red Fish and the Clog of Gold, Papalluga, Pepelyouga, Rashin-Coatie, Rosina in the Oven, Sodewa Bai,* and *Vasilisa the Beautiful*. There are two ballets, *Aschenbroedel* by Johann Strauss (1901) and *Solushka,* the Russian version of the story, by Sergei Prokofiev (1945).

Up till now there have been more than 100 movie versions, the oldest dating from the year 1899 (France), the most successful produced by Walt Disney (1950) anticipating the crowning ceremony of Elizabeth II, another one, live action with animated characters, by Kenneth Branagh for Disney. A modern version of the tale was *Pretty Woman* (1990) starring Julia Roberts. But so far there is only one minor Chinese film version atrociously animated. Most Chinese people never have heard about the tale neither have many people in the West: a big chance for producers between the United States and China. And the Chinese version even has the asset of an animal, a mysterious magic fish with golden eyes.

Just for educational purposes in China, we tried to adapt the tale of *Yeh-Shen* for an animated movie. We found that in the original tale, there is a fish but it is only a supporting character, similar to the cricket in Carlo Collodi's *Pinocchio*, another power animal that was transformed into a major character by Disney.

So we went ahead and tried with the fish what Disney had done with the cricket.

There are only a few people, the blessed ones, those who are pure in heart, who will have close encounters with those fairy-tale power animals that might change

---

[*] Bruno Bettelheim: *The Uses of Enchantment: The Meaning and Importance of Fairy Tales*. New York: Alfred A. Knopf, 1976.

Acting and Character Animation

an entire life. Please recall that fish is a strong sexual symbol, in this case in the emancipation of a young girl from the Middle Kingdom.

Once upon a time, there was a wise carp but he was old and tired. Before he was going to die he was looking for the right successor to watch over the kingdom of the river fish. Three carps were sent out in a contest. Two of them were evil and disciples of black magic, the third, however, was true and honest.

At the same time, there was a girl sitting at the river. She was sick at heart singing a sad song. The necklace she wore was very precious to her and became her lucky charm. It was shaped like a fish bone. It was all that was left to her by her mother who had passed away when she had given life to the baby girl. Her father, a cave thief named Wu, had married a new wife. They had another daughter together, and clearly the new wife preferred her.

The stepmother despised Yeh-Shen, the elder girl from her husband's first marriage, because she was more beautiful and kinder than her own daughter. She treated her poorly and gave her impossible tasks to do.

While sitting at the riverbank she saw that out there was a fish in need. A carp, with scales of pure silver and big golden eyes, that was attacked by two bigger carps. She didn't hesitate to save the fish that began to talk to her. She could understand every word that he said. So she decided to come to the river whenever she was in bad mood to wait for the fish. Then she would play with him, enjoy, and, if only for a brief time, would forget her misfortune that had clothed her in rags.

In Europe, the fish mutated into a fairy but we kept him the way he was and linked him to the tale of *Little Carp That Jumped over the Dragon Gate*. Gradually, the fish became the central character of the story that led the Prince to find the girl of his dreams who lost the slipper. The envious stepmother had used black magic to transfer Chinese Cinderella upstream behind the dragon gate where she was locked in eternal sleep, like Sleeping Beauty.

The Prince accompanies the fish upstream to fight all dangers and the stepmother's black magic. The carp jumps rapids and leaps over waterfalls till they reach the fearful dragon gate. The fish accomplishes the impossible and leaps over the dragon gate. In that moment the carp changes into a fish-dragon. The dragon frees the prince who is caged not by a thorny hedge but by vines from the stepmother's mouth that stretch for miles and swing around like gigantic tentacles, clutching and clinching everything (a nod to Tim Burton), and brings him to Yeh-Shen so that he can kiss her to life again.

Fairy-tale characters have a strong effect on the mind of children and become early companions in understanding the world. As we mentioned, they are initiation tales to womanhood. Disney has a whole bunch of such princesses. First he took the classic, preconceived ones. Then, due to changing demographic data, the company innovatively added heroines according to ethnic groups. They pursued still the *Cinderella* type character but chose to transfer it to an Afro American (*The Princess and the Frog: Tiana of Maldonia* was patterned after Grimm Brothers' *The Frog Prince* and Elizabeth Dawson Barker's *The Frog Princess*) and Native

American (*Pocahontas*) background. Now they even got a Latino Princess on Disney Channel: *Elena of Avalor* was created to please the demands of Hispanic and Latino Americans, the second largest ethnic group in the United States.

Fairy tales are still worthwhile in animation and will remain so. You don't have to introduce them because audiences will know and love them anywhere in the world: cross-cultural, cross-generational. Sometimes they play it safe and cast a famous cartoon character in a well-known fairy tale but Mister Magoo by all means was miscast as Aladdin's uncle Abdul Azziz Magoo in *1001 Arabian Nights* (1959). The poor box office results led to the sale of UPA to entrepreneur Henry G. Saperstein.

Challenging as well as sometimes difficult are comic book protagonists. They are in a way fully developed, outward and inward, and their creators watch any change with envy. Robert Crumb disliked what Ralph Bakshi did to *Fritz the Cat* (1972). Yet what Bakshi, a producer–director not that well liked by animation buffs, did was to open the doors for X-rated animated cartoons and to oppose Disney not only in style (as UPA did) but also in adult content.

Vice versa it seems to be different. Carl Barks (1901–2000) was a storyboard artist at Disney's before he went to work for Dell Comics and created a more sophisticated version of Donald Duck that was much richer and deeper than anything seen in the Donald shorts directed by Jack King or Jack Hannah. There were great mystery and adventure stories with lots of dialogue, nothing like it in the Disney cartoons of the 1940s or 1950s, not even in the feature-length *Three Caballeros* (1944) but the Disneys accepted the changes and didn't interfere as long as Donald looked like Donald and made money for them.

One of the most interesting animated feature films from Europe, *Wrinkles* (2011), is based on an award-winning Spanish comic book. Paco Roca's graphic novel *Arrugas* deals with Alzheimer's disease and portrays the friendship between two aged gentlemen shut away in a care home.

Paco Roca knew what he told and drew. He did his homework.

*"I haven't really made anything up. The real anecdotes are so good they couldn't be outdone. Emilio is the father of a good friend of mine, Roca recalls. I also met a lady who spent all day sat a window convinced she was on a train and to get her to eat something she had to be told she was in the dining coach."** She, too, became part of the comic book and its faithful screen adaptation.

Producer Manuel Cristóbal didn't have much money: just 1.9 million Euros which is next to nothing. He proved that a good animated movie doesn't necessarily depend on the budget. It depends on unconventional stories and memorable characters, same as in life. The animation isn't that outstanding, but the characters are well designed by Roca and they are believable. You like these two guys because they remind you of people who meant something to you.

Emilio is a retired bank manager who suffers from Alzheimer's disease and is taken to the elderly care home by his son. Confused by his new surroundings and

---

* Publicity notes released by Perro Verde Films.

Wrinkles (2011) from a graphic novel by Paco Roca. (Courtesy of Manuel Cristóbal, Perro Verde Films.)

disorientated, he regresses to earlier stages of his life. Emilio unexpectedly finds support in his roommate Miguel.

Miguel is one of the care home veterans. This mischievous and brazen trickster guides Emilio through the different environments within his new home. Having always lived without emotional ties, Miguel finds himself directly witnessing his new friend's gradual degeneration. Involved in all sorts of comical and absurd situations to help Emilio, Miguel now is confronted by his own fears and the decisions that have marked his life up until now.

Together they employ all kinds of stunts to stop the doctors noticing Emilio's ongoing deterioration so that he won't end up on the feared top floor of the care home, also known as the lost causes or "assisted" floor. Through their struggle to stay active as individuals and maintain their dignity, the pair shapes a genuine, strong friendship in resistance and starts a new life.

"*I recall a conversation with a friend who is an animation film director,*" tells Ignacio Ferreras, who directed the film version, *who said: "you spend five or six years working on an animated feature film, then you watch it and think: I've wasted five years of my life on this. I'd be happy making at least one really good film that would make it worthwhile. I am confident that Wrinkles will be my worthwhile film."**

Unfortunately, although it won awards, the movie did not make much money.

---

* *Wrinkles.* Movie Pressbook. La Coruna, Spain: Perro Verde Films, 2011. http://wrinkles.vhx.tv/

30

Animals and Anthropomorphism

While *Arrugas* introduced real people, a lot of animation plays safe and relies still on animal characters. The problem that many animators have is that they have to feel very often neither like man nor like animal but as both at the same time and in the same body. We are talking about anthropomorphic animals. In these cases, the animator has to be familiar with human *and* animal behavior. Human and animal expressions have to shine through the character. There is some help from the fact that human characteristics are associated with certain animals. One particular adjective from the human world will describe the respective animal: Smart as a fox, stupid as a donkey, cocky as a peacock, busy like a bee, and tired as a bear. There already is a human side projected into each animal, a like or a dislike. Disney used this concept even in his so-called *True-Life Adventures,* in the feature-length *Perri* (1958) based on Felix Salten's book about the Youth of a Squirrel. In the same year, in *White Wilderness* that won an Academy Award for Best Documentary Feature, Disney's "Cruel Camera" installed a rotating platform to prove the alleged mass suicide of lemmings and push them into a river near downtown Calgary in the Canadian province of Alberta. Disney re-created nature like God to his own taste.

An animator, of course, has even more ways to approach humanized animals:

The whole physical concept might still be animal-like, however, human expressions and emotions have been added.

The animals might talk while they still remain distinctly animal-like. Disney's most famous characters, in this regard, are more human than animal, while Tom & Jerry remain more animal than human. We expect Mickey the Mouse and Donald the Duck to talk, but we consider it a mistake when Tom the Cat suddenly opens the mouth and says a word or two, as in *The Million Dollar Cat* (1944): "*Gee, I'm throwing away a million dollars. But I'm happy.*" Spike the Bulldog, yes, but Tom? One of the reasons that the feature-length *Tom & Jerry Movie* (1992) was so disappointing was the fact that *both* talked.

Then, with a nod to the pig characters in Halas and Batchelor's animated version of George Orwell's *Animal Farm* (1954), animals might walk upright on two legs. They even may wear clothes and carry props.

Final step is a totally humanized behavior so that you sometimes won't recognize what animal the character was based on. Goofy, for instance, is a dog. What is named Tasmanian Devil in the Warner Cartoons doesn't resemble the original animal that much. They are just metaphors for human "types," even human stereotypes that are associated with animals as we have noticed. In short, these animals are just humans in animal disguise living either in their natural habitat (Bugs Bunny, Woody Woodpecker, and Yogi Bear) or in human suburbs (Mickey Mouse and Donald Duck).

But what is considered varmint throughout the depths of history is often not so in animation: Rats and mice might become so cartoony and witty that even Hitler liked them who killed millions of people like vermin.

We got Mickey Mouse, Mighty Mouse, Jerry Mouse, Rémy the Rat of *Ratatouille* fame. In MGM's *Good Will to Men*, a 1955 CinemaScope remake of their 1939 short *Peace on Earth* created by Hugh Harman, mice survive the nightmare of mankind who killed itself in terrible wars. No, the German dictator wouldn't have liked that.

In real life, we use snap traps, glue boards, and zapper traps that lure mice into enclosures before delivering a lethal electric shock. In Disney's 1953 *Ben and Me*, Amos a church mouse assists Benjamin Franklin in discovering the secrets of electricity.

So many people have cats but in cartoons felines very often are the baddies. There is evil Lucifer chasing *Cinderella's* mice friends or the treacherous Siamese Cats from *Lady and the Tramp* (1955).

There is a biological grasshopper and cricket control. In cartoons, however, Wilbur, a tame grasshopper, proves to be Goofy's best friend helping him to fish in forbidden grounds (*Goofy and Wilbur*, 1939). Jiminy Cricket is dubbed Pinocchio's conscience by the Blue Fairy: lord high keeper of the knowledge of right and wrong, counselor in moments of high temptation, and guide along the straight and narrow path. A supporting character, which only had a cameo in Collodi's book, transformed into a screen star animated by Ward Kimball. The character's name was derived from "Jiminy cricket(s)!," an expletive euphemism for Jesus Christ.

Grasshoppers and crickets yes, but cockroaches? Why not? Even cockroaches! They are the heroes and best companions of Joe (Jerry O'Connell) in *Joe's Apartment* announced in 1996 as *Sex Bugs Rock'N'Roll*. Under Chris Wedge's supervision, Blue Sky Studios contributed CG-animated cockroaches that were blended with puppetry, stop motion, and live cockroaches.

Original animation art: Beetles in *Weather-Beaten Melody* (1943). (Courtesy of J. P. Storm Collection.)

Animals and insects like Jiminy make wonderful *sidekicks* that compensate sometimes for weak heroes. Even Disney heroes occasionally seem to be rather pedestrian, shy and boring and need a strong horse to hold audience's attention. In *Sleeping Beauty* (1959), Prince Phillip's horse Samson, lovable but stubborn, steals his master's scenes. In French cartoons, Lucky Luke and his horse Jolly Jumper are equal and suit each other as do Prince Edward and his horse Destiny in *Enchanted* (2007). Winner is Maximus from *Tangled* (2010), a dedicated personality that not only steals scenes but the whole show.

But there are sidekicks that backfire as did a weird creature named Gurgi, a two-legged furry something with the face of a dog that joined Taran who is introduced as "assistant pig-keeper" on his quest for the *Black Cauldron* (1985) and praised away right to the animation hall of shame.

Apropos of pigs: Eating pork but loving Porky Pig?

Is it a guilt complex? An archaic ritual just to beg pardon from those we kill in masses?

But beware of frogs. The French regard frog legs as delicacy. But frogs rarely make stars. They tried to prove otherwise. Ub Iwerks was asked to sketch a few animals that would make potential cartoon stars. Among them were a mouse and a frog. Disney would take the mouse and name him Mickey. Iwerks, when lured away by Disney's former distributor, Pat Powers, would be left with Flip the Frog. We mentioned this earlier. Disney built a kingdom upon the strength of the mouse. Iwerks failed as an independent and had to return ruefully as employee to his former partner.

He's a secret agent with super powers... A leaping green fighting machine... Defending the world against the forces of evil... He's ... Freddie as F.R.O.7, went the movie tagline for the ill-fated 1992 parody of James Bond, *Freddie as F.R.O.7.* (retitled *Freddie the Frog* in the United States).

In 2013, in association with partners from the North of China, our friend Nelson Shin, the South Korean President of ASIFA, released *Frog Kingdom*, featuring the characters Princess Froglegs and Freddie.

The only frog that survived so far in the media was a simple green hand puppet: Jim Henson's Kermit the Frog.

In the 1980s, another producer got a hold of a property developed by animator Wolfgang Urchs: *Stowaways on the Ark.* It told the story of a woodworm and his family that would arrive on Noah's Ark. That immediately sounds like a funny short, but they wanted to have it feature-length. Although the picture was only mildly successful, the producer, a recidivist, got nuts and immovable in his decision to try a second time and star another woodworm, Pico, alongside Christopher Columbus in *The Magic Voyage* (1992). To make matters worse, the pathetic producer who had directed documentaries but no feature film, let alone an animated one, would claim directorial chores. Some good artists who were involved like Harold Whitaker and Phil Nibbelink couldn't save it. The result was one of the biggest disasters in European animation film history at that time. Well, there *is* an animated worm movie that has some merits coming to our mind. The Danish-German *Disco ormene* is about *Disco Worms*! Sunshine Barry is an outcast rain worm that founds a band to get some recognition and thus provides at least a dashing soundtrack.

Snails are problematic too. They are so slow. There is only one gag possible: to turn the slow ones into fast ones as they did in *Turbo.* In this 2013 DreamWorks picture director David Soren got an ordinary garden snail, another outcast character, involved into a freak accident when sucked into the supercharger of a drag racer, fusing its DNA with nitrous oxide. This way the loser and underdog becomes *Fast & Furious.*

More successful at the box office than frogs, worms and snails are man's best friends—no, not dogs. We mean *cars*! In animation, cars are sometimes humanized too the way animals are.

In 1952, Tex Avery made a short cartoon for MGM: *One Cab's Family* (and Disney later made the VW *Herbie* films) that became the blueprint for Pixar's successful *Cars* that would not only drive but act and even talk like humans, have mouth and eyes and, above all, emotions.

In *Transformers,* robots transform into cars and vice versa, which held a special appeal for audiences in Asia that are fascinated by giant robots that resemble ancient warriors and modern cars. In China, *Transformers* merchandise became a sales hit.

31

Animation, Toys, and Merchandising

We have talked a lot about China.

This is absolutely necessary in our profession because China has become the biggest animation producer in the world. And not only that: China is also the biggest toy manufacturer. About 80 percent of worldwide toys are produced in China.

Chinese animation means selling toys and merchandising per se.

Asked if there would be a future for traditional water-ink animation Cai Zhijun, the managing director of CCTV Animation in Beijing, a former animation director himself, answered that 50 years ago audiences only had few choices because the yearly output wasn't about 10 or 20 minutes. Art still had a chance back then. Some animation may have been great work but nowadays the yearly output has exceeded 2 million minutes. Screening a picture is not enough. The derivative products are more important.

The picture itself accounts for only one-third of the total profits. Derived products make more money.

In a way, *Toy Story* set the pattern.

For some years producers discuss new ways of funding by reversing the Disney merchandising method and introducing successful toys to animation that already have been established with customers.

One of the first to go was *Barbie* [full name: *Barbara Millicent Roberts*], a best-selling small fashion doll created by Ruth Handler (1916–2002) and produced by Mattel Inc. *Barbie* has no character by herself. She is just a mannequin with lots of clothes to buy to change her outwardly. The product was introduced on March 9, 1959 at the *American Toy Fair* in New York City and, as alternative to baby dolls, became an instant albeit costly success and collector's item with girls. Since 2001, more than 30 CGI *Barbie* films (Direct to DVD releases and TV) have been produced that prove unwatchable even for animation hardcore fans. The first video entry was *Barbie in the Nutcracker* directed by Owen Hurtley who came from TV (creative consultant and episode director, *Beast Wars: Transformers; Re-Boot; War Planets* and later with Technicolor's Animation and Games group) and produced by Family Home Entertainment, a company that had specialized in distributing animated series and specials, and Mainframe Entertainment in association with Mattel Entertainment. Conventional fairy tale and ballet titles such as *Barbie as Rapunzel* (2002) and *Barbie of Swan Lake* (2003) followed until new avenues were explored with *Barbie: A Fashion Fairytale* (2010) and Rainmaker Entertainment's *Barbie in Rock 'N Royals* (2015) with the title character switching places with Erika, a famous rock star.

DreamWorks Animation SKG belonged to those who jumped on the bandwagon. In April 2013, it was announced that Katzenberg's company had acquired the image and distribution rights of the iconic *Troll* dolls. This made DreamWorks Animation the worldwide licensor for *Trolls* merchandise, except of Scandinavia. The original *Good Luck Troll* was created in 1959 by Thomas Dam (1909–1986), a Danish fisherman-turned-woodcarver. It was intended as a Christmas present for his daughter. In the early 1960s, thousands of those Trolls, made of natural rubber and filled with wood shavings, traveled into the world. Although quite ugly, with long colorful hair, they became instant girl's items, next to *Barbie* and Co. And like *Barbie* and the *Smurfs*, they became surefire stuff to animate. To top the choice, DreamWorks hired Justin Timberlake to produce a number of songs and to voice, alongside with co-star Anna Kendrick, the two Troll hero characters: Branch and Princess Poppy who are setting forth to rescue some fellow Trolls. But the voices of the teenie stars don't match the tiny characters. They do not fit into this type of movie. And even worse, DreamWorks didn't care much for animation and story values. The narrative is quite odd. It tells of the Bergens. These are monsters that live in a kingdom of misery and cheerlessness. Their only joy is to devour once a year the Good Luck Trolls and experience a brief moment of hilarious happiness. This DreamWorks product is a pathetic mishmash. The characters are no real dramatis personae, they have no true personality. They are simply designed to make money hand over fist.

Disney reportedly continues to bank on the *Princess Line* and with it promotes more female characters but had to halt sales of *Moana* costumes after racism claims. Although their *Moana* (2016) is no princess as such, but the daughter of a Polynesian chief, she certainly belongs in that category. The costume was based on Maui, a key figure in Polynesian oral tradition, and featured full-length brown trousers, a long-sleeved shirt covered in "tattoos," and a "skirt" made of leaves. Chelsie Haunai Fairchild, a native Hawaiian college student, criticized the costume as "disgusting" as it doesn't honor or pay homage to a culture but educates children to pretend to be another race. (Anyway, *Moana*, re-titled *Vaiana* in Europe to avoid confusion with Italian porno queen Moana Pozzi, would have been much better off in live action. It's not the greatest choice for Disney animation. The few animals and creatures are not very strong and could have been added by VFX as well.)

Early on animated figures were starred in advertising films, which meant that you had to have a character that worked in less than a minute on screen. Some of these became legendary: the stop-frame animated, squeaky-voiced Speedy Alka-Seltzer boy named Sparky [originally created in 1952 by Robert Watkins for a magazine ad and in some early commercials appearing with Buster Keaton] or Poppin' Fresh, the Pillsbury Dough Boy of deceptively simple design, complete with replacement faces, animated by Jim Danforth, David Allen, and others, *Frito Bandito* [a Tex Avery character] and, the most famous classic one, *the Esso/ Exxon Tiger* [*Put a Tiger in Your Tank* campaign].

Even on this market there is a big competition. There simply is too much animation to gain the attention advertising characters had, say, 40 years ago. An enduring success story like that of Mickey Mouse today? Impossible!

32

Design, Posing, and Facial Expression

Sometimes the whole story is part of the design, part of the *production bible* or *style guide*. One example comes to mind: Pixar's robot *Wall-E* (2008). Its story is defined in shape, design, and environment. (The setting tells a lot about a character, particularly in series and sitcoms.)

Anyway, in preproduction the design of characters and the development of the story go hand in hand. Character design is the casting of virtual characters that are required by the story. The design should express life in a still image.

A driver, for instance, should look *fast*. Or, think in contradictions: *slow*. A slow person in a fast car would be funny, or a fast guy, but then in a slow car.

In the best case, a single character design will tell a whole life story. In the worst case, not even high-quality animation will save the figure or gain any interest. A well-designed character will speak to the animator itself.

A strong chin, for instance, will make a person or character fearsome and intimidating. Just watch how many politicians have chin. It's like being the *Lion King*.

Posing is essential to both, good feature-length and limited TV animation.

There should be only one or two major poses per scene. The model sheets should give a hint how to pose characters and facial expressions:

Clearly, the design decisions made when creating a character will influence the kind of animation possible. The more restrictive the nature of the designs, the more difficult it will be to animate. The designer must be aware of the job a character has to fulfill and be aware of the difficulties that animators face in the animation process and give them at least a fighting chance to achieve the required performance.

The posing has a lot to do how a character will move in animation. Action analysis will serve as a vehicle for introducing and building the character.

Many years after he photographed animals and athletes, Eadweard Muybridge's chronophotography remained the standard action analysis.

Walt Disney created his own educational program and it included action analysis. Don Graham was hired from Chouinard [Art Institute]† to put these classes together. They examined the films of artists such as Charlie Chaplin and Buster Keaton, frame by frame and discussed how the gags were set up and how they communicated with the audience. They looked at all kinds of films including German Expressionism, films by Leni Riefenstahl, sports films, Hollywood films, nature films, documentaries.‡

This is how they found German actor Emil Jannings towering as giant Mephistopheles over a Medieval Town in Friedrich Wilhelm Murnau's Ufa production *Faust* (1927), an image that became the inspirational source for the Devil on Bald Mountain in *Fantasia*.

Animation director David Hand:

We have been pretty stock-minded in the past. We always made a walk in the same way. That is one thing Don [Graham's] action analysis classes are doing—at least did for me. A few years ago there were only two walks—a regular walk and a Felix walk. Then we began to think and now we find a walk for every different kind of person.§

One has to note that the first individual cartoon walk was that of Felix the Cat thinking.

What was right in silent films—overacting—certainly is not bad for animation as it lives from that kind of exaggeration. Animators should take the time and study the great silents: Lon Chaney as *The Hunchback of Notre Dame* (1923), Conrad Veidt as *The Man Who Laughs* (1928), Max Schreck as *Nosferatu* (1922), the gruesome vampire with rat teeth and pointed ears (originally director F. W. Murnau wanted to have Veidt for the part), the slapstick performances of Chaplin, Keaton, Harry Langdon, and Larry Semon.

* Derek Hayes and Chris Webster, *Acting and Performance in Animation*. Burlington, MA: Focal Press (Taylor & Francis Group), 2013, p. 73.
† In 1961, thanks to Disney, Chouinard merged with the Los Angeles Conservatory of Music to establish the California Institute of the Arts [Cal Arts].
‡ John Canemaker, *Performance and Acting For Animators*. Animation World Magazine—Issue 4.12—March 2000.
§ David Hand, *Action Analysis: Director's Relationship to the Picture and to the Animator*. Walt Disney Studios transcript. August 1, 1936.

Even Douglas Fairbanks, if allowed, could give a hilarious performance as he did in *The Mystery of the Leaping Fish*, a 1916 American short silent comedy written by D. W. Griffith, Tod Browning, and Anita Loos. The acrobatic star played an addictive detective named "Coke" Ennyday who is a parody of that famous sleuth, Sherlock Holmes. This guy liberally helps himself to the contents of a hatbox-sized round container of white powder on his desk labelled "COCAINE."

The way of acting through animated characters is not, as in modern acting, through understatement but by Expressionist acting, a short-lived theatrical style popular in Germany for some time. While the structure of Expressionist theatre consisted of static scenes, the antithesis of a well-made play, the characters bore many similarities to cartoon figures: They were stereotypes, grotesque caricatures, their inner psychological reality was revealed by external means, and their dialogue was truncated, clipped, and fragmented. This exaggerated style, sans dialogue, can be studied especially in German silents like the 1919 *Cabinet of Dr. Caligari* (Werner Krauss as the insane hypnotist and Conrad Veidt as Cesare the somnambulist) or *The Golem* (1920, Paul Wegener and Ernst Deutsch). The style of acting was supposed to match the style of the sets. Sometimes, as in long shots, actors moved in patterns to correspond with the settings, almost dancing or gliding on tiptoe along a wall as Veidt did in a famous scene in *Caligari*. This type of filmmaking was deliberately copied in early American horror films such as *Dracula* and *Frankenstein* that owe a lot to German Expressionism. The main difference to cartoons is the pace: Animation often is fast-pace while the silents, including their preferred way acting, are pretty slow.

It was a deliberate departure from the realism of Stanislavsky. Expressionist film stars endeavored to overact and adopt the stilted, mechanical movements of a puppet: a reversion to the world of animism and nature spirits.

A lot of animation is pretty gruesome. Many cartoon characters are what we may call: action figures.

The violence was graphic. It did not harm the cartoon stars because they were graphic entities. In Golden Age Cartoons, no blood was spilled.

The first one playing around and acting with graphic symbols and cheating physical laws was Felix the Cat.

Of course, there is a big difference between 2D animal caricatures and realistic 3D characters and the characters in computer games. Superficial as they are, they are still caricatures but of 3D realism.

Besides posing, it is facial expression that is most important in the creation of model sheets and the design of characters.

There are comedians who literally had a face that seemed to be made of rubber. Jerry Lewis was easily caricatured and transformed into a cartoon.

Between cultures facial expressions might differ. In Asia, facial expressions are more restrained than in the Western world. But nevertheless basic mime seems to be universal.

It was Dr. Paul Ekman who did a lot of research in facial expression and emotion. His research provided strong evidence that Charles Darwin (*The Expression of Emotions in Man and Animal)* was right when he assumed that facial expressions and with them emotions—we want to add—correspond and are part of all cultural circles. In 1978, Dr. Ekman developed the *Facial Action Coding System* (FACS). The basic emotions are cross-cultural and genetically inherited.

We already have mentioned that there are six emotions plus one:

Anger—disgust—fear—joy—sadness—surprise plus contempt.

Series of facial expressions from puppet film. (Courtesy of Grigori Zurkan.)

A 100 years after James Stuart Blackton's *Humorous Phases of Funny Faces*, animator Chris Landreth who tried to depict the human psyche through the medium of Kafkaesque animation in the Academy-Award winning short of drug-addicted *Ryan* (2004) has developed a 42-hour, 4 week course program *Making Faces: a Masterclass on Facial Animation*: a complete immersion in facial animation, from complex musculoskeletal anatomy to rigging and animation that begins with the insight that every face is special and individual. Yet mimic art depends on 15 muscles of the face that define the six (to seven) characteristics of emotion that are universal across all cultures.[*]

---

[*] According to American psychologist Dr. Paul Ekman, *Facial Expressions of Emotion*. Palo Alto: Annual Reviews, 1979.

Acting and Character Animation

This somewhat mechanical approach to animation doesn't surprise as Chris started in Theoretical and Applied Mechanics at the University of Illinois and experimented in fluid mechanics research. And it shows in his films of people that mutate into nothingness.

In the meantime, thanks to the development of 3D computer animation, facial expression has become top priority. Same as in live-action movies, there are more close-ups in 3D than in 2D that focused more on the body. This is one of the qualities that 3D offers: being more cinematically.

In Hiroshi Teshigahara's feature *The Face of Another* (*Tanin no kao,* 1966), a character named Okuyama (Tatsuya Nakadai), whose face was disfigured in an industrial accident, says that the face is the door to the soul: "*When the face is closed off, so too is the soul. Nobody is allowed inside. The soul is left to rot, reduced to ruins. It becomes the soul of a monster, rotten to the core.*"

33

Understanding Body Language

Body language is the nonverbal essence of a character. Actually, it is the oldest language in the world, our native language, our mother tongue although we don't realize its existence. Mood, health, personality, age, gender as well as cultural and social background—all this and more can be deduced from the way individuals move and behave. Even if we are not aware of it, we cannot disconnect this demeanor to transmit messages through our body. Even if you don't move, you communicate constantly and give signals by way of your body posture. Head downward or keeping the chin up, arms crossed, hunched or sagging shoulders, standing with your knees bent—all this is part of human communication. Via body language, we emit our inner feelings all time even if we want to hide our emotions. Vice versa we read subconsciously other people's mind by the signals transmitted through their body. There are people, of course, who are withdrawn and have a spare body language. But with a little experience, you can read their mind too.

Popular opinion, caricatures and prejudices, however, are not based on understanding of the emotional language of the soul. They focus on physique, disabilities, and body structure and are mainly fed on stereotypes. Many people hold the opinion that someone who is slim is more likely an intellectual and aloof than a stout person who is usually said to be more down-to-earth, jovial, and funny.

Just being fat or slender raises certain expectations in an audience. We think that if you are strong, you don't need much intellect. You simply use your muscles to solve problems. But when you are physically weak you have to use your brain. This is how the Gaulish comic book heroes Asterix (slim, shrewd, and cunning) and Obelix (fat, always hungry, and good natured) work.

In history, personality typologies and friend–foe modes of thought were based on such superficial expectations. For centuries there was the belief that a character would be projected by physiognomy and body frame (and, sadly, color of the skin).

Greek humoral pathology although disproved still is going through countless people's minds albeit in modern disguises. The classification of humans in four basic types—sanguine persons, phlegmatic types, cholerics, and melancholiacs—has its origin in a theory of 400 BCE that puts the Four Humors on the same level with the Four Elements. The theory is ascribed to Polybos, disciple and son-in-law of Hippocrates. His *Corpus Hippocraticum* includes an essay on the nature of man.

According to this theory, air is identified with blood, warm and moist, or the Sanguine humor, water, cold and wet, with phlegm, or the Phlegmatic humor, fire, hot and dry, with yellow bile, or the Choleric humor, earth, cold and dry, with black bile, or the Melancholic humor. The elements of nature are projected onto the human metabolism. All of a sudden it's the percentage of bile fluid that determines your character and humor.

All these prejudices work in animation.

The sanguine type [*sanguis*, Latin: blood] is highly temperamental, warm-hearted, optimistic, and social.

This is typical of *Mickey Mouse* and *Beavis*.

The phlegmatic [*phlegein*, Greek: to burn] is languid and passive.

Garfield is a well-known exponent of this breed. Another one is *Fry*, one of the main characters of Matt Groening's *Futurama*.

The choleric [*khole*, Greek: bile] suffers from too much acid (yellow) bile that makes him hot-tempered and irascible: a true hothead with a chip on his shoulders.

Donald Duck, Yosemite Sam, and *Butt-Head* are typical cholerics sitting on a volcano of emotions.

The melancholic personality is afflicted with *melainachole* (Greek, black bile) and is a wet blanket.

If you think about it, there are more cartoon characters that belong to that type than you would have expected: Tex Avery's stoic *Droopy* and *Charlie Brown* as well as *Moe Slizack*, the bartender of *Simpsons* fame, and *SpongeBob's* antisocial neighbor *Squidward*.

Provided you have a Gang of Four, it is almost certain that you will have a member of each type. The *Dalton Brothers,* convicts and perennial antipodes of *Lucky Luke,* have sanguine Averell, phlegmatic Jack, choleric Joe, and melancholic William. A similar family background pertains to the *Flintstones:* Barney (sanguine), his wife Betty (melancholic), Fred (choleric), and Wilma (phlegmatic). *The Penguins of Madagascar* consists of Skipper (melancholic), Rico (choleric),

Kowalski (phlegmatic), and Private (sanguine). *Homer Simpson* is choleric, Marge phlegmatic, Bart sanguine, and Lisa melancholic.

Medical theory defined them by temperament. At least in the black-and-white microcosm of comics and cartoons, nothing has changed after hundreds of years although no type is exclusively sanguine, melancholic, choleric, or phlegmatic.

To create a connection between physiognomy and character in real life is a highly doubtful and dangerous undertaking. Just take anti-Semitic caricatures and racist fantasies which are always cliché-ridden. A cliché works in comics and comic strips, but if you are going to develop a character based on real psychological features, with a profound psychogram, you cannot resort to caricatures. You have to do research on real people and not stereotypes. You will have to observe life in everyday world and not in fiction.

Cliché characters will not develop. They will stay the same no matter what will happen. This is the reason why they are so popular in series. You don't have to explain their personal and social background. You can go right into a story.

If you want to tell a more complex story, then you have to create equally complex role profiles and shouldn't think of using stereotypes: A cook has to be endomorph with a beer garden physiognomy, a con man is sly, a construction worker sturdy, and beefy. The connection between body structure and character and even profession is based on stereotyped thinking. With today's sophisticated audiences, you cannot go on and rely on compartmentalization but have to get more creative. You shouldn't rethermalize the old (gender) stereotypes such as male and female. This is the twenty-first century.

So forget about prejudices. Study people. And study body language.

An animator needs to understand what the body tells. He has to watch and read people with the eyes, not the ears. Psychological and emotional processes are transformed into movement. Even tiny gestures count, such as a facial shrug or the drooping corner of the mouth.

Once animators and actors have understanding of body language, certain movements will become organic. You will have to fill a part mentally. Prejudices aside, there are differences between people that are objective. A slim person will have different movements than a coarse character. A kid differs from adult, a female from males. The movement doesn't depend exclusively on individual body structure, skeleton, and musculature, but also on age and gender, mood, and culture. Besides that, there are conscious and subconscious gestures.

If you slouch your shoulders, with your head facing down, you signal that you are sad and in a depressed mood. If you are tired you won't talk much and get monosyllabic. An upright position radiates freshness and alertness. There are trained body postures that are supposed to evoke a certain impression. One puts himself up strongly. Chin upward. Hand rubbing is a gesture of expectation. As serviceman you have to learn to stand at attention, to march and salute.

Hand gestures are culturally differentiated. Similar gestures can have different cultural meanings. Sometimes a well-meant gesture can have a derogatory meaning in another culture although we are not aware of it. If you fold the hands, it can mean that you pray or it could be a welcome gesture as well. Some cultures gesticulate more with hands and fingers than others. They say for instance that Italians talk with their hands.

In daily life, words are given a bigger meaning in the system of communication. Information that we hear is processed in the brain and we develop a position to it. But at the same time, a process of subconscious, nonverbal decoding is taking place and mediates a feeling. And if the signals of the body and the information do not match, we get suspicious.

Animator Shamus Culhane had observed that one particular politician who fell into the disgrace of history, Richard M. Nixon, a personal friend of Walt Disney, was clever enough to rehearse body language, but the gestures were out of sync. He emphasized his key words by strong hand movements but they were made without any conviction. Culhane suggested to his readers to study the ex-president's TV appearances as a chance to see some very bad animation in live action.* Even with dialogue it's the body language that counts and will stick in the mind. Also, while talking people act with the body.

A person comes across authentic if body language and words correspond and match.

We have to consider that the visual sense is the one that is highly developed in most humans.

Albert Mehrabian, Professor Emeritus of Psychology, UCLA, claimed that only seven percent of the impression a person makes are based on words, thirty-eight percent: vocal liking, and fifty-five percent: facial liking.

True or not—therefore, body language is more important than words and dialogue.

You have to study body language carefully and if you want to animate a character in motion, then you shouldn't just imitate a superficial movement that you have seen or select a digital program to help you but try to imagine this movement in your own body. You have to feel and explore it inside yourself. Here—and only here—an animator will have a real chance to truly act. Not just gestures and body posture but feeling and empathizing.

Imagine a situation, feel yourself into it. Feel your emotion. Where does your body brace? What movement does it execute following the pattern of emotions? Try to realize this on your own body. You become your own tool, register and understand body language.

Recall a situation that made you angry. Somebody had insulted you. Try to explore how this feeling, how this emotion worked inside your body. On the other hand, try to recall a feeling that made you happy. How does this feel? Don't you feel lighter? Can you differentiate the impulses that move your body? If you are doing exercises like this always finish with positive feelings. These exercises should support and stagger your imagination and creativity and shouldn't make you sad.

* Shamus Culhane, *Animation from Script to Screen*. London: Columbus Books Limited, 1989, p. 208–209.

In the past, many animators used a mirror to study their facial expression. Today, they can use a camcorder or simply their mobile device to study facial expression and record it as reference.

But try to imagine the emotion that you want to express, for instance, joy, not in an abstract way. It should always be part of a situation, a little story that you invent. Acting is always re-acting to a special situation, a so-called stimulus. Anger rises when something or somebody infuriates you. Joy will rise when you are happy about something that happened to you.

But be critical of self-observation because you might repeat the most common beginner's mistake of drama students and animators: They exaggerate because they want to express too much simultaneously.

Reduce, focus on the essential. One step after the other.

This shouldn't inhibit your motivation. Pleasure and joy are necessary prerequisites for your work.

There are also books on anatomy, on body language. Besides watching you can read and learn a lot about it intellectually. This is the right way: experience yourself by exercises *and* read about it. In this context, we highly recommend a book by Desmond Morris: *Bodytalk.**

Many of the old-time animators—including Disney and his staff—adored pantomime. Pantomime is a beautiful art that demonstrates what we can express without words. It emphasizes body posture, facial expression, movement, and gesture and reveals the emotional state of a person nonverbally. Masters of the pantomime are artists of body language.

Many animation characters, especially those that had no dialogue, moved in a non-natural way. It's a synthetic type of movement. It's not spontaneous. It's more like ballet. Pantomime is a special art form of its own that has no naturalness.

In pantomime there is a lot of slowness. Interestingly, many movements are being done in slow motion and, with a few exceptions, would consequently slow down animation that basically (albeit not exclusively) is an art of fast movement.

Pantomime was hot particularly in the early days of animation when they had only little or no dialogue. In those days, they liked to go for pantomime. Today, with low-budget animation, you have to have more dialogue.

Today pantomime has to be used restrainedly in (naturalistic) animation. If there is pantomime, it is part of Expressionist acting. Silent film actors had to have certain pantomime abilities. So there is a relationship that became part of animation in its infancy.

There are wonderful pantomimes such as Marcel Marceau and mime artists like Nola Rae but you will see them rarely on the big screen.

All the big movie stars nowadays are actors, no pantomimes.

Nevertheless, both pantomimes and actors have to understand the body and its language but they use their experience in different ways.

---

* Desmond Morris, *Bodytalk: The Meaning of Human Gestures.* New York: Crown Publishers, 1995.

Usually, an actor will have years to train but an animator who isn't an actor will never find the time and therefore lack the professional background knowledge. If an animator will try acting, it will look clichéd.

What can a poor animator, chained inside his cubicle, do to re-enact what an actor has learned in 3 or 4 years? Will a crash course in body language help him? Or joining an amateur drama group?

If there is no time and no budget, animators will avoid body language at all, do what Chuck Jones called illustrated radio and animate mechanically. Characters have no limbs, no facial features. They become caricatures with pared-down bodies. If you study inexpensive animation series, even Japanese anime, you see that every character has the same walk. The legs look like hinges. They move like jointed dolls. But nobody walks dead straight as these pathetic figures do.

Animator Cliff Nordberg trained young artists at Disney. He let them work with flour sack characters to create mood: anger, happiness, curiosity, fear, indecision, and bashfulness. You can do it all with a flour sack.

But maybe it will look exaggerated and excessive.

The dilemma is: The instrument of actors is the body. They have to learn how to sense emotions. Their body will get automatically into the right position. On stage to determine gestures is the duty of the director, but in animation the director isn't present all time and certainly not trained as a stage director. The animator's tool is the pencil or the computer or a stop-motion puppet. They don't use their own bodies. An animator has to change position but basically his position is, contrary to the actor, not inside but outside a character.

The only way is to watch other people and get familiar with their body language. Real people will not wave their arms and exaggerate. You don't have to become an actor but you have to use your sketch pad. Watch what they do, how they use their hands and feet. Thus, gradually, the understanding of body language is trained.

Don't look excessively at animation. Watch real life.

Lucia (2004). (Courtesy of Felix Goennert and Film University Babelsberg.)

Acting and Character Animation

Acting is a profession. As actors animators are amateurs.

There are no fixed gestures. You can't learn body language from a manual alone.

There are so many unemployed actors and actresses around. Why don't animation producers and directors hire a few of them as consultants, not only as voice artists but to use them in active production with the animators?

They did so in the case of Ed Hooks.

Now let's talk about animals. In most cartoons, animals do not behave like animals. In the best cases, they might move like animals but we know that they are not. We project our own body talk and way of behaving into nature and its creatures and subdue and *Disney-ify* them.

Provided you are not going to humanize animals, you have to consider that animals have their own body language. You can read a cat's mood from how it moves ears and tail. If a cat goes ahead of you, tail up, it wants to tell you that you have to follow. Most likely, the animal will lead you to its feeding dish to tell you that it wants some food.

Pack animals have a more distinct facial expression than lone wolves that generally live or spend time alone instead with a group. Usually wolves demonstrate more facial play than, for instance, bears. You can't read a bear's face.

There are a lot of good documentaries around. Even better is a living pet which will teach you animal behavior.

34

The Eyes Have It!

This was the title of a comedy starring cross-eyed Ben Turpin. It is true for live action as well as animation. Just see the gallery of cartoon eyes.

With their enchantingly large eyes, two big circles, cartoon characters reflect the age of innocence and the purity of childhood. More, these eyes are acting. Sometimes, in combination with the eyebrows, they are the whole performance suggesting that a character is tired, surprised, shocked (with wide opened eyes), angered (with eyebrows angled over), and furious (with red eyes). Sometimes, particularly in crazy Tex Avery cartoons, the eyes pop out when the character flips out, when a wolf spots a beautiful girl on stage as in *Red Hot Riding Hood* (1943) or *Hound Hunters* (1947). Others have dollar signs in their eyes when they speak of money.

People's eyes are in constant movement. They look away when not telling the truth. They wander if the person is thinking.

Cartoon characters are graphic symbols and so they reflect graphic symbols for certain expressions. The expressiveness of their eyes is based, largely, on BIG eyes. So cartoon characters are the proof that the eyes are really the windows of the soul.

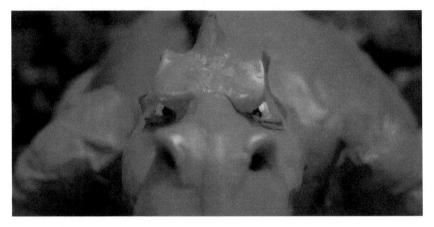

Puppet character. (Courtesy of Grigori Zurkan.)

Our pupils enlarge when we are sexually excited, when we are furious, or lying. There are even bedroom eyes.

These symbolic eye-waves are reflected in the symbolism of cartoon characters.

There are different shapes of cartoon eyes: vertically stretched, footballs, circles, or even pinpoints as in the *Peanuts*.

Or take Ray Harryhausen's constantly enraged one-eyed cyclops from *The 7th Voyage of Sinbad* that inspired, albeit a completely different character, greenish Mike Wazowski in Pixar's *Monsters, Inc.* (2001). Harryhausen used puppet eyes from Germany. The animators of *Anomalisa* (2015) put a special shine into the puppet eyes.

In the beginning, eyes have been a big obstacle in 3D animation. They looked dead. They had no shine. Just take Tom Hanks' digital clone in Robert Zemeckis' *The Polar Express* (2004) with his dead eyes. In an outstanding award-winning short film produced by the National Film Board of Canada, *Madame Tutli-Putli* (2007), the stop-motion model has realistic eyes composed from actress Laurie Maher onto the puppet's face.

Hank the Octopus, one of the animated stars of Pixar's *Finding Dory* (2016), is not so much working by his tentacles but by his eyes and eyelids. In most of his scenes, he is an eye creature. With the fish of *Finding Nemo* and *Finding Dory* it's the same: They are all eyes.

Remember John Lasseter's words? Pixar, in particular, cares for expressive eyes. That's the main difference to other cartoons. Right after *Finding Dory*, we saw the disappointing fifth part of the *Ice Age* series: *Collision Course*. No main character, only supporting actors—they try to perform with the eyes but they do not succeed. Worse some European cartoons: Their characters are waving their arms, flapping lips—but their big eyes remain lifeless.

There is a lot to know about blinking and eye movement. Some of this knowledge is only technical:

If you turn your head, you blink. A blink may emphasize a change of thought.

The regular blink might last in animation for six frames: two frames closing lids, one frame hold eyes closed, and three frames opening. A fast blink to show the character is anxious or angry lasts five frames. A long blink might last nine frames.

Wide-eyed CG character from Felix Goennert's *Lucia* (2004). (Courtesy of Felix Goennert and Film University Babelsberg.)

One should not forget those big eyes in Asian cartoons. They are not part of an inferiority complex but were introduced by Osamu Tezuka who liked Betty Boop so much that he copied her big eyes that became a trademark of Japanese and later Asian animation.

Betty Boop, designed by Grim Natwick, who later animated Disney's *Snow White*, was the first female cartoon star. For many, her girlish voice:

boop-boop-a-doop, her outfits and mini-dress that revealed one gartered leg and her movements seemed to be a synonym for sex and sexual freedom. In 1934, during a copyright infringement suit initiated by actress Helen Kane who felt herself (rightly) copied, a judge described *the broad baby face, the large round flirting eyes, the low placed pouting mouth, the small nose, the imperceptible chin, and the mature bosom: It was a unique combination of infancy and maturity, innocence and sophistication.* It was not so much the animation. It was just the figure as symbol that, for a while, paid the bills: some kind of animated Lolita.

Another famous cartoon character, *Superman*, created by two slight kids, Jerry Siegel and Joe Shuster, became an animated star in Max Fleischer's Technicolor series released in 1941 and 1942. To transform into an average citizen, awkward reporter Clark Kent, Superman only needed a suit and a prop: glasses to cover his X-ray eyes.

You even can freeze a character as long as you keep the eyes alive. Jim Henson once got to the heart of it when he said that without eyes there is no character.

Of course one can easily overdo this eye business like the producers of the Warner Animation Group did in their 2016 3D-animated *Storks*. Besides the stupid premise that storks are still the ones in charge to deliver the babies to mankind, the whole plot is acted out by characters who are constantly staring wide-eyed and signal that the whole show and they themselves are completely insane. This applies in particular to Tulip, an occasionally cross-eyed, grinning, hyperactive orphan girl who seems to suffer from ADHD.

35

It's Personality That Wins

The elder statesmen of 2D animation, Frank Thomas and Ollie Johnston, taught us twelve rules that they said we would have to watch:

1. *Squash and stretch* that defines the plasticity and flexibility of characters and objects, deforming and distorting figures.
2. *Timing* of scenes and characters.
3. *Anticipation* as a start of an action or movement.
4. *Staging* or layout of a scene.
5. *Follow through/overlapping action:* the slowdown of an action. When one movement is about to stop, another one can (overlapping) begin.
6. *Straight ahead and pose-to-pose:* animating straight ahead so that ideas can be injected by the animator.
7. *Slow in/slow out:* soft accelerating, soft stop.
8. *Exaggeration* as part of a caricature.
9. *Arc:* realistic curves to get smooth movements.
10. *Secondary action:* for instance the movement of clothes caused by a person's movements.
11. *Solid drawing* (not that important for 3D animators).

12. *Appeal*: pleasant design, colors, forms, and simplicity. (When we talk about personality, we shouldn't forget that clothes make people. The vulgar Mickey Mouse wore red shorts. Citizen Mouse wears a suit or even a dress coat with top hat. The twiggy carcass of Cruella De Vil in *One Hundred and One Dalmatians* wears a heavy, a very heavy fur coat.)

Well, these are just technical terms that can be mastered with some experience. Above all, there is a quality that is part of the appeal but is strikingly different. It's *personality*. It's difficult to put a personality in words but you can sense it immediately. There is some strange magnetism working.

The Snow Man (1944). Original animation cel. (Courtesy of J. P. Storm Collection.)

Jack Hannah directed many Donald Duck cartoons for Disney, then, when Disney ceased short film production, left for Walter Lantz. He asked himself why actors like Clark Gable or John Wayne became stars and said that it was not necessarily their great acting. It was their personality that made the difference:

Good cartoon characters are like that as well. Donald Duck had a great personality and the audience had a lot of fun with him. However, Donald Duck was an accident. Just like in real life, someone comes on as an extra and then "Boom!" Most of the popular animated characters were accidents. They just seemed to work for an audience.

But what elements does an audience want? On the surface, there seems to be nothing in common between a Donald Duck and a Bugs Bunny and a Woody

Woodpecker. To me, it means that the audience likes more than just one type of personality. Some like a sweeter, gentler character. Others like a rougher one. The audience would sometimes surprise us about which characters they really accepted.

These characters took on a life of their own. Even though some of these characters haven't appeared in years, people are still interested in them.[*]

Jeffrey Katzenberg belongs to those who strongly believe in character. Finally, it's the star, the animated character that is going to sell Katzenberg's product:

The first thing you need is a great character. Whoever the protagonist is, it's got be someone the whole family can connect to, identify with and relate to.[†]

To Katzenberg, *Kung Fu Panda's* Po is one of those characters: lovable, huggable, and charming: *He's got a big dilemma, a difficulty, and we have to be able to relate to it, so we want to be with him on his journey, so we care about him.*[†]

When people ask him why *Shrek* is so popular, Katzenberg tells them that there's a little ogre in all of us. At the core, *Shrek* wants to be loved but he has to learn to love before someone else can love him.

You need to celebrate the values that are the best in humanity: that's something both children and adults can identify with. In the new Panda film [Kung Fu Panda 3], Shifu says to Po: 'If you only do what you know how to do, you can never be better than you are now.' And when you think about that, it's an inspiring notion. Po wants to stand still because he's happy with how everything is going, so why change?

But the thing is that change is life—there's no such thing as standing still. So what Shifu is really saying is, you've got to grow up. You've got to be more than you are today.[†]

Po and even better *Shrek* adapt very well to a vulgar society of losers. Walt Disney himself would have never produced a fairy tale like *Shrek*. He had completely forgotten that the early Mickey Mouse stepped out as vulgar as *Shrek*. Shrek smells, picks his nose, burps, and even finds a bride who likes this and more. People love monsters, so the movie monsters became lovable themselves, as in *Monsters, Inc.*

In the Western world, dragons are regarded as monsters, too. They aren't in Asia. And they aren't in DreamWorks' *How to Train Your Dragon* (2010) and the animated TV series based on the film's success simply titled *DreamWorks Dragons* (started in 2012).

The series' Viking kids are defined by the dragons they ride:

> Self-conscious, devil-may-care Snotlout Jorgenson and fire-breathing Hookfang

* Jack Hannah, *Further Foreword*. John Cawley/Jim Korkis: *The Encyclopedia of Cartoon Superstars*. Las Vegas: Pioneer Books, Inc., 1990, p. 7.

† Joanna Moorhead, *Jeffrey Katzenberg: How to Make a Perfect Family Film*. The Guardian, London, March 12, 2016.

Chubby Fishlegs Ingerman and burly Gronckle Meatlug

Truffnut and Ruffnut Thorston, a pair of twins, and their two-headed Hideous Zippleback with one head named Barf, the other one Belch

Astrid Hofferson and Stormfly, a female Deadly Nadder

Hiccup Horrendous Haddock III, a Viking sort of Luke Skywalker: He is disabled having lost the lower part of his leg but his metal leg combines favorably with Night Fury Toothless that has lost his left tail fin. He demonstrates to the Viking youth how to successfully train dragons.

The series works thanks to effective pairing of kids and dragons.

36

The Score

One day gagman, trombonist and voice actor Pinto Colvig (Goofy) was called in to perform for a special guest who visited the Disney Studio. He improvised Mickey Mouse taking off in an airplane and landing in a barnyard which evoked a wild conglomeration of pig squeals, grunts, dog barks, rooster crows, hen cackles, sheep baas, and moo cows. The guest seemed very pleased with that barnyard orchestra. His name was Leopold Stokowski. He would go on and introduce the Disney people to classic music with *Fantasia* (1940). *Fantasia* was an exception, a single and singular excursion into that field.

Particularly in animation the score underlines emotion. Hanns Eisler, the great German composer, termed this technique of matching movement to music that we know as *Mickey Mousing*, an awful Wagnerian illustration technique.

Scott Bradley, the musical director of MGM's cartoon department, showed film students once a Tom & Jerry cartoon without and then with music and sound effects to demonstrate how his work enhanced the series. The students, however, laughed the first time, when screened again with music the laughs weren't as big because they knew all the gags.

Animation needs speed and a good soundtrack that adds music to lively sound effects. Disney knew about the value of musical contributions. It became the founding stone of the *Silly Symphonies*. It also helps us to empathize with the characters.

Some of the most famous animated films wouldn't exist without music: *Fantasia,* the Ravel *Bolero* sequence in Bruno Bozzetto's *Allegro Non Troppo* (1976), the Beatles-influenced *Yellow Submarine* (1968).

Big movies need big feelings. So they need a big score.

Peter Jackson's *King Kong* remake (2005) had magnificent production values but this didn't help. Everything was bigger, louder, and more expensive than the 1933 original film. Instead of one they got three Tyrannosauri fighting Kong, they had not one but a whole swarm of Pterodactyls to multiply the action. Yet it left the audience cold.

There is a number of reasons. Sure, Jackson's *Kong* had the better technology and budget and a great mocap performance by Andy Serkis, but in other departments it remained uninspired. Besides weak comedy acting by Naomi Watts and Jack Black, the musical score by James Newton Howard (who replaced the much better Howard Shore who after some argument had left the project)—except for a brief sequence with Kong on ice where the tunes fit—was nothing short than terrible. One would sadly realize the shortcoming when a few minutes worth of Max Steiner's score for the original film were cut in for a change.

It was Steiner's 1933 score, one long musical crescendo that created empathy for its animated main character. It's the music that drives the picture through its rather episodic structure and holds audience's attention from beginning to end. Ray Bradbury, a big *Kong* fan and Harryhausen friend, once said that Steiner's music contributed 30 percent to the success of the movie. The emotional moments wouldn't have been so strong without Steiner's work and neither would have been the action. The same is true for the scores Bernard Herrmann created for some of Harryhausen's films, including *The 7th Voyage of Sinbad* and *Jason and the Argonauts*. It gave the animation in otherwise low-budget pictures certain greatness and grandeur and underlined the fairy-tale character.

Jim Danforth remembers visiting *Sinbad* producer Charles H. Schneer on a 1958 movie set on the "Columbia Ranch" and overheard him talk to somebody on the phone who wanted to see *7th Voyage*. Schneer denied the request firmly because sound effects and music weren't finished yet and they were too important to this kind of film: *"No, you can't see it without the music. Absolutely not."*

Good or bad acting techniques notwithstanding, the soundtrack is one of the main ingredients of animation and VFX pictures.

The greatest of animation directors knew how to time their exposure sheets to the score. A Taiwanese professor who once met animation director William Hanna who timed the old Tom & Jerry cartoons told us that the man had hands like those of a pianist.

The production of *Luminaris,* the wonderful Pixilation short by Argentine animator Juan Pablo Zaramella that we mentioned earlier, started with a piece of music by Osmar Héctor Maderna, the Chopin of the tango who died in 1951. The whole picture, the animation of the actors was timed to Maderna's tango tunes.

Next to the music, there are the songs. Some of Disney's best cartoon films are animated musicals and made it later to the musical stage like *The Lion King, The Hunchback of Notre Dame,* or *Aladdin.*

A pleasant surprise is Garth Jennings' *Sing* (2016), which features a merry song contest casting show arranged by a broke, desperate koala impresario named Buster Moon that links funny gags with some good singing voices.

37

Psychological Projection

There is a lot of symbolism in animation. Particularly Chinese think in symbols. Animals, colors—many things have a special meaning.

The same is true for Aesop's or La Fontaine's fables: the fox is cunning and the bear slow and dumb.

Many of us care for the little, cute animals. Contrary to nature—the social Darwinist concept of the "Survival of the Fittest" stressed in Disney's 1943 *Education for Death: The Making of the Nazi*, where little Hans who pities the little rabbit being devoured by the fox gets scolded by a feisty Nazi teacher animated by Bill Tytla—in picture books it is often the small one who outdoes the big one. It is the story of David and Goliath: The mouse outdoes the cat. Tweety Bird wins over Sylvester P. Pussycat.

According to Sigmund Freud, psychological projection is a psychological defense mechanism whereby one "projects" one's own undesirable thoughts, dreams, motivations, desires, and feelings onto animals and inanimate objects. We might add: animated objects and characters. This includes fears of illness and death as well.

This is a pact between filmmakers and audience.

Not so in one Nazi cartoon that fits perfectly in the scheme portrayed in *Education for Death*. In 1941, the Germans founded their own Trickfilm Company, Deutsche Zeichenfilm GmbH, to compete with Disney's productions that were not shown in the German Reich back then but nevertheless appreciated by Reich Propaganda Minister Goebbels and Hitler. They spent millions of Reichsmark to set up a studio in the German capital and trained artists and technical personnel, but the output until 1945 consisted in only one single finished Agfacolor short film of 18 minutes: *Poor Hansi* [*Armer Hansi*]. The original idea was submitted in October 1941 by Hermann Krause as *the story of a little canary that flew into freedom*. In his cage, the canary named Hansi listens to the voice of freedom, love, and adventure. He hears the song of a chickadee and carelessly leaves the birdcage. The canary's wings, however, grow weak too early. And freedom is dangerous. Hunger, thirst, rain, and finally an ugly street cat drive Hansi back to the safety of prison. In the end, it all turns out to be a dream. The parable of a weak canary, a typical cage bird, feeling safe only in prison was outrageously stupid but it seemed to please the Nazi powers-at-be who had prisoned a big part of Europe, at least ideologically, and send millions to the concentration camps. The very thought of freedom, on the other hand, certainly wouldn't appeal to them. It was not part of their thinking. When the movie was finally released, in 1943, Germany was hit by severe bomb raids.

Having read the basic idea, Horst von Möllendorff who belonged to the company's staff of writers was one of the few who realized this matter. He suggested immediate changes and tried to introduce ideas of his own:

> *I want to comment on two important issues:*
> *The canary who only dreams about the flight into freedom leaves an unsatisfied desire.*
> *The ending leaves an unfree feeling, the cage becomes a prison as the canary returns because he is unable to live in freedom.*
> *Therefore I suggest:*
> *Leave the desire for freedom as core of the plot but give the whole another basic idea as follows:*
> *The wish to swap with the life of another.*
>
> 1. *This would give a different meaning to beginning as well as the ending.*
>
> 2. *The canary wants to swap his life with a sparrow, and this not in dream but in real life.*
>
> *After they have lived the life of the other, they are happy to become their old selfs and change again.*[*]

Möllendorff's idea was not that novel: We find it in the story of Doctor Faustus, who trades his soul for a younger self, or in Robert Louis Stevenson's *The Bottle Imp*.

---

* Memo to the leaders of Deutsche Zeichenfilm GmbH. Document saved from the files of the late Horst von Möllendorff and made available by J. P. Storm from his collection.

It also would have changed little because the glorious prison still lured. The story supervisor of the Deutsche Zeichenfilm Company, a man named Frank Leberecht, didn't sympathize with Möllendorff's suggestions and the man himself, but he did change the dream for reality and at the end allowed Hansi, who voluntarily returned to his prison cage, a consolation price in the shape of a female canary, Hansine.

Original animation art from *Poor Hansi* (1943). (Courtesy of J. P. Storm Collection.)

What he didn't do was the only reasonable thing to do: build the character. Have David defeat Goliath, i.e., the hungry cat, and have him triumph in freedom. But letting Goliath chase David back to prison didn't please audiences anywhere.

A tragic irony was that one of the writers who worked on the first *Hansi* draft, a woman named Libertas Schulze-Boysen, had a second identity and fought for freedom. She belonged to a circle of resistance, *Red Chapel*. She and her husband were sentenced to death on December 19, 1942 and executed 3 days later.

Möllendorff in the meantime had left Leberecht's company and sold story ideas to animation producer Hans Fischerkoesen. In 1943, on behalf of Deutsche Wochenschau [German Newsreel], Fischerkoesen created *The Snow Man [Der Schneemann]* from an idea conceived by Möllendorff that pleased audiences to no end and one German cartoon lover in particular: Hitler's Reich Minister Dr. Joseph Goebbels who still hoped to start one day feature-length film production that would rival Disney's work. As in many other fields, the Nazis would fail to do so.

The Snow Man itself was a caricature that consisted of mainly three circles. So there was not that much character animation. Everything was kept very simple. It was tame and slow, including a dog chasing the snow man, not even an original because Fischerkoesen had used the same character briefly in a pre-war Coca-Cola spot. Animation-wise the quality was below Terrytoons. But it was highly sentimental and worked emotionally. It was psychological projection that performed miracles and made it one of the most interesting of all wartime cartoons.

With the success of that short film Horst von Möllendorff was to become Germany's busiest cartoon writer at the end of the war, supervising scenarios in the Reich as well as in occupied Prague and the Netherlands. This all was based on the success of *The Snow Man*.

One evening Möllendorff sat in a Berlin beer garden to find a suitable topic for a cartoon and eventually came up with the story of a Snow Man that had a warm spot in his heart. He wakes up in a full moon night on a quiet market place. After some adventures, he creeps into a house to rest on a sofa. There he discovers a calendar. The calendar page for January shows a snowman like himself, in a familiar winter landscape. He browses through February, March, April, May, June, and stops in July. For the first time he learns about the loveliest of seasons: summer. There is a sentimental feeling in his heart. The Germans have a word for it: *Sehnsucht*. It's difficult to translate: desire, yearning, and longing. This Snow Man is sick for the sweet experience of summer. He gets himself frozen in the refrigerator and leaves it with the advent of summer. Everything looks exactly like the promising picture in the calendar. The Snow Man grins from ear to ear and is all smiles when he leaves the house welcoming "the summer of his lifetime."

The Snow Man picks flowers and spreads them around. He sticks a red rose into his cold breast. He surprises an excited hen with an egg made up of ice and snow. Then the warm July sun begins to burn. Slowly the snowman starts to melt leaving only a top hat and his carrot nose which is picked up by a little rabbit and eaten.

Original animation art from *The Snow Man* (1944). (Courtesy of J. P. Storm Collection.)

Möllendorff had nothing to do with the making. His contribution was the basic idea and the writing but that was enough to create an unforgettable character.

Technically, the *Snow Man* was surprising only because Fischerkoesen's cameraman Kurt Schleicher made use of Max Fleischer's table top process that combined 3D models with 2D animation. But the color short itself worked so well because it was a reflection of death. In some odd way, the Snow Man's tragi-comic death reflected the millionfold death that had become a firm part of the society of the German aggressor. Now the killing had returned to its breeding ground and transformed into a death wish. Some of the leading Nazis were suicidal. Goebbels and his wife Magda took themselves and their children to death. Heinrich Himmler, Robert Ley, and Josef Terboven committed suicide as did their newly wed Führer. "At least 12 years good living," Göring said before he committed suicide to prevent them from hanging him in Nuremberg. So, in a tragic way, the *Snow Man* became an image of the society of its day.

Psychological projection can be used for agitation and propaganda. Right after the *Snow Man's* success, in 1944, Fischerkoesen, this time without the help of Möllendorff, did another short film, *The Silly Goose*. The villain is a fox. He's a bad character, no question about that. And when he seduces a goose we hear a Yiddish tune: *Bei mir bist du scheen*. The 1D villain in this Nazi time cartoon isn't defined by personality acting but just by race.

Dinah Gottliebová was a concentration camp prisoner in Auschwitz. She was an artist and recruited by the infamous KZ physician Dr. Josef Mengele to do portray studies. There was a children barrack and to please the doomed children she would paint a mural in this barrack. As she had seen Disney's version of *Snow White and the Seven Dwarfs* at least seven times in a cinema in the Prague, she chose to paint the Princess and the dwarf characters, the landscape and what else. And in the children's imagination, the characters began to live and gave them a bit of hope in their desperate situation. Gottliebová survived Auschwitz. She went to America and married one of the original animators of the seven dwarfs, Art Babbitt. She died in 2009.

Wartime is rich in such characters and even ethnic stereotypes once you consider the Japanese caricatures in so many American cartoons. They certainly had no profile, they were just—"Japs," but they fulfilled the objective of propaganda and wartime agitation.

What was true back then is true today.

When we spoke to a North Korean animation functionary who came as guest to a conference held at the Beijing Film Academy, we praised, well, not a film they had done but the animation of an eagle that pursued some small animals. We then were instructed by the man that it was all political: Their great supreme leader Kim Jong-il, back then still living, a movie buff in his own right who was mesmerized that much by foreign films that he had a filmmaker kidnapped, had told this story to children and with the eagle he meant U.S. Imperialism! No word about the animators who, in a witty prologue to the *Simpsons,* are seen as cel-washing slaves in subpar sweatshops where kittens are spliced up into Bart Simpson puppets and a gaunt unicorn punches holes into DVDs. (Actually, the *Simpsons* are made in South Korean high-tech workshops by producer Nelson Shin.)

In an anti-Donald Trump *Simpsons* election spot made in 2016, we see a vain Trump in bed with a book containing Hitler's Collected Speeches lying next to him and with a small dog on his bald head. (So far we didn't speak about the importance of hair: The centaur from *Golden Voyage of Sinbad* had a David Bowie hairstyle—said Ray Harryhausen.)

In the days of the Cultural Revolution, the Chinese portrayed heroic young-sters. *Little Sisters of Grassland* (1965) is a tale of two Mongolian teenage sisters, Long Mei and Yu Rong, who risk their lives to protect their commune's flock of sheep during a sudden snowstorm. *We fear neither the cold nor the blizzard,* Yu Rong sings. *Ah, the beacon of revolution is shining in the hearts of the little sisters. To protect the property of the collective we fear neither frost bite nor hunger. Ah, Communist thoughts are beaming over the little heroes.* And even years later, we still saw a soldier boy fighting nasty Japanese stereotypes as in *Little Soldier Zhang Ga* (2005).

In 2015, there was an anti-Israeli propaganda video that was released by the so-called Islamic Revolution Design House, a group of hardline Iranian activists. There is an animated CG part that shows heavily armed militants standing side by side, first a few, then more and more, prepared to march on Jerusalem, the images underlined by a martial score. The activists have no personality, they wear black masks. But the images suggest that they are determined to reach their goal. There is no big difference between a video like this and infamous Nazi propaganda films like *The Eternal Jew (Der ewige Jude)*, a 1940 semi-documentary mix of animated maps, falsely labeled stock footage, and newly recorded footage. It compared Jews with a plague of rats that, so the commentary, moved 2000 years from the Middle Easr to Egypt. It later flooded—the commentary claimed—the entire Mediterranean region, broke into Spain, France, and Southern Germany, followed German colonists and found a "reservoir" in Poland: *"Where rats turn up, they spread diseases and carry extermination into the land. They are cunning, cowardly and cruel, they travel in large packs, exactly the way the Jews infect the races of the world."*

Psychological projection also supports activities in merchandising. Propaganda and promotion have a lot to do with each other. Both political and commercial indoctrination share common roots. Disney convinced his customers that little girls will never forget their first encounter with a Disney Princess and claimed that even long after they're all grown up, they continue to pass along their love for these heroines, introducing them to their own daughters: a case of generation-spanning identification based on the faith in beauty. They found out that in every little girl there should be a desire to feel special and to dream into magic places where costly clothes are spun of silk and gold and where princes immediately come to the rescue as they have fallen in love at first sight. For almost every girl who believes in her beauty, Disney's advertising experts announced, there is a sweet princess to prove that everything is possible (provided she is submissive enough to accept a male hero). Over decades, Disney as we know had monopolized famous fairy tale characters such as Snow White, Cinderella, Sleeping Beauty, or even Pocahontas who were in the public domain and could be re-created and coyprighted. So in 2000, the merchandising department launched the ubiquitous *Disney Princesses* that cover virtually every product category, particularly dolls, toys and dresses, personal care, and consumer electronics. These characters seem to be perennial preschool favorites, thanks to psychological projection. In her 2011 bestseller *Cinderella Ate My Daughter*, Peggy Orenstein, a journalist, criticized this kind of role stereotypes and recommended to talk with kids about the influence of media.*

Preadolescent girls will like the magical girl manga-turned-anime *Sailor Moon* and teenage girls a new movement in manga and anime toward sexy heroines. The artist Go (Kiyoshi) Nakai, the creator of *Goldorak*, the giant robot, often draws these nude but strong willed amazons that serve as role models for the next generation.

---

* Peggy Orenstein, Cinderella Ate My Daughter: Dispatches from the Front Lines of the New Girlie-Girl Culture. New York/London/Toronto/Sydney: HarperCollins Publishers, 2011.

38

The Role of Producer and Director

All of animation is teamwork including storyboarding. Storyboarding and creating animatics is always a collaborating effort and, besides that, has a lot to do with the performance to be seen later on screen.

The work on Disney's *Snow White* was almost reminiscent of a Stanislavsky-style rehearsal. It was very much like staging a play. Animation, as we have said, is a producer-driven medium. Many times the actual animation director doesn't have the say. One producer told us that creating the story and storyboarding is the most delightful time in the process of animation, much more rewarding than production itself, and so he claimed all important creative decisions for himself.

Walt Disney was, as we have seen, a brilliant, naturally gifted actor. He would act it out for the animators while he told the story as he saw it. That's great if a Disney is around. It's a source of inspiration. It isn't when the producer is less talented but still regards himself as the creative force. There are producers around who think that they are story-minded. If this isn't the case and they are not self-critical enough, they virtually destroy preproduction. They are slow, dull, and stiff, and their motionless attitude transfers into the movie.

With a producer around who is not as imaginative and entertaining as Disney, it is sometimes a boring task. If an animated movie doesn't work, then the reason is quite often the producer.

The real duty of an animation producer is to get the best artists on board and create an atmosphere of total freedom so that the artists can rise and find complete expression. It is no wonder that a school of creativity later came to be known as the *Disney Method*, which in turn has a lot in common with Stanislavsky.

At Pixar and other big studios the producers protect the artists, spend up to ten percent of the budget on preproduction. This is paradise, this is an ideal condition. In most of the small cartoon factories, however, where they don't grant this kind of freedom, quite the reverse is true. Here artists and writers do not dare to speak out what they have in mind but just bow to the producer's verdict because they fear punishment. This extends to animation directors who often are not hired to give creative input but as workhorses that keep the schedule.

Companies like Aardman are the exception. On *Chicken Run,* Aardman producer-directors Peter Lord and Nick Park established rules how each stop-motion character should be animated. They would lay down the action, but this didn't mean that the animators had to work like robots. They just determined the key poses to start with and work from. This was similar to handing out model sheets for each character as they do in 2D animation.

Occasionally, Lord and Park would get hands-on with the puppets to demonstrate their intent. Sometimes the best way, as Lord said, to show what you have in mind is to just move the puppet into position yourself rather than talk about it. They also would do a certain performance for the animators (at least stop-motion animators do this occasionally), recording themselves on video. But this was only meant as a reference. Just to give an idea about the performance and a sense of timing because they didn't like them to copy from live action. They said that would crush creativity and encourage dependence. (The opposite is true, of course, for CG animation in live-action films.)

Producer Merian C. Cooper claimed that he often would have acted scenes out to show the animators how to move *Kong.* Ray Harryhausen, himself an accomplished animator, had his doubts about that statement.

Contrary to live-action filmmaking, 3D animators rarely have directors behind them while shooting or animating. I [RG] had the chance to direct stop motion myself, and after I went to the set to discuss a scene with the animator he locked me out. He didn't like me or anybody else around. And in 2D animation, we rarely see directors go through animation cubicles. If they are hired hands, they just turn up from time to time.

Animators are mainly left to themselves. It's the same with stage actors. After a more or less extensive period of rehearsals, when the play is actually on, the director will leave.

39

Feel at Ease While Animating

If the producer-director doesn't find the time to put his team at ease, the animator has to care for himself, has to find individual means to get himself in the right mood.

Imagine animators sitting at their desks in front of computer screens.

They move characters but rarely move themselves.

In the best case, an animator has a single office, in the worst, very often in Asia, we find him in a large office cube where you see hundreds of them: wedged for 8 hours, hunched like in a prison.

No doubt that this position, all day sitting, is unhealthy for your body and it is not optimal to develop your creative mind.

Imagination needs space to find complete expression and fresh air.

All animators should be given the chance to leave their cubicle and temporarily breathe fresh air. The producer should give the animator a chance to relax: ping-pong, refreshments, open a balcony so that they can take time out, look at the sky and widen their horizon before they return to work.

Big companies like Google do this. Animation companies, too, depend on the creativity of their artists. Animation producers therefore should go a step further: Why not have "kid's corners" where people can play, reminders of the places of childhood to enhance their motivation?

Producers should respect their employees. Socially, this is particularly difficult in some Asian countries where they still have sort of a caste system, with producers at the top and artists working like slaves and drawing little wages. An artist is no graphic program. An artist is a highly sensitive individual whose feelings are easily hurt.

If the working conditions are miserable, then, being an animator, you have to plan your spare time very consciously. Don't idle away your time but work on your own dreams, on your own imagination, and on your own portfolio. When a producer-director isn't going to give you freedom (only very intelligent producers would do that!), you have to do it yourself. Maybe the future prospects with a different employer will be better, but first you have to work on yourself. Otherwise you are in danger to lose your passion and interest in animation.

Look for a quiet place that suits your equilibrium and provides peace of mind and soul.

You are important—even if producers and directors don't realize this because they only like to push you.

You cannot change them. They are under deadline pressure too.

Ideal would be an office with not so many people around, flowers, colors you like, places to rest—and, above all, good teamwork. Unless you are working for Pixar, this will remain a dream.

In our school time, we had to sit a lot and be attentive, but now we have to get rid of that behavior. We aren't in school anymore. Physiologically, sitting like a pupil in school will damage your back and your head which is bent forward, a rather depressive position.

This way you won't free your mind.

But you will interject that even in your spare time that should be reserved for recreation you depend on the computer: you have to answer e-mails and serve Facebook accounts, have to check Twitter, write blogs, and what else. The computer occupies a lot of human time, in business and in leisure time. But it is not friendly to your body. So you need to exercise.

Never mind. You don't need much time for these exercises.

Referring to the animator's workplace, the optimal position is:

Hands in the neck and chin a little upwards, not downwards, in a very relaxed position.

This is a position you will often notice when you watch stage directors during rehearsals.

Human positions refer not only to different physical configurations but to different states of mind: In one position you will get sad and be depressed, in another one you will be happy. Automatically.

Try yourself. It's easy.

We noticed that there are many depressing short films around. Sometimes, not always, they are an animator's personal cry for help. Nobody ever thought of that. This type of animation is quite lonesome. You have to focus on your animation but you need to move too provided you are sitting all day in front of a computer's cyclops eye.

40

Computer Graphic Characters, Performance Capture Techniques, and the Future of Acting in Animation

Fifteen years ago, Volker Engel, Academy Award winning VFX supervisor of *Independence Day* and for many years one of the closest collaborators of director Roland Emmerich, told us that he couldn't imagine believable digital actresses and actors to take over. He claimed that physical acting in movies always would have a future. Robert Zemeckis tried to prove otherwise and failed. Watching a plastic 3D clone of Tom Hanks walk through *Polar Express* (2004) was pathetic. But Zemeckis didn't give up. He had other name actors like Angelina Jolie and Anthony Hopkins capture his version of the Anglo-Saxon poem *Beowulf* (2007) and Jim Carrey mime a digital Ebenezer Scrooge in Charles Dickens' perennial *Christmas Carol* (2009). Today, with so many real plastic faces around in our real world (thanks to the use of Botox), we can imagine the final triumph of future performers that are artificially created.

A few digitized light rings round the body, in remembrance of the Robotrix in Fritz Lang's *Metropolis* (1926–1927), and you will magically turn from inhuman pixels into a human being. Hundreds of Hollywood actresses and actors have been already scanned and digitized.

Even with today's technology, you still need real actors and link virtual characters to performance capture because, although there are quite realistic virtual reproductions and simulations of humans, they cannot act. (Well, there are many so-called stars who cannot act too.) But it is likely that in the near future they will be able to develop characters purely out of our stored database. Darren Hendler, VFX supervisor at Digital Domain, is convinced, *We are at the point where we can create a digital version of an actor that is indistinguishable from the real person.*[*] There are serious considerations to substitute real actors, to make virtual "humans" conscious of their environment and (artificially) intelligent, and to have them respond to direction automatically. It would be a breakthrough in computer games, too, to have incalculable virtual opponents.

The Cognitive Modeling group at Tübingen University, supervised by Professor Martin Butz, has developed software to create social skills, based on human thinking and behavior, to favorite video game characters such as Mario, Luigi, Yoshi, and Toad. These experiments show what socially intelligent game characters may be capable of in the future.

Just think of obvious AI agents like NPCs (nonplayer characters, false friends) or enemies and monsters. They will duck and roll away from gunfire and try to be ahead of the gamer.

In his dystopian *The Congress* (2013), freely adapted from a novel by the late Polish sci-fi writer Stanisław Lem, Ari Folman, the Israeli director of *Waltz with Bashir* (2008), tried to depict a future that features digital clones of famous actors:

An actress named Robin Wright (and played by real-life Robin Wright) is scanned, every move and microexpression of her. The artificial version is destined to take over from her completely, being exploited eternally. In the world-building view of the future, reality will become fiction and fiction reality.

So will there be a post-biological future to Hollywood? Walt Disney was considered an idiot when he claimed that audiences would be willing to watch animated characters for 70 minutes and more. Then came *Snow White and the Seven Dwarfs*.

So Folman's nightmare vision is not that absurd. Canadian actress Ellen Page jokingly complained about one of the big gaming blockbusters of 2013, the action-adventure survival horror game *The Last of Us* developed by Naughty Dog and published by Sony Computer Entertainment for PlayStation 3, that she didn't appreciate the (unauthorized) likeness between herself and the main character named Ellie: *"I guess I should be flattered that they ripped off my likeness, but I am actually* [voice] *acting in a video game called Beyond Two Souls, so it was not appreciated."* The producers just used, deliberately or not, a digital figure that looked like the *Inception* and *Juno* star.

Is it an absurd thought that we are nothing more than a computer simulation ourselves being run by post-humanists? This was the premise of Daniel Francis Galouye's groundbreaking sci-fi novel *Simulacron 3* (published in 1964) that became the unofficial blueprint for the *Matrix* trilogy. The *New York Times*

---

* Cited in Lucinda Everett, *When will CGI actors replace human ones?* The Telegraph, August 15, 2014.

devoted an article to the odd (computer) simulation hypothesis of Dr. Nick Bostrom, philosopher and director of the Future of Humanity Institute, Faculty of Philosophy, Oxford University, who assumed that the technological advances could produce a computer with more processing power than all the brains in the world, and that advanced humans, or "post humans," could run "ancestor simulations" of their evolutionary history by creating virtual worlds inhabited by virtual people with fully developed virtual nervous systems.*

This is what Nick Bostrom speculates about:

> *Many works of science fiction as well as some forecasts by serious technologists and futurologists predict that enormous amounts of computing power will be available in the future. Let us suppose for a moment that these predictions are correct. One thing that later generations might do with their super-powerful computers is run detailed simulations of their forebears or of people like their forebears. Because their comput-ers would be so powerful, they could run a great many such simulations. Suppose that these simulated people are conscious (as they would be if the simulations would be sufficiently fine-grained and if a certain quite widely accepted position in the phi-losophy of mind is correct). Then it could be the case that the vast majority of minds like ours do not belong to the original race but rather to people simulated by the advanced descendants of an original race. It is then possible to argue that, if this were the case, we would be rational to think that we are likely among the simulated minds rather than among the original biological ones. Therefore, if we don't think that we are currently living in a computer simulation, we are not entitled to believe that we will have descendants who will run lots of such simulations of their forebears. That is the basic idea.†*

If outrageous ideas like these seem to be at least thinkable, why not have arti-ficial actors who are simulations as well command artificial intelligence and live a virtual life of their own?

Helmut Herbst, a German scholar, filmmaker, and animation expert, specu-lated about the volatilization of images throughout the history of imagery. Ever heard of Étienne-Gaspard Robert who called himself Robertson (1763–1837)? He was a Belgian physicist and showman who introduced black backgrounds to the ghostly images of the *Phantasmagoria* slides he projected so that they stood out in the darkness not having borders that would reveal that they are pictures. This was the beginning of what Stanisław Lem once called *phantomatics*: Could they get away today by digitally placing a Marilyn Monroe double being raped by a gorilla? And these *phantomatics* don't need any image carrier. Ghost images, as Herbst claims, multiply into billions and dissolve like the dead.

In the 1980s, Professor Nadia Magnenat Thalmann, a Swiss Canadian com-puter graphics scientist, who was obsessed by Hollywood faces, re-created her

---

* John Tierney, Our Lives, Controlled From Some Guy's Couch. *The New York Times*, August 14, 2007.
† Nick Bostrom, *Are You Living in a Computer Simulation?* Abstract. In Philosophical Quarterly (2003), Vol. 53, No. 211, p. 243.

personal artificial vision of Marilyn Monroe, co-starring with a plastic-faced Humphrey Bogart in *Rendezvous à Montreal*. From then on, in her own MIRALab Research Laboratory at the University of Geneva, Thalmann tried to refine her *Virtual Marilyn*, as a sculptor would do, by using advanced CG technology.

When Thalmann started her project she had to digitize clay models of the actress' face, hands, and so on, but then a process called *Z-Brush* was introduced. It was like having a lump of digital clay that could be sculptured right in the computer.

People might think that the computer makes things easier for the animator but that is not. Of course the artist can review, change, and refine the animation over and over again, but there is still the question of a good performance. But certainly there *is* one advantage: CG animation is fluid and not jerky.

In the beginning, Nadia Thalmann had peculiar ideas how this specimen of resurrection of the dead could be used: TV anchormen and anchorwomen or even politicians who don't master foreign languages could be substituted and dubbed and wouldn't have to speak themselves.

Do they want to sell the idea of having digitized not only the dead but also the living to get rid of the problem of migration and overpopulation? Raymond Kurzweil, an American computer scientist and futurist who speculated about the "algorithms" of the brain and how it "processes data," believes that the Mind–Body Problem discussed for several thousand years can be solved by simply eliminating the human body. Then we would be acting imprisoned in our own dreams and nightmares: lost in a labyrinth of Virtual Reality like Hansel and Gretel in the cyberwoods. In the realm of the cyberworld, we are confronted with our own doppelgängers and avatars. We constantly split ourselves into different units that exist simultaneously.

Besides niches like that occupied by Studio Ghibli, the days of frame-to-frame animation are over and what we get, especially in the universe of games, is a new type of kinetic animation in a world of mostly standardized imagination (which is a contradiction in itself). We cannot change the course of technological history. 3D animation will prevail and we only can hope that 2D will survive as memory of true art.

It seems that true childlike (not childish) imagination and big money are irreconcilable. The market doesn't need imagination. It needs, as we have said, globalization and standardization. But we shouldn't overlook that it also needs creativity: the creative human mind.

A lot of research is being devoted to the question how the mind works. They are discussing the developmental aspects of the mind and the highly interactive modulatory system found in the brain and with it the computational theory of mind. In the mid-1800s, Hermann von Helmholtz (1821–1894), a German physicist, compared the brain to a telegraph. John von Neumann (1903–1957), a Hungarian–American mathematician, drew a parallel between the components of the computing machines of the day and the components of the human brain.

The human mind, however, is more, *much* more than a computer. The question is not if human mind will go cyberspace and achieve immortality through downloading. This was the idea behind the dystopian *Transcendence* (2014) with Johnny Depp as a scientist whose mind was downloaded to the Internet, with fatal results. Humans are organisms, no computers.

Yet there seems to be no way to stop the train as future already besieges present age. It always astonished us how conservative and less visionary the Dreamsmiths of today's visual media are. They don't like to look into the future, do not want to forecast. They content themselves with the vast market opportunities of the status quo. They forget that we set the course for what will happen the next decades, maybe the next centuries. If they suspect something, they silence their conscience: *Devil-may-care.* But we who do care can do something to preserve past and present and humanity: We have to retrieve poetry, music, empathy, not only as retort but spiritually. In short, we have to keep our imagination going.

Therefore we have to train our mind.

You need to be flexible in the turn of eras and self-confidence. Some day the technique of *Brain–Computer Interfaces* will be developed in a way that we can communicate with computing machines, the computing machine will get access to our mind.

So we really need to train.

41

Perceptions Exercises

Particularly animators should train their own eyes to watch. We have mentioned this primary rule repeatedly.

To foster perception and imagination, it is useful to expand the horizon. To do so you can stretch your arms and try to see the fingertips left and right, with your eyes looking straight ahead. This way you determine the scope of your view.

Perception is equally important to actors as well as animators.

You can exercise yourself or in groups (which is good for teamwork). Two groups of persons might sit opposite of each other. One group has covered the eyes. These persons will have the task to smell various ethereal oils and essences. The other group has to watch them carefully, to record and sketch their facial expression while they react to different scent. There are various olfactory stimuli, some smell good, others distasteful. The persons in the first group have to hold that expression for a moment.

Instead of essences you also can use little fruit parts, sweet or sour, salty stuff as well so that they combine to different tastes.

Finally the sketches the persons who are in the second group have made will be compared. What can you tell about eyes, eyebrows, and mouths you see in those sketches? What are the typical characteristics? Find out which drawing is the best record of what we have seen. And in which sketch does the portrayed person recognize himself or herself best?

Then groups will change, and the experiment is repeated vice versa. The objective is to train exact perception and to focus on extreme facial expression.

Watch eyes and eyebrows. Register different frames of mind: excited, amused, angry, sad, and tired.

Meet in a café or some other public place and describe to each other in a group what you see. Watch people closely. How are they clothed? Try to speculate about the people you see. In what mood are they? Can you tell what occupation the people have and maybe invent some stories that have to do with them? You might see a couple and can speculate about the persons' relationship.

Or go to the zoo to sketch animals. Record movements of animals with a camera and analyze them at home.

Watch: All pedestrians follow the same pattern, but the walking cycles are different from each other: No two people have the same walk. Persons differ in size, weight, and speed.

*If a run is to be convincing, the effect of weight must be considered. Basically, you must always remember that the larger the character, the more weight he has to carry. And the more weight that must be carried, the slower the character must move, and the harder it is for the character to control that weight. The animator, therefore, has far more to consider when drawing a fat man running than a thin man.**

---

* Tony White, *The Animator's Workbook*. Oxford: Phaidon Press Limited, 1986, p. 74.

42

Game of Imagination

Maybe you know *Johnny Head-in-the-Air*, the *Struwwelpeter* tale (written by Heinrich Hoffmann) from your own childhood:

As he trudged along to school,
It was always Johnny's rule
To be looking at the sky
And the clouds that floated by.

You can play this game with others, even in competition, preferably in summer days.

Find yourself a pasture or go to a park. Lie down on a blanket and watch the clouds in the sky. Relax.

Guess what you see. If you are with friends ask each other what your imagination suggests that you see.

Do you see an object? Do you recognize an animal? Aren't these human faces?

Protect your eyes. Don't look straight at the sun.

Your friends have to guess what you see and when they are right they will score.

This game shall stagger your imagination and make yourself aware of your childhood. More than a computer, you will need these qualities to become a good animator.

Why don't you invent games of your own?

43

Visualization Techniques
Creatures of the Mind

Even Arnold Schwarzenegger said, "*It's all in the mind. The mind is really so incredible. Before I won my first Mr. Universe title, I walked around the tournament like I owned it. I had won it so many times in my mind, the title was already mine. Then when I moved on to the movies I used the same technique. I visualized daily being a successful actor and earning big money.*"*

You can use visualization techniques at sports or to get self-conscious but you also can use it in a creative way to experience what's inside you.

We cannot deny that someday in the future the human brain will become a veritable interface. Until then, pencils and computers are just tools to translate ideas and creatures that are in your mind.

This is the most important prerequisite of any person who is going to unleash his or her creativity at work.

Everybody has the power of imagination. If you read a thrilling novel, you sure will see the persons and the scenery in your mind's eye. If the tension and suspense are unbearable, then you might feel as if you are yourself in the scenery and have become part of the action.

---

* Cited in John Kehoe, *Mind Power Into the 21st Century.* New Delhi: Sterling Publishers, 1997.

If you see images of the mind at a certain distance, then you call this perceptual position *dissociative*, if you are a part of the scenery and your point of view is inside the scenery, then your position has become *associative*. If you see things from a distance, then your emotional participation is not as strong as if you were right inside the action.

For an animation designer and the animator, both perceptual positions are equally important. If you develop a character, you will start with the exterior shape: a rough sketch, an inspirational, you give it a shot. Experienced designers will have a prototype of the character in their mind. They have seen and studied so many characters that they will associate a character that appears in the script with something they have seen some time. In the best case, a character designer is a walking encyclopedia of cartoon characters. Of course, he will do research and will have reference maps at his disposal. The designer will know how to use clothes (that make people and cartoons) and props (like Sherlock Holmes' pipe) and he will understand the importance of the setting and environment that is part of the character's background. So he will please the expectations of producers and audience likewise. A two-legged mouse will always be inspired by Mickey. Originality is relative. Everything depends on the emotional effect of the character and the emotional effect is based on the writing and certain details which disassociate the mouse from models you have seen before. The detail makes the difference. Animation designers have an encyclopedia of characters recorded in their mind and should know how to use effective details to make the character different. If you have a nice dog, then it maybe will resemble Tintin's white Wire Fox Terrier Milou (or, English: Snowy), if you have a vicious dog then it might be an offspring of the Hound of the Baskervilles. Will a bear look like Baloo? You bet!

Try to dive deep into memory and see the character with your mind's eye.

Once you got your individual Milou, you can try and communicate with the character and learn more about him. He can be your spirit animal guide through the *terra incognita* of your mind.

But until you have reached this level, you will have to train your imagination.

Just try yourself: Take a chair. Sit down. Relax.

Visualization is mental rehearsal. It is the creative skill to imagine. Practice it once a day. Five minutes should be enough.

Of course, some people have greater ability to imagine than others.

You don't need *Pokémon Go*. But this game that links real and virtual world thanks to GPS and Google maps demonstrates how important visualization is, but it's designed for people who like to leave their imagination in the cloakroom: *Get on your feet and step outside to find and catch wild Pokémon. Explore cities and towns around where you live and even around the globe to capture as many Pokémon as you can. As you move around, your smartphone will vibrate to let you know you're near a Pokémon. Once you've encountered a Pokémon, take aim on your smartphone's touch screen and throw a Poké Ball to catch it.*

If you try to imagine something, it is like placing it in front of you. You don't need a *Pokémon* device. We have this mental gift from childhood. So everybody has this ability. It is like dreaming. Everybody dreams.

Just imagine you are lying at the beach.

Different persons will choose different perspectives. One associates, the other will disassociate.

One will see it from the view of the person who actually lies on the beach seeing the water and the sun. This viewer associates. He or she will be one with the person who is on the beach. The other disassociates and will see the scenery from outside. So everything is a question of perspective. Mind the perspective you prefer and try later another one.

For the animator, we will first select an outside perspective because this will be the position the spectator will take.

Try to imagine something else: an object in a certain environment.

Take something that you are familiar with.

Take something very simple.

Imagine a ball.

Focus on it. Don't let anything distract you.

What is the color? Is the ball red, yellow, green, or blue? Does it have dots?

If you see it in front of you, try to turn it around. Try to see it from all angles. Zoom in, zoom out.

You also can try an apple. Cut it in the middle. End the exercise by smelling and tasting the apple. Bite, take three deep breaths. Count from one to five. Then open your eyes.

Select a series of objects of your own choice. Once you master this, you can take the next step which is the important one for animators.

You might now invite an animal. Take it from your own imagination, based on your own criteria. Maybe you will take a white puppy and project the character in front of you.

This might have the effect of a slide or a hologram. Just like this *Pokémon*, that is put into reality but this time not using a mobile device. How big is the animal? Can you try and change the distance of the projected image? As a rule, these imagined objects and animals have often the size of a TV screen but try to make it bigger. If it is small try to zoom in and then try to find out where the character actually is. Is it outside or inside a certain room? We got a myriad of images saved in the library of our brain. When you have determined the location—if it is in a rural landscape or in a certain building—the images will develop in your imagination.

Back to our white puppy. You see him sitting in front of you. Speak softly and say hello to him. Unlike Pokémon, this creature of the mind is living. What does he do? Does he react? Does he answer? What mood he's in? Is he happy?

How does the dog move? How is the tail? Low? Tucked away? Whipping? Swishing? Body language will express the dog's sentiments and needs.

Do you see the animal in 3D? If not, switch to 3D.

Look at the character and say thank you that it appeared without raising your voice.

Take the character that you have invented inside yourself. And wake up.

Rub your face, move your arms, your legs. Shake your limbs.

Return *slowly* to daily life. Do not rush. Take your time. Take a mental break.

This was your first encounter with a character you have invented by your own projection.

You have to study the animal's body language. You don't have to use your own body as an animator but you have to perceive the typical expression and mood. You know it from your watching exercises.

You can exercise to get into a character. And you always will be as good as your imagination was in your childhood.

For these exercises, you need a sober mind (no alcohol, no drugs). You will have your head on straight and can stop the process any time. You will stay in the here and now. You will know that even if you are going to be a bird, you cannot fly in reality. You are like an actor who is taken up in his part. But take your time before you leave your home or do any driving. (The authors cannot accept any responsibility. So please be careful. Finish the exercises well.)

Some rules concerning conversation with imaginary characters: Ask simple questions. Be patient. Don't push. Don't use negations. Be honest and respectful.

Potential Problems with Visualization

Visualization doesn't work like television: Push a button and the movie starts.

You need to be prepared. You have entered a quiet room. You are completely relaxed and you are able to focus on the exercise. Your eyes are closed. But nothing happens. No living characters show up. You want to meet this little dog again. But after 10 minutes there is no dog. You have prepared an imaginary room just for that dog, with a bowl of delicious food. But still no animal.

Maybe the puppy is too shy. Ask yourself if there is a reason why the dog doesn't show up. Maybe it had bad experiences resulting from encounters with other humans. Wait a little and if you don't get an answer say thanks to the dog that he found time for you because the animal is sure nearby. You can make a new appointment and ask if the dog will have time for you later. If the puppy still doesn't come, just imagine a different animal. Maybe there is a cat that wants to get your attention.

But it might be that you are not a cat's person, that you dislike cats. In this case, your subconscious mind will refuse to let a cat in. Interestingly enough, many households have cats but in myths as well as in animation cats, as we have seen already, are often antagonists.

All living beings, real as well as imaginary ones, do not appear at the flick of a switch. They ask for your full attention. These characters have to be treated with utmost respect. Never ever humiliate them. There might, for instance, a character be around that looks quite funny to you, but don't ridicule him. Don't laugh about, laugh *with* him. The friendlier you treat these imaginations, the more will show up and your subconscious mind will have a ball calling them up.

Now invite a human. Take somebody you know well, a relative maybe.

Take other characters so that you can switch roles.

Try to get inside the various characters. Try to understand and feel them.

You will argue and say that as an animator you have to work with fixed characters. So if you are able take one of those or a scene you are involved in.

Try to imagine the area where the scene is going to take place.

Maybe it's the forest, with trees, bird song, and scents. Locate the setting on a mental map. Add more and more details: moisture after rain—you smell it—, moss—you feel it under your feet—, a small river—you hear it fleet—, a lake, maybe some obstacles.

After a while, you will arrive at a clearing.

Imagine you were asked to create a fox hunt which was popular in many old cartoons. Have you seen Donald Duck and Goofy in *The Fox Hunt* that was released in 1938?

This time, however, you will have a realistic fox hunt, no comic.

Imagine the various characters, the hunters and the hunted: the riders, the mixed field of horses, the hounds, and the fox.

Try to get in touch with them.

How do they feel? Try to switch roles. You have to understand both, the hunters *and* the hunted.

Hunting the fox, you see him as a red spot from behind. After a while, you might have a cut and change your point of view. You are now, so to speak, inside the fox. You don't have to become a Charles Foster who wrote a book *Being a Beast*.* Foster is an eccentric British naturalist who really has been on all fours to become a badger, an otter, or an urban fox, and live like an animal to reconnect with his inner beast.

Feel hunted yourself. Feel the hunting instinct of your pursuers in your neck. Change of perspective is important, inwardly and outwardly.

There are questions that both, actors and animators, will ask in the beginning to understand a character: Where do I come from? Where do I go to? What mood I am in?

If you are inside the character, it becomes *you.*

Acting is always reacting. You are reacting to an insult or mental scars. Then you will have a motive for doing something. The reaction can explode into some action. You might try to punish, hit the person who has hurt you. I have become one with the character I am going to portray.

Very important: Deep respect, understanding, empathy, maybe a little love are absolutely essential for the creative treatment of your characters.

* Charles Foster, *Being a Beast*. London: Profile Books Ltd., 2016.

Do you realize that by visualizing you are telling a story, that you are acting through separate characters?

Talk to your characters and let them act on your imaginary stage.

Tricks You May Use in the Process of Visualization

Let's suppose that you are going to imagine some particular scenery, for instance a child at a kitchen table eating soup. You are relaxed. But you see—nothing. Why? Well, maybe the whole scenery is located behind a wall in another room. Try to imagine you are in a theater, in the orchestra, and in front of you there is a curtain. Open the curtain to see the scene. If this doesn't work and nothing is to be seen, turn the light on.

Sometimes a scene is hidden behind a door. Now there always is a reason why characters don't show up immediately. Respect your subconscious mind, the location of your imagination. If you don't feel well simply, stop the exercises and try again later. Maybe you regard all of this as too childish. Then stop too. There are other ways to find access to your characters.

Very often, these mental blocks are a result of our education. As children we often heard our parents tell us: *Don't dream!* Of course there was a meaning to bring us kids back to reality because we had to focus on what we had to do in school. But, alas, imagination would suffer. So ask yourself if there is somebody who forbids you to do these exercises: Parents? Teachers? Get it straight to your mind that you have to get access to the full potential of your imagination to make your work better. There is nothing to fear but fear itself. You have made your way from school to a professional career to everybody's pleasure. You can master the real tasks at each time. You can draw, you can operate a computer. But assure yourself that you don't lose touch with reality. Differentiate between fiction and reality.

Fear of Your Own Imagination

Is there an anxiety to meet a certain imaginary character? Zoom out. The image and with it the character that has intimidated you a moment ago will get smaller. The fright will disappear. Now you can ask yourself what made the character so awkward and change him.

Many years ago, I (AK) taught drama students who were in the final year of their education how to lose mental blocks by means of mental training. These students were trained and sensitized but didn't know about mental training. One of them had the problem that he spoke with a voice that rang as clear as a bell. His voice was so beautiful because it was excessively soft. He spoke stilted and clearly would have failed in a naturalistic theatre performance. The student and I were in a large room that was absolutely quiet. I asked him if he had a block and where this block was. Suddenly he saw a dwarfish creature jumping out of his body. For a moment he was shocked and cried, *"Kill him! Kill him!"* His visualization was so intense and specific that both of us saw this gnome. I comforted the young actor, took his hand and both of us left the gnome. Then we compared our images and realized that the character we imagined looked similar. The gnome, the poor creature, was stunned himself about what had happened.

Of course such spectacular sessions are very rare. Particularly actors are trained for years concerning sensitivity and imagination. Besides his handicap, speaking way too beautiful, the drama student was naturally gifted. During our exercise, we carefully approached the gnome until the student could empathize with the dwarf. Playing the gnome himself, the young man could experience how maltreated the gnome was whom a short while ago he wanted to kill. He would identify with the gnome, reconcile with him and accept him as part of his own personality. This exercise lasted for one-and-a-half up to 2 hours. The acceptance of this seemingly negative part of his own self helped the student.

A psychiatrist would have asked: Where does the gnome come from? But our duty is to understand the mental block and to visualize it, to enter a communication with its product and re-integrate it into the own personality. (At that time I re-assured, however, with a psychoanalyst who wasn't present during the sessions.)

After these exercises, the young actor underwent a change. He would grow and become more virile. He became a good actor. He dared to play ugly, not only beautiful parts.

He fundamentally lost his mental block.

This was an exception. But it tells us that we shouldn't be afraid to see what we are seeing.

As an actor you are tied to your body and a single person that you portray, as an artist you have much more creative freedom (and power over different characters, like a director has). Unless you improvise or you ad-lib as an actor, you have a structure, you have co-players, and you have lines. Everything is fixed when rehearsals are finished. The artist, however, will draw and then, somehow, there will be a moment of magic when a character will look to you.

The animator doesn't have to learn and know what an actor has to train for years: voice training, physical training, dancing, fencing, and what else. All this he doesn't need.

Criticism wouldn't harm an animator less than an actor because he can change and draw another character.

Artists are much more abstract. Their work consists of stylization and their perception of art. It's important that an animator knows anatomy, but he doesn't need to become a physician. Different from live action, you are able to stretch and squash your characters. You are able to do more than live actors. Much more. Like Phoenix out of the ashes, your characters seem to have more than one life. Each time they are finished off, they rise from the dead. Animation conquers death, overcomes it a hundred times while theatrical plays celebrate death.

This is the freedom of animation: to fool reality and see the things behind.

Now you enter the realm of fantasy, the state of the shaman.

In shamanism, trance is an antenna to have mystic experience without using drugs. It is similar to a natural view of the world. Trance in its extreme is an extra-physical experience. The spirit world is, according to one's own point of view or religion, experienced as real. Trance is an ancient kind of spiritual experience. We follow a different pattern and see in the state of trance the means of supporting creativity. Trance exists on different levels. The daily conscience is blanked out and the subconscious will receive space. This is the whole potential of imagination: the material that dreams are made of. Animators are no necromancers. They are people of imagination. The only question is how to set it free. The subconscious shall be fully "exploited." But how will I get into that state?

This state is between dreaming and being awake. It is a state of absolute quietness and concentration. Fade out daily routine. Past and future are irrelevant. You are only here and now.

Sit down on a chair or lay down on a sofa or bed and close your eyes. Focus on your breath. Try to relax. For creative work, deep relaxation with deep concentration at the same time is a prerequisite. This technique is used too when coaching athletes or actors to cure stage fright. Some actors use that technique in preparation for film scenes and in preparation of role studies. Certain film scenes are mentally prepared. This is a dry run.

We suggest that you use the same technique for imagination, for dreaming up characters. The imagination is being trained in a way that you will enter into straight communication with the character. You even can take a step further. You can have a dialogue with these characters. Although these are figures that come from your own imagination, they are linked to the subconscious mind. You have cut back everyday consciousness. In this process of visualization, it is important to stay relatively unprejudiced. Do not be too critical. Do not suffocate imagination. Be patient and exercise to enter this state, preferably in a quiet room, relaxed, no mobile phones, no computer, or TV screen around. Just focus on yourself.

In Edgar Allan Poe's *The Masque of the Red Death* (made into a 1969 short by Zagreb Film), Prince Prospero entrenches behind the walls of his castle. Follow him through rooms of different color: blue, purple, green, orange, white, violet, and black (illuminated by a scarlet light) where fate strikes. Each color makes you feel different.

Maybe you will have problems to imagine a villain, an evil character. You might be afraid because inside yourself you won't feel any evil. The knowledge of the gallery of the biggest villains in world history will not help you. Did you ever meet a baddie or a corrupt person? Sure. There always is somebody who has hurt you? Try to remember. Well, you found the guy you love to hate. This person will guide you to understand villainy. And suddenly the feeling is inside me because I remember how angry I was. With such a feeling it will be easier to imagine and invent a villain. It's not about evil in general but the individual understanding of evil.

But at the same time, being inside the villain, you have to understand his deeds to make him believable and not a cliché.

Well then, the character has appeared and you could watch him from all angles, heroes as well as villains.

You were able to establish a contact with the character.

You have given the character space to develop his own personality and have treated him in a friendly and polite manner.

You have given him life of his own.

Due to respectful treatment of the imagined character, you can extract more information out of your subconscious mind.

Imagination is given more space. The imagination is being trained. And you can control your imagination with this technique.

Not only will you make a figure visible, you develop a deeper understanding of the character.

Now you can proceed.

You may ask the imagined character to help you.

You can ask the character (silently) to support you to carry out his optimal creation, to describe a situation he is involved in: scenario, background, scent, and the whole state of mind.

You can ask the characters to cooperate with their own design.

You can ask and make a deal with the figure, while you sleep, to continue developing on his own character according to role profiles and a certain scene or given situation.

Ask the character to agree.

Then say thanks, open your arms and take the character in.

After that, return to daily life.

Don't think about what happened. Let your subconscious mind work.

The next day you will realize that "he" has worked strongly inside you. Something has evolved. Maybe unusual solutions have been found. Often these characters show humor. They are unconventional and develop funny ideas. You will be astonished.

You also can ask the character to bring a friend. You will realize how your stage, the cinema in your head is filling.

What advantage is it to treat an imagined character like a living being?

If I grant the characters life of their own I allow them access to my whole knowledge, even that which is buried in my subconscious mind.

In daily life, our brain inhales incredible amounts of information. But we are forced to fade out big chunks of this information immediately just to master our daily affairs. Otherwise, our brain would overheat.

People who are suffering from the savant syndrome give us an example. Sometimes they have incredible abilities. Some of them are able to learn an unknown language in brief time. Others have mind-boggling mathematical skills. One sees briefly a location (a town) and can draw an exact map of the place.

These genius people, however, have problems to manage their daily affairs. To keep social contacts is a real problem for them.

Normal people use a big part of their brain capacities for managing their social life. Therefore, they eliminate other important parts. We are totally occupied with the little things of daily life which absorb our mind.

In principle, this proves the great but unexplored abilities of the human brain.

The lively contact will bring the experience of new expressions. It will surprise you and you will not remain trapped in the narrow repertoire of standard facial play and gestures.

This is the problem an actor has when repeating his role for the span of a hundred performances or more. Each evening anew, actors must naively immerse themselves into a role and certain situation. This way the character will not rust but remain fresh as in the first performance.

Even if you are only a small cog in the entertainment machine of show business, you will find that your part and contribution will not develop that uninteresting cleanness but offer new challenges.

Art needs creative freedom.

We mentioned the Disney Method. That means that in a creative process all ideas should be allowed: no self-censorship. Out of hundred ideas, one will work. A heady critic will cut out a possibly absurd idea immediately. This means you will sacrifice worthwhile ideas too early, like that of having a rat in the kitchen.

Disney is credited with granting this mental freedom to his artists, but the reality in the Disney Studios was different when it became a factory with hundreds of employees. The family atmosphere would slowly vanish.

The exercises mean to keep the critic inside us in check so that no flower is culled too early. Creativity is highly vulnerable. Persons who work in creative fields are highly sensitive and feel easily hurt.

By respectful and relaxed treatment of characters, we give them time to develop in our mind.

So producers have to be psychologists, no steamrollers. Time is money—but you cannot churn out good ideas. You don't need to be rushed (as you are in many low-production productions and series).

Remember the words of the great Max Reinhardt who compared acting with mementos from the childhood. There should be no end to childhood. For a child it is easy to bring a toy alive in his or her imagination. If a kid has a small plastic knight, he might envision a medieval fortress. Or by playing with a little toy horse, children might dream themselves into the Wildest West.

Good examples are the crudely animated plastic toys from the French-language Belgian stop action *A Town Called Panic (Panique au village)*, a series of 5-minute shorts: the everyday events of the small figurines of three roommates, Cowboy, Indian and, as the main character, Horse, in a rural village. There certainly is not much animation used to move these mostly stiff figures, but they have character and personality. The producers, Stéphane Aubier and Vincent

Patar, play it out like children who have toy figures. Everything will end in a mess and anarchic madness, from village to inferno.

In 2009, a 75-minute *Panic* feature was released and amazingly it was not boring to watch the hilarious stop action:

Everybody talks like little kids. Indian and Horse are on the same scale, about twice as tall as Cowboy, though nobody notices this. They get around fine on their little platforms, even climbing stairs. Horse, who has four legs and can balance without a platform, takes Farmer's kids to Madame Longree for music lessons and falls in love with Madame, who is also a horse and plays the piano with her hooves pretty well.

The most frequent line of dialogue in this enchanting world is "Oh, no!" One strange thing happens after another. You wouldn't believe me if I told you how Horse, Indian and Cowboy all end up perched precariously on a rock slab above a volcano at the Earth's Center, or how they get from there to the middle of an ocean and the North Pole, or how they happen upon a mad scientist and his robot, named Penguin, or the excuses Horse uses on his cell phone to explain to Madame Longree why he hasn't turned up for his piano lessons. Or why it rains cows.

Like children, they've been constructing their own absurdist, chaotic world. Here it's really *Cloudy with a Chance of Meatballs*. No computer has been used. The budget was comparatively low. To be fully creative, you first and foremost need a kid's corner to set your imagination free.

As adults we will have to re-learn childlike imagination: what they call the sense of wonder.

You have to be on the same wavelength with your characters.

It is as if *Pinocchio* would get alive and speak to you. You sit across and breathe life into him. You are like mad Stromboli, the owner of the puppet theater in Disney's film, who sees his marionettes including Pinocchio dance by themselves.

We mentioned Argentine stop-motion filmmaker Juan Pablo Zaramella repeatedly in the pages of this book. In 2004, he did a lovely 17-minute stop-motion tale titled *Viaje a Marte* that summarizes the whole essence of what animation should be: Watching Sci-Fi on TV, Antonio, a little boy, has the dream of travelling to Mars. His grandfather tells him that he knows how to get there. In his truck, he takes the boy to an unearthly spot (that was amazingly created by tabletop animation!). At school, the classmates tease the boy when he claims to have been on Mars with his grandpa. When he has grown up, a family man who has almost forgotten the adventure trip with grandpa who has passed away since, astronauts are finally on their way to Mars. Suddenly—miraculously—he finds his tow truck stranded on the same unearthly ground that he has visited as a child—and sees the astronauts landing in front of him: Animation to stagger the imagination. (Zaramella told us that the plot was based on the true story of

---

* *A Town Called Panic* (2009), reviewed by Roger Ebert on January 13, 2010. Review originally published in 2010 in *Chicago Sun-Times*.

a Latin American boy who dreamed of living in California and was taken by his grandfather to a place that looked like California.)

You are going to play with externalized characters, but they come from your own subconscious mind. And you are going to join these characters exploring strange new worlds, boldly going where no man has gone before.

This will be the future of *imagination*. We should be capable to create our own type of animation that will not be tied to a cinema or TV screen but straight to imagination. The human mind will create new worlds populated by colorful creatures mentally—and you will be part of the action.

Not today, not tomorrow but certainly the day after tomorrow.

Then our mind will become a cinema in its own right. But it shouldn't replace, no, it should enhance real life. We have to be aware that there are great dangers: the dangers of a virtual matrix. Yet our thoughts, experiences, and behavior should evolute and blossom by the power of creativity and imagination.

That it will happen one day, we are sure—and beyond that, we are certain, later generations will look upon our early efforts as upon childish stuttering.

Hahn Film & Super RTL present   ARABIAN NIGHTS - THE UNTOLD STORIES

Designs from *Sherazade: The Untold Stories* that started as a 2D project (images above) and was cancelled in the aftermath of 9/11. Fifteen years later it was revived and made in 3D (images below). (Courtesy of Hahn Film, Germany/ Chocolate Liberation Front, Australia/Toonz Entertainment, India.)

PART III
Q & A

We have sent out questionnaires to animators, producers, directors, VFX practitioners, historians, and scholars around the world not only to receive a response from different positions in filmmaking and film reception but also to get an intercultural point of view to the topic from people in the United States, New Zealand, China and Asia, and various European countries.

44

The Animation Film Historian

Giannalberto Bendazzi

Giannalberto Bendazzi (born in 1946 in Ravenna, raised in Milan) is a leading animation historian. In 1994, he published *Cartoons: One Hundred Years of Cinema Animation*, and in 2016, the 3-volume *World History of Animation*. In 2002, the Animafest Zagreb honored him with the *Award for Outstanding Achievement in Animation Theory*.

Q: What is it that makes a cartoon character a personality? Is it the acting? Is it the writing, the design, or just the emotional tie to the audience?

A: I would say "a star" instead of "a personality." In my opinion, what makes a star out of a character are of course all the things that are listed in the question. PLUS special, uncontrollable charisma that radiates from that drawing, or that actor or that actress. Nobody ever could create a star using a recipe. Mr. Magoo (for instance) was born exactly by chance. In John Hubley's *Ragtime Bear* (1949) we see an old, shortsighted and grouchy man with his nephew up in the mountains. He has to do with a well designed and psychologically appealing bear. Everybody thought that this was the pilot for a series on the bear. The public roared at the old pest, instead.

Q: Are there any particular cartoon characters that have impressed you—and why?

A: I have a soft spot for Miyazaki Hayao's *Porco Rosso*. I think it is just a personal reaction to the setting and the story and the times. As far as acting is concerned, I love Mickey Mouse in *Brave Little Tailor*. The performance is outstanding.*

Q: More than any live actors, cartoon characters seem to express their feeling with their eyes.

A: Let me be horrendously down-to-earth: a live actor has much smaller eyes, in proportion with the rest of the body, than the average cartoon character!

Q: How have cartoon characters changed from 2D to 3D?

A: A 3D character has many more body and face muscles to move, in order to act. The beautiful cat of the Shrek theatrical series would have been much weaker in 2D.

Q: What would you recommend animators should do to create, visualize, and feel themselves into cartoon characters?

A: They should act themselves! And later, exaggerate what they have acted.

Q: As a historian: What can a new generation of cartoon creators learn from animation film history?

A: Character animation is a specifically American contribution to the international art of animation (I'm quoting John Canemaker). There is a century-long tradition for young American animators to learn and understand. They should behave with this tradition the way a creative mind should behave with any tradition: either contradict it, or renew it. Copying the masters is for unimaginative people.

---

* Mickey Mouse was animated by Fred Moore (1911–1952), who also redesigned Mickey for his appearance in *The Sorcerer's Apprentice* segment in *Fantasia* (1940).

45

The VFX Artist

Robert Blalack

Robert Blalack (born in 1948 in Canal Zone, Panama) has one Academy Award to his credit having done the optical composites for the original George Lucas *Star Wars* (1977), using (before the advent of the digital age) an optical printer that was designed by another award winner, Larry Butler. Robert Blalack is now living in Paris.

Q: We seem to be on the threshold to a new Virtual Age, in the stone age of what they call Virtual Reality which must be a challenge for animators and pretty tough for traditional actresses and actors. What changes will that bring to the movie industry?

A: How will VR change the movie industry? The movie business model is rooted in the audience thirst for empathetic characters and engaging story. The movie audience participates via observation of and empathy with a condensed, focused replication of real or imagined life.

VR is a technique platform that delivers an unrestricted visual and audio view of a real or synthetic world, presented today on a screen that encompasses peripheral vision, usually with goggles, wherein the VR audience can interact with people or objects with tactile feedback.

VR needs to answer the question of what it offers to satisfy the thirst of the movie audience. If I'm a gamer, I may hunger to be deep up inside the game world and its inhabitants? If I'm a porn enthusiast, I may ache to imagine breaking the third wall, so I can "reach out and touch someone"?

If I'm a movie lover, I wonder why VR is not just Stereo 3D on steroids, which I know has not enhanced the core of any movie story and smells like marketing perfume sprinkled on the Emperor's funky clothes? Have I not been conned before by the movie marketing promises of thrills never delivered?

VR has impacted the movie business as a tool for pre-production design and production, used to visually articulate a movie's environment, actor performances, camera lighting and framing. VR used for this purpose empowers filmmakers with another iteration tool, different from the perennial hand-drawn storyboard but fulfilling the same role as a clarifying tool. There's enormous power in clear communication, no matter what the message. VR iterations can help refine a filmmaker's interior vision, which lives in its own non-reality, and bring those usually hazy visions into the specific and concrete components that make up a movie.

VR can be a creative and production cost clarifying and savings tool, when employed for Hollywood visual extravaganzas, so it's going to get more development and use in movie production. Today's consumers get a taste of this iterative visualization use of VR with Augmented Reality enabled smart phones, where the consumers can, in real time, place various 3D models of IKEA furniture in their home and decide what fits. Or the soon to be realized business opportunity of CG models of potential Internet dates/mates, fit in real time into the buyer's home or bedroom?

To appeal to the movie audience, VR will need to engage and merge the solo headset audience into one interconnected virtual world? VR will not challenge the traditional movie experience until VR morphs into a communal "VR Movie Theater," where hundreds, thousands, or millions of people are simultaneously experiencing the same VR regardless of where the VR audience is.

WHY I want to spend my money and my time in a VR movie is the question VR artists have to answer by delivering the "revolutionary" Star Wars of VR.

Q: Is this new age the beginning of a new art form that is going to challenge the human brain or will it restrict the human mind because to most people it might be a network of social fake?

A: Any technique becomes an art form only when worked by artists? VR artists struggle with every artist's challenge: WHY must an audience spend its time and money experiencing my CONTENT? If VR artists can deliver compelling answers to both these enduring real world questions, VR will progress from a technique to an art form.

VR will "challenge the human brain" in expansive or constrictive directions depending on the particular VR artist's skill and objectives. For some, it may offer no more than claustrophobic nausea.

46

The Creator from Italy

Bruno Bozzetto

Bruno Bozzetto (born in 1938 in Milan) created his first animation short, *Tapum, the History of Weapons* in 1958 when he was 20. When only a few companies in Europe tried to compete with Disney on the animated feature film field, between 1965 and 1976, he produced *West and Soda, Vip, Mio Fratello Superuomo,* and *Allegro Non Troppo.* In 1987, in *Trouble in Paradise,* he worked with live actors too. Today, he devotes his time to 2D as well as 3D computer animation. In 1991, his film *Cavalette* was nominated for an Academy Award for Best Animated Short. His most famous character is named *Signor Rossi.*

Q: At the time you created Signor Rossi there was a change in animation, artistically: from Disney to UPA and Zagreb style, economically from full to limited TV animation. Did it help you cost-wise and what did it mean in regard to designing characters that were human, no anthropomorphic Disney animals?

A: The creation of Rossi and his graphical simplicity surely helped a lot from the economical point of view. I can say, though, the idea to switch to human beings in particular is Canadian-rooted, if you think of the National Film Board, and was partly inspired by Zagreb Film. I got to know their festival films of which I grew enthusiastic. The decisive inspiration came from Ward Kimball (*Toot, Whistle, Plunk and Boom*) from Disney.

Q: What "typical" Italian features does Signor Rossi reflect? Is he sort of a prototype Italian?

A: I can't really tell. He originated from a real story that I personally lived. In the beginning Rossi was supposed to be a sort of caricature of myself, of my friends and of my father, too. The character was the mirror of everybody's daily attitudes that I used to observe and that I myself at times had. Then, with the passing of time, he changed and, having to adapt to what the television demanded, he underwent a sort of transformation becoming fit for the young audiences.

Q: *West and Soda*, at that time one of the first big feature-length animated productions in Europe, parodies the genre of Italian (or Spaghetti) Western, even before *Django* came out. Did you study the work of Sergio Leone and how did you design the characters according to their counterparts in feature films?

A: I didn't know Sergio Leone back then. We began making parodies of the Western films simultaneously. My biggest inspiration was, above all, the movie *Shane* featuring Alan Ladd and Jack Palance, and the great classics by John Ford. Anyway, *West & Soda* is the result of the everlasting passion I, as a boy (and still now), had for the Western films as a genre.

Q: Did comic books, as fumetti an acknowledged part of Italian culture, serve as a springboard when you prepared *VIP, My Brother Superman* (1968) about two brothers, the Adonis-like SuperVip and slim MiniVip?

A: MiniVip originates from the *Phantom* (by Lee Falk and Ray Moore), a comic strip I loved as a kid.

Q: What can you tell about the work with your voice actors and actresses?

A: During the making of our films we had no original voices of our own. At the end we had them dubbed by Italian dubbers who were very famous back then. [Oreste Lionello, one of the founders of modern Italian cabaret, as MiniVip. Among those he dubbed were Chaplin, Groucho Marx, Dick Van Dyke, Peter Sellers, and Woody Allen.]

Q: You also worked with live actors in front of the camera. What's the difference between directing live and animated characters?

A: I think the difference consists in the fact that it is much easier to direct a sketch than an actor. This is because drawing requires time and thinking while interacting with an actor implies immediate decisions. And for someone who comes from the animation industry this is very difficult.

Q: *Allegro Non Troppo* had that wonderful, masterful evolutionary *Fantasia* spoof, where all living emerges from a Cola bottle. Was it difficult to time movement and action to classic music (Ravel's famous *Bolero*)? How important is musical score to you? How important is it to underline action and define characters?

A: To respect the time movement is always very difficult but it rewards you with great satisfaction because you have the chance to work on highly valuable material which grants to keep the film together within a solid structure. Music is very important to me and it sort of opens the way to both, the story and the characters.

Q: How did 2D and 3D computer animation change your work?

A: 3D adds up more technology but sensibly increases the costs of production. Personally, I still don't see any change in the way a story is being told. The framings, the acting and the actions depend on the story and not on the used technique.

Q: Animation-wise, are there any characters outside your work that you find interesting and worth studying?

A: I believe that it is important and interesting to study mankind and its behavior. It is and will always be the biggest source of inspiration for the subjects and the stories.

Q: Is there anything in particular you would like to save from the days of classic animation into the digital future?

A: The direct human contact, the exchange of views and of personal information that today we risk losing because of the impersonality and distance between the artists working on a project.

The Replacement Animators from Argentina

Alberto Couceiro and Alejandra Tomei

Born in Buenos Aires, the couple lives in Berlin since 1992. Alberto Couceiro studied animation in Potsdam-Babelsberg and specialized in stop motion, while Alejandra Tomei focused on directing, character design, and digital image processing and compositing. After the great success of their stop-motion *TV City* at the Cannes Film Festival in 2003, they founded their own studio Animas Film. *TV City* was screened at the Museum of Modern Art in New York, the puppets were on display at the Jilin Animation Institute in Changchun, China. At the Berlin Film Festival in 2015, another short film, *Automatic Fitness*, was shown that won awards at film festivals round the world.

Q: **You don't work in front of a computer screen. You still favor the traditional process of replacement puppet animation. What's the challenge to work physically with puppets and not with all those digital tools?**

A: Alejandra Tomei: I like the real world most, the world of objects, a world that is haptic, a world that you can touch. This is the place where I feel well, about which I can talk most.

Every man-made object has its story, an existence that talks to me. These objects have their own logic. The objects which we create in our studio develop by and by their own "soul" which we try to understand. The challenge is to share these stories through our films with other people.

Alberto Couceiro: Stop motion is one of the oldest techniques in cinematography. It combines various other techniques.

To create armatures for instance one must gain expertise in metal working and for the puppet construction you need to combine a lot of materials. The task to build sets and models is a world of its own. Then there is the traditional craftsmanship like photography and lighting and now we got digital image processing.

In all these fields we have to experiment, master each technique, we have to know the various materials to produce a result of high quality. This is one of the challenges working with puppets and working physically. It's real handiwork in a world which as a result of digitalization becomes more and more abstract and incomprehensible.

For independent artists and filmmakers it is a great obligation to maintain and develop all these techniques more or less under one roof.

We are moving into a wide and open world of objects for which you need time and space, a scarce commodity in our era.

Q: Do you consider it a niche that allows you to work as individuals?

A: Alejandra Tomei: That was not meant to be our marketing concept. By experimenting we developed over the years a style of our own so that I know for sure how things and figures should look like and how ideas should be realized.

Alberto Couceiro and Alejandra Tomei. (Courtesy of Animas Film.)

Alberto Couceiro: After so many projects that we did there certainly evolved something like an individual style. The more you build an animation studio and develop the technical infrastructure as means of creativity, the more ideas you will get and develop a way how to produce your individual kind of images.

Q: How do you establish a relationship with the puppets, how do you determine their performance, not only technically speaking but mentally? How do you time and visualize the movements and the performance in advance?

A: Alejandra Tomei: Ideas grow out of little things, out of certain situations that we have watched carefully. Daily life delivers lots of ideas out of which absurd and funny images and reflections will evolve. These impressions become concrete visions of film plots. This is the basic material for the animation.

Alberto Couceiro: In our early stages we had prepared exposure sheets, we made notes and used other aids. Often we used a stop watch, a metronome, and pantomime. We reenacted and timed scenes so that we could translate the structure of the plot into a series of images and make a plan. These were means to get confident in abstract animation.

Specifically in productions we did with 35 mm cameras and analogue technique we needed more preparation before shooting a take than today. The shooting process was connected with big technical expenditure and high costs.

The digital technique and digital photography has opened up enormous new possibilities for stop motion. Small and light equipment is sufficient to shoot high-quality images. You get the result at once. You can process the images in different ways and much more… We are able to work spontaneously and use our intuition.

Usually I start animating now without much preparation and thoughts given to the movement.

Of course the many years of experience and the new developments of technology are helpful.

I get involved almost casually into intuitive play with animation. One image brings me to the next and the animation often moves by itself. Breaks are made where rhythm needs them, and we let the movements flow.

If everything goes well and animation is done with the utmost concentration (in a time of diversion and distraction this is a mental state that is not self-evident) you get a feeling for images and the length of scenes. You are like a sculptor who carves as if the form is already engraved in the stone. You take pot luck by the movements that develop frame after frame in front of your camera.

Q: There are those tiny, unexpected details that seem to make up the distinctiveness of a puppet and charm the audience, right?

A: Alejandra Tomei: Although usually everything is thought out beforehand it is the discovery of little details that gain our attention.

Alberto Couceiro: Surprise is the fascinating and magical part about animation. The unexpected is what makes animation special. One cannot easily reproduce these moments. Puppet play and movements are being built in one session, a scene in a few hours, in front of the camera, frame by frame. It depends on many other factors. It is a "live-play" which takes place between animator and figure, and the whole movement can be seen several hours after single-frame shooting. Then it's the details that determine beauty and charm. One is always looking for such moments. It's a subtle perception. You cannot say why a certain animation scene is beautiful. The reason must be that it has the certain something that is so hard to describe. It's always these tiny details that make us recognize life and charm. This is our motivation to go on and animate and bring these figures to life: to look for a human character and find yourself.

Q: Are there any outstanding achievements in the history of stop motion or more recent examples that you would like to recommend to fellow animators?

A: Alejandra Tomei: I'm seeing always new animation films at festivals that surprise me. Often I forget the titles and names involved. Regarding stop motion and animation in general it's often the short films that inspire and motivate me to start a film project. In this field filmmakers experiment a lot so that you can discover always things that you haven't seen before. There are numerous animation films that you see exclusively at festivals, films that are really mind-blowing.

In film history most names that come to my mind are not related to animation and stop motion. I would like to mention Murnau, Fritz Lang, Hitchcock, Bunuel, David Lynch. These are directors that inspired me a lot.

Alberto Couceiro: I would like to mention the old films of Ray Harryhausen and the old Czechoslovkian films by Karel Zeman and Jiří Trnka. Also the 1970s and 1980s with Jan Švankmajer, the Brothers Quay, Barry Purves, and the cut-out animation by Terry Gilliam that had an influence on us. Of course names such as Nick Park and Tim Burton are extremely important too.

Q: You are working in extremely confined studio spaces.

A: Alberto Couceiro: As a beginner you always can work in small rooms and accomplish something working with little figures. But then the time will come that a room proves to be too small, but beginners will continue to work out of small cabins, in garages, basement rooms. These are locations where one will begin.

Alejandra Tomei: You can always do something in the room that you have. I have seen this by watching colleagues. Everybody must deal with the possibilities he got.

More ideal would be larger rooms and professional studios. But small rooms must not be an obstacle. The ideas have to correspond with the conditions of limited studio space. Important are quiet workshops where you can work over a long time.

Q: As stop-motion animators you are like long-distance runners. You are animating everything yourself, with no assistant's helping hand. This affords even more time.

A: Alberto Couceiro: Our strength is endurance and self-discipline. We work on our films as long as necessary, according to requirements and aspiration. Sometimes the conditions are not optimal, and there is a certain kind of self-exploitation.

I have to admit that the production conditions of our last projects were not always the best ones to save production time. We were forced to interrupt shooting to do commissioned work which will bring in the money we need to finance our own productions.

Alejandra Tomei: The means we had at hand were extremely low. We couldn't pay a big team. There was no other choice than to produce in the long view and do many things yourself.

Q: This process requires a lot of patience and humility we guess.

A: Alberto Couceiro: Patience is a prerequisite in any technique of animation.

Q: What can you tell about the international stop-motion scene? Is there something like a renaissance of stop motion thanks to films like *Anomalisa* and *Kubo & the Two Strings*?

A: Alberto Couceiro: There are many new small studios that spring up like mushrooms, and there is a new generation of filmmakers that is very interested in puppet animation. At the same time we see more and more stop motion in advertisement and TV.

Q: Can you describe some of your previous projects?

A: Alberto Couceiro: Our first film, *The Shirt*, was more of an exercise. We didn't have exaggerated ambitions. It was our first encounter with the medium of film. The idea was to show a shirt at breakfast. We worked with real objects, including live sequences. This helped us to learn more about objects and how to animate them and how to use 35 mm film technique.

Out of this exercise evolved a nice six-minute film that we finished in six months. We submitted it to festivals where it won several awards. That motivated us to start something new.

TV City was a big project right from the beginning [a satire about TV broadcasters and their audience]. It was a coproduction with Film University Babelsberg and became my graduate film. We built many figures and developed stories for them. We wanted a film with dialogue and many locations: a world of its own. We didn't economize on ideas. We worked on it for a long time. We were younger than and had much time. We used age-old 35 mm technique and camera equipment that weighed 50 pounds but produced beautiful images. The film got longer and longer and more and more elaborate. We spent a lot of time and had our fun over a period of six years. The film run 27 minutes and turned out a successful festival entry.

Automatic Fitness was the first completely independent production we did at our studio Animas Film. We were our own writers, animators and producers. It's a film about stress, optimization of work processes and the high pressure to perform in a fast and rapidly changing working environment.

Q: Do you consider 3D computer animation a competition or an equal?

A: Alberto Couceiro: No, I don't consider it a competition. I think it is a completely different technique to produce moving images.

Alejandra Tomei: With 3D computer animation the world of objects looks different than in stop motion.

Alejandra Tomei working on *TV City*. (Courtesy of Animas Film.)

Acting and Character Animation

Q: Considering techniques like motion capture: Is it easier for CG animators to provide a naturalistic performance? You seem to work with exaggeration, the Expressionist way of performance, the big gesture.

A: Alberto Couceiro: I like caricatures, expressive gestures which get the gist. I don't like naturalism in animation that much. For me naturalism and animation is a mix that doesn't succeed too often. I have noticed that with gestures and expressions done in the way of a caricature simple lines come off livelier and stronger so that emotions and the human factor become clearer.

Alejandra Tomei: Our technique allows for more freedom. I have a preference for such techniques because they foster the imagination of the audience. They offer more space for association and one's own thoughts. At the same time you can establish a kind of own logic without feeling a stranger while watching. There is more space for absurdity and humor which can unfold under these conditions. From a creative point of view there are no bounds that we are not allowed to overstep. For us animators this is a good feeling.

Q: So stylization is the basis of your type of animation, not photorealism.

A: Alberto Couceiro: In our previous projects we used photo-realism more in a surrealist way. Of course this depends on the idea and the creative choice. There are ideas that work better in other aesthetics.

Alejandra Tomei: I'm not predetermined. I think that depending on the project we could do both. We have used stylization in preference to photo-realism because it suited our projects.

48

The Spanish Animation Producer

Manuel Cristóbal

Manuel Cristóbal (born in 1969 in Madrid) is a producer who introduced 3D animation to his country with *El bosque animado (The Living Forest)*. He has won three Goya Awards in the best animation feature category. In 2012, he produced one of the most memorable (but least successful) animated feature films of Europe: *Arrugas (Wrinkles)*. He is a member of the European Film Academy. At the time of this interview, Manuel Cristóbal was preparing a Spanish–Chinese co-production *Dragonkeeper* and an animated arthouse film project about Luis Bunuel.

The young Luis Bunuel in an animated biopic titled *Bunuel in the Labyrinth of the Turtles*. (Courtesy of Manuel Cristóbal.)

Q: Not many people abroad seem to know European animation. Even in Europe it's not considered a premier brand. It's mainly American blockbusters that seem to conquer audiences. Is this only a question of marketing?

A: I just do not think "European animation" is a needed brand, or at least I am not interested in that. Animation is international, animation is cinema. What we need are directors and studios that are a "brand" and recognized worldwide. There is a great example in *Despicable Me*. The original story comes from Sergio Pablos, a Spanish animator who sold it to Universal and Illumination, then later it was produced in France with French directors, so does it mean it is European? Does it even bother? It is a question of distribution and finding a partner that can secure worldwide distribution. In this case Universal did an excellent job but you always need three ingredients: a great story with great writers and a great director, a solid studio to give you the needed quality and a distribution partner with the power to reach the whole world.

Q: Nevertheless, there is a lot of support for European animation from Cartoon Brussels and national subsidies. Some claim the strength of European product is variety. Variety, however, is often a different spelling for fragmentation. Do you think it would be worthwhile to find a handwriting in animation, to find a type of film that is identifiable— just like anime are identified with Japan?

A: I think certain art house projects can only come from Europe and we should keep that, but I also think we should use animation to entertain a family and mainstream audience. Balance is important, and finding the right dimension for each project is crucial. In a certain way family animation is football, a great market with great demand where you need big budgets plus a franchise potential and if you don't have them don't bother to show up. Art house animation is like ice skating: a much more reduced market but there certainly is one and it is worth it only if you are able to find unique stories and produce them with a very competitive budget.

Q: Sometimes European productions seem to have problems of even being shown in Europe. Spanish films are successful in Spain, German in Germany, and so on but not so often vice versa. Is this the effect of what the Americans call "local production?"

A: I think if a film is good it will travel. It would be helpful to support local distributors that want to release European animation films because distribution is the key.

Q: How did you become a producer yourself? And what are the qualities an animation producer should have?

A: I was trained as theatre and film director. I just saw I wasn't a genius at it, produced some shorts and also began working as manager in a producer's association in Spain. Suddenly I went from serving coffee TO the producers to having coffee WITH the producers and listening to them. One of the members of the association was the owner of the studio where we did *The Living Forest*. I started helping him out, and he offered me a position as executive producer. I was 29 at the time and I think it was such a crazy project that no one else wanted to take it. I just saw that the one who puts the project together is the producer and that is something fascinating and rewarding. The training available from the MEDIA Programme of the European Union [a subsidized initiative designed to support the development and distribution of films, training activities, festivals, and promotion projects throughout Europe] also helped me a lot, it helped a great deal.

An animation producer should know both worlds, animation and production, mainly production, and should be able to listen, to believe and to persist. Animation is very tricky and budgets are normally higher than live action. Preproduction is key as we can't make the films twice like a regular studio would do, therefore facing the problems far in advance is mandatory.

Q: Do you prefer to buy properties for screen adaptation or to develop stories and characters from scratch?

A: I do prefer pre-existing properties but I am not closed to original stories. I think that when you work with adaptations you have three great advantages: first you have something that most of the times is a production value with readers to support you plus something that moved them emotionally, second is that you have something to talk with the talent (possible writers and possible directors) to find out if you see the same film and third, you have a selling tool as you can send the book even before writing the script to test interest from investors. When I buy something it is because I love it and I see how to try to make it possible. Also I know that there is a great leap of faith from the author to give you his or her "baby" and that for me is very rewarding that although the story may change, because film is a different medium and the director needs its space, the author is proud of the result.

Q: How do you work as a producer with the animation director, writers, and animators?

A: As a producer I work mainly with the writer and the director and they have to be different persons, it doesn't mean that the director is not involved in the script but I think it is important to have an extraordinary scriptwriter. In Europe the writer-director sometimes is a good combination but many other times just hides a lousy writer. I do not write and I do not direct but I do choose the projects and I know what I want. If you have the right team and it works well my opinion is the opinion of the team and I fight for it. I do not work with animation directors and animators as I think a producer has to be very involved in development and just check that the studio is working ok. He should be there only if problems need to be solved. I am also very much involved in marketing and distribution. The film does not end when the animation ends, till a certain extent begins there.

Q: You were the first Spanish producer to work with 3D animation. What were your experiences?

A: *The Living Forest* (directed by Angel de la Cruz, 2001) is a very dear film to me, not only because it was the first CGI animation film in Europe, but because it was also the first success of Spanish animation in its theatrical market. I was hired in 1999 by the owner of Dygra Films and producer of the film as executive producer and enjoyed every moment. We were a very young team in La Coruna, north east of Spain, and for most of us it was our first feature, so we gave everything. I dealt with script development, packaging, financing, marketing and even acted as sales agent of the film. We were very lucky that Javier Vasallo, head of Buena Vista Spain at the time, was interested from very early on and I could work on the marketing of the film with Alvaro Curie, who was Marketing Director of Buena Vista.

Q: *Wrinkles*, 2D-animated, was developed from a comic book. It's about Alzheimer's disease and tells its story with a lot of emotion and empathy. Many animated films seem to project more empathy than any live-action film.

A: I already had done three family films and I saw *Wrinkles* as a wonderful new challenge. I read an article in the newspaper that this comic book got its author the National Comic Book Award in Spain and I thought that if with those ingredients (a retirement home and Alzheimer) it had been awarded many prizes and was selling there should be a great story, and with no doubt there was one. I also had met [director] Ignacio Ferreras and he was somebody I wanted to work with, so I bought the book for him as I thought he had that sensitivity for it. Animation in a certain extent can be more poetic than live-action film and also in animation they become unique films. The empathy in this case is due to Ignacio Ferreras, the director, who was able to make you laugh and cry with the characters, and it was his first film.

Q: You didn't have a big budget when you made *Wrinkles*. Nevertheless, there is great character animation. How was that possible with such a low budget?

A: I think *Wrinkles* is great storytelling and some journalists have compared the animation with films that cost ten times as much, just because it has great characters. I knew that I could raise almost two million Euros in Spain for a film like that. I talked to the director and we found a way to do it for that budget. Ignacio Ferreras did the whole animatic by himself and we just animated the animatic. We couldn't afford more and it paid off.

Q: Right now you seem to be one of the few European animation producers trying to cooperate with China. What can you tell about it?

A: I am lucky to have a partner like Larry Levene who has been working with China for many years. Of course, it is tricky but like I heard somebody say, "China now is like Hollywood in the 30s, anything can happen." It is crucial to go to China often, listen a lot, find the right partners and persist.

Q: In adapting *Dragonkeeper,* part of a bestselling trilogy of novels, you deal with Chinese characters. Would you please share with us problems in design, acting, and research?

A: *Dragonkeeper* is the first of the three novels we bought. This story takes place in China and was written by Carole Wilkinson, a wonderful Australian writer. In design we did concept art with Sergio Pablos but early on it was clear that we had to have a Chinese art director to have not only the accuracy but also the Chinese talent. We took on board BASE FX

Wrinkles. (Courtesy of Manuel Cristóbal, Perro Verde Films.)

with a team led by Tony Zhang and the work took off. The main problem is getting the story right when dealing with Chinese elements and making them work for a Chinese audience but at the end of the day you have to take your chances and go for a great story.

Q: Right now there is only one very successful Chinese animation character on the international market and that was developed not by Chinese but by Americans: *Kung Fu Panda*. Do you think Chinese producers will be able to place their own product on international markets or will they content themselves with their own vast domestic market?

A: I don't know if Chinese producers would like to stay in their market. What I do know is that the challenge is to make something that works in China as well as in the rest of the world. Animation is the perfect vehicle to try that and also is the vehicle to aim for a franchise.

The Stop-Motion Animator and VFX Director

Jim Danforth

Jim Danforth (born in 1940) was one of the leading traditional American stop-motion animators and visual effects directors. He animated big parts of *Jack the Giant Killer* (1961), did most of the dragon sequence in *The Wonderful World of the Brothers Grimm* (1962), the Beetle Man (and matte art) for *Flesh Gordon* (1973), and Pegasus for Ray Harryhausen's final movie, *Clash of the Titans* (1981). He was twice nominated for an Academy Award: for *Seven Faces of Dr. Lao* (1964) and Hammer-Seven Arts' *When Dinosaurs Ruled the Earth* (1971).

Mike Jittlov: "*Absolute genius! Boosted me out of some really low moods, he's been through Hollywood hell, and shrugs off the flames like a summer's breeze.*"*

Q: There was some short stop-motion test you once did on spec. It seemed to be, if we remember the footage correctly, a recreation of a situation from Norse mythology, showing a winged-helmet god or hero in front of a live, rear projected waterfall in a mountainous region. The stately, imposing figure didn't move much, but you could recognize the

---

* *Mike Jittlov Can Do Everything!* In Fantastic Films Collectors Edition #20. December, 1980.

Wotan. (Courtesy of Jim Danforth.)

character immediately in the 30 seconds you did. Can you describe this particular animation?

A: The scene to which you are referring shows a young version of Wotan. As you will recall from the legend, Wotan, although a god, is not immortal, so I chose to show him in his younger days. In the scene he turns and walks up the mountain trail toward the camera. What I tried to do was make the animation slow and majestic. I also had to give some animation to Wotan's cape.

Q: Ray Harryhausen, when asked to explain how he would handle the task of animation technically, said that it becomes your second nature. Did he mean he did animation instinctively and not mathematically, just counting frames to outline the action?

A: I know that Ray sometimes used a stop watch to time actions. I think that was mostly in his younger days. I tended to count seconds to myself—one-thousand-and-one, one-thousand-and-two, etc. Then I multiplied by twenty four to get the number of frames. After some practice, I learned that some actions were predictable—eight frames for a quick puppet-like step, twelve frames for a more human like step; more frames for a slow step or for a large giant.

Q: Ray took acting lessons in his youth, even said that he had stage fright and that it was one of the reasons that he preferred to animate instead of appearing on stage himself. Did you do research on acting? Do you feel like acting it out via puppets or do you consider yourself more of directing a certain character?

A: I did do research on acting, and I believed that animation was a dramatic performance, but I also approached the design of animation sequences from a directorial perspective.

Q: How do you mentally explore a character? And how do you visualize it? Does the puppet become an avatar to you?

A: I think about the character's motivation or goals. Usually, the goals are simple: get from one side of the shot to the other, for example. Sometimes there is more drama to it. In my career, the scenes with the most drama were in the Art Clokey TV series *Davey and Goliath*. In the feature films with creatures, most of the drama was situational—meaning that the human characters were menaced by the animated creatures, so that a simple roar might seem very dramatic in context, even though the action might not be inherently dramatic. I tried to avoid bold, stylized characterizations for 'naturalistic' creatures, which made my animation seem less powerful. Ray tended to be very broad in his characterizations, except with the Troglodyte in *Sinbad and the Eye of the Tiger*.

Q: By the way, we re-read your proposed script *Theseus and the Minotaur* for the ill-fated series project *Ray Harryhausen's World of Myth & Legend* and included portions in this book. Everything was in the writing, and you could imagine and visualize the fight between the Greek hero and the mythological creature just from reading; every movement, up to the dapper wave of the hand we dare to say. If you compare these pages to screenwriter Kenneth Kolb's description of the cyclops/dragon fight from *The 7th Voyage of Sinbad*, Kolb's writing seemed uninspired and weak.

A: Keep in mind that Kenneth Kolb was not directing the animation, only writing something for Ray to base his direction on. In my Theseus script, I was predirecting the filming and editing of the story. I thought the sequence in which Theseus fights the Minotaur was the best example of that, with each cut specified in the writing. By the way, I rewrote *Theseus and the Minotaur*, adding two monkey characters as pets for Ariadne— one dyed red, the other dyed blue (there is a fresco at Knossos showing a blue monkey).

Q: How did you approach the movements of extinct animals, of dinosaurs? In some cases, you were able to give the dinosaurs—well, character: the baby dinosaur from *When Dinosaurs Ruled the Earth,* the fat tyrannosaur from *Caveman.* And, on the contrary, how did you do research on living animals and humans to be animated? Did you study Muybridge? What does movement mean to you? Your animation always was so full of live and so imaginative.

A: As it happens, the two examples you mentioned were largely animated by others. Dave Allen did some of the animation of the baby Dinosaur in *When Dinosaurs Ruled the Earth*, and Randy Cook did most of the animation of the tyrannosaur in *Caveman.* However, I did study Muybridge—particularly when animating Pegasus for *Clash of the Titans.* I've always been very interested in movement and dance, and I thought that designing stop motion was like choreographing the sequences in which animation was to appear. Because some of the 'dancers' were actors, and only one or two were puppets, and because of the prohibitions of the Directors Guild, I was not always able to get the choreography performed according to my design. In pure puppet films, the choreography was easier, although I understand that conditions for animators are now more restrictive than they were in the past.

Q: What do you think about classic, stylized Czech animation like Trnka and some fine Japanese stop motion?

A: I'm a big fan of Czech animation—particularly that of Jiří Trnka (although I don't know whether Trnka himself ever animated any of his puppets). Trnka was more a director, I believe. Some of the Japanese animator/directors I found to be very good—particularly Kihachiro Kawamoto.

The Belgian Animation Director

Piet De Rycker

Piet De Rycker (born in 1957 in Antwerp) is a Belgian animator and animation director who worked all over Europe, animating in Ireland for Don Bluth (*Rock-A-Doodle*, 1991), directing in Germany as well as in Great Britain. His most famous animated feature films in Europe were *The Little Polar Bear* (2001) and *Laura's Star* (2004). He came from 2D animation but directed 3D as well. Thanks to the organizers of the Cartoon Forum, we met Mr. De Rycker in Toulouse and spoke to him.

Q: Can you tell us a little bit about your background?

A: Since age 12 I wanted to be in the animation industry. At that time I had no clue about the many disciplines one must master, nor did I know about the amount of people involved or the talents one must have. I just liked the idea of creating emotions through moving drawings. Those 1960s Disney movies could make me weep every time, over and over again. Being a kid that was born with a pencil in his hand it was only logical to steer all my studies from then on into that direction. But it was until I was in my early thirties that things started to turn. I had moved in the meantime to Ireland and worked for the Don Bluth Entertainment Studios. Don Bluth, being a former classical Disney animator, had left the Disney Studios together with half of the animation staff and had founded his own company wherein he wanted to prove that excellent classical animation combined with storytelling that went straight to the heart had still a great potential to move people from all over the world. In those days 3D animation was just glancing around the corner and was still an oddity and only used to simplify the animation of props. Character animation was still done as in the old days: on paper.

Another input I had was through my work as a comic book artist and illustrator for magazines in which I could train my own way of storytelling.

The combination of these two skills made me move up fast to scriptwriting and directing. First in my own studios, after having returned from Ireland some years later, then more important for Cartoon Film, a Berlin-based animation company that was back then only producing TV series but wanted to get into feature family entertainment as well. The combination of Cartoon Film (being supported by Warner Bros. Germany) working with local talents mixed with internationally trained European animation artists as myself made it possible to produce movies that were outstanding.

Q: **You have directed a number of successful animated feature films for kids, mainly preschoolers. So you work around children's imagination. What is the difference between children's and adult's animation? Did you do research in child psychology?**

A: In principle not much and Pixar proves this. Unfortunately, under the influence of TV formats, we have split up the audience in all kinds of age groups forgetting that a good story should be able to hold the attention of any spectator, being kid or adult alike.

This doesn't mean that all adult stories can be told for children, because their life experience is not sufficient to understand the deep content of it. But every children story can be told in a way that also adults can be touched by it. That asks, of course, for daring storytelling and not patronized storytelling or parent-proof storytelling. As real life is for all ages, a movie should be too.

Q: **Concerning this do you realize differences in various European countries?**

A: From my own experience in feature animation (I leave preschool TV out of the discussion), there is a big difference between working for a German project or a British. It is all about culture and about what one thinks entertainment is or should be. I have the impression British culture understands entertainment as a challenge to explore the grandness of a project, not limited by predetermined ideas if it is of educational value or parent-proof. This state of thinking means that there are a lot of wild, funny, grand ideas on the table that might be hilarious, even over the top which makes the work process hilarious, too. Of course not all of those ideas make it to the screen. But somehow it influences the way how you look at a project. By trying to be parent-proof, however, as they do in Germany, educationally and politically correct, a lot of potential is cut already out before one starts a project. It means that there is a stop toward high adventure, not only by the false idea of not having the money to visualize it but just because there is a certain fear to impress, to excel in entertaining filmmaking. This idea of social rightness I see as a self limitation. In Germany there seems to be an unwritten law that says we need to protect future generations from crazy irrational behavior. So we will educate them well and if things would go out of hand nobody can blame us. This doesn't mean that German movies can't be successful. On the contrary, they might be very popular, on the home market. But elsewhere, they will be hard to sell. Maybe because when one doesn't go for the educational, one might go for the burlesque. And that is a style that has also an audience attraction in Germany. As a Belgian, I am in the middle of those two cultures. I understand them both, but the British tongue in cheek, laughing about your own stupid self, holds a charm that we all should embrace in our working life.

Q: Can you describe the work of an animation director and the problems he or she has to face?

A: Firstly, a director must have a vision. Secondly, a language that is deeply connected to the particular story he wants to tell. Thirdly, the courage to fight for his vision, because the amount of high-risk money at stake in this industry makes it possible that in the course of the daily work he might have forgotten the initial sparkle that generated the whole reason of making the movie anyway. There are many ways a boat can sink. Fourthly, he must be able to stir a team, through arguments and not feelings, and mediate the way the story should be told. There are still too many pictures made in a ground soap of ideas driven by team decisions that lack a good view on strong and bold storytelling. Fifthly, he must be capable to listen very, very carefully to all what is being said by any person working on the project. One might be surprised by the amount of accidental input given for free by all those nice people at only an arm length away from you. In short, one must have a brain to have a vision, an eye for a view, a mouth to express the ideas and an ear to hold you back from making mistakes that your brain wasn't able to grasp: A heart to be brave. A belly to feel. Strong legs and feet for emotional storms coming in from nowhere.

Q: You worked with preconceived characters from popular children's books but developed also figures of your own. Do you develop the story, in the best case, out of these characters, limitations included?

A: There are two ways to tell stories. One is to narrate a tale character-driven, the other is story-driven or structure-driven. And in the middle you will find infinite options. Best is to find a combination wherein both will have their perfect moments. But in all cases it must be believably unique.

Another approach I use is that I can't write a story or define a character without having at least an idea of the visual look and feel. This means that during the writing process we also draw character models to see what would work best. Sometimes a character doesn't come from design but is a pose one finds that will fill in the right personality.

Once the story is storyboarded one can fine-tune the rough models into more precise models, but most of the time they don't change too much, since everybody in the meantime got used to them.

It is more or less the writer of live-action movies who writes a role with a specific actor in mind. If for one reason or another it is not possible to hire that particular actor most of the time the script has to be re-written.

Q: Do you consider acting theories helpful for animation directors and animators?

A: They are extremely important and will help you to create believable and unique scenes. One must become an encyclopedia of gestures in well defined moments of life to avoid generic fill-ins of none telling poses which won't evocate an emotion in the spectator. A moment is always connected to the character's behavior, its outlook and the believability of its action, given under these specific circumstances.

Q: How do you create the emotional part, the empathy?

A: I think "build" is a better word than "create." It is a fine planning of the right elements that makes the audience first feel for the character, understand its dilemma and then hit at the right moment the string where the character will fall apart and lose all it was standing and hoping for. If the first part is poorly done, it will be hard to convince any audience to feel empathy, regardless of the amount of weeping violins one likes to place on top of it. That means if you don't feel for the character at that crucial moment late in the movie, one has to do his homework again in the first and second act.

Q: In some of your children's films, you had to do without antagonists. Isn't it difficult to develop a story without a villain?

A: I don't believe that it is possible to tell a story, to do a book, film, stage play without a villain. But if the villain should always be the Joker from

Batman or a brutal, devilish person with a silly sidekick and a sardonic team member that has no connection to any reasonable human argument, I'm not convinced. When using this kind of villains, it becomes always the same kind of structured project: very hero-driven with a big party at the end arranged in the community that was saved. Some films are better off with an internal villain that one has to overcome. Or a set of combined evil forces, being it a sum of characters or a sum of disasters (volcano, lost on a wild river, a bear, a pack of wolves). Like *Inside Out*, or *Pinocchio*, or *Laura's Star*, *Princess Mononoke*, *Totoro*, *Kiki's Delivery Service*. In live action the range of storytelling has a much bigger spectrum than what's allowed in animation. Probably because merchandising isn't a necessity to recoup the invested money.

This would lead to the question: Is it difficult to write a story that doesn't follow the archetypical structures of a hero movie? Then the answer would be: Any movie is difficult to write being it a hero movie in a landscape of fierce competition or being it an internal conflict story in an unknown landscape. Personally I feel more at ease with projects where humanity is in the centre of storytelling instead of: I killed the beast. Although I might like to watch one of those, once in a while.

Q: **There is a lot of bad, standardized animation around. In spite of all the digital tools, some of it looks as if they have done it in the early days of animation. What does good character animation mean to you?**

A: Evoking emotions! Creating moments one can relate to as if you were there, together with the other characters, waiting to say your own lines. This can't be done with poor design. This can't be done in poor light conditions, but it can be done in limited animation if the type of characters is symbolic archetypes, in a design as simple as the animation and backgrounds will be. The problem is that a lot of animation has a kind of humanized realistic character style without the budget to animate them believably or without the budget to place them properly in the background.

Real art is a fine chemistry wherein all elements, such as style, color sets, brushstrokes, the blackness of shadows, the fluency of successive troughs and on and on, are combined in the right amount of values creating one specific visual language that could only be this one to tell this particular story.

Another story, another style. Another style, a different kind of storytelling.

Q: **You directed a well-liked animated feature, *Laura's Star* (2004), with an aesthetic bow to Japanese anime and you did a sequel, *Laura's Star and the Mysterious Dragon Nian* (2009) that was a Sino-German co-production. What about intercultural approach?**

A: Belgium is a center of comic books, a culture very open-minded toward visuals, from the French to the American to the Manga. All influences from children comic strips to graphic novels are familiar to our cultural background. It means we were visually raised eclectically. The range of art goes from copying styles to mixing styles to finding an own style. Without this inner path that we all somehow have to follow, one can't come into his or her own bloom. I place myself for the moment on a spot between Miyazaki and Disney. I was brainwashed by Disney's great movies till the age of 30, and all I wanted to do was to work in the classic animation industry. But around 40 the work of Miyazaki was introduced to me. That was really an eye opener. One can tell stories based on totally different parameters in design, animation style and story concept and still be successful. I don't mean necessarily in money terms but more meaningful to a wide audience. This has influenced my own art toward something that I can see now as a marriage between East and West, and maybe just because I'm a European filmmaker, it was possible to see the beauty of both ends and combine them to an own style.

Q: **Please tell us about the difficulties adapting children's books: illustrating kids' imaginary world.**

A: Animation properties are about world-building. It isn't just enough to have a funny character or a story idea. One must be able to translate it to a world people like to wander in. The exploration of that world is part of the fun, and the better one can create such a world the longer you can hook your followers. Which means one has to make a choice at the start. With a lot of questions to ask oneself. Where do the characters live? Are they like us? Or are they timeless and ageless? Is the real world wherein kids dream the thing we want our audience to feel and see and explore? So if you enter such a project you have to be aware that the only way to succeed is to deliver something that is unique, believable, empathic, and, if possible, doesn't resemble something that already exists. Success is not only guaranteed by the greatness of an idea but also by the capability to get imbedded in the daily life, with all its merchandising potential. One cannot sell if one cannot communicate. And communication is all about hope, dreams, wishes.

Q: **Can you name a few movies that have influenced your work considering role profiles and character animation?**

A: *Totoro, Princess Mononoke, Kiki's Delivery Service, Ratatouille, Pinocchio, Iron Giant, The Secret of NIMH, Thumbelina, Tobias Totz, Tekkonkinkreet, Grave of the Fireflies, Cinderella, Peter Pan, Jungle Book.* As you see these are all well-controlled animated features, hardly any television work.

51

The Game Expert
Thomas Dlugaiczyk

In 1999, Thomas Dlugaiczyk founded the *Games Academy* in Berlin, the first and foremost educational and training institution for computer game developers in Europe. In 2010, he co-founded the Games Academy Vancouver, Inc.

Q: **For some time now computer games seem to overshadow anything that the movie industry has achieved commercially. And yet this is only the beginning. What do you think of a joint venture between games and film industry? We often speak about games in money terms. The worldwide success is that astonishing. If you would write science fiction, where would you see the end?**

A: There is no science fiction. George Lucas was the first Hollywood producer and director, who played both pianos very well: games and movies. In 1982 he founded Lucasfilm Games to develop games, first as standalone projects, later more for the purpose of licensing products for his own Star Wars story.

Lucasfilm is regarded as the most important representative of games-related filmmakers and an impressive example for chances and boundaries of the exchange from movie picture art and games.

What about the money? You can't compare apples and oranges. Movies stand in the long-time tradition of the theatre, whereas games are pure software and have a strong link to the culture of rituals because of the extended possibilities to play an active role in the scenes.

Why make games more money? On one hand: Games are provided by a completely different and very complex and sometimes strange system of monetarization you really don't want to have in the movie industry. On the other hand: Games are software and this allows the distribution of the products in other technical ways. More money, but an instable and more volatile business.

The end? In the future games and movies will influence each other in a positive way. Many games are very cinematic today—from graphics to story. Many movies tend to create a multimedia product concept to find more investors and attract a growing audience.

But I cannot see the "merge" of movies and games before Stanisław Lem's or Gene Roddenberry's vision of the holodeck will come true. And this is when? Which star date?

Q: **The synthetic characters in computer games get more and more realistic. But we don't know as much about their motivation as we do in movies.**

A: Yes, the optical resolution on the PC and video console systems screens has exploded in the last decade. Is this really more "realistic?" Yes, the production pipelines of cinematic games like *L.A. Noir* or *Godfather II* and CGI-animated films like *Avatar* are very similar. Games have genres too: In action movies like *The Expendables* and 3D-shooters happens the same, at least on the first look. But: One is reception and the other interaction.

Q: **Do you think it might be someday possible to create synthetic characters with artificial intelligence?**

A: From time to time we can read articles about artificial intelligence in games. Well, this is a myth. What we have are script-based engines that are generating interaction systems between the player and the machine. Okay, it feels like intelligence. But on the way the secretary of Joseph Weizenbaum was removing Weizenbaum from his office because she was talking with his brand-new computer program Eliza at MIT in 1966.

Q: **Are there maybe ideas to hire the digital avatars of famous actors? They all are digitized already in Hollywood.**

A: One of the first films that explored the possibilities of animated digital art was Robert Zemeckis' *Polar Express* from 2004. Tom Hanks himself appeared in an animated movie—this was impressive, but the style was not my taste.

Q: What about empathy games? Do you think that empathy can have a part in hard competition?

A: Very often playing is confronting me with the decision between cooperation and conflict. Our postmodern society is extremely competitive. But this has nothing to do with games or playing. This is the impact economical systems leave on mankind.

Q: What do you think about the discussion concerning first-person shooters? Many gamers are said to present addictive behavior.

A: Oh goodness! I've co-founded the USK, the German age ratings system for games and interactive media. In an age of over 50 I'm going to be more and more critical about new technologies, especially digital ones. And I have kids in the age between 20 and 30. Let me try to answer with Paracelsus, "All things are poison, for there is nothing without poison. It is only the dose which makes a thing poison or not." Electronic games have no qualities to create massive addiction, no more than sugar, sports or very extensive movie consumption.

Q: Internationally, the military brass and intelligence services are going to recruit young gamers and hackers for cyberwarfare. There seems to be a big need.

A: Games are a kind of virtual reality. In games we can train our skills, the social ones for instance, but also the skill I need to become a good soldier to pay a visit to foreign countries and kill people over there. I have no idea where the main markets for those games are and how big the opportunities are.

Computer and video games are just a technical extension of playing. And this is what man is doing from the moment he opened his eyes. Training is a part of the biological use of playing, of course. For what we will be ready to train is our personal decision.

Q: We guess it won't take long when they will use the human brain as interface. Will future games take place in the human mind?

A: Yes, like today as well. If you are dreaming at night, you have a complete video console in your brain. In HD, full color, with super sound and very realistic.

52

The Artist from the Zagreb School of Animation

Borivoj Dovniković-Bordo

Borivoj Dovniković-Bordo (born in 1930 in Osijek, the fourth largest city in Croatia) is an animation director and animator, a cartoonist, illustrator, comic strip, and graphic designer who began to work for Zagreb Film, then one of the leading animation places in the world. He was also involved in the World Festival of Animated Films in Zagreb as well ASIFA, the International Association of Animated Films.

Q: You were there at Zagreb Film right from the beginning. Can you talk a little bit about your own career?

A: After finishing high school in Osijek in 1949, I moved to Zagreb, capital of the Republic of Croatia, to study at the Academy of Fine Arts. At the same time I joined the satirical weekly Kerempuh and very soon became a professional newspaper cartoonist (on a monthly payment!). Obviously, working for newspapers and illustrating books interested me more than the Academy. When in the following year (1950) I got the offer to take part in the production of an animated film I left the Academy and became a filmmaker, besides doing newspaper cartoons, illustration, comic strips and graphic design.

Q: While most American cartoons up to the 1950s and 1960s focused on anthropomorphic animals UPA (United Productions of America) and then Zagreb preferred "mechanomorphic" humans. And while UPA artists were more interested in slapstick, Zagreb put the individual in a changing society in the foreground. Why did it happen, of all places, in Zagreb, in Yugoslavia? What made this place so special that an own school emerged from it that was acknowledged with an Academy Award for Dušan Vukotić (for the short film Surrogat, 1961)? Why you of all people?

A: After finishing the first independent art film *The Big Meeting (Rally)* in the weekly Kerempuh (1951), the Croatian Republic Government (in the Federative Yugoslavia) gave the financial support for the foundation of the new company that specialized in producing animation films (Duga Film/ Rainbow Film). *The Meeting* and other films of the new company were made, of course, in the classic Disney manner, like all animation in the world at that time.

Already in the first year, young animators, uninfected by the Disney style, started to talk about new possibilities in animation—in everyday spontaneous discussions off-time. It was the privilege of a common work and life in one production house. Today, under conditions of computer animation, where animators are working alone in their private spaces, mainly at home—that wouldn't be possible. One of our colleagues, Vlado Kristl, started drawing sketches for a thoughtful animated picture with characters in the manner of Honoré Daumier. We all thought that it was unusable for animation. (Nine years after that Vlado created the exceptional film *La Peau de Chagrin* in that style!)

1956, in the newly formed company Zagreb Film, new authors and directors Nikola Kostelac, Dušan Vukotić and Vatrosvlav Mimica, designers Aleksandar Marks, Boris Kolar and Vjekoslav Kostanjšek, and animator Vladimir Jutrisa abandoned their teachers (Walter Neugebauer, Vladimir Delać, Borivoj Dovnikovic...) and moved toward non-Disney animation. When they found some texts with illustrations in an English magazine in the British Consulate Library about the new animation that was done at UPA, and stylized drawings in illustrated books by Mary Blair—they got the confirmation for their ideas. Foreign newspapers and books weren't imported to the country. One bookshop in Zagreb and the English Library were the only places to find cultural news from the West. It was in the 1950s. Later, after the total break from Stalin's block, Yugoslavia opened to the idea and the art from the Western countries. But otherwise, at that time there were not many books about animation in the world in general. We saw the animated films by UPA later when we already started doing films in non-Disney style.

Why did it happen in Zagreb? Zagreb was a well-known cultural center of that region, especially in comic strip, and many artists (painters, illustrators, musicians, architects, filmmakers…) were interested in the new art—animation. Except for that, animation movement was financed by the government and was completely free in the artistic creation. It resulted in fast recognition in the cinema world. At the Cannes Festival, in 1958, the screening of the first seven animated films from Zagreb got big attention and this movement was named the Zagreb School of Animation.

Q: What made caricaturists who worked for that satirical magazine titled Kerempuh go for animation and film? Besides Walter Neugebauer who later went to Germany to work on comic books for a guy named Rolf Kauka, there weren't many experienced artists and technicians in Zagreb in those days.

A: The caricaturists who responded to the call of the Kerempuh manager Fadil Hadžić and artist Walter Neugebauer were at the same time comic strip designers (Vladimir Delać and Borivoj Dovniković). They were the only ones who agreed to take part in the uncertain adventure of starting the animated film. Other colleagues (even Dušan Vukotić) considered this attempt not serious. After finishing *The Big Meeting (Veliki Miting)* and the foundation of the company Duga Film, many colleagues approached us. One of the first was Vukotić (to whom I personally introduced the basic secrets of animation, as he was my close friend).

Walter Neugebauer revealed to me privately in the 1970s that he had planned the production of animated films in Zagreb as a commercial venture. In fact, he was not interested in artistic animation. Because of that he abandoned Zagreb and devoted himself to comic strip work in Munich, hoping to install his own studio for advertising animation. But he didn't manage to realize his plans.

Q: What exactly did you do at Zagreb Film?

A: From the beginning until 1960, I worked at Zagreb Film as a designer and head animator working for other directors. But at that time I also was very active in drawing comic strips for Zagreb magazines. In early 1960, the idea came up that designers and animators can create their own films. So very soon our group of designers began to work on our own animated pictures. We would write our own scripts, design, animate and direct. We had total control of our work, like painters control their pictures on linen—what is quite logical. Of course, such was possible only in independent short films. And many of the directors who weren't designers and animators vanished from our animation scene in the next years. Only the real artists among the non-designers were kept working with their designers and animators. The traditional division of functions is normal in the production of animated feature films even now.

Q: In a caricature, the whole personality of a character is squeezed in the design. This, of course, makes animation easier and less complex. But how did you make the movements of a character more interesting in spite of this simplification?

A: The animator's skills are crucial here. A good animator can give soul and expressiveness even to the simplest character. This is where many young animators make mistakes these days. They think that animation means to move the character, but, even the direct translation from the Latin language says that it means to give soul and life to the character, not just move it. The audience must trust the animated hero in all he is doing, not just watch him move.

Q: Are you an avid watcher? Do you like to watch people and how do you find their Achilles' heel, their weak spot?

A: As a caricaturist, during my whole professional life, I'm watching and commenting people's characters and their manners. In doing animation I am still the caricaturist. Many of my pictures are devoted to people's and society's weaknesses. Because of that I became known as a master of psychological animation.

Q: What changes did the advent of 3D animation bring to Zagreb?

A: It's very interesting—the nineties were historical. At the same time it was the end of socialist Yugoslavia and the beginning of, the foundation of an independent and capitalistic Croatia, and with it the computer appeared in our animation. Officially, I became a retired artist. 3D animation brought essential changes to film animation. The computer dramatically depreciated and expanded animation production all over the world. And with it the number of animated film festivals increased. We can say that animation (not so much in art but in games) overflowed the globe. I have no relations to the new animation, not at all. My film career was finished with the classical cel animation. That's it! Today the youngsters do miracles in animation. I'm delighted seeing fantastic technical results in pictures. But, unfortunately, very often the technical progress is not followed by quality of direction. Many of these films are indistinct and poorly narrated. Young animators get the technical skills very quickly, but they don't become artists at the same time. I would say that we have quantity but not the adequate quality.

Q: Zagreb is still a place of art and animation. How does the Zagreb School of Animation survive in a world of powerful digitized giant corporations?

A: I think you have to put this question to the leaders of Zagreb Film studios. As a retired artist in animation, I can only say what I personally think. Zagreb Film exists in the independent Croatia for 25 years. Croatian government still finances the animation film production through its film fund. As a state culture institution, in competition with many other new private animation studios, Zagreb Film is satisfied with the financial support for some art animation projects and has no aspirations for spreading the production, making commercial attempts—animated games, series, advertising films, etc. I am completely out of recent animation and I cannot explain this case in detail. Today digitalized giant corporations in the world maybe remember the old Zagreb School only as a nice memory from the last century.

Q: For ASIFA, you have travelled around the world and seen many places. Can you talk a little bit about the cultural differences in animation and also about the commonalities and similarities that make it a global community?

A: I was travelling all over the world for ASIFA, but more as animation author who was part of that Zagreb School. During a 2 month tour with my films through the United States in 1994 I had nice experiences concerning animation. Not only the ordinary people, the students of animation, too, knew only American animation films, in fact mainly Disney productions. After screening my films at Harvard University, one student said, "After seeing your animated films one must think!" That is what modern (not only Zagreb), non-Disney animation is all about: Make one think!

A good piece of art will be understood and appreciated in the whole world, sooner or later!

53

The Animation Scholar from Hong Kong

Daisy Yan Du

Daisy Yan Du is Associate Professor at the Division of Humanities at the Hong Kong University of Science and Technology. She is building an association for Chinese animation studies, kind of a resource center for researchers. The aim is to promote Chinese animation to the English-speaking world.

Q: After more than 10 years of re-building Chinese animation and establishing literally thousands of studios all over the country, China has become the biggest animation-producing nation in the world. But why is it that we don't know that much about Chinese animation in the Western world?

A: It is true that thousands of animation studios were established in contemporary China, but most of them are profit-driven and marked by a lack of originality and creativity. In order to achieve commercial success, Chinese animators are more than eager to be international. They emulate Hollywood and Japanese animation, to the extent that they lose their own national style and national identity. Film scripts, which are often quickly prepared without literary and philosophical depth, do not have a good quality. The stories are neither coherent nor touching. The artistic details are not handled well. Some companies or studios also work on projects outsourced from Japan and the West, which also influence the aesthetic taste of Chinese animators and hinder the originality and productivity of their own creative work. This is embarrassing because since these films just superficially emulate Hollywood and Japanese animation, they cannot enjoy the same commercial success and share the international market as Hollywood and Japanese animation have done.

In sharp contrast to the large-scale and profit-driven animation companies or studios, there are many talented independent animators who still insist on the "art film" approach. These animators, such as Liu Jian and Ray Lei, are more sensitive to the artistic and thematic subtlety of animation and are more visible at international film festivals, but it is difficult for them to achieve commercial success and global popularity. After all, the number of audiences for art films is quite limited.

The lack of universal theme and style, the lack of literary and humanitarian depth, the poverty of artistic innovation, and the lack of a market and mass audience for art films can explain the relatively low visibility of Chinese animation in the world. In addition, although the Chinese government attaches much importance to animation and enthusiastically protects and promotes Chinese animation to domestic audiences, it has not done much work in promoting Chinese animation to the English-speaking world, such as cataloguing, archiving, and supporting the production of DVDs with English subtitles. Except a few animated films, the majority of Chinese animation can't be watched in English versions. When I taught Chinese animation in the U.S. and Hong Kong, I was really frustrated by the lack of English subtitles for Chinese animation. If the Chinese government and animation studios would do a better job with English subtitles, things would improve significantly. There are also government-sponsored animation associations and organizations in mainland China, which are just limited to domestic animators and scholars and tend to be insular, conservative, and bureaucratic. Because of these experiences and frustrations over the years, I developed the idea of establishing the Association for Chinese Animation Studies, an open and democratic international organization built with the aim of introducing and promoting Chinese animation to the English-speaking world (http:acas. ust.hk).

Despite the challenges, I still feel very positive about the future of Chinese animation. The Chinese government now realizes the "soft power" of animation on the global stage and is trying to do something, and the younger generation of animators is learning and maturing. With the decline of the Shanghai Animation Film Studio since the mid-1980s, people have thought that Chinese animation might have met its dead end. However, recent blockbuster animated films, such as *Monkey King: Hero*

Is Back (2015) and *Monster Hunt* (2015), had unprecedented high box office revenues in the domestic market, which does give us tremendous hope. In terms of animation technology, they are on a par with Hollywood and Japanese animation. If they address more universal themes and target an international audience, I am sure they will be as commercially successful around the world as Hollywood and Japanese animation.

Q: The Chinese box office receipts for some animated products rank among the highest in the world. Is it the family aspect that attracts Chinese audiences to animation?

A: It may be the family reason because generally speaking animation is safe for all family members to watch, but I think it needs more statistics and research to prove the hypothesis.

Q: Chinese animation is related to the merchandising and toy industry. How are they connected with each other?

A: In my opinion, Japanese animation did a better job in terms of connecting animation with the merchandising and toy industry. Think about Astro Boy, Doraemon, Hello Kitty, Pokémon, and many others. They have their own animation stars, who are promoted further with toys and other related cultural products.

Chinese animation is now developing its merchandising and toy industry, but most of it targets a domestic market. Chinese animation has few, if any, world-renowned animation stars like Astro Boy and Doraemon, so it is very difficult to reach the international market. Yet Chinese animation is now on the road and full of potentials and possibilities.

Q: *Pleasant Goat and Big Big Wolf, Blue Cat, Monkey King,* and others seem to be successful in China alone. *Kung Fu Panda* is basically not a Chinese but an American brand. In the Chinese animation industry, there seems to be little thought given to and less time spent on preproduction and development and an intercultural perspective that would work throughout the world. It's mainly mass production. What is being done to inspire quality products? Are there companies whose work should be watched?

A: The phenomenon takes place not just in animation industry, but also in other industrial sectors in China. Products "Made in China" are often associated with low price, low quality, and quantity. However, this does not mean that China cannot produce an animated film with good quality. Many famous Hollywood and Japanese animated films were actually "Made in China." Hollywood and Japanese animators did the preproduction work and designed everything, and then outsourced the projects to Chinese companies for lower labor cost. The quality of these "Made in China" animated films was as good as those produced in Hollywood and Japan. There is no problem with animation techniques or technology in China.

In my opinion, the major reason for the low quality of recent Chinese animation is the monetary and fast-food culture in contemporary China. Animation companies or studios are often profit-driven and do not want to spend time and resources on the preproduction work, such as film script, character design, stories with literary and humanitarian depth, and artistic sophistication. They are often jerry-built to receive fast returns. I think Chinese animation is now still struggling with the issue of quality.

Q: What can you tell about Chinese animation producers and their motivation?

A: There are roughly two groups of animation producers in China. The first group works for relatively large scale animation companies, which strive for commercial success in the market. The second includes independent animators, who strive for artistic excellence and try to win recognition at international film festivals. If the two groups of animators collaborate with each other perfectly, the quality of Chinese animation will be improved significantly and they will become more visible on the global stage.

Q: There is a whole new generation of animation students trained all over China, more than in any other country in the world. How is the social situation of animators and artists?

A: They probably share the same social situation with other college students in contemporary China. The job market might be more challenging for them, because they are art students. I think animation students in other countries might have a similar, if not the same, social situation.

Q: There was a great tradition in Chinese animation before the advent of 3D. Is there anything you can save to keep the tradition alive and how could this be achieved? Japanese anime have a handwriting which we often miss in modern Chinese animation.

A: I think the masterpieces, such as the ink-painting animated film *Little Tadpoles Look for Mama* (1960) and the cel-animated *Uproar in Heaven* (1961) produced in socialist China (1949–1976), are best representatives of "Chinese" animation. They were carefully made with a strong national and ethnic style and a high degree of artistic quality.

Contemporary Chinese animation is still struggling between being international and being Chinese at the same time. Most of them lose their Chineseness in trying to be more international.

Q: There is the internet. There are future developments in software and digital media. How will animation change due to the new possibilities? Is this a chance for new talent?

A: I think this will provide opportunities for animation. In the past, we have paper animation, cel animation, and stop motion (such as puppet) animation. I think this is good because it expands the horizon of animation and provides more opportunities for talented animators who are good at computers and software.

54

The Disney Expert

Didier Ghez

Didier Ghez runs the Disney History blog (http://disneybooks.blogspot.com), the Disney Books Network website (https://www.didierghez.com), and serves as managing editor of the Walt's People book series. Books include *Disneyland Paris: From Sketch to Reality, Disney's Grand Tour,* and *They Drew As They Pleased: The Hidden Art of Disney's Golden Age.* He lives in Florida.

Q: **What is it that makes a cartoon character a personality? For Disney it seems to have been an important question. Is it the acting? Is it the writing, the design, or just the emotional tie to the audience?**

A: Walt, as we know, saw his animators as actors. So the acting is definitely an important part of the mix. This is what Frank Thomas and Ollie Johnston argue throughout their seminal book, *Disney Animation: The Illusion of Life* (Abbeville, 1981).*

---

* Frank Thomas and Ollie Johnston, Disney Animation: The Illusion of Life. New York: Abbeville Press, 1981.

But there is a lot more to it than this, as Walt well knew. The design of the characters is also critical since that design needs to reflect their "soul." Here are two Walt quotes that illustrate this.

On November 11, 1938, in a *Fantasia* story meeting, while talking about the members of a planned bug orchestra, Walt explained:

> We've got to get characters in our bugs, and if we could get bugs that are sort of like people in an orchestra—you study a symphony orchestra and there's a serious fellow that plays a bassoon—to me a bassoon is a funny instrument, yet you see a bassoon player—he wears glasses and he looks like he has liver trouble, a very serious guy—and the drummer, the guy that holds the cymbals, is always some big fat guy that should be playing the tuba; and the tuba player is always a little guy—you get those caricatures with these bugs. That's why I am crazy about this Praying Mantis thing, because it's a caricature of a harpist, with a bug. Now if we can do that with our other bugs some way—that's what your spider is, a caricature of a guy with all his sticks in his hand—It's why I like the bugs with the three arms and fiddles, that's something that's funny as it is. You don't have to go outside to get gags. Here's this fellow, he's very serious and he's playing the top one very slowly, and the next one down is a bouncing bow and the next one is pizzicato. And it's all right there, if you went down the line—this one little fellow still has, while he's playing up there, he still has one arm free to scratch. It's all right because it's right in character [...] and he wouldn't pay any attention to it, he would go right on playing, but with this one hand he could scratch his leg and get back for the other notes.
>
> Just to have bugs, and they all look the same and they're all sort of stylized cartoon bugs, we'll have nothing; so we've got to try to find bugs or little insects that fit these various parts.

Earlier, in December 1935, he had written director Dave Hand:

> We should try to develop models of the characters that express more actual personalities, or caricatures of personalities. I do not mean caricatures of prominent personalities, but bringing out a caricature of the personality we are trying to express...
>
> I think we should utilize the talent of [story artist] Joe Grant for the making of these models. A good example of what I mean is in the model of the St. Bernard dog to be used in the Alpine picture [*Alpine Climbers*]. We had practically every sketch artist try a model on the St. Bernard dog, and in my opinion there were only two who achieved a real caricature of the St. Bernard. Joe Grant drew the face that seemed really to express the caricature that a St. Bernard suggests to a person, and [Ferdinand] Horvath had the feeling in the body that a St. Bernard seems to give the person looking at him. I think it will be very helpful to the animators if Joe handles most of these models. A different personality will be picked up from the sketch that Joe gives them.*

---

* Didier Ghez, *Walt's People—Volume 1. Talking Disney with the Artists Who Knew Him.* Bloomington: Xlibris, 2005.

Q: Are there any Disney characters in particular that have impressed you—and why?

A: One of my personal favorites is the Brazilian José Carioca.* Being married to a Brazilian, I am obviously biased.

But aside from the personal connection, there is the fact that the character was animated by one of the Studio's geniuses, Bill Tytla. In a 1967 interview conducted by Louise Beaudet, Tytla explained:

> One day, on the Disney lot they happened to have a bunch of Brazilian people there, in an advisory capacity. At lunch we were strolling around and we happened to be watching several Brazilians talking to each other and they were very animated. They are very flexible. When they talk, they talk with their whole bodies. And one Brazilian happened to see another Brazilian that he knew and he went "AAAAH! OOOOH!" I can't tell you the way he did it, but [I used this] for José Carioca when he met Donald Duck. All emotion, all exuberance!†

Q: Disney cartoons depict rather expressive acting in front of naturalistic backgrounds.

A: In many ways, the naturalistic backgrounds help focus your attention on the characters themselves. And the "caricature" in the characters, paradoxically, helps humanize them and make them more real.

Q: What did Disney in his heyday do to introduce his animators to the art of performing? What did he do to make them feel themselves into cartoon characters?

A: Here is what Disney artist Marc Davis explained to historian Armand Eisen in 1975, in answer to this question:

> We saw every ballet, we saw every film. If a film was good, we could go and see it five times. At one time, Walt rented a studio up in North Hollywood and every Wednesday night we would see a selection of films—anything from Chaplin to unusual subjects, anything that might produce growth that might be stimulating—the editing, the staging, how a group of scenes was put together. Everybody here was studying constantly. We had models at the Studio and we'd go over and draw every night...
>
> The comedies were always marvelous—Chaplin, Edgar Kennedy with his slow burn, Laurel and Hardy, Fred Astaire's dancing, from pose to pose—animation is pretty much like that, always with an attitude. We would all study the acting of Charles Laughton. We all read Stanislavsky. We didn't miss a trick, really. There was always someone around to bring something to

---

* The anthropomorphized parrot from Rio de Janeiro that starred in *Saludos Amigos* (1943) and *The Three Caballeros* (1944) was voiced by José Oliveira.
† Louise Beaudet passed away in 1997. The interview was not published during her *lifetime*. Part of it was released in The Disney Blog in 2008.

your attention. We tried to understand Matisse and Picasso and others, even though our end result shows very little of that literally.

You have to realize the vitality of all these young men who were, for the first time in their lives, paid for drawing all day. They had an educational system where the director would come over and explain what he did; the story men would explain who and why, how you build a certain gag and why the laugh is where it is; the musicians would tell us about the musical end of it.*

Q: Asking you as a historian: What can a new generation of cartoon creators learn from the evolution of animation and especially from Disney film history?

A: Walt Disney and his artists invented an art form. They were not the first ones to animate, of course, but the Studio was the first studio to create characters and animated cartoons that connected deeply and universally with the audience.

Understanding what worked and did not work in the way Disney artists built stories, designed the characters, animated them and made them come to life is therefore critical to new generations of cartoon creators, to avoid making mistakes that could be avoided.

In fact, studying Disney history is not only critical for new artists, it also makes sense if you are an animation executive. The move from the old Hyperion Studio to the modern Burbank Studio in 1940 in many ways destroyed the team spirit that existed in the cramped quarters of Hyperion. The new studio was a very modern and functional one but the artists had less chance of interacting and therefore felt isolated, which led to a sense of disaffection, which was part of what led to the 1941 Disney strike.

When Michael Eisner and Jeffrey Katzenberg decided to build the new animation building, which opened on the Disney lot in 1995, they committed a very similar mistake by commissioning a very functional but impersonal space. The artists, when they moved in, felt as isolated as their predecessors had in 1940. John Lasseter and Ed Catmull, from Pixar, on the other end had designed a new building which encouraged interaction and collaboration. The fact that John and Ed are both Disney history enthusiasts is no coincidence, of course.

---

* *Walt' People—Volume 4: Talking Disney with the Artists Who Knew Him.* Marc Davis by Armand Eisen. Bloomington: Xlibris, 2007.

55

The 3D Animator from Germany

Felix Goennert

Felix Goennert (born in 1975 in Lüneburg, Germany) is a professor at the Film University in Potsdam-Babelsberg, where he has studied too. He was the lead character animator for the CGI-animated feature *Lissi und der Wilde Kaiser (Lissi and the Wild Emperor, 2007)*. He won more than 30 awards for his 3D-animated short films.

Q: Your short films *Lucia* (2004), *Apollo* (2010), and *Loup* (2016) show 3D-stylized children's characters that move and behave absolutely natural and in a child way. Even the small insect in your movie *BSSS* (1999) seemed to be a child. The role profiles work 100 percent. If you plan animation, do you start with the characters or a situation?

A: My stories usually develop from a character whom I have "met" before. These meetings start for example with sketches in notebooks or by modeling a character in clay. Sometimes while doing this, ideas develop for situations that often already bear conflict potential. Lucia was a little girl who has to spend a night in a hospital, and BSSS was a fly that discovers an elephant in a children's book doing a "trunk stand."

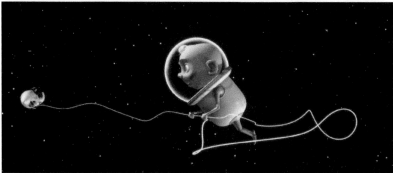

Apollo. (Courtesy of Felix Goennert.)

Q: You work around children's imagination. In *Apollo*, a boy plays with a toy rocket and finds himself in outer space. Do you have a straight approach to your own childhood dreams? And if, is this helpful to animation?

A: Animation has a lot to do with dreams. I guess this is one of its most essential characteristics. Besides their natural curiosity, children have a more unprejudiced approach to imagination than us adults. They have no problems to dream, any time, even daydream. In one of my school reports there is a note: "Felix has problems to concentrate on the class." I preferred to look out of the window and imagine what I could do outside. Although it is a lot of work to make an animated film, the films that you mentioned opened the chance to return somehow to this state of mind. I am sure this attitude has helped me with the animation. The spaceship, by the way, is made of metal and fully functional, with a hatch that can be closed and little light bulbs in the panel.

Q: Have you done research in children's psychology or do you create your characters instinctively, from gut feeling?

A: Characters are like real human beings, they have a life of their own. Of course one can think a lot theoretically and sometimes one has to find out why an animation doesn't work correctly. Basically, however, to me during the process of animation there is no such thing as theory, more internalized insights from previous research. I have absolutely no idea about children's psychology. I find it interesting to see how actors approach their parts. Stanislavsky's definition of authenticity in my opinion applies the same to the play with a character in animation. As animators are not on the stage themselves this is a slightly different process. It doesn't happen in real time as is the case in film and theatre. It does develop in space and time through a character that you bring to life. Then I really have the feeling that the character determines what is going to happen. I am only the one who pushes the buttons or moves the pencil into a certain direction.

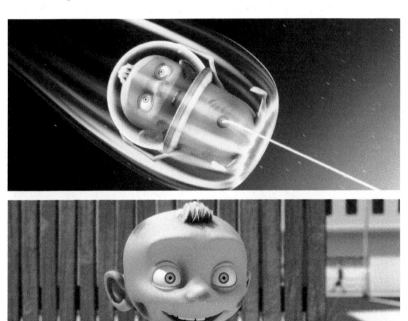

Apollo. (Courtesy of Felix Goennert.)

Q: In your animation one notices many little details and gestures that are missing in standardized mass animation. Are these those details that are omitted in series production, those little things that bring a character really to life?

A: I guess with mass animation you mean commercial production? I don't know if my animation differs from it so much. My working method is usually based on layered animation. For each particular scene you animate the most important parts of a character. The animation of the less important parts will follow. This approach forces first to abstraction and to reflection about how to approach timing and spacing, the elementary parts of animation. After that I descend in several steps to a more intuitive, flowing type of work which evolves into a more natural movement than the frame-based process would allow. Perhaps a more personal style develops out of that. Finally, in the productions that you have mentioned I intend to communicate most clearly to the audience what the characters think and feel and why they act that way.

Q: One notices the large, expressive eyes of your characters.

A: The eyes of my characters are often that large because sights tell a big chunk of the stories. Mostly I eschew dialogue so that it is helpful that a viewer recognizes immediately where to and why a character looks, even if it occupies only a small part of the frame.

Q: The most prominent character you have animated, however, you haven't developed yourself. Your short film *Der Bonker [The Bunker]* watched by millions on YouTube is a spoof about Adolf Hitler who was caricatured by Walter Moers showing the German dictator and "Fuehrer" singing in his bathtub a short time before his suicide in the bunker of the Reich Chancellery. How did you approach this caricature as an animator and hired hand?

A: There were already two essentials for *The Bonker* when they asked me to do the project. On one hand there was a storyboard by Walter Moers himself, on the other hand there was a song by Thomas Pigor. Walter's drawings often consist of cursorily sketched lines. Nevertheless, he puts the expression of the character straight. Therefore it was quite easy for me to bring the character to life, together with Carla Heinzel. Thomas' song determined the rhythm and creates a catchy tune on the sound level to the rubber ducky theatre on the image level. The main challenge was to translate the charm of Walter's drawings into the 3D world of computer animation. By the way, the clip remained in the drawer for one year before it was finally published in 2006 and one day later it was uploaded by somebody in the internet. At that time YouTube and consorts had just started in Germany.

Q: You are a teacher too. What do you recommend your students concerning creation and direction of characters who should develop their own personality on screen? Do you talk about acting theories or are these not so important for animators? Is it more important to watch and observe humans and animals and reproduce them with digital tools?

A: I believe that everything that helps to understand why things work or maybe not should be part of the animation training. In part I introduce acting theories. Exact observation and feeling of the body are highly important. These are things that you can learn in exercises. I notice, however, that the ones who get special results command both characteristics. Besides the kinetic basics, for instance how to animate a walking cycle, it is most important how to get inside a character. While doing this one sometimes grimaces, screws up the face or crooks on the chair. With that the whole process becomes livelier and you will have fun immediately. Video references, too, help with more complicated movements. To get to satisfactory animation you need both: intuition and analysis. Only when I know what's behind a movement I will be able to determine its meaning and have it correspond with the story that is being told. Of course, good character design helps with the animation. Especially as computer graphics tend to photo realism and the opportunities to navigate complexity increase with the modern tools I recommend that you keep it clear and simple. To create good animation one should deduce the design from the story and from the resources you have at your disposal. In the best case, an artistically exciting and surprising performance will evolve.

Q: **Can you please name a few movies that contain role profiles and/or character animation that left an impression on you?**

A: It's difficult to draw up a shortlist. Sometimes it's only a moment that excites me. Many of my inspirations come from feature films, comics, art and photography. In the realm of computer animation I follow the output of Pixar since the 1980s. Two short films that have impressed me in particular were *Luxo Jr.* (1986) and *Knick Knack* (1989).

56

The European Producer
Gerhard Hahn

Since 1980 Gerhard Hahn (born in 1946 in Rehburg, Germany) is one of the leading European animation producers and directors and was one of the first in Europe to open an animation studio in Asia (Saigon). Consequently his studio Hahn Film AG, since 1986 located in Berlin, relied on series characters on TV as well as on the cinema screen: *Werner-Beinhart* (1990), *Astcrix Conquers America* (1994), *Bibi Blocksberg* (since 1994), *The Pirates of Tortuga: Under the Black Flag* (2001), *SimsalaGrimm, School for Vampires, Mia and me: Adventures in Centopia*. In addition to TV and cinema, Hahn Film launched internationally successful merchandising brands such as the *Worry Eaters*. The company also produced animated advertising spots, music videos, and computer games in house and, with Hahn Graphics, specializes in graphic solutions for brand identity, product development, books, packaging design, and retail.

Q: As one of the few important European animation studios, Hahn Film has consequently focused on series characters. How influential is the European comic strip culture and what about using tested merchandising characters in cartoons?

A: Considering films produced by Hahn Film, there is only a minor influence of comic strip culture—be it European, Anglo-Saxon or Japanese—and this for two reasons: We attach great importance to the universality of characters and stories. Our productions are developed, not least because to get them financed, for the international market, and therefore should be understood by audiences in all parts of the world. That's why our series are mainly inspired by characters and stories that found their way into international popular culture in the widest sense of the word: vampires from *School for Vampires*, elves, unicorns and Pans in *Mia and me: Adventures in Centopia* right up to the tales of Arabian Night in *Sherazade: The Untold Stories*. Here we have characters and stories that are comparatively easy to pitch internationally. This is true for other projects too that we currently work on: *Ganesha, help!* is a series that is being developed in association with a partner from India. In the center we have an Indian deity of the same name. Our approach is to shape this ancient Indian topic attractively in design and storytelling for the international market.

The second essential reason is the age of the target groups. Depending on the series it's either intended for 4 to 6 years, i.e., preschool, or for 6 to 9 years old. In this age comic strips and their stylings play not that role as they do for the 10 to 12 years old—but for this age group there are no firm time slots on TV. We all know that kids in this age watch programs wherever they are, that means online. The double-etched formula therefore reads: no time slots, no co-funding from broadcasters, ergo no products.

Regarding the adaptation of approved merchandising characters we make a point developing, producing and marketing our own intellectual properties. Apart from the distinctively greater creative pleasure in developing own properties, options in financing and re-financing play an important, if not the important part. Considering the funding, let's suppose we have a German broadcaster who contributes to the production of a series. That means that we as producers are forced to put up more than 80 percent of the budget by ourselves. Therefore a participation in potential license agreements and merchandise receipts is almost inevitable. We have to keep in mind that the relatively low input of broadcasters makes it necessary that we have to calculate our production budgets as low as possible to obtain funding reliably. This results in the fact that an animation producer today cannot recoup his efforts—which in case of a series might extend over a period of two to three years—solely from producing. A merchandising license deal as early as possible is a relevant factor. We know both extremes from our own work: In the early history of Hahn Film besides feature films such as *Werner* and *Asterix Conquers America* there were successful series like *Benjamin the Elephant (Benjamin Bluemchen)* and *Bibi Blocksberg*. This was commissioned work without shares or any additional revenues. 30 years ago that made sense. Today's situation is different. The other extreme is our series *Worry Eaters*. In order to pitch the series idea I had presented stuffed dolls some years ago—with the result that the dolls and related products became an instant international sales hit before the first screenplay was written. The relatively absurd or at least untypical effect is that the merchandising recoupements from marketing the dolls now are a significant part of series financing which in turn hopefully will further fuel the merchandising success.

Q: You were actively involved in the evolutionary step from 2D to 3D animation. Your studio uses both techniques. What experiences did you make? What differences do you see in designing cartoon characters?

A: Generally speaking the truth is that 2D wasn't removed by 3D. Out of the projects that we currently have in development or preproduction two series are in 2D. Once we have developed the characteristics of certain figures and the story concept so that they sort of awaken to life one feels what technique is the adequate one—I shouldn't speak of technique but rather call it style. The development of characters is done from an aesthetic point of view. The mere technical aspect is added when it comes to efficiency in realization which starts with the work on the screenplay in which one has to take into consideration the number of characters and sets in the respective episodes. The advantage of 3D is that characters and sets, once modeled, can be re-used easier from episode to episode. If I travel in each episode through different sets and meet new characters, then 2D is better—but as I say, this is only dictated by production economics. Our guideline, however, is: style and aesthetics come first, not the technique.

Q: In the case of series the characters you have to work with and create stories for have preconceived, prefabricated role profiles. Can it be an advantage to tailor stories to such characters?

A: Neither one nor the other is, taken by itself, the case; the work on the Design Bible and the Writer's Bible go hand in hand and cross-fertilize. When we start with a topic and have, for instance, to create a children's series from One Thousand and One Nights we develop the main characters and their antagonists and their motives and objectives first. Considering the adaptation of more or less famous tales we want to break of course with traditional role images. I have to define this primarily in the design of the character. And then our authors will write this character exactly this way. The characters, their motives and their constellations come first in our company. There is a simple rule of thumb that we find confirmed ever when we release a pitch book. At the first glimpse of the character designs I discover the tonality of the series (if the character design suggests something completely different than the stories promise, the concept sure cannot be consistent).

Q: Once you have founded a studio in Vietnam and acquired experiences with filmmaking in Asia early on. How does European animation production position itself today between Asia and America? How would you judge the development of intercultural projects?

A: There is a rather mundane, banal reason for the previous and still practiced cooperation between Europe and Asia: the labor costs. This simple fact implicated that our partners in Far East always were service producers. There was no partnership on a creative level which would have led to a coproduction partnership. The situation is changing currently. The artistic potential of companies in Asia begins to grow. Nevertheless, as I see it, the situation will continue for some time that European producers will handle the creative part, from design and script development to animatics, and our Asian partners will do the actual production.

China, on the other hand, rates high alone for the size of the market. But one should not blend oneself by this Klondike-like hype and only have Yuan signs in the eyes. For some time, we are in touch with Chinese studios but haven't found the likewise artistically and economically compellent case to cooperate necessarily.

The question of chances for intercultural projects can be answered both for and against. Culturally we are looking back at different pictorial and different narrative traditions. Stories and characters that answer a claim of interculturality run the risk of being neither fish nor fowl. When I watch Asian and American series then I am expecting either an Asian or an American series, with all their respective specifica, and nothing else. I think that one shouldn't enforce artificially interculturality and drag it in by the head and shoulders—which will bring us back to the question of European positioning between America and Asia. From my standpoint the specific idiosyncrasies and individualities are significant and this will remain so for some time. The three cultures and particularly these three markets work differently. A comparison of the production terms and budgets in America and Europe alone doesn't place, literally speaking, apples against pears but, considering the sheer volume, melons against lemons. We are well advised [in Europe] to make the best out of lemons and in the most successful case this will be lemonade.

Q: You are very close to the audience. What can you say about audience reception? What insights did you win? Which features does the audience appreciate?

A: This directness between us and the audience doesn't—alas—exist completely because there are the broadcasters in between. The broadcasters receive the mails from the audience. If we develop characters and stories convinced that they will please children internationally we have, provided the case of conventional funding, at first the hurdle of the editors of our national TV broadcasters. We have to convince them and have them confront us with their own insights. Pointedly expressed, it is the reception behavior of TV editors that we could comment on. It is similar when our colleagues in sales and distribution offer our productions on international trade fairs. The colleagues in distribution face a test audience that doesn't consist of kids but buyers who make decisions based on their own insight too.

The idiosyncrasies of our characters—no matter whether they are human or animal with humanoid behavior—are the same that we appreciate at humans and particularly children: friendship, trust, affection but they are also allowed to make mistakes. The path is being laid by the design. Once a character is so well-designed that it is received as a completely autonomous entity with own idiosyncrasies we have done our job well.

Q: You have successfully animated girl characters, from *Bibi Blocksberg* to *Mia and me*. What do you have to observe considering character development, story concept and animation when aiming at an audience of young girls?

A: As the target group of these series consists in fact of young girls the question is easily answered: The main characters like Bibi or Mia must be designed in a way and have idiosyncrasies that the young viewers can accept them and wish to have them as their best girl friend. And the stories that characters like Bibi or Mia experience must be told in a way that as a young girl you want to experience these together with the fictional character. That sounds trivial but must be accomplished first.

Q: One of your most interesting projects is a series called *Sherazade: The Untold Stories*. That was developed years ago, but you had to put it on hold for quite some time. Why?

A: I had the idea for Sherazade already in the late 1990s. The original working title was Arabian Nights and used themes from the Arabian Night tales. We had the contract with a broadcaster already in our pocket and had aroused international interest for license. Then came 9/11, and from one (terrible) day to another the word "Arabian" in the title became box-office poison. The project was dead. But I was still convinced of the basic concept—Sherazade is not the story teller of the framework plot but the heroine herself who experiences all adventures and then later projects them onto figures like Sinbad or Aladdin—and haven't lost faith in the project. Over five years ago we said farewell to the (at that time) 12-year-old 2D designs—with a tear in our eyes and a smile—and reworked the project completely for a 3D series. Then we went to a local broadcaster and found open ears. The work on screenplays began and now *Sherazade: The Untold Stories* is in postproduction. So you see, we do not only tell fairy tales, sometimes we experience fairy tales ourselves.

57

The Stop-Motion Historian

Mike Hankin

Mike Hankin (born in 1948 in Morden, Surrey) is an expert on stop-motion films. He has written a highly acclaimed 3-volume *Ray Harryhausen* biography and is preparing another book devoted to George Pal's *Puppetoons*.

Q: Ray Harryhausen took acting lessons. Do you recognize a particular Harryhausen pattern of acting in his pictures?

A: There is a wonderful story of how Ray would act out various moves of the gorilla model, such as thumping the ground, while working on his first feature film, *Mighty Joe Young* (1949). All animators are actors by proxy, whether they were trained in the art, or just transferring movement into their creations through their own observations. Many friends of Ray have been witness to naturally performed body actions, such as gestures, that had unconsciously found their way into his animation. Artists working in drawn animation would often have a mirror close by to work out facial expressions, so it follows that model animators would occasionally use their own bodies to time a movement. It is doubtful that the classic Harryhausen humanoid walk pattern: shoulders back, arms bent at the elbows, used in creations such as the Ymir and Cyclops can be directly attributed to Ray's own forward movement, but that is, where imagination comes into play.

Q: When one asked Ray about animation, he always said the way how he animated became his second nature but he couldn't define his style of animation.

A: It is very difficult to define Ray's animation style. He worked very hard to make the manipulations of his models instinctive. We are fortunate to be able to view his earliest experiments and how the movements of his creations progressed from the stiff-legged walk of his first dinosaur figures to the point where his acquired knowledge of the mechanics of locomotion was transferred to the anatomically correct creations in such films as *The Valley of Gwangi* (1969). This, of course, is not only attributable to his increased proficiency as an animator, but also as a model designer and builder. It is well known that Ray religiously studied the movement of various living entities that were close approximations to the creature he was working on, but the art of animation also comes from within. Maybe this could be termed his "style," taking his knowledge of movement and coupling it with something of himself, acting out how he himself would react to a certain situation.

Q: In later years, while living in Britain, he denied the certain grotesqueness that he had introduced himself into *The 7th Voyage of Sinbad*. He wouldn't go anymore for his fanciful comic book *Cyclops*, wouldn't show much sympathy for the creature, but would say that Cyclopes are just people like you and me, no hooves and pointed ears, only overgrown and with a single eye. Do you feel there is a difference between the American and the British Ray Harryhausen?

A: *The 7th Voyage of Sinbad* (1958) was the first of Ray's films that readily lent itself to a parade of grotesque creatures. If you take into consideration one definition of the word grotesque as "extravagantly formed" then Ray certainly exploited this phenomenon in his later, British-made films. His first Sinbad film seemed to establish a template for his future cinematic adventures, which apart from the single animated squirrel in his next film, *The 3 Worlds of Gulliver* (1959), would feature multiple creatures. Grotesque can be aligned with memorable, which is why most admirers of Ray's work retain stronger images of his creatures in their mind than the films in which they featured.

Q: You interviewed many people who acted in Ray's films. What did they tell you about his methods of working with actors? How would they prepare to act with things that were not visible on the set but added later in postproduction?

A: Every actor I talked to agreed that Ray was an enthusiastic director of scenes involving his creations. He would go to great pains to show through his illustrations the creature they were supposed to face, so that they could picture it in their mind's eye. He would also ensure that they had a visual reference, which actress Caroline Munro, in *The Golden Voyage of Sinbad* (1973), lovingly called a "Monster Stick". Intrinsically, a long pole cut to the height of the missing creature adorned with the image of an eye painted at the top, which would give the actor a point of reference to maintain eye-line, whenever possible. Tom Pigott-Smith, Thallo in *Clash of the Titans* (1981), remembers that Ray, on occasion, would forget that he was dealing with actors rather than models, asking him one time to fall backward, slowly, after he had been stabbed by the absent, animated character Calibos. Perhaps the best image to conjure up in your mind is Ray directing Raquel Welch in *One Million Years B.C.* (1966), when from the back of a truck he made the action of flapping wings to represent the Pteranodon that was about to snatch her up from the volcanic poolside.

Q: Do you see an evolution from Ray's films to present-day CGI?

A: Many of today's practitioners in CGI confess to being influenced and to reference Ray's work. If there is a need to create an apparent living being, the portrayal of accurate movement is paramount to maintain believability. Ray was a master of the movement, perfected over years of careful study and countless experimentation. His method of creating this movement through model animation may now be seen as outdated, at least as far as supposedly living creatures are concerned, but how they moved is still a specialized skill. CGI is only a progression of technique. I have little doubt that the thousands of film industry artists in the past that built, painted, manipulated images and all the other skills that combine to make moving pictures would have loved to use today's technology if it had been available to them. In reverse, many of the people who presently work in the industry yearn for the tactile satisfaction of creating something by hand. The sad fact is that in most cases the public will not accept less than perfect effects. The destruction of obvious miniatures, hand-painted backdrops, objects held aloft by wires and, dare I say it, creatures created through the use of model animation are now regarded with a degree of derision. The public can still enjoy and admire films made with physical effects in the past, but in a sort of tolerant, nostalgic way.

Q: While Ray animated anatomically correct, George Pal, one of his early mentors, preferred cartooniness over anatomy. His replacement animation technique was like 2D-turned 3D. So he must have had an enormous influence on today's computer-animated films, perhaps even more so than Ray.

A: I think a line can be drawn between the influence of the George Pal puppet films and the genus of film with which Ray Harryhausen is associated.

One of the reasons that Ray came up with the name Dynamation was to differentiate his type of film to that of drawn or pure puppet animation. The characters in Pal's Puppetoon films were never meant to be viewed as living entities, whereas the Harryhausen creatures were intended to be part of the real world. The lines did cross, with Ray producing his pure animated puppet fairy tale films at the beginning of his career and Pal using single animated figures that were meant to be living creatures, such as the squirrel in *The Great Rupert* (1949) and the Loch Ness Monster in *7 Faces of Dr. Lao* (1964), but in general they were known for differing types of animated figures. Shades of Pal's Puppetoons can be seen in CGI films such as the *Toy Story* series, although the humor is vastly different. The influence of Harryhausen permeates everything from *Jurassic Park* (1993) to *Avatar* (2009) and beyond.*

Q: **Pal later turned to feature films, but some critics and reviewers say he handed his actors like puppets. Do you know anything about Pal's approach to acting? He started out as a caricaturist.**

A: Previous to his role on *Tom Thumb* (1958), George Pal's only other live-action directorial exercise was with the actor Wam Heskes in *Hoe Een Reclame-Affiche Ontstond (How an Advertisement Poster Came Into Being)* (1938) and two of his Puppetoon shorts, *A Date With Duke* and *Rhapsody in Wood* (both 1947). His decision to direct *Tom Thumb* only came about through a mixture of economics (making the film in England brought it in on budget) and his connection to the project that he had been trying to make from as early as 1943. His involvement with all aspects of movie-making from the very beginning of his career gave him the experience that a director needs, and although none of the films he directed can be described as breaking new ground, they all have a certain charm in execution. *The Time Machine* (1960), in the opening Victorian London scenes with the future time-traveller, George and his group of friends exudes a feeling of warmth and camaraderie that immediately draws you into their world. This shows a director in tune with his subject matter.

Q: **What can we still learn from seeing animation done by George Pal, Ray Harryhausen, or Jim Danforth?**

A: George Pal, Ray Harryhausen and Jim Danforth are among the few film-makers whose diversity of skills contributed to the overall look of films on which they worked. These rare individuals stand apart from so many other gifted artists in the film industvry, because each created their own niche and body of work that in turn has influenced so many others.

* The living skeletons in Tim Burton's *Miss Peregrine's Home for Peculiar Children* (2016).

58

The Late Stop-Motion Legend Himself

Ray Harryhausen

Ray Harryhausen (born in 1920 in Los Angeles) passed away in London in 2013, 2 months before his 93rd birthday. For more than 30 years, I (RG) was associated with him while I curated the different exhibitions in Germany (where his family name came from: Harriehausen) that had his animation artifacts on display. A great deal was written about him. He was the only VFX and stop-motion artist who had several books and countless articles devoted to his work. Digging in our files we found an extensive career interview that I had conducted for an exhibition of his work in the German Film Museum Frankfurt in 1988. It is virtually unknown as it was published in German language.* From my notes I have added remarks that he made to me over the years, facts that involved his models, actors he worked with, and composers who were very important to enhance his animation.

---

* Rolf Giesen: *Sagenhafte Welten. Der Trickspezialist Ray Harryhausen*. Frankfurt/Main: Deutsches Filmmuseum, 1988.

Q: It didn't start with Eve, it started with Kong, right?

A: I've seen *King Kong* in 1933. Rather innocently, I went to Grauman's Chinese Theatre in Hollywood to see this picture, and I haven't been the same since. The screening changed my life completely. Months, years went by until I had found out how *King Kong* was really made. The whole thing fascinated me. I made it my hobby and finally my profession.

Q: The premiere of King Kong at Grauman's Chinese in March 1933 must have been a big show.

A: Of course. The Chinese and the Egyptian Theatre were two very important cinemas in Hollywood. They got always previews of the top movies. Sid Grauman who had built the theatres was a master showman. *King Kong* opened with a live on-stage prologue in the jungle: drums, acrobats and trapeze artists, all in full costume. That was highly impressive. The show went on for an hour before the movie began. Then the curtain opened, and Max Steiner's great crescendo was to be heard. Before one entered the cinema one had to pass the atrium where the footprints of the famous stars are—and in this atrium they had the giant bust that was used in *King Kong*: The mouth moved, the eyes rolled, the nostrils inflated. Beneath the bust a group of pink flamingos stalked through the jungle scenery. Sure, it was a terrific sight, particularly way back in 1933. Something I will never forget. This is proof that a movie can change a whole life.

Q: So it was the grandeur that impressed you as a child. Which films have influenced you besides *King Kong*?

A: There were many movies. A very early impression was *The Lost World*, the silent version. Then *Metropolis* although we didn't understand it at that time because someone* had butchered the American release beyond comprehension and taken out a lot of footage so that we thought it was just a German art movie. And some other foreign films whose titles I don't remember. Later, *She* and *The Last Days of Pompeii*, both produced by Merian Cooper, come to mind. [In other discussions, I've had with him he mentioned *The Golem* starring Paul Wegener, *Dracula*, *Frankenstein*, *The Bride of Frankenstein*, *Dr. Jekyll and Mr. Hyde* featuring Fredric March, and *Deluge*, which we saw together as he had an VHS tape of the print that they had found in Italy.] Merian Cooper was a super showman too. He knew how to stage a spectacle, how to develop large-scale action and build drama, abilities he demonstrated to the utmost as a producer of *King Kong*. I am jolly glad that it wasn't Edward G. Robinson and *Little Caesar* who attracted my younger self. Otherwise I might have become a second Godfather.

---

* Channing Pollock, an American playwright.

Q: Thirteen years later, right after the War, on *Mighty Joe Young*, you found yourself working with Willis O'Brien [OBie], the chief technician of *The Lost World* and *Kong*, and Merian C. Cooper himself. What did impress you more in your life: the birth of your daughter Vanessa or the day OBie called to invite you to work on *Mighty Joe*?

A: [Laughs.] When OBie called. Both, Coop and OBie, were, in many ways, my mentors—especially Willis O'Brien since I had found out that it was him who was in charge of the technical side of *Kong.*

Q: How did you find out?

A: I studied souvenir books, magazines, Popular Mechanics—and always the name Willis O'Brien turned up.

Q: That's amazing that somebody studied technical credits because in those days, if at all, the only ones working behind the camera that people were interested in were the directors.

A: After all, *King Kong* was a highly technical movie. There were exhibitions devoted to the work of Willis O'Brien. So his name stuck out. Merian Cooper also, as producer of the film, received a good deal of publicity. It was very exciting to work with both of them, also with director Ernest Schoedsack. But he and OBie seemed to have some problems. There were days when OBie would return from story conferences and damn Schoedsack.

Q: You were not the only animator on *Mighty Joe.*

A: There were several people who tried animating Joe. Buzz Gibson and his brother [Carl] came in. They had worked on *Kong.* They were there for a month. I didn't see what they did, but from what I heard their footage was unusable. Gibson said that the Joe Young models were too small compared to Kong. The brothers [Marcel and Victor] Delgado tried. Scott Whitaker [who worked as special effects animator at RKO and as story artist and writer at Walt Disney Studios in Burbank] tried. All to no avail. So I ended up doing about eighty-five percent of the animation because I seemed to be the fastest. Only one other guy, Peter Peterson, a grip who watched me animating, did succeed. He later suffered from multiple sclerosis I heard. There was only one of the four Joes that I felt comfortable with. As nearby they shot a movie with Jennifer Jones I named the model Jennifer.

Q: You first met Willis O'Brien when he worked at MGM on a project titled *War Eagles*, which wasn't finished. Do you remember this project? The protagonists were Vikings who lived in a fantasy land somewhere at North Pole where they hunted dinosaurs and who, riding on huge eagles, would save New York City from an attack of German airships.

A: From a classmate I learned that he and Cooper worked on a new project at MGM in 1939. So I called him and told him about my interest in model animation and asked him if he would allow me to show him some of my models. He graciously invited me over to the studio. So I went to MGM and was guided into his office. He had three rooms full of artwork, paintings, and drawings. I was overwhelmed. There must have been about 200 paintings and drawings for the projected *War Eagles*: highly impressive. Eagles sitting on the areola of the Statue of Liberty. OBie's wife, Darlyne, was around too. He was very interested and offered a lot of constructive criticism. I had brought a Stegosaurus model and he advised me to study anatomy. The legs of that model indeed looked like plums.

Q: Personally, are you economically minded?

A: Oh yes! I think that one should do anything as reasonably as possible. I don't believe that it makes sense to throw big sums out of the window, just for an effect that is to be seen on screen only 20 seconds. Or 10 seconds. So I tried to find a way to make movies of this type for a reasonable budget without having it all look cheap.

Q: In 1953, *The Beast from 20,000 Fathoms* started a cycle of films with monsters that were awakened and created by nuclear tests.

A: That's right. Sometime later the Japanese produced their *Godzilla* from practically the same concept. In America there were Them! and other films that warned against the elemental force of the atomic bomb, a whole group of films that evoked subconscious fears of what might happen if they would drop the bomb. The creatures just worked as personification of the horror that the atomic bomb could bring about the civilized world.

Q: You, too, continued the cycle that you had begun and started a long-term partnership with producer Charles H. Schneer who worked for Columbia Pictures.

A: Charles saw *The Beast from 20,000 Fathoms*. A friend of mine with whom I was in the Army [Harryhausen served as camera assistant under Joe Biroc and others in the Signal Corps] called and said that there was a producer who wanted to destroy the Golden Gate Bridge in a film and introduced me to Charles. The idea sounded interesting—particularly as there was a giant octopus involved that should create all havoc. Otherwise, *It Came from Beneath the Sea* was a variation of the basic concept of *Beast* with the slight difference that the nuclear test happened under water. That led the octopus grow to enormous proportions. It invaded San Francisco and, among other horrible deeds, pulled down the Golden Gate Bridge.

Q: Economically minded, as you are, you reduced the number of tentacles for animation, right?

A: An octopus as we know has eight tentacles but we thought if it would have less it would reduce costs, time and construction work. My father [Fred

Harryhausen] made all those armatures from my designs. So this octopus became a sixtopus as it had only six tentacles which, of course, nobody realized as it was never seen in all its tentacled glory—until someone published it.

Q: Someone?

A: Someone named Forry Ackerman who edited a magazine called "Famous Monsters of Filmland." Carelessly I gave away the internal secrets and since then it haunts me. Sam Katzman was the executive producer of Columbia's B-Picture Unit. When I showed him my octopus designs, he was aghast and started to draw a thing that resembled a balloon with tentacles. "That's what an octopus looks like," he said. Instead it looked like something out of a Popeye cartoon. He also wanted me to do *The Giant Claw* [an interplanetary buzzard that was as big as a battleship], but I turned him down. But back to Charles: After *It Came from Beneath the Sea* we did *Earth vs. the Flying Saucers*, which Charles developed, inspired by all the headlines about Flying Saucer sightings. At that time there was no other chance than to make the aliens in the saucers villains. What they later tried in *Close Encounters* was almost impossible back then as nobody seemed to be interested in such a concept. Retrospectively, *Earth vs. the Flying Saucers* was one of those cliché concepts, which went back to H. G. Wells' formula that each creature from outer space had to be aggressive.

Q: You shot some test footage for a proposed film version of War of the Worlds.

A: I did an alien with a huge head crawling on its tentacles out of a spaceship. I tried to get [producer] Jesse Lasky interested. Later George Pal made a version of his own for Paramount that didn't have any animation [released in 1953].

I did some concept art for *Earth vs. the Flying Saucers* that had the Venusians with bodies like snakes brainwash earthlings. On a research trip I even went and visited George Adamski [then a well-known, infamous UFOlogist]. The second time, I saw him he was building a brick wall mural, a rather mundane thing to do for a man who claimed to have met with aliens.

After this picture, looking for a new project, I took my old drawings for a project tentatively called *The Giant Ymir* out of the drawer. Charles was impressed, a screenwriter rewrote the treatment that I had written with Charlott Knight, my former acting coach, and I added new illustrations. *The Giant Ymir* was retitled *20 Million Miles to Earth*. Eventually, my dream became true. We went to Europe, to Rome where all second unit scenes were shot. I was fascinated by all those ancient relics, but Larry Butler, the second unit director, only called it a bunch of old stones. Then we returned to Hollywood, hired a director [Nathan Juran] and finished the production. Charles had separated in the meantime from Sam Katzman and founded his own company, Morningside Productions. *20 Million Miles to Earth* was his first film as independent producer.

Q: The perennial childhood favorite, however, was *The 7th Voyage of Sinbad* in 1958.

A: Sinbad, yes. Of course we couldn't film the Arabian Nights in black and white. Something like this had to be produced in color although there were a lot of problems as I had to work with dupes for the effects. In spite of the technical difficulties, we brought the film in for less than a million dollar. I guess we spent 650,000 dollars. For an Arabian Nights Fairy Tale! Nowadays, they spent that budget on a single scene! Even at that time Sinbad was true low budget. Luckily, we got magnificent costumes from Columbia which, by the way, were left over from a cancelled Rita Hayworth project. If I recall correctly that project was *Joseph and His Brethren*. We were one of the first American production companies that shot in Spain. For the location shooting we had four or five weeks. Six months later we shot the interiors at the studio. And then I had another 4 or 5 months for the animation.

Q: Many young people my age were as much intrigued by *7th Voyage* as you were by *Kong* (and a later generation by *Star Wars*): John Landis, Dennis Muren, and many more. Even Wim Wenders seemed to have liked it as I once heard. What was it that made this film so unique?

A: I don't know. I tried to show things in *The 7th Voyage of Sinbad* that people hadn't seen before. While we were in production on Mighty Joe, Douglas Fairbanks, Jr. did *Sinbad the Sailor* (1947) for the same company, RKO, but he only talked about the giant Roc. All those miracles were not on the screen. Dale Robertson did another one, *Son of Sinbad* (1955), for Howard Hughes, which became a girlie show. Lili St. Cyr started out as a stripper in night clubs. Even the first *Thief of Bagdad* (1924), the silent one with Douglas Fairbanks, Sr., wasn't that much effects-wise. Well, they had a flying carpet and a few special effects sequences but nothing that really reproduced the fantastic world of 1001 Nights.

In *The 7th Voyage of Sinbad*, however, we wanted to reproduce the fairy tale world as lively and faithful as possible on the screen. Originally I had a drawing done of an unnamed hero fighting a skeleton. I took it, named him Sinbad and added more drawings that I showed around: Sinbad fighting a dragon, the seamen cracking a giant egg and pulling out a two headed Roc chick, two Cyclopes fighting over tiny human victims, and another one which showed one Cyclops cowering behind his barbecue roasting a sailor. I showed the drawings to various producers: George Pal and Jesse Lasky. I think I have shown it to Merian Cooper. Edward Small—I couldn't get past his secretary. But nobody was really interested. So I filed them. Years later, during a meeting with Charles Schneer, I took them out again. Charles became enthusiastic. I then made some changes to have the production less costly.

Q: You had a drawing that showed a Cyclops armed with a club prepared to attack a giant snake wrapped around a tree, with little sailors hanging in the branches.

A: We had to omit that. Charles hated snakes.

Anyway, Charles sent me to Spain for location scouting. When that was finished he came himself with key members of the team. From England we got Wilkie Cooper as director of photography and a few technicians. Other members of the crew we hired in Spain. It was a truly international picture. *The 7th Voyage of Sinbad* became a sleeper and one of the biggest box office hits Columbia Pictures had at that time.

Q: Incredibly enriched was the picture by Bernard Herrmann's powerful, fantastic score.

A: I was very pleased about that. When we began production I told Charles that we would need a good composer, somebody who would give to the picture what it deserves. Charles knew Bernie Herrmann and talked to him. Bernie came and saw the rough cut. He seemed to like what he saw at least so far that he didn't turn us down. He had turned down many film offers. He said he could do something for the picture, and I think that he composed an extraordinary score for *The 7th Voyage*.

Q: Technicolor, too, was important.

A: Color was very important. When I see the film today again on a big screen, the film stock proves to be relatively grainy, but I don't think that people go primarily to the cinema to see something technically perfect. They want to get thrilled and carried away by a story.

Q: Unforgettable was Torin Thatcher's magnificent presence as Sokurah the Magician.

A: Oh, Torin! He had a lot of stage experience and gave the part what it needed. Kerwin [Mathews], too, was convincing as Sinbad. He offered a different incarnation than Douglas Fairbanks, Jr. And we had Kathy Grant who gave the movie a lot of charm.

Q: Then, of course, besides the human actors, there were two wonderful stop-motion characters: the fire-breathing dragon and, above all, the horned Cyclops.

A: Yes, most people seem to remember the Cyclops. The dragon, too, was unique when it appeared on screen. People hadn't seen creatures like that before.

Q: Like many others, it was the Cyclops on the Beach who took me off when I was a child.

A: Really? You should have seen him. But I wished I would have had more time for animation back then. Well, it was the walk that made him.

Q: A clever design idea to have him not only one-eyed but one-horned too.

A: That was a last minute decision. Originally, he was supposed to have two horns. The unicorn [another mythological creature] has one.
[Harryhausen showed me a black-and-white photo of an earlier clay version of the Cyclops that looked god-awful. I've never seen anything so awkward. He would never ever have allowed somebody to publish this picture.]

Q: The steel armature was much bigger than your usual models, almost the same size as the original Kong. The second Cyclops, a roaring, bellowing hulk that was killed by the dragon was smaller. I heard that he was constructed by using the Ymir armature.

A: He had to be in proportion with the dragon. I should have made him different from the first one. Most people thought he was the same.

Q: There was a rumor that you offered Willis O'Brien a job to be your consultant on *7th Voyage*.

A: No. That's not true. He wouldn't have accepted it.

Q: When did you see OBie the final time? He passed away in November 1962.

A: When we made *The Animal World* for [producer] Irwin Allen. Originally, I was to contribute some of my early 16-mm test footage that I had made for a proposed dinosaur picture named *Evolution*. It was blown up to 35-mm film and looked quite good. But there was not enough of it. So they decided to animate new footage and hired OBie to design the sets, the animals, and the armatures for the models. The armatures were made in the Warner Bros. Machine shop. For close-ups Irwin Allen had mechanical dinosaur heads built. Obie and I looked at each other and wouldn't agree. An articulated stop-motion head would have been much better, but this way the director could yell while he manipulated it, "Roll the eyes! Do this, do that!"

Q: Which of your models would you call memorable from the point of character animation?

A: They all had their own personality. The Ymir had character, people remember him. The Cyclops had a very dynamic appearance. Trog in *Sinbad and the Eye of the Tiger*. I don't know if people thought he was a man in a monster suit. But he was an animated figure who had individual characteristics and left a high impact on screen.

Q: Even *The Beast from 20,000 Fathoms*, your first solo effort. At that time you and OBie had split already.

A: Yes, at the end the Beast gained a lot of sympathy, so to speak a victim of circumstances. Even Gwangi the Allosaurus from *The Valley of Gwangi* earns a certain sympathy. It is difficult to embrace sympathetic features to a reptile. With a gorilla it's easier because he looks more human, but with a lizard or an animal to which humans react with disgust it is very difficult. OBie always waited for the big picture. Many of his projects collapsed like *War Eagles*. When he had to move to a new, smaller house he would give away drawings as a present to kids in the street. And the kids would sell them for 10 cents a piece.

Q: You worked together on a project called *Valley of the Mist* that never got made.

A: After he received the Oscar for *Mighty Joe* people told him that now he could lean backwards and wait for the best offers. It never happened and I had to tell him that I would have to start my own business.

Q: You have a tendency to dare intriguingly complicated animation sequences: the fight with the living skeleton in *The 7th Voyage*, the seven skeletons in *Jason and the Argonauts* in 1963.

A: These were real milestones because something like that hadn't been tried before.

Q: A challenge for your animating skills?

A: Oh yes! I have visualized these scenes before and listened to my inner voice if I could translate this vision convincingly. To me it was with great satisfaction that the result on screen was even better than what I had imagined.

Q: The heads of the Hydra…

A: That's true for the Hydra too. It had seven heads and it was a challenge to animate them in a certain harmony. A creature with a multitude of heads is so eccentric that it would appear ridiculous, if one doesn't take care.

Q: How would you memorize each frame while facing such complicated animation sequences?

A: It becomes your second nature after having done more and more of it. You must have it in your blood.

Q: But there must have been mishaps and accidents during animation. Maybe you forgot a certain movement or the armature wouldn't work.

A: Very often so. Not that I would have forgotten something, but in the midst of shooting a joint or a leg would break or similar things would happen.

Sometimes you can continue after the damage has been repaired if the position of the figure has been registered, but most often you have to start from scratch.

Q: You once said that among your films, *Jason and the Argonauts* is your personal favorite.

A: I think it lasts. There are always scenes that you are ashamed of and you tell yourself: You should have spent more time. But we worked with the restraints of a certain budget and time pressure. With a big budget one can allow to test as long as everything is right. We never had the chance, however, and in 9 of 10 cases it's the first take that we use because we don't have the time and the money for a retake. All in all, we had maybe less than eight percent retakes of shots when the animation was too jerky or the split screen matte wasn't right or the image wasn't steady. Sometimes we were forced to approve results that normally wouldn't be accepted. There are people who don't compromise, but I think if you are in this business you have to.

Q: In the mid-1960s, you did two dinosaur films, one right after the other. The first, *One Million Years B.C.*, was a big success in 1966/1967, the second, *The Valley of Gwangi* in 1969, from an original idea by the late Willis O'Brien that didn't get made in its time, flopped. What did happen?

A: *One Million Years BC* was an interesting project. A Hammer production that, with good marketing, became very successful.

Q: It was *Raquel Welch vs. the Dinosaurs.*

A: In a way, yes. When Charles and I started *Gwangi*, the management of the distributor, Warner Bros., approved of our concept but 2 years later when the movie was finished there was a changeover of power—and very often the new management will not agree with projects the old regime has approved. They were not interested in *Gwangi* and just released the movie without any big advertising.

It was a shame because this film had many entertaining elements: cowboys, back then still popular, a western film scenery, and of course dinosaurs that most kids like. But nobody noticed when the movie was released. My wife's sister-in-law lived next to the cinema and didn't know that they showed the film. The publicity was disastrous and the movie was screened in a double feature as second movie. Most people who see Gwangi like it and find it very entertaining. It had a pretty good score by Jerome Moross.

Q: And there was the famous roping sequence when the cowboys lasso Gwangi (like they did in *Mighty Joe Young*). How was that done?

A: That was one of OBie's original ideas. We had a jeep with a pole inside, and they would lasso it. Then we did a split screen to cut the jeep out. Parts of the lasso were animated frame by frame.

Q: Was this the first time that you experienced the unpleasant changes in film industry?

A: No, not the first time. I have made these experiences before. There was the problem of block booking. If you made a picture in Europe then it was shown automatically on the double bill as Number 2, right after an American film. It was disappointing to have several years invested in a project and to see that it played second-string after an American cowboy film. Problems like these we had all the time. *Mysterious Island* was an exciting picture—and was shown in 1962 as a double feature with some Hammer film. If I recall correctly it was *The Pirates of Blood River.*[*] Really disappointing because most people came to see *Mysterious Island*, a well-made film with a great score again by Bernie Herrmann. Back then one was victim of a certain distribution style. I am convinced that Gwangi, with a clever PR man on board who would have had confidence in the picture, could have been a success for Warner Bros.

Q: Was it your idea to return to Sinbad in the early 1970s with *The Golden Voyage of Sinbad*?

A: Yes, we were looking for a new story and I suggested a new Sinbad story. I went again through 1001 Nights and wrote a 20-page treatment that I sold to Charles. We hired a screenwriter, Brian Clemens, with whom I collaborated closely—and so we developed the screenplay for *The Golden Voyage*. We tried a different Sinbad type this time. We didn't want to repeat the Douglas Fairbanks type: a grinning face, two rows of full teeth, moustache. Time ago it was okay but you couldn't repeat it permanently. This time our Sinbad was John Phillip Law. The colors were subdued which made the look more realistic, not as colorful as *The 7th Voyage of Sinbad*.

Q: In the mid-1970s when you made a third Sinbad, *Sinbad and the Eye of the Tiger*, you were the only special effects star. Your name was on the posters, in the advertisements, and program books. For some time there was also a fan magazine devoted exclusively to your Œuvre.[†] When you did *Clash of the Titans*, there was a wave of brand-new, highly expensive effects pictures: VFX suddenly were en vogue. They even compared the sounds of your mechanical owl Bubo (in *Clash*) with those of R2D2.

A: Yes, there was a new wave. SFX pictures we had already in the silent era. There was *Noah's Ark*, big effects in Cecil B. DeMille's *King of Kings*, and in *Metropolis*. In the 1930s, there was the disaster sequence of *Deluge*. In the 1950s, *The Rains of Ranchipur*, followed by other disaster pictures. Everything returns in a cycle. When audiences will become weary they

---

[*] Britain's biggest grossing double bill of 1962.
[†] *FXRH* (Special Visual Effects Created by Ray Harryhausen), published from 1971 to 1974.

will turn to something else like love stories. We were able, through all cycles, to make our pictures because we produced them always at reasonable prices so that there never would be a big loss.

Q: Are there any projects you regret that you couldn't make them?

A: There are several projects that I would have loved to do. Once I wanted to do the Russian legend of *Ilya Muromets*, using Symphony No. 3 by [Reinhold] Glière—until I found out that they had done it already in Russia [directed by Alexander Ptushko, in America released as *The Sword and the Dragon*, the first Russian scope picture]. A very expensive project would have been *Dante's Inferno* if one had it made properly. But I don't know how many people would have gone to see other people in hell... There would have been certain nudities, however, because you don't go to hell in clothes. Gustave Doré's renderings of *Dante's Inferno* have always impressed me. But today I wouldn't touch such a project. Once Hammer wanted to do a remake of *King Kong*, but they couldn't secure the rights.

The World's Leading Performance Capture Expert

Joe Letteri

Joe Letteri (born in 1957 in Aliquippa, Pennsylvania) graduated from the University of California in Berkeley in 1981. In 2001, he joined Peter Jackson's company Weta Digital in New Zealand. As a senior visual effects supervisor in charge of creative, artistic, and technical direction, specializing in performance capture technology, he won four Academy Awards (*The Lord of the Rings: Two Towers* and *The Return of the King; King Kong;* and *Avatar*) and was five more times nominated, won four BAFTA awards and four Visual Effects Society Awards.

Q: Is there any type of acting that applies best to performance capture? What type of qualifications must actors have to get into it?

A: The goal of the process is to capture everything the actor is doing and the emotions actors are expressing through their performance. The tools and workflow are designed to make sure the actor is uninhibited and can stay in the moment. Any actor's approach or technique can work in a motion capture context.

Q: Is it helpful for *Mocap* acting to be able to visualize, for filmmakers as well as actors, because everything that you act with is virtual and green screen? Of course, there is *previz* but that's virtual and not physical. What can you do to support the director and get the actors in the right mood for the respective part?

A: We've evolved our motion capture setup to be much more compact and mobile. This allows us to use it on a live-action set, even in adverse conditions, without disrupting principal photography. We really established this workflow with the Planet of the Apes franchise where the director was focused on working with the actors, knowing that if the emotion was there in the performance, we would translate it into the digital apes.

In other cases, a simulcam workflow is useful. With the simulcam setup, the director and actors can choose to see a live-action or digital version of the set and the actors depending on what is most important for the shot. There are many different permutations of these tools, but ultimately it is about providing a virtual approximation of the desired shot to aid the decision-making process to onset production.

Q: Some traditional animators seem reluctant to identify performance capture with animation. Of course it is more kinetic and creates movement in real time against painstaking frame-by-frame animation but what they mean is: They use live models only as reference while in the case of performance capture the actors in a way are animating themselves. Or are you considering yourself a virtual marionette player? Then, of course, you would be an heir to Willis O'Brien, Ray Harryhausen, and other artists who were close to puppetry.

A: Performance capture is far less polarizing than it was, in part because artists now have a broader understanding of the process. The data that are gathered through the performance capture process is a starting point for animators to craft a performance. Nothing is determined by the data.

Even when the creative decision is made to replicate an actor's performance with a digital character, there is a tremendous amount of talent and skill that goes into translating the nuances of a human performance onto a digital character that, in most cases, does not share the same physical characteristics.

Performance capture is an additive process; it gives the animator another tool to work with. Traditionally, the animator must rely only on his/her eyes to match reference. Performance capture gives animators a representation of motion that may include subtlety of movement or a slight asymmetry of posture or gate that adds to what we perceive subconsciously. Sometimes we don't know why something looks "right," only that it does. In some cases, performance capture can help you get there more quickly by doing the basic work more efficiently, freeing the animator to spend more time polishing the extra 10% that make a performance.

Q: You had many great evolutionary steps in your career that reflect the progress of technology: *I, Robot—King Kong—The Hobbit—Batman v Superman: Dawn of Justice*. What do we have to expect the next years while you are working on sequels of *Avatar* (I guess until 2024)? There's only one case you were involved in a project that had no naturalistic rendering of characters and environments. That was the comic book adaptation of *The Adventures of Tintin*.

A: It's always the films that drive the requirements. You look at the script and talk to the director about his vision for the film and you have to determine if the tools you have are sufficient to achieve that vision. Obviously Jim Cameron is a director with a great imagination and a thorough understanding of the visual effects technology and process. I would certainly expect his films to continue to push our process to evolve.

In recent years we have been working to make our capture setup more versatile to handle more adverse onset conditions and also more robust in terms of how many actors we can process in real time. Larger ensemble casts with full facial capture put a strain on any system due to the sheer amount of data being processed but we're getting more and more efficient with our setup. We've also integrated much more realistic lighting for the virtual production stage because lighting is a critical component to a performance and having a good approximation of the lighting onset is invaluable.

We mainly associate performance capture with the necessities of the entertainment industry, but there are many other fields to use that technology. The basic idea didn't come from entertainment industry as well.

Most of the techniques that we use, including motion capture, come from the field of Computer Graphics. But much of the continuing research and development is driven by the requirements that we have for creating characters, environments, and stories. Which is why you tend to see their most visible uses in entertainment.

Q: How are you going to advance 3D technology beyond movie-making: cross-media? Do you think that there will be synthespians one day who will act like real people and, above all, will be equipped with artificial intelligence? Maybe in interactive games?

A: Our focus is on film but obviously others will take these tools into new areas. Creating a believable digital human requires extraordinary skill over a long period of time. Once you start asking a computer to make acting choices, you enter a whole other level of difficulty. Certainly for film-making, it relies on a team of artists to create the final result and can't be done by computers alone.

Q: How should film schools train young people in a field that is going to change considerably the next decades?

A: Everything starts with understanding the principles of good storytelling. This is as true in visual effects as it is in any other part of filmmaking. An understanding of how shots are framed, the use of lighting for tone and motivation and the fundamentals of composition will always be an essential part of filmmaking. Starting with the basic language of film will always serve you as well.

For visual effects in particular, having a good balance of art and technical skill is extremely valuable. Computing skills that enable you to extend and get more out of the software you use is part of mastering your tools.

The German Animation Producer

Tony Loeser

Tony Loeser was born in Liverpool in 1953 but raised in GDR (East Germany), where he worked as a stop frame cameraman at DEFA Studios Babelsberg. After reunification, he became a producer and founded MotionWorks, a production company based in Halle in Lower Saxony. He did TV series as well as feature films (*Mullewapp 1* and *2*) that all aimed at a young audience.

Q: As a European animation producer you have the benefit of state support, but we guess you still have to overcome a lot of obstacles.

A: The biggest barrier for all people who are creative is the increasing administration in the media. It gets more and more complicated to raise funds. Everything is being bureaucratized. Some bloated machinery has been built up. And the more money they spent for this bureaucracy, the less is available for the creative aspects of production. Unproductive work soaks up parts of the budget that doesn't go into production. Decision-making processes are slowed down and delayed over periods of 1 to 1.5 year. This bureaucratic superstructure paralyzes creative animation production and results in unnecessary compromises.

Q: On all levels in Europe, mediocrity seems to be on the rise. Mediocrity, however, is the arch enemy of creativity, not to mention the employment situation of the creative personnel and animators, social security, and old-age provision. In a way, they have to live from hand to mouth.

A: That's right. Our system causes forty to fifty percent outsourcing to foreign countries due to shrinking funds, severe competition, and overproduction. But it looks as if Germany will become a low-wage country too. We have producers from Spain coming to us and asking if we got excess capacities. We don't have tax incentives in Germany as they now have in Italy where they offer up to thirty percent tax relief for film productions.

Q: And in this economically serious situation, you continue to focus on an audience of little kids and do preschool entertainment. Why do you neglect big family audiences?

A: On the contrary, I consider this very young audience group highly important. We shouldn't ignore the kids. In this age, the foundation is laid for social competence and cultural education.

In media there is a big problem with globalization: We have program without end. The Americans have succeeded in adapting European content, fairy tales, and so on, and have transformed it into a global formula. That kills local content in Europe, in India, and everywhere in the world. In France they still have a good cultural policy and reach sufficient quota for French movies. But this is an exception based on a strong national tradition.

Q: You have produced two parts of an animated feature film series from children's books by Helme Heine: Both parts of *Mullewapp*, the first (*Friends Forever*) released in 2009, the second one in 2016, deal with a rural community of animals: a trio of friends consisting of a mouse, a cock, and a pig.

You put a lot of effort into the second part. Did you reshape Helme Heine's very simple picture-book animals for the needs of animation?

A: Yes, in the picture-books the eyes of the animals were mere dots. We spent some time on the eyes as they are the mirror of the souls.

Q: Despite your hard work Part 2 didn't perform at the box office as expected.

A: We knew that we wouldn't get an audience of half a million but we hoped for 300,000. We got 200,000. That was very disappointing.

Q: These preschool films are very tame. Aren't they too infantile even for the youngest? They seemed to have been commissioned by mothers who

Animal characters from *Mullewapp 2*: Franz von Hahn, a rooster and Waldemar, the pig. (Courtesy of MotionWorks.)

fear for the salvation of their kids. Today the Brothers Grimm would have big problems in a number of European countries we guess.

A: We have no other choice than to turn to the persons who actually buy the tickets at the box office, and these are the mothers.

Q: Why shouldn't kids see things that are frightening provided it's not autotelic but cathartic?

A: I remember that this discussion, in East Germany too, started sometime in the 1960s and 1970s when they developed a different attitude toward scenes of violence in fairy tales and began to listen to pedagogues. Children, if they are not directly confronted, have no conception of death. So death is cut out.

Q: You avoid death and at the same time change nature considering animal behavior.

A: As an antagonist in *Mullewapp 1* we had a wolf that was after the pig. Parents but also some reviewers considered him too radical.

Q: We guess this wolf was no vegetarian. The Big Bad Wolf was our favorite in Disney's *Three Little Pigs*. The same is true for the Russian series *Nu Pogodi* that told of the perennial controversy between wolf and hare.

A: Right, but we shouldn't forget what kind of powerful experience the first visit to the movies is for little kids. It gets dark and you are alone, even with Mom and Dad sitting beside you. And the screen is so large. On the audio side of things there is Dolby Surround. The impression is overwhelming. The visual and audio effect is way too big. So there are many parents who care about what their children are watching.

Q: **Among your TV series is one that is very interesting under intercultural aspects:** *The Travels of the Young Marco Polo.* **The episodes of the first season were released in 2013. Here you had a famous name, a brand so to speak, and a Eurasian topic linked by the Silk Road.**

A: Right now we are working on the second season which is being produced exclusively in Germany, with some Canadian input.

Q: **The first season had everything one could wish for with regard to an exotic background. But we found it a little bit too stiff and educational.**

A: That was my idea. I am the one to blame. But I think it was a good adventure series. In Cannes we were approached by a Chinese buyer who had seen one episode. For a moment we feared she had seen a pirated copy on the Chinese internet, but then we learned that the young woman had seen this episode in an Arabian studio and became very interested.

Q: **The animation is very simple for this type of series.**

A: I wanted it that way. I didn't want Pixar-type animation. I would like to have something that is in style and animation similar to the Flintstones. But there are not many animators around who are really able to animate that way. Everybody wants to work on Pixar level, but they all will fail trying to achieve that. They never will come near that quality. Sadly we have no tradition regarding the simple line. Characters that are intended for full animation will not work drawn in simple lines. But if you have a well-designed simple character raising the eyebrow, it will get noticed. These characters will not do much, but what they do will have an effect on the audience. Yet there are not many people around anymore who are able to keep it simple and good.

Q: **Characters such as** *Mister Magoo* **or** *Signor Rossi* **that are real types born from simple designs. By the way, with a nod to Marco Polo, what do you expect from China animation-wise?**

A: We have to adapt ourselves in the future more and more to China. In Germany we have a TV entertainer named Harald Schmidt who joked: My child is going to learn Chinese that someday he can serve Chinese guests in a Chinese restaurant.

The American Expert in 3D Scans

Karl Meyer

Karl Meyer is founder and CEO of Gentle Giant Studios, which is part of 3D Systems, a leading provider of 3D printing centric design-to-manufacture solutions. The company is nestled near the major studios in Burbank, California. Business started with designing toys, but when Meyer purchased the first scanner and 3D printer in 1997, he gradually became involved in scanning and collecting data for film, television, and games. Since then the company scanned virtually everybody including *Lady Gaga* and participated in almost every major VFX movie working with Industrial Light & Magic, Rhythm & Hues, Sony Imageworks, and other companies: *Star Wars, Harry Potter, Lord of the Rings, Spider-Man, King Kong (2005), The Chronicles of Narnia, X-Men, Hulk (2003), Transformers, Ratatouille, Coraline, Avatar, Toy Story 3, TRON: Legacy, Terminator Genisys, Gravity, Fast & Furious 7, Ant-Man,* and *Batman v Superman: Dawn of Justice.*

Q: You are working in the field of digitizing actors. Can you describe the process and estimate how many actresses and actors you have scanned in the meantime and have digital data of?

A: Digitizing people has many benefits and applications. Capturing the "real geometry" of a human provides an indisputable dataset that becomes an asset which can be utilized across multiple platforms. Data can be processed and refined using a myriad of software and tools to create the "digital thespians" we see in most action sequences in feature films today. There are many different approaches and often various VFX houses will develop their own proprietary pipeline for producing their models. This includes texture capture and refinement, animation rigging, and sophisticated lighting controls to simulate any environment. The tools are ever evolving, from the early laser scanners, white light grid projection to the flexibility and versatility of high-resolution camera photogrammetry. Over the last couple of decades, Gentle Giant Studios has 3D scanned thousands of people. Many people we have captured are actors, athletes, and other notable celebrities. This is significant because along with their life's body of work, they leave behind 3D information that contributes to their immortality. Combined with motion and sound capture synthesis, the digital double can participate in media long after the life of the original host.

Q: **Obviously, this is not the end but the beginning of digital clones. If you look to other media, not only the movies, do you see a chance that virtual actors, maybe commanding artificial intelligence, might act out of their own? Can you speculate a little about the future of digital acting? Will it always rely on performance capture, on a human "marionette player" so to speak?**

A: Today we see the results of leveraging "real geometry" into the most accurate toys, statues, and bio medical physical reproductions. The fast progress of 3D printing has elevated the quality and authenticity of transposing digital data to the physical form in an expanding scope of materials. One day possibly living flesh and bone. This is driven by the progression of content collection. Virtual reality, augmented reality, and the "fourth dimension" cross the boundaries of new experiences.

I believe it is not far in the future where AI (artificial intelligence) will be a common driver of sophisticated geometry. Today there are amazing immersive video games and films that project a clear vision of what's to come. The more that can be captured and collected, the more can be multiplied and emulated providing an almost indistinguishable reality with unpredictable outcome.

The Managing Director from Hungary

Ferenc Mikulás

In the spring of 1957, Ferenc Mikulás (born in 1940)—because of his participation in the Revolution—was dismissed from secondary school. From 1970 on, after writing scripts and directing short films, he was getting acquainted with animated cartoon films at the Pannónia Film Studio. Since June 1, 1971, he has been the head of the Kecskemét Animation Studio, where he produced several films and series. Since 1993, he has been Director of the Kecskemét Animation Film Festival. Between 1997 and 2000, he was member of the Board of Directors of ASIFA. For his activities, he received the Golden Cross of Distinction of the Hungarian Republic in 1995.

Q: How did you get involved in animation? What was it that fascinated you personally in creating life artificially on screen?

A: By accident, from the field of documentaries. The discovery of other languages and metacommunication was significant for me.

Q: Were there special movies and series that impressed you?

A: The work of numerous film directors had a great effect on me: e.g. Disney, [Yuri] Norstein, Miyazaki, [Paul] Driessen, the Hungarian [Sándor] Reisenbüchler, etc.

Q: In Europe, Hungary for some time was a very important animation-producing nation. How did you secure funding in the past? How did you train young aspiring animators and technical personnel?

A: Before the change of the Hungarian political system (1989), the budget for Hungarian films was distributed—based on thematic plans—among the state-run studios by the Ministry of Culture. Public television also allocated a significant amount to the production of animated series.

In this period, between 1970 and 1990, 20 full animated feature films, several dozens of animated film series and numerous artistic short films that received significant festival awards were made at Pannónia Film Studio and in the Kecskemét Studio.

In this period there was still no animation faculty at the universities, so the training of the animators and directors took place in the film studios during production.

Q: How is the state of the Hungarian animation industry today? How is it positioned at home and on the global market?

A: Today, the Hungarian animation industry is weak, due to a recession which started with the 1989 change of the political system.

Instead of the distribution of funds by the state, tenders could only be submitted to the Hungarian National Film Fund, where the power of feature film makers forced the animation genre into the background.

One sign of the recession is that during the past 25 years only a total of 5 animated feature films could be made. The Hungarian Television does not commission animated films at all and does not want to be involved in co-productions and the production of TV series.

The state-owned Pannónia Studio disbanded. The Kecskemét Studio was privatized. We purchased the share of the state with my colleagues. Currently, it is the only such studio that has been continuously operating with almost a constant staff number for 45 years.

In Europe, the Moholy-Nagy University has its presence with its graduation films, while Kecskemétfilm Ltd. operates primarily with its services (Irish—*The Secret of Kells*; Spanish—*Chico and Rita*; French–Japanese—*The Red Turtle*), as it participates in the production of full animated feature films requiring character animation.

Q: What about co-producers you worked with then and now? Is it mainly about money and outsourcing? And what happened when the competition from Asia got strong and stronger?

A: The Hungarian co-producers operate an enterprise established for a certain film, and if needed, we can help each other by providing working capacity.

For Kecskemétfilm Ltd., there are orders from Western Europe requiring high-quality character animation almost continuously. The situation in Asia does not affect us.

Q: TV participation has become hard to obtain in Europe. Do you see options in new digital media and maybe in developing characters that work well in merchandising?

A: Due to the lack of new television series the significance of merchandising is minimal. The new media is likely to take over the role of television in the future among young people.

Q: Can you describe how the evolution from 2D to 3D did work in your country? What problems did you have? Is 2D still an equivalent?

A: In Hungary, the number of films made in 3D is not significant. Currently, 2D and 3D go hand in hand peacefully in Hungary. In the Kecskemét Studio, we successfully apply 3D technology to 2D productions, and a new and unique film language has developed.

Q: What is the main quality a good cartoon character should fulfill?

A: A good example: the appearance of a character evokes a feeling of déjà vu, and the posture, movement, and gestures of the character reflect his/her personality without words.

Q: Very often you were commissioned to animate cartoon characters that were copyrighted by someone else. Did you have enough creative freedom to develop even these figures?

A: No, in such cases we do not have the opportunity of development. However, in the process of animation the characters often get perfected, and we follow the best example.

Q: Working with low budgets: What is the best method of getting a good performance out of the characters? Is it more based on writing and dialogue or on a design or is there anything the animator can do above the usual?

A: Based on my experience, storytelling is getting a greater role today, and the quality and nature of animation has a lower priority. With the aid of the visual cues, many things are up to the imagination of the viewer; thus, audiences are more involved in the acts, rather than showing everything to them.

Q: What can producers and directors do to support and inspire the creative personnel?

A: This largely depends on the person. Based on my experience, it is the difficulties that make people truly creative. I give them tasks and opportunities. I send them to festivals, and certain films they watch wake up something in them many times.

Q: Just being curious: How do you see the future of European and Hungarian animation and how do you judge the evolution of digital technology in this field? Why is it that character animation in some of the old cartoons is so much better than nowadays' animation, in spite of all the digital tools?

A: Currently, in several countries of Europe, I do not see such a problem. I think it depends on who is using the digital technology: if it gets into the hands of a talented artist, there is no need to worry.

"Old" character animation was better due to the lack of dialogue and the joyful satisfaction given by the exploration of a new form of language. A great deal of knowledge was needed: to draw well, to know anatomy, to think spatially, etc. Talent and thinking cannot be replaced by software and machines.

The German Puppet Animator

Heinrich Sabl

Heinrich Sabl (born in 1961 in Görlitz/GDR) started out as a locksmith. His objective was to work in the theatre as a technician. It was then that he became interested in puppetry. He studied puppetry at Ernst Busch Drama School in East Berlin and turned to stop-motion filmmaking, producing animated short films (including *Père Ubu* and *Mère Ubu*), and devoting most of his lifetime to finishing a stop-motion feature film titled *Memory Hotel*.

Q: In your practice you have decided to work with animated puppets. What do puppets mean to you? What do puppets relate to you while you are animating them? Do you feel comfortable within the tradition of the puppet play and the classic stop-motion puppet film? Do you watch what's going on in international puppet play?

A: At first I want an exact terminology. This has to do with my socialization. While I was trained as a puppeteer back in the 1980s, the puppet play tried to emancipate and this was underlined by some theoretical work, for instance, by Konstanza Kavrakova Lorenz. Puppetry discovered the adult audience. And we understood "the puppet" as our tool—as a material which, depending on the story, could be replaced through other materials which include an actor. In the process of work with the material, a terminology was established that has since accompanied my work. The lifeless material (it might be a thing, it might be a puppet) becomes a character by means of animation. In this regard, the term puppet doesn't exist for me. It is just material, a tool that transforms by the process of animation/ life giving into a character. A figure with regard to screenplay/the literary source, however, that ceases the right to be a character if we, the recipients, won't believe in it.

When I animate I have to embrace the material. In the material I find all information for the camerawork, the choreography, and, related to that, the animation. This approach takes place from different angles as I have been for the past 15 years behind the camera (cinematography, direction) and as animator in front of it. Although some of these three working areas overlap, it was helpful to separate and distinguish these three activities very well from each other. The first impulse is the issue what I am going to tell. This is ever an action, for instance, if the protagonist will enter a room or something like that. Is the action defined I search for the best-as-possible camera angles. This process is complex. At one hand, the camera shall capture that action understandably for the spectator, and at the other hand, the material (the puppet, the object, or the prop) doesn't stand any closeness and proximity, any angle, any lens. Then there is the lighting which—at least in my work—subordinates to the scene, to the narrative. The final decision is about aperture and focus.

Then it needs free ways to be able to animate and the adventure can begin.

I don't feel within the tradition of stop-motion film. I can't because I don't share that term. A 24 fps moving image was nothing else inside the film camera than film transport—exposure—film transport—not different from stop motion.

My first roots are indeed those of puppetry. This is what I studied. It was like learning in a hard school and the best prerequisite for my job. I feel connected to puppetry as spectator and attend, sporadically, from time to time, stage plays.

Q: **Before you entered the field of puppetry, you wanted to go to the theatre to become a technician. How would you see the difference between stage play and puppetry?**

A: Let me try to explain it backward. I have realized that certain fabrics are very useful for puppetry. Whenever something is more model and exemplary, an abstraction in the story which is to be told, then one ends very fast at puppetry or animation. That works for me only provided the abstraction is reinforced by a plausible narrative.

I differentiate not so much between show and puppet players. The decision for this one or that one I am always searching in the source, in the story that is to be told.

The reason for being a technician is not by chance. If I want to possess material and to animate it there is a technical aspect too. There are lighting and shooting techniques. The question is how to use the machinery for my story. This is a lifelong process of searching which still forces me to my knees in spite of my many years of experience.

Q: Are there any examples in the field of stop motion that have influenced or impressed you? Were there films you didn't like?

A: There is a film that left an effect on me continuously: Balance by the Lauenstein Brothers. I like films with a position which sure has to do with my East German background (Friedrich Wolf's "art as weapon" has an effect on me until today). Regarding this, Jan Švankmajer's *Death of Stalinism in Bohemia* and, on an Expressionist level, Food [an animated documentary short] are very close to me.

In 2D animation, there are Andreas Hykade's *Ring of Fire* (although I haven't really understood it) and the groundbreaking [abstract] work by Raimund Krumme and Phil Mulloy.

Then it gets difficult. Of course, *Chicken Run*—but since then there was nothing by Aardman that fascinated me.

Actually, there is almost nothing I like, neither in style nor in story—I am waiting for Tarantino to make a stop-motion film or Lars von Trier. Both would hopefully please me, this I would like to watch.

Q: What qualities should a good puppeteer and a good stop-motion animator have?

A: This question hits my heart. As I said I had a training to become puppeteer: acting lessons, dancing, movement, pantomime, acrobatics, speech training, Materials Science, just to name some of the disciplines.

This education became an essential basis for my work today.

I think that the abilities of an animator and a puppeteer are very close to each other. Both have to know how a movement works, where the center of mass displacement is, they have to abstract and beat the bush. They have to think straightforward and in concrete terms have to be able to transfer their ideas onto whatever material. Never mind if you use a puppet or a match box.

Q: How do you approach a character when you animate it? Do you observe a lot? Do you work with a stop watch to time movements?

A: In the moment of animation, I am interested solely in the action that has to be told. Everything else is craftsmanship. If a material/puppet stands

Memory Hotel. (Courtesy of Heinrich Sabl.)

safely, the difficulty of a certain movement, etc.—all this doesn't count because in the end it's a mixture of craftsmanship, intuition, and experience. You can rely on these abilities. More important is what's under the surface, how my protagonist moves from A to B. What does he have in his luggage? In actor's school, we called that subtext. This is what really interests me. I never animate original text/dialogue but always the so-called subtext. In the forefront, I don't time any movement, not even camera movement, which has to be segmented into single frames too.

In the past years, I didn't have much opportunity to observe. But yes, I do, on the way to the studio and back. But actually what I'm doing more is to study the possibilities that are in my materials, what they allow me to do. Then the searching starts. I am convinced that how a thing/puppet moves is still part of the material itself.

This requires lots of patience, humility, and devotion. One has to be concerned with the material.

Q: You are regarded as perfectionist. For many years, you are working to finish your most ambitious film: *Memory Hotel.* **What can you tell about the project and the story? Was it a challenge or did it culminate in a series of disappointment and frustration considering the enormous difficulties?**

A: I don't think there is a difference between perfection and precision. In my work on *Memory Hotel* I made some effort to avoid the perfection; I worked with an old 35-mm film camera and denied high-resolution images and total control of animation, I worked under open sky and deprived the safe atmosphere of the studio, I even widely quit story-boards and dashed into the adventure of improvisation. I didn't animate any classic lip sync but trusted in the power of the subtext—short, I faced danger. This was and is part of a creative process that is continued in postproduction. During this process, I work as long as possible with the sketchy. My objective is to shove as much sketch as possible into the final product to keep the space for reception as open and big as possible. This process will not be in the way of precision while selecting the devices.

To talk about *Memory Hotel* is not easy in the moment. The work/genesis involves many groups of themes: to tell a story with the means of the animated film, the question of financing it, analogue technologies, the digital changes in image, sound and communication, social questions, time, aging, etc. It's useful to consider all this separately and it needs a structure.

The first idea for the project came up in the 1990s. In 1995, the first application for film subsidies was filed, and in 1999, we began physical production. That's now 17 years; there was no single day when the film project was not part of daily thinking and acting. During a long learning process, I developed some kind of resistance to frustration. Nevertheless, there were and are declines that weight heavily—but there still is—unswerving—besides a straightforward surrounding of supporters, a central driving force that doesn't let me give up: THE IMAGE and increasingly again THE STORY which this film is about to tell. And the security to live in Germany; I was and I am still able to continue in this highly unusual type of work. I regard this as a great privilege.

Q: **You had a story, set among Germans and Russian troops in the ruins of a Berlin hotel in the aftermath of World War II, but as you said, contrary to many commercial animators, you improvise a lot during your work.**

A: I don't know many commercial animators, so I don't know much about their work process. As I said, there is craftsmanship which I have to master and extend. Then the fun begins; similar to instrumentalists whose play we hear and recognize from their own style during a music recording, I am looking for my own style. I always felt the requirement to create strong characters. These I inflict with my own handwriting and this must be strong. For this I need space. This space I grant to my figures, this is why they become characters. In the moment of shooting, of animating I give all to them. This mostly is an arduous live performance. It isn't necessary that the animation is perfect but the power, the motivation, and the impulse must be right.

So animation can become a preplanned process. It would bore me to exchange the so-called replacement faces for consonant sounds and vocals to put perfect lip sync into the mouths of the characters. It would bore me too if an animatic would dictate a movement.

I listen to my material. I react to and use alleged mistakes. Siegfried Kracauer attributed the "affinity to unstaged life" to film. This is what I want to bring into my studio and therefore I leave, among else, the unprotected room of the studio and animate under open sky.

Q: **What's your relationship with the hybrids of live action and 3D animation, with the blockbusters that dominate currently the global screens?**

A: This is a question I cannot answer because I haven't seen such films.

Q: **Which qualities of your work would you like to see "saved" in the future which undoubtedly will be digital and virtual? Which status will stop motion have? What kind of audience do you wish?**

A: If I type the term "Stop Motion" in the search field of YouTube, I encounter Lego films, Tutorials, etc. I do not want to call the creative efforts of the makers into question as these trials are well-meant. Software easily accessible and approachable for anybody besides camera technique makes it possible. The line of demarcation between hobby and professional aspiration seems to be fluent or seems to disintegrate. A determination of the position is difficult. This is not meant derogatorily, but what is needed is delimitation and differentiation. Anybody can do it,—and yet, to myself, filmmaking is breadwinning and art production at the same time. I myself can get the inspiration that is part of my life only from the material. And from the stories that I hopefully will be able to tell in the future. From my own stylistics and from my way of animation which, so I hope, I will be able and will be allowed to develop further. These abilities are completely independent from questions of technology. These are questions of physical nature and afford my presence, my senses, and my abilities.

I previously only had the brief pleasure to use digital technology. Regarding the total control it made my work very simple; there were still stage fright and a certain tension which were always part of my film work. In the realm of digital filmmaking, I have to search a new focus.

I guess that in spite of all commercial efforts and the box office receipts of the American Laika [producers of *Coraline, ParaNorman, Boxtrolls,* and *Kubo*] or the British Aardman Studios the so-called stop-motion technique will remain a niche product. The global networking, however, is, considering the distribution of animated films, a true chance, but the creators shouldn't have to wait for getting reimbursed.

A source of inspiration I always found in musicians, creative artists, filmmakers, and writers. They have carried me, their work has touched me.

Maybe in the future there will be young film enthusiasts who will take *Memory Hotel* as a source of their inspiration. Then I would have had accomplished something.

64

The Animation Student from Romania

Veronica Solomon

Veronica Solomon (born in 1980 in Tirgu Mures/Romania) is an animation student at Film University Babelsberg, which is located on a studio lot near Potsdam, Germany. We thought it would be interesting to interview not only professionals but students too.

Q: Do you develop your projects out of the characters or do you prefer to explore them through a finished story?

A: I would say I explore characters out of certain situations. Usually at the beginning I have no precise story, but I must know what it is all about to see the characters in my head. I have no defined style. It depends on how the story is going to develop. But the characters are the first that become clear.

Q: How do you get into the mood, into the spirit of a certain character when you animate? Do you animate 2D or 3D?

A: I understand myself as 2D animator, using digital tools. But it turned out that I make my final assignment now as claymation.

Q: Do you watch humans and animals? Do you do caricatures?

A: I always watch humans and animals, but I haven't done it explicitly while designing a character. My characters come so to speak from my own personal universe of mythology, which consists of everything I have read, seen, or heard. I like to mix these ingredients.

Q: We noticed that many projects of young animation filmmakers and students are quite ambitious, sometimes overly pretentious, but relatively limited in animation, in spite of all digital tools.

A: I can only tell what I have watched in my own personal neighborhood. At the Film University Babelsberg, you don't have to finish a project of your own, but there is this tradition and they all want to become filmmakers [auteurs]. Rarely people are pleased to play a certain supporting part: character designer or background designer or just being an animator for a fellow student. Then you have to do everything yourself: screenwriting, directing, designing, modeling and rigging in case of 3D, animating, compositing, editing, and 9 times out of 10 handling the production chores. So you start very carefully on designs, backgrounds, characters, props, and what else—and then you realize that there is no time for extensive animation. You have to finish your degree. In the professional world, similar things will happen, but this has to do with lack of money I guess.

Q: Are there examples of character animation that have impressed you?

A: The encounter with God scene from *Mind Game*. And all from *Tekkon Kinkreet*. Otherwise classic Disney films such as *Jungle Book, Robin Hood*, and *Aristocats*. Character-wise I also like Emperor's New Groove. I am very influenced by Japanese animation—there is a special kind of character movement—they have a different rhythm.

Q: How do you judge hybrids of live action and 3D animation, these blockbusters that currently dominate our screens? Do you consider performance capture a legitimate tool of animation?

A: I must admit that I haven't seen a lot. I don't consider it real animation but cannot tell why. I recall when *Polar Express* came out, I think that was one of the first features that used motion capture, that I thought: Hey, man, that's terrible, I don't want to see it. But recently I have seen a Making of *The Hobbit* with Benedict Cumberbatch who played the dragon. Very impressive. Maybe a good animator would have been able to deliver the same performance, but it would have lasted longer and would have been more expensive. I don't know. But that's certainly no art.

Q: Given the fast evolution of digital technology, how do you see the future, including your own? Will you have to change artistically and economically to reproduce yourself?

A: I find everything very exciting and frightening at the same time. I don't know if I am flexible enough. Changing and reproducing don't have to be bad things. I am very grateful for the Undo function. Technology is just a bunch of tools. I hope that at the end the story is what counts and not the glitter.

65

The Czech 3D Producer

Jan Tománek

Jan Tománek (born in 1978 in Prague) experimented with 3D computer animation since he graduated from the High School of Arts in Prague in 1996. In 2003, he became the first Czech filmmaker to produce a feature-length 3D animated movie: His *Goat Story—The Old Prague Legends (Kozí příběh—pověsti staré Prahy)* was finished by his Art And Animation Studio in 2008. A sequel, *Goat Story with Cheese,* was released in 2012.

Q: **Prague has always been an interesting playground for all kind of puppetry, the illusions of the Black Theatre, and, of course, animation and stop motion. How were you influenced personally by this tradition? You were born 10 years after Jiří Trnka's death.**

A: Really? I didn't think about Jiří Trnka's death like that…

But in fact, when I was younger there was Communism here in Czech Republic. That meant: no commercial U.S. cartoons, just traditional Czech animation that was of very good quality and Russian films.

It was natural for kids here to see quality traditional animation like Trnka, [Hermína] Týrlová, [Jiří] Barta.

But the main influence for me was my family. Both of my parents are artists. My mother [Dagmar Doubková] is a very famous director of animated movies with awards from the famous festivals like Hiroshima, Bilbao, etc.

So I grew up with puppets and animation.

Q: You were among the firsts to experiment with 3D computer animation, the first to produce a feature-length 3D animated film in the Czech Republic: *Goat Story*. Can you talk a little about the challenges and the difficulties?

A: The whole movie took me 5 years of my life. The most difficult part was collecting the money. I got small funds from the EU MEDIA program for development, but all other financing I had to secure from private investors. Czech government, Czech funds, even the City of Prague didn't participate in financing.

Q: Did you have problems to find 3D animators and how did you train them?

A: It's a paradox situation compared to the long Czech animation history, but we have here no 3D animators. There are some elder classical animators, but they don't know computers, and the new ones are educated by these old ones… Worse was to accept students from Czech animation schools. We had to teach them from scratch on how to animate by modern standards.

Q: You chose not a modern topic for *Goat Story* but based your work on *Old Prague Legends*. Was this a distinctive move on your part not picking an international adventure yarn?

A: Prague as location was and is interesting for foreign audiences. The only problems were some adult jokes in the movie and the dark atmosphere. The buyers had problems how to classify the picture. Nevertheless, we sold the movie to many countries and territories, but mainly DVD and TV.

Q: You had to work on a miniscule budget as you have said. What did this mean for designing the characters and, above all, for the animation itself?

A: Concerning the design I had a very accurate idea and I stuck to it the whole movie. The money didn't prove limited for design at all. But when I tell somebody that the movie was produced for less than 2 million USD and the whole picture was made by 15 people (3D models and animation), nobody believes it. *Shrek* cost 150 million USD, and even Shrek's animated credits were made by more people than worked on our whole movie.

Q: How do you approach the acting part in 3D animation?

A: Each animator has its own character, same as an actor in live films. I tried to distribute the main characters between our animators according to their own character and style of animation.

It was the same with certain moods—some person is more qualified for a funny scene and another is better handling slow and scary ones.

I think it's also a benefit to work with a small team because I talked with all animators personally and showed them what I wanted them to do acting-wise. There was no "interface" like a senior animator who would step in and translate my emotions to them. I did it myself.

Q: How do you see the future of 3D animation in Europe as well as other territories?

A: Notwithstanding that *Goat Story* was the most successful Czech animation movie I didn't hardly recoup the budget, without any profit...

It's getting harder and harder. When I created *Goat Story 1* in 2008, I knew that I would get the money back from releasing the movie to Czech cinemas. When I did *Goat Story 2* in 2012, it was 50/50 to get the money. Now I know that if I would create a new movie and even provided all goes very well, Czech cinemas will never pay this movie back. It's getting worse and worse.

We have to look for new distribution channels. I gave both movies to YouTube for free. This act generates some money for the advert. It's paradox but this act didn't spoil DVD and TV sales.

Q: Can you please name a few 3D-animated films that have impressed you recently?

A: I like Pixar movies but I have to say that the last one that I saw, *The Good Dinosaur*, is the worst entry Pixar ever produced.

The last movie I saw with my kids was *The Secret Life of Pets*. It was fun—because of the great animal characters.

66

The Experimental Stop-Frame Animator

Grigori Zurkan

Grigori Zurkan (born in 1986) is a freelance animator specialized in stop motion including editorial, art direction, camera work, and solo projects. He graduated from Film University Babelsberg, Germany and worked on Frank Gessner's expanded animation project *Alias Yederbeck*. He was invited to China to work on a solo stop-motion project at Jilin Animation Institute in Changchun.

Q: You have studied animation. What insights did you win during your study?

A: The most important discovery I made during my study was that technique and even more expenditure only partly have an influence on animation films as end product. Whether the final film was several years in production or not is relevant for me to know only after I have evaluated the work.

Q: You are focusing on puppet animation. Do you design your puppets in a certain style? What about facial expression and what about the eyes?

A: I can say that I have a certain style of my own: partly because I have difficulties to imitate others. Regarding the facial play of a puppet, it is of course important that it corresponds with the character. The eyes play a very important role. While creating a puppet, it is crucial how the eyes are "positioned" in the face of the puppet. That includes how high or deep compared to the forehead, the distance between the eyes, between eye and eyebrow, how big the eyes are, and the facial angle. All these things must work for a character and be noticeable even without animation, in a still.

Q: Is animating for you like slipping into the role of the puppet? Or is it more a communication process with the puppet?

A: It's more communication. I must get to know the puppet and its abilities, technically and from the design point of view. I know then as a matter of fact where I have to change things, especially technically.

Q: Shall a puppet move like a human or do you have your own stylized type of movement?

A: As most of the puppets I have built so far are human they should move at least anatomically comprehensible. I have noticed that the more lifelike and realistic a puppet and its movements are, the more it feels as if it acts, just compared to a more stylized puppet. It's likely that it is extremely difficult to imitate a realistic human movement a hundred percent.

Q: Do you have a stop watch in mind when you are animating? Do you think in frames and time? Or do you explore the movement of a character intuitively?

A: In my own work I animate more intuitively.

Q: Have you seen recent animation films like *Anomalisa* and *Kubo?*

A: Both films are, in their own way, very impressive.

   With *Anomalisa* it's, besides the plot, the design of the puppets. For the facial expression, they eschewed deliberately elaborate image processing so that you can see that these are puppets with replacement faces although the design is quite realistic. This certain kind of "sincerity" makes this film so sympathetic for me.

   Kubo is just the opposite in this regard. This film is indeed special and to me in particular as I appreciate and like Far East cultures. And yet it is not the stop motion which makes this picture so special because visually it doesn't differ from 3D.

The Miracle Doctor (Der Wunderdoktor). GDR 1958. Director: Herbert K. Schulz. Puppet: Willibald Hofmann.

Anton the Musician (Anton der Musikant). GDR 1968. Director: Dietrich Nitzsche. Puppet: Dietrich Nitzsche.

Rübezahl. Puppet series. GDR/ČSSR 1979. Director: Vins Zdenek. Photographed by Rolf Hofmann. (Courtesy of Deutsches Institut für Animationsfilm/Archiv [German Institute for Animated Film/Archive.])

The Suitcase (Der Koffer). GDR 1983. Director: Kurt Weiler. Puppet: Martina Grosser. Photographed by Rolf Hofmann. (Courtesy of Deutsches Institut für Animationsfilm/ Archiv [German Institute for Animated Film/Archive.])

The Falling Shadow (Der fallende Schatten). GDR 1986. Director: Stanislav Sokolov. Puppets: W. Dudkin, A. Melik-Sarkisian. Photographed by Rolf Hofmann. (Courtesy of Deutsches Institut für Animationsfilm/Archiv [German Institute for Animated Film/Archive.])

Fairy Birds (Feenvögel). GDR 1987. Director: Monika Krausse-Anderson. Puppets: Klaus Schollbach. Photographed by Rolf Hofmann. (Courtesy of Deutsches Institut für Animationsfilm/Archiv [German Institute for Animated Film/Archive.])

Q: How do you see the future of stop motion compared to 3D computer animation?

A: It gets more and more difficult to judge the future of animation in general. But I got the impression that stop motion still has a future regarding auteur filmmaking with an intensely defined individual style.

Q: What do you think is the special quality of animation compared to live action?

A: The quality of animation, particularly stop motion, I see in the fact that I have much more control over the whole process. It is my responsibility what a puppet should be able to do. So I cannot blame the puppet for "bad acting."

Selected Filmography

1912
HOW A MOSQUITO OPERATES
The first triumph of character animation in the cinema: A partly humanized Mosquito plagues a sleeper. Still a masterpiece, animated by the brilliant Winsor McCay.

1914
GERTIE THE DINOSAUR
Elements of this already appeared in Winsor McCay's comic strip work, *Dream of a Rarebit Fiend*. Made in the "McCay Split System": with key frames being done first, then the inbetweens.

1926
THE ADVENTURES OF PRINCE ACHMED
(**Die Abenteuer des Prinzen Achmed**)
Comenius Film GmbH
Lotte Reiniger's sensitively animated delicate silhouette characters.

1933
KING KONG
RKO Radio Pictures
He was a king and a god in the world he knew, but now he comes to civilization merely a captive—a show to gratify your curiosity. Ladies and gentlemen, look at Kong, the Eighth Wonder of the World. Although you see the fingerprints of animators Willis O'Brien and Buzz Gibson on the rabbit fur that model maker Marcel Delgado was given for the two Kong models, it's still the most memorable screen monster. The 18″ armatures of the models are not exactly the same: One

Kong that was built earlier had a long face and looked a little bit human, while the other one with a rotund face looked more like a gorilla.

1933
THREE LITTLE PIGS
Walt Disney Productions
The breakthrough in Disney color animation, this *Silly Symphony* won the 1934 Academy Award for Best Animated Short Film. The pigs all look equal, but they differ in character: Fiddler Pig and Fifer Pig, the care-free ones, and Practical Pig, the foresighted one.

1934
PLAYFUL PLUTO
Walt Disney Productions
Norman Ferguson animated a brief (one-minute-and-half) sequence that shows Pluto's tussle with a piece of flypaper.

1935
LONESOME GHOSTS
Walt Disney Productions
The blueprint of *Ghostbusters:* Mickey, Donald, and Goofy make a good trio. The Technicolor short was animated by Isadore Klein, Ed Love, Milt Kahl, Marvin Woodward, Bob Wickersham, Clyde Geronimi, Dick Huemer, Dick Williams, Art Babbitt, and Rex Cox.

1937
SNOW WHITE AND THE SEVEN DWARFS
Walt Disney Productions
The first big success of Disney character animation: the dwarfs and the witch (Norman Ferguson).
Honorary Award, Academy of Motion Picture Arts and Sciences, 1939, recognized as a significant screen innovation, which has charmed millions and pioneered a great new entertainment field (one regular Oscar statuette and seven miniature statuettes for the dwarfs).

1938
BRAVE LITTLE TAILOR
Walt Disney Productions
Mickey Mouse, as Grimm Bros.' Valiant Little Tailor animated by Fred Moore, outwits a giant that was animated by Vladimir "Bill" Tytla.
Nominated for an Academy Award for Animated Short Film, 1939.

1940
PINOCCHIO
Walt Disney Productions
Disney once asked Albert Whitlock, who was one of his matte artists, "Al, what's your favorite Disney picture?" Albert said, "*Pinocchio*." Disney seemed to be pleased, "Mine too." Ward Kimball became the supervising animator for Jiminy Cricket. Bill Tytla animated Stromboli, the brutal puppeteer.

1940
FANTASIA
Walt Disney Productions
Bill Tytla animated Chernabog and projected his own powerful and self-confident character onto the Devil of the *Night on the Bald Mountain* Sequence.

1941
DUMBO
Walt Disney Productions
Bill Tytla's animation made you cry for the little elephant with the big ears.

1943
EDUCATION FOR DEATH: THE MAKING OF THE NAZI
Walt Disney Productions
Milt Kahl, Ward Kimball, Frank Thomas, and Bill Tytla, who did a Nazi teacher, were in charge of animating this authentic anti-Fascist short.

1944
THE SNOW MAN
Der Schneemann
Fischerkoesen Film Studio
A snow man longs for the melting experience of summertime.

1947
KING-SIZE CANARY
Metro-Goldwyn-Mayer, Inc.
Tex Avery's surreal play with proportions: A bottle of *Jumbo-Gro* transforms a hungry cat, a tiny bird and a dog to creatures of monstrous size. If there ever was Expressionist acting with characters staring wide-eyed and mouths dropped open to indicate surprise, then this is it.

1950
GERALD McBOING-BOING
UPA United Productions of America/Columbia Pictures
Not the limited animation but the boy's Sound FX makes this short and its title character that is based on a story by Theodor Seuss Geisel.
Academy Award, Best Animated Short Film, 1951.

1952
NEIGHBOURS
National Film Board of Canada
Pixilation by Norman McLaren.
Academy Award, Best Animated Short Film, 1953.

1956
EARTH VS. THE FLYING SAUCERS
Clover Productions/Columbia Pictures
Flying Saucers became living objects in the hand of master craftsman Ray Harryhausen.

1957
THE BLACK SCORPION
Amex Productions/Warner Bros. Pictures
Eerie underground cavern sequence with giant scorpions and a lively spider that rockets around the ground in pursue of a human victim, with stop motion conceived by Willis O'Brien and executed by Peter Peterson.

1958
THE 7TH VOYAGE OF SINBAD
Morningside Productions/Columbia Pictures
Ray Harryhausen's stop-frame animation of a Cyclops and a Skeleton swordfight are the highlights of this (in its days) spectacular although low-budget Arabian Nights adventure, the equivalent to the age of *Star Wars*.

1959
SLEEPING BEAUTY
Walt Disney Productions
Maleficent, the evil fairy, designed complete with a collar that made her look like a bat and devil horns, was animated by Marc Davis for this Super Technirama 70 production.

1959
A MIDSUMMER NIGHT'S DREAM
Sen noci svatojánské
Studio Kresleného a Loutkového Filmu, Prague
Ambitious puppet film version of Shakespeare's play directed by Jiří Trnka.

1963

JASON AND THE ARGONAUTS

Morningside Worldwide/Columbia Pictures

Ray Harryhausen multiplied the one sword-wielding skeleton from *Sinbad* and gave us seven. While animating he averaged less than a foot of film a day, only 13 to 15 frames. The 4-minute sequence took 4.5 months to do.

1967

THE JUNGLE BOOK

Walt Disney Productions

Milt Kahl's animation of Shere Khan, young Mowgli's nemesis, was a milestone of 2D animation. The Disney people tried to remake it in 3D CGI (released in 2016), but in spite of incredible technical resources weren't able to capture the light spirit of the 2D original.

1981

CLASH OF THE TITANS

Peerford, Ltd./Metro-Goldwyn-Mayer

Not a great film but a superb Medusa with snake-body and snakes in the hair, Ray Harryhausen's swansong as animator.

1988

GRAVE OF THE FIREFLIES

Hotaru no haka

Studio Ghibli

Isao Takahata's tragic tale of a 14-year-old Japanese boy and his little sister who don't survive the last days of World War II.

1988

MY NEIGHBOR TOTORO

Tonari no Totoro

Studio Ghibli

Hayao Miyazaki sure understands the imaginary world and the souls of kids.

1988

WHO FRAMED ROGER RABBIT

Touchstone Pictures (Disney)/Amblin Entertainment (Spielberg)

Robert Zemeckis' picture, in its time, was an inventive project mixing 2D animated characters and live action: Bob Hoskins co-starring with the residents of animated Toontown.

Academy Awards, Best Effects, Visual Effects (Ken Ralston, Richard Williams, Ed Jones, and George Gibbs), Special Achievement Award for animation direction and creation of the cartoon characters (Richard Williams), 1989.

1988
THE WIZARD OF SPEED AND TIME
Jittlov/Kaye Productions
The ultimate in Pixilation which grew out of a 1979 short film by Mike Jittlov.

1989
CREATURE COMFORTS
Aardman Animations
Clay-animated zoo animals talk in this short like ordinary people about their homes.
Academy Award, Best Animated Short Film, 1990.

1995
TOY STORY
Pixar Animation Studios
The clean surface of toys was easy to render in those days.
Academy Award, Special Achievement Award (John Lasseter), 1996.

1995
GHOST IN THE SHELL
Kokaku Kidotai
Bandai Visual Company
Mamoru Oshii's anime of the year 2029 that anticipated everything from the age of the internet to Cyborgs and the Matrix.

1997
PRINCESS MONONOKE
Mononoke-hime
Studio Ghibli
Hayao Miyazaki's romantic epic fantasy was based on his early sketches from the 1970s that had a princess living in the woods.

1997
PERFECT BLUE
Pafekuto buru
Studio Madhouse
Satoshi Kon's directorial suspense debut based on a novel by Yoshikazu Takeuchi: The picture focuses on a pop idol who decides to pursue an acting career and becomes a victim of stalking.

1999
THE IRON GIANT
Warner Bros. Animation
Brad Bird's tale of a boy who saves a robot from outer space from government agents is often described as a prime example for outstanding acting in animation. Well, it's good but not outstanding. The robot itself is an oversized *E.T.* rip-off.

2001
MILLENNIUM ACTRESS
Sennen joyu
Studio Madhouse
Satoshi Kon's postmodernist comedy-drama features two documentary film-makers who are going to investigate the life of a retired actress.

2001
MONSTERS, INC.
Pixar Animation Studios
Two colorful monstrous scaremongers: top scarer Sulley and his one-eyed friend Mike become attached to a little girl they name "Boo" and hide the kid from their fellow monsters.

2001–2003
THE LORD OF THE RINGS:
THE MOTION PICTURE TRILOGY
WingNut Films/The Saul Zaentz Company/New Line Cinema
Andy Serkis' captured performance as Gollum became a milestone in mocap acting. Won 17 out of 30 total Academy Award nominations.

2003
FINDING NEMO
Pixar Animated Studios
Not so much the fish but the animation of an Australian pelican, Nigel, fascinated the animation community.
Academy Award, Best Animated Feature (Andrew Stanton), 2003.

2004
TERKEL IN TROUBLE
Terkel i knibe
A. Film/Nordisk Film
Maybe not everybody's choice: Simple 3D teenage animation from Denmark but great fun and lots of sarcasm.

2004
RYAN
National Film Board of Canada
The gradual deconstruction of a drug addict.
Academy Award, Best Animated Short Film, 2004.

2007
RATATOUILLE
Pixar Animation Studios
The delicious adventures of a rat in French cuisine.
Academy Award, Best Animated Feature Film of the Year (Brad Bird), 2008.

2007
THE PIANO FOREST
Piano no mori
Studio Madhouse
Manga-turned-anime: A teenage boy dares to play a mysterious piano in the middle of a forest.

2009
CORALINE
Laika Entertainment
Henry Selick's stop motion illustrates a girl's nightmare.
Nominated for an Academy Award, 2010.

2009
FANTASTIC MR. FOX
Twentieth Century Fox/Indian Paintbrush/Regency Enterprises
2009 was an exceptional year for the art of stop motion: Wes Anderson's adaptation of Roald Dahl's children's novel featured the voices of George Clooney and Meryl Streep, but the real stars were animated puppets.
Nominated for Golden Globe and Academy Awards for Best Animated Feature and Best Original Score.

2009
AVATAR
Twentieth Century Fox Film Corporation/Dune Entertainment/Ingenious Film Partners
James Cameron's commercial triumph of performance capture.
Academy Award, Best Visual Effects (Richard Baneham, Andrew R. Jones, Joe Letteri, and Stephen Rosenbaum), 2010.

2010
HOW TO TRAIN YOUR DRAGON
DreamWorks Animation
The friendship between a Viking boy and a black dragon, a Night Fury, based on a book by Cressida Cowell.
Nominated for an Academy Award, Best Animated Film, 2011.

2010
CHICO & RITA
Isle of Man Film/CinemaNX, Estudio Mariscal
Havanna in the 1940s: Jazz and love in a melodrama that tells of Cuban Dancing and hot music.
Nominated for an Academy Award, Best Animated Film, 2012.

2011
WRINKLES
Arrugas
Perro Verde Films
Alzheimer's disease is the topic of a very touching Spanish comic book that became an astonishing low-budget 2D animation film.
Nominated for European Film Award, 2012.

2012
PARANORMAN
Laika Entertainment
An 11-year-old Norman is not only thrilled by horror movies, he actually can see ghosts. *ParaNorman* was stop-frame animated by a crew of 300.

2012
ERNEST & CÉLESTINE
La Parti Productions/Les Armateurs/Maybe Movies
This very poetic film is about an unlikely friendship—Ernest is a bear, Célestine a mouse:
If you don't eat me, I'll give you whatever you most want in the world.
Nominated for an Academy Award, Best Animated Feature Film, 2014.

2015
ANOMALISA
Snoot Entertainment/Starburns Industries
Charlie Kaufman (screenplay, *Being John Malkovich*) and animation director Duke Johnson teamed to create one of the most unusual stop-motion films. Puppets become people as they never were.

2016
FINDING DORY
Pixar Animation Studios
Great 3D animation of Hank the octopus.

2016
KUBO AND THE TWO STRINGS
Laika Entertainment
Amazing stop-motion story about a Japanese magic boy who fights the spirit of his evil grandfather, the Moon King.

Bibliography

Béla Balázs, *Early Film Theory. Visible Man and The Spirit of Film.* Edited by Erica Carter, translated by Rodney Livingstone. New York/Oxford: Berghahn, 2010.

Tom Bancroft, *Creating Characters with Personality. For Film, TV, Animation, Video Games and Graphic Novels.* New York: Watson-Guptill, 2006.

Joe Barbera, *My Life in 'Toons: From Flatbush to Bedrock in Under a Century.* Atlanta, Georgia: Turner Publishing, 1994.

Michael Barrier, *Hollywood Cartoons: American Animation in Its Golden Age.* New York: Oxford University Press, 2003.

Michael Barrier, *The Animated Man: A Life of Walt Disney.* Berkeley, CA: University of California Press, 2008.

André Bazin, *What Is Cinema?* Berkeley and Los Angeles, CA: University of California Press, 1970.

Jerry Beck, *"I Tawt I Taw A Puddy Tat": Fifty Years of Sylvester and Tweety.* New York: Henry Holt and Company, Inc., 1991.

Giannalberto Bendazzi, *Cartoons: One Hundred Years of Cinema Animation.* London: John Libbey and Company Ltd., 1994.

Giannalberto Bendazzi, *Animation: A World History. Volumes I–III.* Boca Raton, FL: CRC Press Taylor & Francis Group. A Focal Press Book, 2015.

Bruno Bettelheim, *The Uses of Enchantment: The Meaning and Importance of Fairy Tales.* New York: Alfred A. Knopf, 1976.

Preston Blair, *Cartoon Animation.* Irvine, CA: Walter Foster Publishing, 1994.

Jaroslav Boček, *Jiří Trnka, Artist and Puppet Master.* 1st Eng. Ed. Prague: Artia, 1965.

Richard Boleslavsky, *Acting: The First Six Lessons.* Original: New York: Taylor & Francis, 1933. Literary Licensing LLC, 2011.

363

Peter Brooks, *The Shifting Point: Theatre, Film, Opera 1946–1987.* New York: Theatre Communications Group, 1986.

Oksana Bulgakowa and Dietmar Hochmuth (eds). *Sergei Eisenstein, Disney.* Translated by Dustin Condren. Berlin: Potemkin Press, 2016.

Leslie Cabarga, *The Fleischer Story.* Rev. ed. New York: DaCapo Press, 1988.

Roger Caillois, *Man, Play and Games.* Translated from the French original by Meyer Barash. New York: Free Press of Glencoe, 1961.

John Canemaker, *Winsor McCay: His Life and Art.* New York: Abbeville Press, 1987.

John Canemaker, *Felix: The Twisted Tale of the World's Most Famous Cat.* New York: Pantheon Books, 1991.

Sharon M. Carnicke, *Stanislavsky in Focus: An Acting Master for the 21st Century.* London: Routledge Theatre Classics, 2008.

John Cawley/Jim Korkis, *The Encyclopedia of Cartoon Superstars.* Las Vegas, NV: Pioneer Books, Inc., 1990.

Michael Chekhov, *On the Technique of Acting.* New York: Harper Perennial, 1993.

Pinto Colvig, *It's a Crazy Business: The Goofy Life of a Disney Legend.* Edited and Introduced by Todd James Pierce. Oregon: Southern Oregon Historical Society/Theme Park Press, 2015.

Donald Crafton, *Before Mickey: The Animated Film 1898–1926.* Cambridge, MA/London: The MIT Press, 1987.

Donald Crafton, *Shadow of a Mouse: Performance, Belief, and World-Making in Animation.* Berkeley and Los Angeles, CA/London: University of California Press, 2013.

Shamus Culhane, *Talking Animals and Other People.* New York: St. Martin's Press, 1981.

John Culhane, *Walt Disney's Fantasia.* New York: Abradale Press/Harry N. Abrams, Inc., Publishers, 1987.

Shamus Culhane, *Animation from Script to Screen.* London: Columbus Books Limited, 1989.

Jim Danforth, *Dinosaurs, Dragons & Drama: The Odyssey of a Trickfilmmaker. Vol. 1 and Vol. 2. CD Books.* Los Angeles: Archive Editions, 2012/2015.

Walt Disney, Growing pains. *American Cinematographer* 22, 3 (March 1941): 106–7, 139–42.

Robert D. Feild, *The Art of Walt Disney.* New York: Macmillan, 1942.

Christopher Finch, *The Art of Walt Disney: From Mickey Mouse to the Magic Kingdoms.* New York: Harry N. Abrams/New American Library, 1973.

Richard Fleischer, *Just Tell Me When to Cry: A Memoir.* New York: Carroll & Graf Publishers, Inc., 1993.

Richard Fleischer, *Out of the Inkwell: Max Fleischer and the Animation Revolution.* Lexington, Kentucky: The University of Kentucky, 2005.

Friz Freleng, with David Weber, *Animation: The Art of Friz Freleng.* Newport Beach, CA: Donovan Publishing, 1994.

Didier Ghez (ed.), *Walt's People. Talking Disney with the Artists Who Knew Him.* Volume 1–12. Bloomington, IN: Xlibris, 2005–2012.

Didier Ghez, *Disneyland Paris from Sketch to Reality.* London: Neverland Editions Ltd., 2012.

Didier Ghez, *Disney's Grand Tour: Walt and Roy's European Vacation Summer 1935.* Theme Park Press, 2014.

Didier Ghez, *They Drew as They Pleased: The Hidden Art of Disney's Golden Age.* Chronicle Books: San Francisco, 2015.

Rolf Giesen/Claudia Meglin, *Künstliche Welten.* Hamburg and Vienna: Europa Verlag, 2000.

Rolf Giesen/J. P. Storm, *Animation Under the Swastika: A History of German Trickfilm, 1933–1945.* Jefferson, NC: McFarland, 2012.

Rolf Giesen, *Chinese Animation: A History and Filmography, 1922–2012.* Jefferson, NC: McFarland, 2015.

Eric Goldberg, *Character Animation Crash Course!* Los Angeles, CA: Silman-James Press, 2008.

Daniel Goldberg and Charlie Keil (ed.), *Funny Pictures: Animation and Comedy in Studio-Era Hollywood.* Berkeley and Los Angeles, CA: University of California Press, 2011.

Orville Goldner and George E. Turner, *The Making of King Kong: The Story Behind a Film Classic.* New York: Ballantine Books, 1975.

Jonathan Gottschall, *The Storytelling Animal: How Stories Make Us Human.* New York: Mariner Books, 2012.

Donald Graham, *The Art of Animation.* Unpublished manuscript dated July 20, 1955, held at Walt Disney Studios.

John Halas and Roger Manvell, *The Technique of Film Animation.* New York: Hastings House, 1963.

Mike Hankin, *Ray Harryhausen: Master of the Majicks. Volume 1: Beginnings and Endings. Volume 2: The American Films. Volume 3: The British Films.* Los Angeles, CA: Archive Editions, 2008–2013.

Derek Hayes and Chris Webster, *Acting and Performance for Animation.* Burlington, MA/Abingdon, Oxon: Focal Press, 2013.

Gordon Hendricks, *Eadweard Muybridge: The Father of the Motion Picture.* Mineola, New York: Dover, 2001.

L. Bruce Holman, *Puppet Animation: History & Technique.* South Brunswick and New York: A. S. Barnes and Company. London: The Tantivy Press, 1975.

Ed Hooks, *Acting for Animators: A Complete Guide to Performance Animation.* Revised edition. Portsmouth, NH: Heinemann Drama, 2003.

Johan Huizinga, *Homo ludens: A Study of the Play-Element in Culture.* London, Boston and Henley: Routledge & Kegan Paul Ltd., 1949.

Leslie Iwerks and John Kenworthy, *The Hand Behind the Mouse.* New York: Disney Editions, 2001.

Ollie Johnston and Frank Thomas, *Walt Disney's Bambi: The Story and the Film*. New York: Stewart, Tabori & Chang, 1990.

Chuck Jones, *Duck Amuck: The Life and Times of an Animated Cartoonist*. New York: Macmillan, 1999.

Buster Keaton and Charles Samuels, *My Wonderful World of Slapstick*. Garden City, NY: Doubleday, 1960.

Isaac Kerlow, *The Art of 3D Computer Animation and Effects*. 4th edition. Hoboken, New York: Wiley, 2009.

Klaus Kohlmann, *Der Computeranimierte Spielfilm: Forschungen zur Inszenierung und Klassifizierung des 3-D-Computer-Trickfilms*. Bielefeld: transcript Verlag, 2007.

David Krasnar, *An Actor's Craft: The Art and Technique of Acting*. London: Palgrave Macmillan, 2012.

Trish Ledoux (ed.), *Anime Interviews: The First Five Years of Animerica Anime & Manga Monthly (1992–97)*. San Francisco, CA: Cadence Books, 1997.

John A. Lent (ed.), *Animation in Asia and the Pacific*. Bloomington and Indianapolis: Indiana University Press/John Libby Publishing, 2001.

Esther Leslie, *Hollywood Flatlands: Animation, Critical Theory and the Avant-Garde*. Verso: London/New York, 2002.

Sergey Levine, *Body Language Animation: Synthesis from Prosody*. An Honors Thesis submitted to the Department of Computer Science of Stanford University, May 2009.

Judy Lieff, Performance and Acting for Animators. *Animation World Magazine*, 4.12, March 2000.

Peter Lord and Brian Sibley, *Creating 3-D Animation*. New York: Harry N. Abrams, 1998.

Jonathan Lyons, *Comedy for Animators*. Foreword by John Canemaker. Boca Raton, FL: CRC Press Taylor & Francis Group, 2016.

Mark W. MacWilliams, *Japanese Visual Culture: Explorations in the World of Manga and Anime*. Foreword by Frederik L. Schodt. London and New York: Routledge Taylor & Francis Group, 2008.

Marcel Mauss, Techniques of the Body (1935). In: *Techniques, Technology and Civilization*, ed. Nathan Schlanger. Trans. Ben Brewster, 77–95. New York: Berghahn Books, 2006.

Helen McCarthy, *Hayao Miyazaki: Master of Japanese Animation*. Berkeley, CA: Stone Bridge Press, 1999.

Sanford Meisner and Dennis Longwell, *Sanford Meisner on Acting*. New York: Random House, Inc., 1987.

Albert Menache, *Understanding Motion Capture for Computer Animation and Video Games*. San Diego/San Francisco/New York/Boston/London/Sydney/Tokyo: Morgan Kaufmann/Academic Press, 2000.

Alice Miller, *The Untouched Key: Tracing Childhood Trauma in Creativity and Destructiveness*. Translated from the German [Gemiedene Schlüssel] by

Hildegarde and Hunter Hannum. New York: Anchor Books. A Division of Random House, Inc., 1991.

Alice Miller, *The Body Never Lies: The Lingering Effects of Hurtful Parenting.* Translated from the German by Andrew Jenkins. New York and London: W. W. Norton & Company, 2006.

Tracey Miller-Zarneke, *The Art of DreamWorks' Kung Fu Panda 2.* San Rafael, CA: Ensight Editions, 2011.

Hayao Miyazaki, *Starting Point: 1979–1996.* San Francisco, CA: VIZ Media LLC, 2009.

Desmond Morris, *Bodytalk: The Meaning of Human Gestures.* New York: Crown Publishers, 1995.

Eadweard Muybridge, *Animals in Motion.* New York: Dover Publications, 1957.

Eadweard Muybridge, *The Human Figure in Motion.* New York: Dover Publications, 1955.

Gerald Peary and Danny Peary, ed., *The American Animated Cartoon. A Critical Anthology.* New York: E. P. Dutton, 1980.

Floriane Place-Verghnes, *Tex Avery: A Unique Legacy (1942–1955).* New Barnet, Herts: John Libby Publishing Ltd., 2006.

Barry Purves, *Basics Animation: Stop-Motion.* Worthing: AVA Publishing, 2010.

Hannes Rall, *Adaptation for Animation: Transforming Literature Frame by Frame.* Boca Raton, FL: CRC Taylor & Francis Group, 2017.

John Howard Reid, *Hollywood Movie Musicals: Great, Good and Glamorous.* Hollywood Classics 16, Raleigh, North Carolina: Lulu Press, Inc., 2006.

Lotte Reiniger, *Shadow Theatres and Shadow Films.* London and New York: B. T. Batsford and Watson-Guptill Publications, 1970.

Valliere T. Richard, *Norman McLaren: Manipulator of Movement. The National Film Board Years, 1947–1967.* An Ontario Film Institute Book. London and Toronto: Associated University Press, 1982.

Richard Rickitt, *Special Effects: The History and Technique.* Foreword by Ray Harryhausen. New York: Billboard Books An imprint of Watson-Cuptill Publications, 2007.

Roger C. Schank, *Tell Me A Story: Narrative and Intelligence.* Evanston, IL: Northwestern University Press, 1995.

Steve Schneider, *That's All Folks! The Art of Warner Bros. Animation.* London: Aurum Press, 1994.

Walt Stanchfield, *Drawn to Life: 20 Golden Years of Disney Master Classes.* New York and London: Focal Press, 2009.

Konstantin Stanislavsky, *An Actor Prepares.* New York: Taylor & Francis, 1989.

Bob Thomas, *Walt Disney, the Art of Animation: The Story of the Disney Studio Contribution to a New Art.* New York: Simon and Schuster, 1958.

Bob Thomas, *Disney's Art of Animation: From Mickey Mouse to Beauty and the Beast.* New York: Hyperion, 1991.

Frank Thomas and Ollie Johnston, *Disney Animation: The Illusion of Life*. New York: Abbeville Press Publishers, 1981.

Tony Thomas, *Gene Kelly: Song and Dance Man*. Foreword by Fred Astaire. Secaucus, NJ: The Citadel Press, 1974.

Patrick Tucker, *The Secrets of Screen Acting*. 3rd edition. Routledge: Theatre Arts Book, 2014.

Bill Warren, *Keep Watching the Skies! American Science Fiction Movies of the Fifties, the 21st Century edition*. Jefferson, NC: McFarland, 2009.

Tom Weaver, *A Sci-Fi Swarm and Horror Horde: Interviews with 62 Filmmakers*. Jefferson, NC and London: McFarland, 2010.

Peter Weishar, *blue sky: The Art of Computer Animation. Featuring Ice Age and Bunny*. New York: Harry N. Abrams, Inc., Publishers, 2002.

Paul Wells, *Understanding Animation*. London: Routledge, 1998.

Paul Wells. *Animation: Genre and Authorship*. London and New York: Wallflower, 2002.

Harold Whitaker and John Halas, *Timing for Animation*. Updated by Tom Sito. New York and London: Focal Press Taylor & Francis Group, 2009.

Tony White, *The Animator's Workbook*. Oxford: Phaidon Press Limited, 1986.

Pat Williams with Jim Denney, *How to Be Like Walt: Capturing the Disney Magic Every Day of Your Life*. Deerfield Beach, FL: Health Communications, Inc., 2004.

Richard Williams, *The Animator's Survival Kit: A Manual of Methods, Principles and Formulas*. London: Faber and Faber, 2001.

S.S. Wilson, *Puppets & People: Large-Scale Animation in the Cinema*. San Diego, CA: A.S. Barnes and Co. Inc., 1980.

Index

Note: Page numbers followed by "*fn*" indicate footnotes.

A

Aardman, 42, 206, 333, 337
Abbott & Costello, 106
Abbott and Costello Cartoon Show, 106
Abel, Robert, 115
The Absent-Minded Professor, 23
The Abyss, 10
Ackerman, Forry, 309
Acting, 135, 181, 225
    with animated characters, 69–74
    against odds of visual effects, 109–111
    theories, 49–52
Action analysis, 172
Adamski, George, 309
Adamson, Andrew, 36, 42
Adamson, Joe, 38*fn*
Adler, Stella, 51
Adobe After Effects, 110
Advanced humans, 213
The Adventures of Prince Achmed,
    13–16, 353
The Adventures of Tintin, 42, 120, 319
Advertising films, 169
Aesop, 36, 91
Aesop's Fables, 91, 197
AI, *see* Artificial intelligence
Aladdin, 27–28, 38–39, 195
Alakazam the Great, see Saiyu-ki

Alan Young Show on NBC Radio, 56
Aldrin, Buzz, 57
Alias Yederbeck, 347
Alice in Cartoonland, 69
Alice in Wonderland, 55
Allegro Non Troppo, 241, 243
Allen, David, 169
Allen, Irwin, 312
Allen, Woody, 106
Alois Nebel, 18
Alpine Climbers, 286
American 3D animation, 114
*The American Animated Cartoon: A
    Critical Anthology*, 56*fn*
American short silent comedy, 173
American Toy Fair, 168
Anchors Aweigh, 65
Anderson, Wes, 360
Andrews, Julie, 67
Anger, 45
Anger, Kenneth, 100
Animafest Zagreb, 235
Animal Farm, 164
Animals, 163–166
The Animal World, 77, 312
Animated characters
    acting with, 69–74
    around world, 91–97

Animatics creation, 205
Animation, 16, 29, 41, 59, 131, 133, 136,
     167–169, 231–232, 255, 258
   feel at ease in, 207–209
   future of acting in, 211–215
Animator(s), 35, 131–133, 143, 145, 228
   developing kinesthetic sense, 36
   Disney's principle, 37
   at Disney studio, 38
The Animator's Workbook, 113*fn*
Animism, 29
Anka, Paul, 57
Anomalisa, 186, 348, 361
Ant-Man, 325
The Ant and the Grasshopper, 91
Anthropomorphic
   animals, 36, 91, 274
   cartoon animals, 29
Anthropomorphism, 163–166
Anticipation, 189
Antiheroes, 99–101
Antisocial, 124
Anton the Musician, 349
Apollo, 289–290, 291
Arabian Nights, 299–300, 310
Aristocats, 340
Armstrong, Robert, 70
Armstrong, Todd, 71
Arrugas, 160, 163, 253
Artaud, Antonin, 46
"Art film" approach, 280
Artificial intelligence (AI), 270, 326
   agents, 212
The Art of Kung Fu Panda 2, 58*fn*
Ashman, Howard, 55
Ashpei, 158
Ashpitel, 158
Assault on a Medieval Town, 88
Associative position, 222
Astaire, Fred, 287
Asterix, 42, 43
Asterix and Obelix, 42, 178
Asterix Conquers America, 295, 296–297
Astro Boy, 92, 281
Atkinson, Rowan, 105
Atta, Mohammed, 100–101
Aubier, Stéphane, 230
Audley, Eleanor, 100

Augmented reality, 238, 326
Auschwitz, 58
Authenticity, Stanislavsky's definition
   of, 291
Automatic Fitness, 245, 250
Avatar, 113–122, 270, 317, 319, 325, 360
The Avengers, 74
Avery, Tex, 55, 166

B

Babbitt, Art, 21, 51–52
Babes in Toyland (1934), 107
Bacher, Hans, 38
Backus, Jim, 56
Bacon, Kevin, 115–116
Badham, John, 124
Baker, Rick, 26
Bakshi, Ralph, 118–119
Ballerina, 67
Ballets Russes de Monte Carlo, 13
Bambi, 55
Bancroft, Anne, 51
Baneham, Richard, 360
Barbara Millicent Roberts, see Barbie
Barbera, Joseph, 37, 41, 66, 106
The Barber of Seville, 31
Barbie: A Fashion Fairytale, 168
Barbie, 168
Barbie as Rapunzel, 168
Barbie in Rock 'N Royals, 168
Barbie in the Nutcracker, 168
Barbie of Swan Lake, 168
Barks, Carl, 160
The Barn Dance, 25
Barta, Jiří, 344
Baskett, James, 65
Batman, 10, 267
Batman Forever, 116
Batman v Superman: Dawn of Justice,
   319, 325
The Beast from 20, 000 Fathoms, 78,
   308, 313
Beast Wars: Transformers, 168
Beaudet, Louise, 287
Beauty and the Beast, 38–39, 55
Bee Movie, 144
Beijing Film Academy, 202
Being a Beast, 225

Being John Malkovich, 361
Belcher, Ernest, 21
Belcher, Marjorie Celeste, 21
Believe It or Don't, 106
Belling, Rudolf, 10
Bell, Margie, 21
Ben, 144
Benaderet, Bea, 55
Ben and Me, 164
Bendazzi, Giannalberto, 235–236
Ben Hur, 70
Benjamin the Elephant, 296–297
Benn, Sean, 123
Beowulf, 211
Bertel, Daniel, 87
Best, Ahmed, 116
Bettelheim, Bruno, 158*fn*
Betty Boop, 187–188
Betuel, Jonathan R., 124
Beyond: Two Souls, 120
Bibi Blocksberg, 295, 296–297, 299
Big Bad Wolf, 323–324
The Big Meeting, 274, 275
The Big Sleep, 146
Biomechania, 50
Bird, Brad, 36
The Birds, 26
Biroc, Joe, 308
Black Cauldron, 165
Black, Jack, 57, 147, 194
The Black Scorpion, 76–77, 356
Blackton, James Stuart, 9, 174
Blair, Mary, 274
Blair, Tony, 57
Blalack, Robert, 237–239
Blanc, Melvin Jerome "Mel", 55
Bletcher, William "Billy", 54
Bliefert, Ulrike, 61, 62
Blue Cat, 95, 281–282
Blue Sky Studios, 165
Bluth, Don, 264
Böcklin, Arnold, 11
Body language, 177
   Disney-ify, 183
   hand rubbing, 179
   personality typologies and friend–foe
      modes of thought, 178
   stimulus, 181
   visual sense, 180

The Body Snatchers, 117
Bodytalk, 181
Bogart, Humphrey, 145
Boleslavsky, Richard, 37
Bond, James, 166
The Bonker, 292
The Book of Life, 97
Bonsels, Waldemar, 323
Bordo, *see* Dovniković, Borivoj
The Borrowers (fantasy novels), 92
Bostrom, Nick, 213
Bowers, Charles R., 106
Bowie, David, 203
Boxtrolls, 337
Bozo the Clown, 105–106
Bozzetto, Bruno, 42, 136, 241–243
Bradbury, Ray, 194
Bradley, Scott, 193
Brain–Computer Interfaces, 215
Brando, Marlon, 51
Brandon, Henry, 107
The Brave Little Tailor, 25, 236, 354
Brecht, Bert, 50
The Bride of Frankenstein, 3, 306
The Brocaded Slipper, 158
The Broken Pitcher, 158
Brook, Peter, 10
Brothers Quay, *see* Quay, Stephen and
    Timothy
Browning, Tod, 173
Brown, Treg, 55
BSSS, 289–290
Bugs Bunny, 56, 106
Bunuel in the Labyrinth of the Turtles, 253
Bunuel, Luis, 253
Burton, Tim, 36, 116, 304*fn*
Butler, Charles Dawson "Daws", 54–55
Butler, Larry, 237, 309
Butt-Head, 178
Butz, Martin, 212

C

Cabinet of Dr. Caligari, 173
Café d'Amour, 60, 61
Caillois, Roger, 126
Caiman (project), 137
Call of Duty: World at War, 123, 124

Cameron, James, 116, 121, 319
Campbell, Joseph, 99
Canemaker, John, 236
Capra, Frank, 104–105
Captain Blackbeard, 23
Captain China, 150
Carrey, Jim, 120, 211
Cartoon Forum, 136–137
Cartoon(s), 41, 235
    aficionados, 31
    characters, 38, 53, 185
    creators, 288
    famous cartoon animals, 29–33
Castaneda, Carlos, 145
Castellaneta, Daniel Louis "Dan", 57
Catmull, Ed, 288
Cavalette, 241
Caveman, 81, 262
Cavett, Dick, 57
*Cendrillon ou La Petite Pantoufle de
    Verre*, 158
CGI, *see* Computer-generated imagery
A Chairy Tale, 59
Chandler, Raymond, 146
Chaney, Jr., Lon, 104
Chaney, Sr., Lon, 172
Chan, Jackie, 57
Chaplin, Charles, 29, 42, 172, 104–105,
    106, 107
Character
    character-driven storytelling, 266
    design, 171
    designer, 222
Character animation, 236, 264
    peak of, 21–23
Charlie Brown, 178
Charly Vet (*project*), 137
Cheng, Tang, 155
Chicken Run, 57, 206, 333
Chicken with Plums, 36
Chico & Rita, 328, 360
Chinese animation, 167, 279–280, 282
Chomet, Sylvain, 107
A Christmas Carol, 120
The Chronicles of Narnia, 325
Churchill, Frank, 93
Cinderella, 25, 27–28, 55, 100, 158, 159,
    164, 268

Cinderella Ate My Daughter, 204
Clampett, Robert, 32, 54, 55
Clark, Les, 22
Clash of the Titans, 259, 262, 303, 357
    bust from, 79
Clausen, Jürgen, 86
Clokey, Art, 261
Clooney, George, 360
Close, Glenn, 57
Cloudy with a Chance of Meatballs, 231
Coco, 61, 62
Cognitive Modeling group, 212
Cohl, Émile, 9–10, 59
Cohn, Harry, 70
Collins, Eddie, 21
Collodi, Carlo, 158
Columbus, Christopher, 166
Colvig, Pinto, 54, 105, 193
Comedy and comedian, 103–107
Computer-generated imagery (CGI), 114
The Congress, 212
Contempt, 29, 46
Contradictions, 143–147
Cook, Randy, 262
Cooper, Gary, 70
Cooper, Merian C., 70, 206, 306, 310–311
Cooper, Wilkie, 311
Coppola, Francis Ford, 100
Coraline, 325, 337, 360
Cornillón, Gustavo, 60
Corpus Hippocraticum, 178
Couceiro, Alberto, 84, 245–251
Cowell, Cressida, 360
Cox, Rex, 354
Cox, Vic, 76*fn*
Coyote & Roadrunner, 41, 96, 106, 145
Cozzi, Luigi, 154, 212
Crafton, Donald, 354
Crawford, Cheryl, 51
Creativity, 230
Creature Comforts, 358
Creature from the Black Lagoon, 10
The Crimson Pirate, 70–71
Cristóbal, Manuel, 253–258
Culhane, Shamus, 180
Culliford, Pierre, 43
Cultural Industries, 91–92
Cumberbatch, Benedict, 111, 340

Curie, Alvaro, 256
Cutout-style animation, 136

D

Daffy Duck, 32, 55, 106
Dafoe, Willem, 57, 120
Dahl, Roald, 360
Dalton Brothers, 178
Dam, Thomas, 168
Dance, Charles, 123
Danforth, Jim, 72, 72fn, 73fn, 81, 82, 86,
    103, 137–138, 169, 194, 259–262,
    304–305
Daniels, Chris, 110
Dante's Inferno, 316
Darby O'Gill and the Little People, 109
Darwin, Charles, 173
A Date With Duke, 304
Daumier, Honoré, 274
Davey and Goliath, 261
David and Goliath principle, 29, 142, 197
Davis, Marc, 287, 356
Davis, Mark, Dr., 125
Davis, Virginia, 69
Davy Crockett, 23
Deadly Creatures, 123
Dean, James, 51
Death of Stalinism in Bohemia, 333
de Basil, Wassily, 13
Debray, Régis, 124
de Chomón, Segundo, 59
DEFA Studios Babelsberg, 321
Defoe, Daniel, 157
Deja, Andreas, 38, 39
de la Cruz, Angel, 256
Delać, Vladimir, 274, 275
de la Pena, Nonny, 125
Delfs, Holger, 80
Delgado, Marcel, 353
Delgado, Victor, 307
del Toro, Guillermo, 97
DeMille, Cecil B., 315
De Niro, Robert, 51
Denney, Jim, 69fn
Denver, Bob, 57
DePatie, David H., 136
Depp, Johnny, 111, 215
Der ewige Jude, see The Eternal Jew

Der Trickfilm: A Survey of German Special
    Effects, 12fn
DeRycker, Piet, 263
Design, 171–175
Despicable Me, 254
Deutsch, Ernst, 173
Deutsche Zeichenfilm GmbH, 198
Devane, William, 115
DeVito, Danny, 57
di Caprio, Leonardo, 103
Dickens, Charles, 120, 211
Diehl, Ferdinand, 87
Diehl, Hermann, 87
Dietrich, Marlene, 114–115
Dinosaurs, 74
Dionysos, 49
Disco ormene, 166
Disco Worms!, 166
Disgust, 46
Disney-Pixar, 45, 145, 171, 186, 324
Disney, 94, 100, 106, 163
    animators, 21
    character animation, 38–39
    method, 206, 230
    Princesses, 203–204
    Studios, 230
    style, 274
Disney Allen, Alice, 22
Disney Animation: The Illusion of Life, 285
Disneyland, 23
Disney, Walt, 18, 21–23, 25, 37, 65, 69, 142,
    172, 180, 205, 288
Dissociative position, 222
Ditko, Steve, 111
Django, 242
Dlugaiczyk, Thomas, 269–271
Docter, Pete, 45
Doctor Faustus, 3
Doctor Strange, 111
Donald Duck, 25, 32, 53, 65, 160, 178,
    190, 225
Donen, Stanley, 65
Donner, Richard, 57
Döpfer, Peter, 87
Doraemon, 281
Doubková, Dagmar, 344
Douglas, Kirk, 22, 57
Dovniković-Bordo, Borivoj, 273–277

The Downfall, 58, 101
Dracula, 22, 173, 306
Dragonkeeper, 253, 257–258
Dragonslayer, 80, 81
Dragon Trouble (project), 137
DreamWorks Animation, 94, 22, 166, 168, 191
Driessen, Paul, 328
Droopy, 178
Dr. Seuss, *see* Geisel, Ted
Duck Amuck, 4
Du, Daisy Yan, 279–283
Duga Film, 274, 275
Dujardin, Jean, 109
Dumas, Alexandre, 10
Dumbo, 355
Dune, 123
Dykstra, John, 116
Dynamation, 304

E

Earth vs. the Flying Saucers, 309, 356
Eastwood, Clint, 145, 155
Ebert, Roger, 93
Eddy, Nelson, 144
Edison Manufacturing Company, 9
Education for Death: The Making of the Nazi, 47, 197, 198, 355
Efira, Virginia, 109
Egged On, 106
Eisen, Armand, 287
Eisenstein, Sergei, 27
Eisler, Hanns, 193
Eisner, Michael, 288
Ekman, Paul, 173, 174*fn*
El bosque animado, 253
El Cid, 70
The Elder Scrolls: Oblivion, 123
Elena of Avalor, 28, 160
Elmer Fudd, 55
Emmerich, Roland, 211
Emotions
    emotional effect, 222
    infants, 45
    older persons, 45
Empathy, 125–126
Empathy games, 125
Emperor's New Groove, 340

Enchanted, 165
The Enchanted Drawing, 9
Engel, Volker, 211
Ernest & Célestine, 360
Esso/Exxon Tiger, 169
Estabrook, Howard, 91
Eternal Jew, 203
Evolution (project), 312
Exaggeration, 189
The Execution of Mary Queen of Scots, 9
The Expendables, 270
Expressionist acting, 173
The Expression of Emotions in Man and Animal, 173–174
Eyer, Richard, 66

F

The Face of Another, 175
Facial Action Coding System (FACS), 174
Facial expression(s), 171–175
FACS, *see Facial Action Coding System*
Fairbanks, Jr., Douglas, 310, 311
Fairbanks, Sr., Douglas, 30, 173, 310
Fairchild, Chelsie Haunai, 169
Fairy-tale characters, 159
Fairy Birds, 351
Falk, Lee, 242
The Falling Shadow, 351
Fallout 3, 123
"Famous Monsters of Filmland" magazine, 309
Fantasia, 12, 22, 172, 193, 194, 355
Fantastic Beasts and Where to Find Them, 111
Fantastic Mr. Fox, 360
Fantomas, 10
Farrell, Colin, 111
Fast & Furious, 166
Fast & Furious 7, 325
Father Knows Best, 41
Faulds, Andrew, 71
Faust, 172
Favreau, Jon, 122
Fear, 46
    of own imagination, 226–232
Felix in Hollywood, 105

Felix the Cat, 105, 114
Ferguson, Norman, 354
Ferreras, Ignacio, 161, 256, 257
Feuillade, Louis, 10
Fields, W. C., 56, 114–115
Film Fantasy Scrapbook, 80
Final Fantasy: The Spirits Within, 120
Finding Dory, 186, 361
Finding Nemo, 115, 186, 359
Finney, Jack, 117
Fischerkoesen, Hans, 200
Fleischer, Dave, 17–20
Fleischer, Max, 4, 17, 21, 69, 116, 201
    rotoscoping process, 116
Fleischer, Richard, 18*fn*
Flesh Gordon, 259
The Flintstones, 41–43, 178
Flip the Frog, 30
Flushed Away, 94
Fly Me to the Moon, 157
Flynn, Errol, 92
Foghorn Leghorn, 55
Folman, Ari, 212
Fonda, Jane, 51
Fonda, Peter, 114
Food, 333
Foray, June, 55
Ford, John, 242
Foster, Charles, 225
The Fox Hunt, 225
Fox, Terry Curtis, 49
Franco-Belgian comics, 91–92
Frankenstein, 3, 4, 10, 173, 306
Franklin, Benjamin, 164
Franquin, André, 42
Freberg, Stan, 54–55
Freddie as F.R.O.7, 166
Freleng, Isadore "Friz", 32, 56, 136
Freud, Sigmund, 197
Friends Forever, 322
Frito Bandito, 169
Fritz the Cat, 160
Frog Kingdom, 166
Fulton, John P., 3, 110
Funny Girl, 66
Futurama, 178
Futureworld, 114
FXRH, 315*fn*

G

Gable, Clark, 70, 190
Gallopin' Gaucho, 30
Galouye, Daniel Francis, 212–213
Games Academy, 269
Ganesha, help! (project), 296
Ganz, Bruno, 58
Garfield, 178
Geisel, Ted, 58, 356
Gemora, Charlie, 26
Gentle Giant, 120
Gerald McBoing-Boing, 58, 356
Gerber, Craig, 28
German Expressionism, 173
Geronimi, Clyde, 354
Gerron, Kurt, 58
Gerson, Betty Lou, 100
Gerson, Dora, 58
Gertie the Dinosaur, 5, 115, 353
Gessner, Frank, 347
Ghez, Didier, 22*fn*, 285–288
Ghost in the Shell, 92, 358
The Giant Claw, 309
The Giant Ymir, 309–310
Gibbons, Tom, 115
Gibbs, George, 357
Gibson, Buzz, 307
Gibson, Mel, 57
Giesen, Rolf, 12*fn*, 305*fn*, 80
Gigantis, the Fire Monster/Godzilla Raids Again, 26
Gil, Carlos, 72
Gilliam, Terry, 248
Gladiator, 116
Gladstone, Frank, 36
Gladstone Gander, 32
Glière, Reinhold, 316
Goat Story-The Old Prague Legends, 343, 345
Goat Story 2 (Goat Story with Cheese), 343, 345
The Godfather, 100
The Godfather II, 270
Godzilla, 26
Goebbels, Joseph, 46–47
Goebbels, Magda, 202
Goennert, Felix, 289–293

Gojira no gyakushu, see Gigantis, the Fire Monster/Godzilla Raids Again
The Golden Touch, 54
The Golden Voyage of Sinbad, 3, 74, 77, 203, 303, 315
Goldner, Orville, 70*fn*
Goldorak, 204
The Golem, 10, 173, 306
Gollum, 118
Good Dinosaur, 145
The Good Person of Szechwan (play), 118
Good Will to Men, 164
Goofy, 21, 51, 54, 225, 164
Goofy and Wilbur, 164
The Goose That Laid the Golden Eggs, 91
Gorillas in the Mist, 26
Goscinny, René, 42
Gottliebová, Dinah, 202
Graham, Don, 172
Grand Theft Auto: San Andreas, 123
Grant, Joe, 286
Grau, Albin, 16
Grave of the Fireflies, 268, 357
Gravity, 325
The Great Rupert, 304
Green, Seth, 123
Greystoke: The Legend of Tarzan, Lord of the Apes, 26
Griffith, David Wark, 173
Groening, Matt, 42
Gromit, 42
Guest, Lance, 124
Guest, Val, 73
Gutierrez, Jorge R., 97

H

Hackett, Buddy, 137–138
Hadžić, Fadil, 275
Hagen, Louis, 13
Hahn Film, 232, 295–296
Hahn, Gerhard, 295–300
Hahn Graphics, 295
Halo: Combat Evolved, 124
Hamill, Mark, 71–72
Hand, David, 172, 286
Hand gestures, 179
Handler, Ruth, 168
Hand rubbing, 179

The Hand, 4
Haney, Carol, 66
Hankin, Mike, 71, 301–304
Hanks, Tom, 57, 120, 186, 270–271
Hanna-Barbera, 106
Hanna, William, 37, 41, 66, 194
Hannah, Jack, 160, 190
Hansel and Gretel, 85
Hara, Setsuko, 93
Hardaway, Ben, 31
Hardy, Oliver, 106
Harlan, Veit, 46
Harman, Hugh, 164
Harmon, Larry, 105–106
Harryhausen, Fred, 77, 308–309
Harryhausen, Ray, 12, 26, 66, 75, 186, 206, 259, 304–305, 305–316
Harry Potter, 111, 325
Hausner, Jerry, 56
Havoc in Heaven, 154, 155
Hawking, Stephen, 57
Hawkins, Emery, 31
Hawks, Howard, 146
Hayes, Craig, 115
Hayes, Derek, 136
Hefner, Hugh, 57
Heidi, Girl of the Alps, 92
Heine, Helme, 322
Heinemann, Art, 31
Heinzel, Carla, 292
Hell and Back, 107
Helmholtz, Hermann von, 214
Hendler, Darren, 212
Henson, Jim, 122, 188
Herbst, Helmut, 213
Hergé, 42
Hero of Alexandria, 77
Herrmann, Bernard, 311
Herzog, Werner, 57
Heskes, Wam, 304
Hippocrates, 178
Hitchcock, Alfred, 26
Hitler, Adolf, 58, 101, 292
The Hobbit, 118, 319, 340
Hoe Een Reclame-Affiche Ontstond, 304
Hoffman, Dustin, 51, 57
Hoffmann, E. T. A., 78
Hoffmann, Heinrich, 219

Holland, Tom, 35
Holloway, Sterling, 55
Hollow Man, 115–116
Hollywood Babylon, 100
Holmes, Sherlock, 173
Homer, 135
Homer Simpson, 41, 42, 179
Homo Faber: Man the Maker, 126
Homo fictus, 135
Homo Ludens: Man the Player, 125–126
Homunculi, 3–4
The Honeymooners, 41
Hooks, Ed, 26, 36*fn*, 37*fn*, 101, 131, 133, 144
Hopkins, Anthony, 211
Hopper, Dennis, 123
Horikoshi, Jiro, 93
Horsley, David Stanley, 3
Horvath, Ferdinand, 286
Hoskins, Bob, 110
Hound Hunters, 185
How a Mosquito Operates, 6, 353
Howard, James Newton, 194
How to Train Your Dragon, 191, 360
Huang Weiming, 96
Hubley, John, 56, 235
Huckleberry Hound, 55
Huemer, Dick, 38
Hughes, Howard, 310
Huizinga, Johan, 125–126
Hulk, 325
Humorous Phases of Funny Faces, 9, 174
The Hunchback of Notre Dame, 104, 145, 172, 195
Hunt, Helen, 57
Huntington, Samuel P., 94
Hurter, Albert, 25
Hurtley, Owen, 168
Hykade, Andreas, 333

I

Ice Age, 115, 186
Ice Age: Collision Course, 186
The Illusionist, 107
I Love Lucy, 41
Ilya Muromets, 77, 316
Independence Day, 211
Infants, emotions, 45
Inside Out, 267

Interactive environments, 120
Invasion of the Body Snatchers, 117
Invasion of the Pod People, 117
The Invisible Ray, 109–110
Invitation to the Dance, 65, 66, 67
I, Robot, 120, 319
The Iron Giant, 268, 358
Irony, 107
Islamic Revolution Design House, 203
It Came from Beneath the Sea, 78, 308, 309
It's a Bird, 106
Iwerks, Ub, 29–30

J

Jack Benny Show, 55
Jackson, Michael, 57
Jackson, Peter, 117, 118–120, 194, 317
Jackson, Samuel L., 123
Jackson, Wilfred, 22, 53–54
Jack the Giant Killer, 35–36, 70, 137–138, 259
Jack the Giant Slayer, 120
Jacobsson, Oscar, 42
Jannings, Emil, 172
Jason and the Argonauts, 71, 79, 194, 314, 357
Jeffrey Katzenberg: How to Make a Perfect Family Film, 22*fn*
Jennings, Garth, 195
Jerry Mouse, 66, 164
The Jewelled Slipper, 158
Jew Suss, 46
Jiminy Cricket, 164
Jin Guoping, 155
Jittlov, Mike, 60, 259
Joe's Apartment, 165
Johnny Head-in-the-Air, 219
Johnson, Duke, 361
Johnston, Ollie, 100*fn*, 189
Jolie, Angelina, 57, 211
Jones, Andrew R., 360
Jones, Chuck, 32, 106, 144, 182
Jones, Davy, 120
Jones, Ed, 357
Jones, James Earl, 57
José Carioca, 65, 287
Joseph and His Brethren (project), 70, 310
Journey to the West, 154
Jouvet, Louis, 101

Joy, 45, 181
Judex, 10
Judge Dredd, 116
Jungle Book, 145, 268, 340
The Jungle Book 3D, 55, 121–122, 357
Juran, Nathan, 70–71, 309–310
Jurassic Park, 10, 80, 81, 115
Jutrisa, Vladimir, 274

K

Kabuki Theatre, 50
Kahl, Milt, 354, 355, 357
Kane, Helen, 188
Karloff, Boris, 110
Kasday, David, 66
Katzenberg, Jeffrey, 22, 94, 136, 191, 288
Katzman, Sam, 309
Kaufman, Charlie, 361
Kauka, Rolf, 275
Kavner, Julie Deborah, 57
Kawamoto, Kihachiro, 93–94, 262
Kazan, Elia, 51
Keaton, Buster, 104, 106, 169, 172
Keaton, Joe, 104
Kelly, Gene, 65
Kendrick, Anna, 168
Kennedy, Edgar, 106, 287–288
Kerempuh, 275
Kermit the Frog, 166
Khrushchev, Nikita, 23
Kiki's Delivery Service, 92, 267, 268
Kilmer, Val, 116
Kimball, Ward, 164
Kim Jong-il, 202
King-Size Canary, 355
King, Jack, 160
King Kong (1933), 70, 74, 80, 81, 137, 145,
    306, 307, 317, 319, 353–354
King Kong (2005), 120, 194, 325
King, Larry, 57
King of Kings, 315–316
Kinney, Jack, 31
Kleinbach, Heinrich von, see Brandon,
    Henry
Klein, Isadore, 143
Kleiser, Jeff, 116
Kleiser–Walczak Construction
    Company, 116

Knick Knack, 293
Knight, Charlott, 309
Knock Knock, 31
Ko-Ko the Clown, 69
Koenig, Wolf, 60
Kolar, Boris, 274
Kon, Satoshi, 92–93, 358, 359
Kostanjšek, Vjekoslav, 274
Kostelac, Nikola, 274
Kracauer, Siegfried, 336
Krause, Hermann, 198
Krauss, Werner, 173
Kristl, Vlado, 274
Krumme, Raimund, 333
Kubo and the Two Strings, 155–156, 337,
    348, 361
Kung Fu Panda, 57, 94, 145, 147, 258,
    281–282
Kung Fu Panda 2, 148
Kung Fu Panda 3, 148
Kung Fu Rabbit, 146
Kurosawa, Akira, 155
Kurzweil, Raymond, 214

L

La Cava, Gregory, 36
La Cenerentola, 158
Ladouceur, J. P., 60
Lady and the Tramp, 164
Lady Gaga, 325
La Fontaine, Jean de, 197
Lahr, Bert, 25–26
Landau, Martin, 51
The Land Before Time series, 81
Landreth, Chris, 174
Langdon, Harry, 104–105, 172
Lang, Fritz, 16
L. A. Noir, 270
Lansbury, Angela, 55
Lantz, Walter, 31, 105, 147, 190
La Peau de Chagrin, 274
Lasky, Jesse, 309
Lasseter, John, 115, 186, 288
The Last Days of Pompeii, 306
The Last of Us, 212
The Last Starfighter, 124–125
Laughton, Charles, 287–288
Laura's Star, 263, 267

Laura's Star and the Mysterious Dragon Nian, 267
Laurel & Hardy, 106, 107
Laurel, Stan, 76, 106, 107
Law, John Phillip, 315
Leberecht, Frank, 199
Lee, Christopher, 56
Lee, Stan, 111
Le imprese di una spada leggendaria, 70–71
Lei, Ray, 280
Lemmon, Jack, 57
Lem, Stanisław, 212
Leone, Sergio, 145, 242
Les Jeux et Les Hommes, 126
Letteri, Joe, 317–320
Levene, Larry, 257
Le Vicomte de Bragelonne, 10
Lewis, Jerry, 173
Lewis, Robert, 51
Ley, Robert, 202
Li, Jet, 116
Lilo & Stitch, 38–39
"Limited" animation technique, 37
Lindbergh, Charles, 30
Lin Yuting, 6, 96
Lionello, Oreste, 242
The Lion King, 38–39, 171, 195
Little Caesar, 306
Little Carp That Jumped over the Dragon Gate, 159
Little Nemo in Slumberland, 5
The Little Polar Bear, 263
Little Red Riding Hood, 85
Little Rural Riding Hood, 55
Little Sisters of Grassland, 203
Little Soldier Zhang Ga, 203
Little Tadpoles Look for Mama, see Where Is Momma?
Liu Jian, 280
Live-action movies, 175
The Living Forest, 253, 256
Lloyd, Harold, 105
Loeser, Tony, 321–324
Lofgren, George, 25–26
Lommel, Andreas, 26
Lonesome Ghosts, 354
Looker, 114

Loos, Anita, 173
Lord of the Rings, 117, 118–119, 317, 325, 359
Lord, Peter, 206
Lorenz, Konstanza Kavrakova, 332
Lorre, Peter, 22
The Lost World, 306
Loup, 289–290
Love, Ed, 354
Low-budget filmmakers, 18
Lucasfilm Games, 269–270
Lucas, George, 269
Lucia, 182, 289–290
Lucky Luke, 43, 178
Lugosi, Bela, 22
Lukas, Paul, 22
Luminaris, 60, 194
Lundy, Dick, 21
Luo Yinggeng, 96
Luxo Jr., 293
Lynch, David, 248

M

MacMurray, Fred, 23
Madame Tutli-Putli, 186
Maderna, Osmar Héctor, 194
Magic of first moment, 107
The Magic Voyage, 166
The Magnificent Seven, 155
Maguire, Tobey, 110
Maher, Laurie, 186
Mailer, Norman, 124
Make Mine Music, 144
Making Faces: a Masterclass on Facial Animation, 174
Maltese, Michael, 32
The Man in the Iron Mask, 10
Man Made Monster, 109–110
Man of Steel, 120
Man, Play and Games, 126
The Man Who Laughs, 172
Mao Zedong, 155
Maraun, Frank, 86
Marceau, Marcel, 181
Marks, Aleksandar, 274
Marlowe, Philip, 145
Marsupilami, 42, 43
Martin, Kevin H., 57*fn*
Marvel Comics, 116

Marvin the Martian, 55
Marx, Groucho, 242
Mary Poppins, 67
The Mask, 10, 120
Mason, James
The Masque of the Red Death, 228
Mathews, Kerwin, 71
The Matrix, 212–213
Mauss, Marcel, 153
Maverick, 57
McCartney, Paul, 57
McCay, Winsor, 5, 6, 9–10, 353,
McDowell, Malcolm, 123
McLaren, Norman, 59, 60
McLuhan, Marshall, 114
McQueen, Steve, 51
"Mechanomorphic" humans, 274
The Meeting, 274
Mein Kampf, 47
Mehrabian, Albert, 180
Meisner, Sanford, 51
Melancholiacs, 178
Méliès, Georges, 9, 11, 59
Memory Hotel, 331, 334–335
Mendelssohn Bartholdy, Felix, 47
Mengele, Josef, 202
Mental delusions, 30
Mephistopheles, 172
Merchandising, 167–169
Mère Ubu, 331
Messmer, Otto, 105
Metropolis, 306
Meyer, Karl, 325–326
Meyerhold, Vsevolod, 50
Mia and me: Adventures in Centopia, 128,
    130, 295, 296, 299
Mickey Mouse, 25, 29, 54, 56, 164–166,
    193, 193, 222, 354
Midler, Bette, 57
A Midsummer Night's Dream, 118, 356
Mifune, Toshiro, 155
Mighty Joe Young, 75, 301–302, 307,
    313, 314
Mighty Mouse, 164
Mikkelsen, Mads, 111
Mikulás, Ferenc, 327–330
Millennium Actress, 92–93, 359

The Million Dollar Cat, 164
Mimesis, 26
Mimica, Vatrosvlav, 274
Mimicry, 126
Mio Fratello Superuomo, 241
The Miracle Doctor, 349
*Misadventures of Charley Zhang
    (project)*, 153
*Miss Peregrine's Home for Peculiar
    Children*, 304fn
Mister Magoo, 56, 136, 148–149, 324, 235
Miyazaki, Hayao, 91–92, 93
Moana, 168–169
Mocap, 318
Modern Times, 42
Moers, Walter, 292
Möllendorff, Horst von, 198, 201
Monkey King, 155, 281–282
Monkey King: Hero Is Back, 280–281
Monroe, Marilyn, 51, 214
Monster Hunt, 280–281
Monsters, Inc., 359
Monster Stick, 71–72, 303
Moore, Fred, 236fn, 354
Moore, Ray, 242
Moorhead, Joanna, 22fn
Moross, Jerome, 314
Morris, Desmond, 181
Mother Goose Stories, 85
MotionWorks, 321
Mr. Bean, 105
Mr. Jinks, 55
Mulan, 97, 155–156
Mullewapp, 322, 323
Mulloy, Phil, 333
Munro, Caroline, 303
Munro, Grant, 59–60
Murders in the Rue Morgue, 26
Murdoch, Rupert, 57
Muren, Dennis, 115
Murnau, Friedrich Wilhelm, 16, 172
Musumeci Greco, Enzo, 70–71
Mutt & Jeff series, 106
Muybridge, Eadweard, 18, 172, 262
My Neighbor Totoro, 357
Mysterious Island, 315
The Mystery of the Leaping Fish, 173

N

Nakadai, Tetsuya, 175
Nakai, Go (Kiyoshi), 204
The Naked and the Dead (novel), 124
Naruse, Mikio, 93
Nash, Clarence Charles, 53
National Film Board of Canada, 59, 186
Natwick, Grim, 187–188
Neeson, Liam, 123
Neighbours, 59, 356
Neugebauer, Walter, 274, 275
Newman, Paul, 51
Nibbelink, Phil, 166
Nighy, Bill, 120
Nimoy, Leonard, 57
Nixon, Richard M., 180
Noah, 135
Noah's Ark, 315–316
Nonplayer characters (NPCs), 212
Nordberg, Cliff, 182
Norstein, Yuri, 328
Norton, Mary, 92
Nosferatu, 16, 172
NPCs, *see* Nonplayer characters

O

Obelix, 42
O'Brien, Conan, 57
O'Brien, Darlyne, 75
O'Brien, Willis, 26, 75, 81, 121, 307,
    314, 353
O'Connell, Jerry, 165
Oldman, Gary, 123
Oliveira, José, 287*fn*
Omnibus Computer Graphics, 116
One Cab's Family, 166
One Froggy Evening, 144
One Hundred and One Dalmatians, 100, 190
*One Hundred Years of Cinema
    Animation*, 235
One Million Years B. C., 303, 314
The One, 116
Oooops! Noah Is Gone, 46
Orenstein, Peggy, 204
Orwell, George, 164
Oshii, Mamoru, 358

Oswald the Lucky Rabbit, 29–30
O'Toole, Peter, 101
Our Gang comedies, 54
*Out of the Inkwell: Max Fleischer and the
    Animation Revolution*, 18*fn*
Out of the Inkwell, 4, 17, 69
Ozu, Yasujiro, 93

P

Pablos, Sergio, 254, 257
Pacino, Al, 51
Page, Ellen, 212
The Pajama Game, 66
Pal, George, 83, 85, 103, 301, 303–305, 309
Panda Jing Jing, 147–148
Pantomime, 181
Paracelsus, 3
ParaNorman, 337, 361
Parker, Fess, 23
Park, Nick, 206
Pasternak, Joe, 65
Patar, Vincent, 230–231
Patterson, Ray, 66
Pauli, Peter, 60, 62
Peace on Earth, 164
Peary, Danny, 144*fn*
Peary, Gerald, 144*fn*
Pena, Nonny de la, 125
The Penguins of Madagascar, 178–179
Pepe Le Pew, 55
Perception, 217
    exercises, 217–218
Perceptual positions, 222
Père Ubu, 331
Perfect Blue, 93, 358
Performance capture, 18, 318, 319
    techniques, 211–215
Perlman, Ron, 111
Perrault, Charles, 158
Perri, 163
Persepolis, 36
Personality, 189–192
Peter and the Wolf, 55
Peter Pan, 268
Peterson, Peter, 307, 356
Petzold, Frank, 115–116
Phantasmagoria, 213

Phantomatics, 213
Phantom of the Opera, 104
Phantom of the Rue Morgue, 26
Phlegmatic types, 178
Photo-realism, 114, 251
Photographic effects, 27
Physiognomy, 179
The Piano Forest (2007), 360
Pickley, Leonard, 21
Pigor, Thomas, 292
Pigott-Smith, Tom, 303
Pillsbury Dough Boy, 169
The Pink Panther, 32–33
Pinnacle System's Commotion, 110
Pinocchio, 21, 25, 27, 158, 231, 267, 268, 355
The Pirates of Blood River, 315
Pirates of the Caribbean: Dead Man's Chest, 120
The Pirates of Tortuga: Under the Black Flag, 295
Pixilation, 59–63
pi ying, 14
Plane Crazy, 30
Planet of the Apes, 145
Plato, 49–50
Playful Pluto, 354
Pleasant Goat and Big Big Wolf, see Xi Yang Yang Yu Huitai Lang
Pluto, 27
Pocahontas, 27–28, 160
Poe, Edgar Allan, 228
Poitier, Sidney, 51
Pokémon, 222, 281
Polar Express, 120, 186, 211, 270–271, 340
Pollock, Channing, 306*fn*
Ponyo, 92
Poor Hansi, 198, 199
Popeye, 51
Porco Rosso, 92, 236
Porky Pig, 55
Posing, 171–175
Post humans, *see* Advanced humans
Poultry in Motion, 57*fn*
Powell, Michael, 80
Power Animals, 26, 27
Power of imagination, 221
Powers, Patrick A. (Pat), 166
Pozzi, Moana, 169

Prejudices, 179
Preproduction, 255
Pretty Woman, 158
Previz, 318
The Princess and the Frog, 159
Princess Mononoke, 267, 268, 358
Ptushko, Alexander, 316
Puppetoons, 301
Purves, Barry, 248

Q

Quaid, Dennis, 81
Quay, Stephen and Timothy, 248

R

Rae, Nola, 181
Ragtime Bear, 235
Rainbow Film, 274
The Rains of Ranchipur, 315–316
Ralston, Ken, 357
Rango, 145
Rapunzel, 28, 85
Ratatouille, 27, 101, 144, 268, 325, 359
Ravel. Maurice, 194
The Raven, xiv
Ray Harryhausen's World of Myth and Legend (project), 77
Reason and Emotion, 45–47
Red Hot Riding Hood, 185
Redmayne, Eddie, 111
The Red Turtle, 328
Reinhardt, Max, 12, 13, 125–126, 230
Reiniger, Lotte, 13–16
Reisenbüchler, Sándor, 328
Rendezvous à Montreal, 214
The Return of the King, 317
Rhapsody in Wood, 304
Rhys-Davies, John, 123
Richard III, 101
Riefenstahl, Leni, 172
Ries, Irving G., 66
Rimsky-Korsakov, Nikolai, 66
Rise of the Planet of the Apes, 118
Roach, Hal, 105
Robert, Étienne-Gaspard, 213
Roberts, Julia, 158
Robertson, Dale, 310
Robin Hood, 340

Robinson Crusoe 3D, 157
Robinson, Edward G., 306
Roca, Paco, 160–161
Rocch, James, 118*fn*
Rock-A-Doodle, 263
Roddenberry, Gene, 270
Rogue Warrior, 123
Rooney, Mickey, 57
Roosevelt, Franklin Delano, 54–55
Rosenbaum, Stephen, 360
Rotoscoping, 17–20, 59
Rourke, Mickey, 123
Rowling, J. K., 111
Rübezahl, 350
Rudiš, Jaroslav, 18
Ruff and Reddy, 55
Ruka, 4
Rutsch, Edwin, 101
Ryan, 359

S

Sabl, Heinrich, 331–337
Sadness, 46
Safety Last, 105
Sahara Hare, 32
Sailor Moon, 204
Saiyu-ki, 154
Salten, Felix, 163
Saludos Amigos, 288*fn*
Sammy's Adventure, 157
The Sandman, 78
Sanguine persons, 178
Saperstein, Henry G., 160
Satrapi, Marjane, 36
Sausage Party, 145
Schatten, 16
Schleicher, Kurt, 201
Schlesinger, Leon, 55
Schmidt, Harald, 324
Schneer, Charles H., 66, 70, 194, 308,
    310–311
Schneider, Rob, 116
Schneider, Walther, 30
Schoedsack, Ernest B. "Monty", 74, 307
School for Vampires, 295, 296
Schreck, Max, 172
Schtroumpfs, 43
Schulze-Boysen, Libertas, 200

Schumacher, Joel, 116
Schwarzenegger, Arnold, 221
Scott, Ridley, 116
Seawright, Roy, 105
Secondary action, 189
The Secret Life of Pets, 345
The Secret of Kells, 328
The Secret of NIMH, 268
The Secret World of Arrietty, 92
Seeber, Guido, 12
Selick, Henry, 360
Sellers, Peter, 242
Semon, Larry, 172
Sennett, Mack, 105
Serkis, Andy, 117, 118
Sethi, Neel, 122
7 Faces of Dr. Lao, 259, 304
Seven Samurai, 155
The 7th Voyage of Sinbad, 66, 70–72, 77,
    78, 80, 81, 186, 194, 302, 310, 311,
    312, 313, 315, 356
Sex Bugs Rock'N'Roll, 165
Sexy Robot, 115
Shadow, 13–16
The Shadow, 10
Shadow Theatres and Shadow Films, 16*fn*
Shakespeare, William, 49, 356
Shamanism, 25–28, 228
Shane, 242
Shanghai Animation Film Studio,
    280–281
Shanghai Super Kids (project),
    150–151, 153
Sharpe, Albert, 109
Shaun the Sheep, 42
Sheen, Martin, 123
Sherazade: The Untold Stories, 232, 296,
    299–300
Sherlock Holmes TV series, 111
Shin, Nelson, 166, 202
The Shirt, 249
Shore, Howard, 194
Shrek, 136, 191
Shuster, Joe, 188
Siegel, Don, 117, 188
Siegel, Jerry, 188
Signor Rossi, 42, 241–242, 324
The Silly Goose, 202

Silly Symphonies, 32, 38, 54, 194, 354
The Simpsons, 42, 57, 202
SimsalaGrimm, 295
Simulacron 3, 212
Sinbad:Beyond the Veil of Mists, 116–117
Sinbad and the Eye of the Tiger, 261, 315–316
Sinbad the Sailor, 66, 310
Sing, 195
Siodmak, Curt, 104
Slapstick, 107
Sleeping Beauty, 100, 165, 356
Slow burn, 106
Slow in/slow out, 189
Small, Edward, 310–311
Smith, David, 22
Smurfs, 43, 168
The Snow Man, 190, 200, 201, 355
Snow White and the Seven Dwarfs, 21, 58, 93, 100, 187–188, 202, 205, 212, 354
Solomon, Veronica, 339–341
Song of the Prairie, 82
Song of the South, 65
Son of Kong, 74
Son of Sinbad, 310
Sony Pictures Imageworks, 110
Soozandeh, Ali, 18, 20, 110
The Sorcerer's Apprentice, 25
Soren, David, 166
South Park, 136
Speedy Gonzales, 55
Spider-Man, 99, 110, 143, 150, 325
Spielberg, Steven, 115
Spirited Away, 27
SpongeBob, 51, 145
Stadtmaus und Feldmaus, 88
Stafford, Grace, 55
Stallone, Sylvester, 116
Stanislavsky, Constantin, 26, 50
Starevich, Ladislas, 82, 85
Starfighter, 124
Starr, Ringo, 57, 81
Star Trek, 135
Star Wars, 18, 99, 116, 135, 237, 325, 269
Stassi, Mike, 122
St. Cyr, Lili, 310

Steamboat Willie, 56
Steiger, Rod, 51, 57
Stevenson, Robert Louis, 198
Stewart, Patrick, 57, 123
"Stillness", 93–94
Sting, 57
Stokowski, Leopold, 193
Stop-frame technique, 59
Stop motion, 246
    animation, 114
    puppets, 59
    technique, 336–337
"Stop trick" technique, 61
Storks, 188
Storyboarding, 205
The Story of King Midas, 85
Stowaways on the Ark, 166
Strasberg, Lee, 51
Streep, Meryl, 57
The Student of Prague, 12
Studio Ghibli, 214
Sturm und drang, 30
Stylization, 227, 251
The Suitcase, 350
Sullivan, Pat, 105
Summer, Eric, 67
Sun Li Jun, 146
Sun Wu Kong, 154–155
Superman, 188
    comics, 143–144
Surprise, 46, 248
Surrealism, 107
Surrogat, 274
"Survival of the Fittest", 197
Suspense, 221
Sutherland, Donald, 57
Sutherland, Kiefer, 123
Švankmajer, Jan, 248, 333
Švejdík, Jaromír, 18
The Sword and the Dragon, 316
Synthespians, 116, 120
Syria, 125

T

Table top process, 201
Takahashi, Ryosuke, 92
Takamine, Hideko, 93
Takeuchi, Yoshikazu, 358

Tale as Old as Time, 55
A Tale of Two Kitties, 106
Tangled, 28, 165
Tanin no kao, see The Face of Another
Tapum, the History of Weapons, 241
Tashlin, Frank, 31–32, 36
The Tasmanian Devil, 55, 164
Tati, Jacques, 107
Taylor, Elizabeth, 57
"Techniques of the body", 153
Tehran Taboo, 18, 19, 110
Tekkon Kinkreet, 268, 340
Temple, Shirley, 93
Terboven, Josef, 202
Terkel In Trouble, 359
Terminator 2, 10
Terminator Genisys, 325
Terry, Paul, 91, 144
Teshigahara, Hiroshi, 175
Tetsuwan Atom, see Astro Boy
Te Wei, 95
Tezuka, Osamu, 92, 187
Thalmann, Nadia Magnenat, 213–214
Thatcher, Torin, 311
Théâtre Robert-Houdin, 9
Theseus and the Minotaur (project), 77,
    137–138, 261
The Thief of Bagdad, 85, 310
Thomas, Frank, 100fn, 189
1001 Arabian Nights, 160
The Three Caballeros, 65, 160, 287fn
Three Little Pigs, 38, 54, 96, 354
The 3 Worlds of Gulliver, 302
Thumbelina, 268
Timberlake, Justin, 168
Time for Beany, 54–55
The Time Machine, 304
Tintin, 42, 43
Tippett, Phil, 115
Tirard, Laurent, 109
Tischlein deck dich, 88
Titanic, 103, 116
Tobias Totz, 268
Tolkien, J. R. R., 118–119
Tom & Jerry, 32, 37, 41, 66, 164, 193
Tom & Jerry Movie, 164
Tománek, Jan, 343–345
Tomei, Alejandra, 84, 245–251

tom thumb, 304
Toniolo, Benedikt, 62
Toot, Whistle, Plunk and Boom, 242
The Tortoise and the Hare, 32
Tortoise Wins by a Hare, 32
Totemism, 25–28
Totheroh, Rollie, 107
A Town Called Panic, 230–231
The Town Mouse and the Country
    Mouse, 91
Toys, 167–169
Toy Story, 115, 304, 358
Toy Story 3, 325
Trance, 228
Transcendence, 215
Transformers, 166, 325
The Travels of Young Marco Polo, 154
Trier, Lars von, 333
Triplets of Belleville (2003), 107
Trnka, Jiří, 4
Trolls, 168
TRON: Legacy, 325
Trouble in Paradise, 241
True-Life Adventures, 163
True Crime: Streets of LA, 123
Trump, Donald, 202
"Trusted authorities", 153fn
Tsuburaya, Eiji, 26
Turbo, 166
Turner, George E., 70fn
Turpin, Ben, 185
TV animation, 136
TV City, 245, 250
Tweety & Sylvester, 55
Tweety Bird, 106, 197
20 Million Miles to Earth, 309–310
20,000 Leagues Under the Sea, 18, 22, 152
Two by Two or All Creatures Big and
    Small, 46
Týrlová, Hermina, 344
Tytla, Vladimir "Bill", 37, 197, 287, 354

U

Uderzo, Albert, 42
United Productions of America (UPA),
    42, 274
Universal, 94
Updyke, Hubert, 56

Up for Love (Un homme à la hauteur), 109
Uproar in Heaven, see Havoc in Heaven
Urchs, Wolfgang, 166
Ustinov, Peter, 23
Utnapishtim, 135

V

Vaiana, see Moana
Vallée, Rudy, 54–55
The Valley of Gwangi, 80, 81, 302, 313
Valley of the Mist (project), 313
Van Dyke, Dick, 67, 242
van Hessen, Frieda, 58
The Vanishing Lady, 9
Vasallo, Javier, 256
Veidt, Conrad, 172, 173
Verhoeven, Paul, 115–116
Verne, Jules, 22, 152
Viaje a Marte, 231
Video game industry, 116
VIP, My Brother Superman, 241, 242
Virtual camera, 121
Virtual Reality (VR), 237–239, 326
Visualization techniques, 221, 222, 228
Visual sense, 180
Vitagraph Company of America, 9
Voight, Jon, 111
Volpone, 118
Voltaire, 47
von Neumann, John, 214
VR, see Virtual Reality
Vukotić, Dušan, 274, 275

W

Walcazk, Diana, 116
Walken, Christopher, 123
Wallace, Edgar, 137
Waltz with Bashir, 212
Wan Brothers, 154
Wan Lei-Ming, 154, 155
Wang Borong, 147–148
Wanted: Dead or Alive series, 92
War Eagles (project), 121, 124, 307–308
War Games (1983), 124
Warin, Éric, 67
War Planets, 168
Warren, Bill, 77

Warren, Gene, 103
Waters, John, 57
Watkins, Robert, 169
Wayne, John, 190
Wazowski, Mike, 186
Webster, Chris, 136
Wedge, Chris, 165
Wegener, Paul, 11–12, 17, 173, 306
Weiss, Lawrence, 105–106
Weizenbaum, Joseph, 270
Welch, Raquel, 303, 314
Wen Jiabao, 94
Werner-Beinhart, 295
West and Soda, 241, 242
Weta Digital, 317
When Dinosaurs Ruled the Earth, 72, 259, 262
Where Is Momma?, 95, 282
Whitaker, Harold, 166
Whitaker, Scott, 307
White, Tony, 113
White Wilderness, 163
Whitlock, Albert, 355
Whitney, Jr. John, 114
Who Framed Roger Rabbit, 110–111, 357
Wickersham, Bob, 354
Wiene, Robert, 16
Wile E. Coyote, 32, 55
Wilkinson, Carole, 257
Willard, 144
Williams, Dick, 354
Williams, Guy, 23
Williams, Pat, 69fn
Williams, Richard, 357
Williams, Tennesse, 101
Willie the Operatic Whale, 144
Willie Whopper, 30
The Wind Rises, 93
Winnie the Pooh, 55
The Wise Little Hen, 25
The Witcher 3: Wild Hunt, 123
The Wizard of Oz, 25–26
The Wizard of Speed and Time, 60, 358
Wolf, Friedrich, 333
The Wolf Man, 10
The Wonderful World of the Brothers Grimm, 103, 137–138, 259
Woods, James, 123

Woodward, Marvin, 354
Woody Woodpecker, 31, 32
World History of Animation, 235
Worry Eaters, 295–297
Wray, Fay, 70
Wright, Robin, 212
Wrinkles, 160–161, 253, 256–257, 361
Wu Cheng'en, 154
Wyndham, Anne, 71–72

X

Xi Jinping, 94
Xi Yang Yang Yu Huitai, 96
X Men, 325

Y

Yan Dingxian, 155
Yeh-Shen, 158

Yellow Submarine, 194
Yogi Bear, 55, 164
Yosemite Sam, 55, 178
Young, Aida, 73
Yuting, Lin, 96

Z

Zagreb Film, 242, 277
Zagreb school of animation, 273–277
Zaramella, Juan Pablo, 60, 194, 231
Zeman, Karel, 248
Zemeckis, Robert, 120, 186, 211,
    270–271
Zhang, Tony, 258
Ziemer, Gregor, 47
Zootopia, 104–105
Zorro, 23
Zurkan, Grigori, 347–352